MW00533174

THAT YOU MAY PROSPER
Dominion By Covenant

THAT YOU MAY PROSPER
Dominion By Covenant

Ray R. Sutton

Institute for Christian Economics
Tyler, Texas

Copyright © 1987 Ray R. Sutton
Second printing, 1992
Third printing, 1997

All rights reserved. Written permission must be secured from
the publisher to use or reproduce any part of this book, except
for brief quotations in critical reviews or articles.

All Scripture citations are from the New American Standard
Version, unless noted otherwise.

Published by Institute for Christian Economics
P.O. Box 8000, Tyler, Texas 75711

Printed in the United States of America

Library of Congress Cataloging-in-Publication Data

Sutton, Ray R., 1950-
    That you may prosper : dominion by covenant /
Ray R. Sutton.
        p.   cm.
    Includes bibliographical references and index.
    ISBN 0-930464-11-7 (alk. paper).
    1. Covenants—Religious aspects—Reformed Church.
2. Dominion Theology.   3. Law (Theology)   4. Reformed
Church—Doctrines.   5. Sociology, Christian (Reformed
Church)   6. Calvinism.   7. Bible. O.T. Deuteronomy—
Criticism, interpretation, etc.   8. Success—Religious aspects—
Christianity.   I. Title.
BT155.S87   1991
231.7'6—dc20   91-22625
                                                        CIP

To One So Suitable For Me
Susan
My Beloved Wife

TABLE OF CONTENTS

FOREWORD

by Milton C. Fisher[1]

Pick up your Bible and ask, "How do I get hold of the message of this Book? How do I apply it to life — not just *my* life, but to *all* life in this complex world in which we live?" Many approaches to "dividing the word of truth" have been proposed. Both complex and simple systems have been developed, propagated, and tried out. Tried, but found wanting. *That You May Prosper* is not just one more experimental system for organizing Bible content. It clearly expounds and applies the Bible's own structure in a way that demonstrates its intent.

Cleverly concocted analyses of the Bible, though often containing scattered elements of truth (out of focus and disproportionate in emphasis), fall short and distort for one reason. They fail to take into account the essential nature of the written Word of God. They miss the should-be-obvious fact that the Bible is by design and intent a covenant document.

Jehovah God called His servant, Moses the Lawgiver, at the bush in the desert. Moses was the prepared agent, learned in all the wisdom of the Egyptians, whom God used to deliver His people from bondage and also to encode the revealed constitution for a new nation, His people Israel. Hence it is most likely that the very first words written *as Bible* were those inscribed by God's own hand: "I am Jehovah your God, who brought you out of the land of Egypt, . . .

---

1. Professor of Old Testament (retired) at Philadelphia Theological Seminary. Education: B.A. (Phi Beta Kappa) and M.A. from the Oriental Seminary department of Johns Hopkins University (under William F. Albright). M.Div., the Theological Seminary of the Reformed Episcopal Church (now "Philadelphia Theological Seminary"). B.D. and Th.M. from Pittsburgh-Xenia Theological Seminary (under James L. Kelso). Ph.D. in Mediterranean Studies from Brandeis University (under Cyrus H. Gordon). Specialties: missionary linguistics and comparative Semitic philology applied to biblical exegesis of the Hebrew Scriptures, plus Bible history and archaeology.

you shall have no other gods before Me." The heart of the Covenant Law is the Decalogue, which these words preface and introduce.

Sutton's Book

The book you now hold in your hand is doubtless the clearest exposition of Bible-as-covenant (that is, Bible as meant to be understood) that you've ever read. That's because the author has spelled out in no uncertain terms the implications of historic reformational covenant theology in the light of current scholarship. The discovery and application to biblical studies of the suzerain treaty parallels to Sacred Scripture, contemporary to and confirmatory of the Pentateuch, has been extremely enlightening and valuable for appreciation of the orientation of the Word of God in its entirety.

Others, such as Meredith G. Kline, have published helpful suggestions concerning archaeological and philological discoveries in this area. But Ray Sutton has now both simplified and expanded upon the rich lode made available through modern research. This he does by citing the biblical reasons for historic successes and failures in human history. In the realms of family, church, and state — covenant institutions by divine design — only when there is conformity to the biblical pattern and requirements of covenantal relationships is divine blessing to be expected and experienced.

Whether you agree with every idea propounded in this volume by its author, experienced pastor and enthusiastic Christian educator that he is, it will surely make you think. Its commanding logic demands your interaction with the flow of reasoning and its often surprisingly fresh suggestions will prove a stimulus and assistance to your formation of judgments of your own. For example, not everyone will readily accept the seemingly facile manner in which several Books of the Bible are outlined on the same covenantal pattern readily found in Pentateuchal Books like Exodus and Deuteronomy. At least not the first time around. But when one becomes convinced of the centrality and importance of the covenantal form and content (structure and specifications) so vital to Holy Scripture as a whole and in its parts, some such analysis of portions of the Bible makes real sense.

Fresh insights into God's Word are sure to be gained, to say the least, through Sutton's work. I found it to be so, after nearly half a century of serious study and teaching of the Bible. Thinking through this book will enable you to focus upon and relate by covenantal

principles certain details of Scripture which you have either over-
looked or found puzzling. For example, I recall the shock of reading
Mark 10:30 for the first time, *in Greek*, searching out words in the
Greek lexicon. Here Jesus promises to those who leave all and follow
Him ". . . a hundredfold now in this time — houses and brothers and
sisters and mothers and children and lands, WITH PERSECU-
TIONS. . . ." What's that!? "Persecutions"? How did *that* get in
there? Sutton's treatment of the "sanctions" aspect of covenant, and
how it explains not only the supreme sufferings of our Savior but
those of His covenant children as well clears up such questions.

Similarly, as I read for about the thirtieth time in my life the
eighteenth chapter of II Kings, about the life of King Hezekiah, I
was struck by how it (along with many other passages) bears out the
title, from Deuteronomy 29:9, of Sutton's book. We are told that
since this Davidic heir "did what was right in the sight of the LORD"
(vs. 3), "removed the high places. . . ." (vs. 4), "trusted in the LORD
God of Israel" (vs. 5), and "held fast to the LORD" (vs. 6), "The LORD
was with him; he PROSPERED wherever he went" (vs. 7).

So, a revived interest and excitement in Bible study is an assured
byproduct of reading this book. But equally helpful is its application
to all areas of private and corporate life, in family, church, and state
— home, religion, and politics. I leave it to the author himself to explain to you why this is so.

In particular, the five aspects and parts of covenant, so thoroughly
discussed and widely applied throughout *That You May Prosper*, are
easy to latch onto — to understand and to remember. But the way in
which these were compared to issues in modern management theory
by Gary North in the *Publisher's Preface* to the original edition of the
book bears repeating. North speaks of how the endless arguments
over details of political theory, as well, boil down to disagreements
over the answers to five questions:

1. Who's in charge here?
2. To whom do I report?
3. What are the rules?
4. What do I get for obeying or disobeying?
5. Does this outfit have a future?

Memorize these five simple and logically sequential questions,
and you'll have no trouble remembering the five point outline in
Sutton's treatment of covenant. You may even start to see it every

where, as it were, as does the author. I'll confess, after I wrote the paragraph about Hezekiah, I discovered to my own amazement that I could see the five points. You just have to switch the last two statements (or verses). I challenge you to return to that paragraph, after you've read the book, and see if you don't think the same thing.

Fully one-third of the text of this volume is comprised of a series of short appendixes. Disconcerting at first, perhaps, but you will come to appreciate how the author keeps you on the track and properly paced for learning as you go through the body of the study. By consigning peripheral issues and demonstrations relating to the covenant outline to the appendix, he moves you at a steady pace through the basic argument of his thesis. I believe you will enjoy running the course, as did I, and you should cross the finish line the stronger for it.

PUBLISHER'S PREFACE
(1992)

by Gary North

Because of the impact which *That You May Prosper* has begun to have on the broader Church, I have decided to scrap my original Preface and substitute a more generic one. The Foreword by Dr. Fisher presents the case for the five-point covenant model from both a biblical standpoint and a practical one. His Foreword should silence several academically inclined critics who have treated Sutton's discovery with something bordering on contempt. Here I wish only to recall the conditions under which the first edition was written and then discuss several applications of Sutton's thesis.

The manuscript began in 1985 as a study on the symbolism of baptism. As the editor, I told him that it needed extensive rewriting. What I eventually got was a completely different book. The manuscript went through at least four revisions. As it began to take shape, I realized that Sutton had stumbled onto something of great importance. When the manuscript was completed, I was convinced that the book would make a major theological contribution. How major? I discussed that in my original Preface, which readers may wish to consult. Some readers felt that I overestimated its importance. Time will tell. (So will eternity.) One thing is sure: Sutton offers us a precise definition of covenant theology, for which the Protestant world had been waiting for a long, long time.

Covenant Theology

Calvinism is known as covenant theology, yet it is one of the great ironies of history that for over four centuries, no Calvinist author before Sutton had spelled out in detail precisely what a biblical covenant is. A legal bond, yes. A personal bond, yes. A kind of contract, yes. But the judicial details that make a covenant legally

xiii

different from a contract — above all, the presence of a self-maledictory oath — were never dealt with clearly prior to Sutton's book. Not one Calvinist theologian had gone back to the Old Testament and returned with a tightly drawn, easily identifiable, biblically defendable covenant model. I said this in my 1987 Preface, and while some critics thought I exaggerated, I have yet to receive photocopied historical evidence to the contrary.

Louis Berkhof

Typical is Louis Berkhof's *Systematic Theology* (1939). His only discussion of the covenant appears in an eight-page chapter on the covenant of works, a theological construct that many Calvinists find difficult to defend exegetically. Two pages — one long paragraph — of the chapter are devoted to a sketch of the history of the doctrine. He confines himself to a discussion of the idea of federal headship, or legal representation. Almost the whole section is a string of names: Olevianus, Gomarus, Trelcatius, Ravensperger, "and especially Cloppenberg," who was a forerunner to Coccejus, who was followed by Burmannus, Witsius, Voetius, Mastricht, De Moor, Ball, Blake, Gib, and Boston. So far, the hapless seminary student does not know anything specific about the doctrine, but he has a string of unfamiliar names (without dates) to memorize.

Then Berkhof takes up "The Scriptural Foundation for the Doctrine of the Covenant of Works." He mentions Genesis 1-3, but cites nothing specific. Here is his only description of the covenant: "In the case under consideration two parties are named, a condition is laid down, a promise of reward for obedience is clearly implied, and a penalty for transgression is threatened" (p. 213). He calls these "all the elements of a covenant." There was a promise of eternal life in God's covenant with Adam, he says. The student might well ask: Then what was the tree of life all about? Was "forever not eating from the tree of the knowledge of good and evil" covenantally the same as "eating from the tree of life"? If so, then what unique positive blessing did eating from the tree of life impart — a tree identified in the New Testament with Jesus Christ?[1] If not, then what exactly was the covenant of works?

Finally we get to the point: "Elements of the Covenant of Works." Prepare to be disappointed. Here are the elements. 1. Contracting

---

1. "Blessed are they that do his commandments, that they may have right to the tree of life, and may enter in through the gates into the city" (Rev. 22:14).

parties: God and Adam. They were in a natural relationship: master and servant (no Bible verses cited); and a covenantal relationship: representative headship, on probation (no Bible verses cited). 2. A promise of the covenant: eternal life vs. eternal death. 3. A condition of the covenant: the moral law (ten commandments). Berkhof proves this in the most powerful way he could imagine: by quoting Bavinck in Dutch (without a translation). 4. A penalty of the covenant (no Bible verse). 5. A sacrament (maybe two) of the covenant: the tree of life.

He ends his discussion by saying that Arminians do not believe in the continuation of the covenant of works; God established a new law. Some Reformed scholars (none named) speak of a covenant of works, and in one sense it was not abrogated: man must obey God. But in another sense it is abrogated: we are under the covenant of grace. End of chapter. End of all mention of the covenant.

Understand, Berkhof's book, nearly 800 pages long, is the most widely read Calvinistic systematic theology of the twentieth century —indeed, it is just about the only one. It is not just that Berkhof's book is representative; it is virtually the lone example.

Sutton's Discovery

Into this near-vacuum came Sutton's *That You May Prosper.* He uses Deuteronomy as his primary exegetical example, but he also appeals to other Bible passages. He appeals also to history. He discusses all three institutional covenants: church, state, and family, appealing to both the Bible and history. For the first time, the student has set before him a comprehensive, biblically grounded, and coherent presentation of the five aspects of the covenant: the sovereignty of God over history, yet His immanence in history; the hierarchical authority of God over His creation, with designated human representatives over other men; the law of God; the dual sanctions of the covenant, established by an oath: blessing and cursing; and covenantal succession: inheritance or disinheritance in time and eternity.

After the publication of the book, one correspondent wrote to Sutton and proposed a helpful memorization tool: an acronym, THEOS. This is the Greek word for God. The acronym stands for Transcendence, Hierarchy, Ethics, Oath, and Succession: the five points.

It is also worth noting that the famous five points of Calvinism correspond to the five points of the biblical covenant. Its acronym is

TULIP: Total depravity, Unconditional election, Limited atonement, Irresistible grace, and the Perseverance of the saints. The five
points of Calvinism are a theological application — soteriology — of
the five points of the covenant. Here is how they match up:

Total depravity	Ethics (man's)
Unconditional election	Oath (God's)
Limited atonement	Hierarchy (representation)
Irresistible grace	Transcendence (sovereignty)
Perseverance of the saints	Succession

Sutton began his monthly newsletter, *Covenant Renewal*, in January of 1987. Each month, he applies the five-point covenant model
to a biblical passage. At some point, he will be able to produce several books with the exegetical evidence he has accumulated. His
newsletter provides monthly confirmation: the five-point model is no
mere "procrustean bed," as one theonomic critic has described it. It is
in fact the key that unlocks the Scriptures.

England's Central School of Religion awarded Sutton the Th.D.
in 1988 on the basis of *That You May Prosper*. In 1991, Sutton became
the president of Philadelphia Theological Seminary, the seminary
of the Reformed Episcopal Church.

Applications of the Model

As soon as I saw the next-to-last version of Sutton's manuscript, I
spotted a mistake. Not a theological mistake: a rhetorical mistake.
He had neglected to appeal to the most important piece of biblical
evidence for his case: the Decalogue. I had just finished proofreading
the page proofs of my book, *The Sinai Strategy: Economics and the Ten
Commandments* (1986). I realized that the five-point biblical model
governs the so-called two tables of the law.[2] The so-called First Table
is the priestly code; the so-called Second Table is the kingly code.

I hastily wrote a Preface for *The Sinai Strategy*, which was due at
the printers. I outlined the two sections as follows:

---

2. I agree with Meredith Kline: the two tables of the law were in fact two copies:
one for God and one for Israel. Both were placed in the Ark of the Covenant. The
"two tables of the law" do not refer to two sections: laws one through five and six
through ten. Still, the terminology of the two tables is almost inescapable today.

Priestly Code

Transcendence: prohibition of false worship
Hierarchy: no graven images (representation)
Ethics: prohibition against misusing God's name[3]
Oath: sabbath as day of judgment (baptism, Lord's supper)[4]
Succession: honoring father and mother; long life as the promised inheritance[5]

Kingly Code

Transcendence: prohibition against murder (God's image)
Hierarchy: prohibition of adultery (covenant authority)
Ethics: prohibition against theft
Oath: no false witness
Succession: no coveting of another's property, which constitutes family inheritance

Next, the covenant's five-point structure became the integrating framework for six of the ten volumes in the Biblical Blueprints Series.[6] Two of the authors submitted manuscripts that instinctively conformed to it, even before they had seen *That You May Prosper*: Gary DeMar's *Ruler of the Nations* and George Grant's *Changing of the Guard*. As the general editor, I reversed two chapters in each book (with the authors' permission) to produce a pair of books, each with two parallel sections of five chapters corresponding to the five-point model.

To date, the most spectacular application of the five-point model is David Chilton's masterful commentary on the Book of Revelation, *The Days of Vengeance* (1987). I had hired Chilton to write this book three and a half years earlier. He had written *Paradise Restored* (1985) in the meantime, but he was bogged down on *Days of Vengeance*. Then, in a Wednesday evening prayer meeting in 1986, Sutton presented his five-point model. Chilton was in attendance. Sutton's outline clicked in Chilton's mind. He approached Sutton immediately after the meeting and began to ask questions about Sutton's model

---

3. The key issue here is property rights, although I did not see this at the time. God's name is declared "off limits," just as the tree of the knowledge of good and evil was. He places a "no trespassing" sign around His name.

4. In the Preface, I used "Judicial/evaluational (sanctions)."

5. In the Preface, I used "Legitimacy/inheritance (continuity)."

6. Gary North (ed.), Biblical Blueprints Series (Ft. Worth, Texas: Dominion Press, 1986-87).

and the Book of Revelation. He kept asking questions for many weeks, as he restructured his manuscript.

Chilton recognized that the Book of Revelation is at least two things: a covenant lawsuit against Old Covenant Israel and a model for church liturgy. He used the five points of the covenant to restructure the commentary with respect to both the covenant lawsuit and covenantal liturgy. Perhaps for academic reasons, Chilton appropriated Meredith G. Kline's terminology for the first two points: preamble and historical prologue, but the actual content of the commentary indicates that Sutton's usage is dominant, not Kline's. Chapter 1 is "King of Kings," indicating transcendence. In the Introduction to Part 1, he writes: "The purpose of the covenantal Preamble is thus to proclaim the lordship of the Great King, declaring *transcendence and immanence* and making it clear from the outset that his will is to be obeyed by the vassals, his servants. Biblical treaties set forth God's transcendence and immanence by referring to one or more of three activities: creation, redemption, and revelation."[7] Chapter 2, which begins Part 2, "Historical Prologue," is titled: "The Spirit Speaks to the Church: Overcome!" Chapter 3 is "The Dominion Mandate." Chilton's focus here is hierarchy and authority, not historical prologue.

For those who doubt the applicability of the five-point model beyond the Book of Deuteronomy, Chilton's *Days of Vengeance* is required reading. The book's Foreword, written by English evangelical theologian and Old Testament specialist Gordon Wenham, added authority to Chilton's creative application of Sutton's discovery. Chilton's *Days of Vengeance* is one of the most impressive secondary support volumes ever written in defense of another author's primary thesis. It may be the most impressive back-up book ever published in the same year as the primary book. In fact, it was published first.

Kenneth L. Gentry's book, *The Greatness of the Great Commission* (1990) also applies the five-point model to an important New Testament theme. He adopts the acronym THEOS. He describes the ancient suzerainty treaties by using the THEOS outline, and writes that "God's covenant follows the same pattern."[8] Part II of the book consists of five chapters: The Declaration of Sovereignty, the Exercise of Sovereignty, The Terms of Sovereignty, the Commitment of Sovereignty, and the Continuance of Sovereignty.

---

7. David Chilton, *The Days of Vengeance: An Exposition of the Book of Revelation* (Ft. Worth, Texas: Dominion Press, 1987), p. 49. Emphasis in original.

8. Kenneth L. Gentry, Jr., *The Greatness of the Great Commission: The Christian Enterprise in a Fallen World* (Tyler, Texas: Institute for Christian Economics, 1990), p. 18.

The Challenge

There are those who argue that there are other structures to various biblical covenants, with six, seven, or even more points. I say in response: "Let's see one example that does not overlap two or more of the points." So far, I have seen none. There have been several attempts. In every case, the extra points obviously overlap, leaving Sutton's five points.

There is a tendency among scholars to reject new findings on the basis of the familiar "too good to be true" argument. Underlying this argument all too often is the NDH agenda: Not Discovered Here. They are correct regarding the latter point: the biblical covenant model was discovered in far-off Tyler, Texas, by a full-time pastor who was painfully recuperating from a very serious burn. The lesson: just because a man is an overworked and underpaid pastor does not mean that he cannot make a major theological discovery. This should serve as an encouragement to full-time pastors rather than as a discouragement to full-time theologians.

INTRODUCTION

A young Israelite king was sitting on his throne one day. He may have been bored; he may have been worried. But he decided to spend his day counting all the money that had come into the treasury. In those times, the money was kept in the Temple, so he sent a messenger to perform the task.

When the messenger arrived, he and a priest began to calculate the king's wealth. As they moved the great chests of gold back and forth, the king's messenger found a strange object. He found something resembling a "time capsule."

The messenger called the priest. Slowly they unrolled the ancient manuscript found inside. In it was a message from their ancestors. Both knew immediately what had been found. They wept, as their eyes raced through the document, reading of a time gone by that obligated them to greatness.

The king had to be told.

The priest was selected to take the document to him. At first he walked; then he ran. The guards outside the king's palace were instructed to move out of the way, for he had a message from the past.

Running into the king's court and interrupting the proceedings, the priest bowed and held the document up to the king. Reaching out, the teenager clasped the manuscript in his hand. He stood, frozen like a statue for what seemed like time without an end. Everyone in this great court covered with gold, silver, and precious jewels waited speechlessly to see what the king was going to do. Then he looked up. But his eyes did not meet the numbed faces encircling him. They stretched up to the heavens.

Then he cried out before all the court, "God, forgive me and my people." He tore his clothes and fell on his face, pleading for God's mercy.

What had happened?

1

King Josiah had discovered the "Book of the Covenant" (II Kgs. 22:8ff.). What was it? Judging by Josiah's response to this book (II Kgs. 22:3, 13; II Chron. 34:3-8), it was the Book of Deuteronomy, itself the summary of the covenant.[1] Deuteronomy is the second giving of the Law (Deutero = twice + nomy = law) stated in the form of a *covenant*. He read, "So keep the words of this *covenant* to do them *that you may prosper* in all that you do" (Deut. 29:8).

Josiah, however, did not stop at the reading of the covenant. He re-instituted it and brought about great reform in his society. Only then could he begin to change his culture. Only then could he re-establish the dominion of the Lord. Only then could he truly prosper! For his commitment to God's law, God identified Josiah as the *greatest* king in the history of Israel: not David, and not Solomon. "And **before** him there was no king like him who turned to the Lord with all his heart and with all his soul and with all his might, according to the law of Moses; nor did any like him arise **after** him" (II Kgs. 23:25).

Rediscovering Our Biblical Roots

That You May Prosper is a book about the covenant: what it is and how it works. It is designed to help create what happened in Josiah's day. Like his time, "covenant" has been forgotten. Unlike his day, it has not yet been rediscovered. (Yes, a lot of Christians *talk* "covenant" and *talk* "accountability," but the doctrine simply has not been discussed in terms of what the Bible actually teaches.) Covenant is *the* answer at a time when we stand at the threshhold of the death of a culture.

In the late 1960s I began to read Francis Schaeffer. He came to a conservative seminary in my home town. I will never forget the day

---

1. Scholars have debated whether the "Book of the Covenant" was actually the Book of Deuteronomy. For a while, this notion was seriously contested. Now, however, most Old Testament scholars agree that the "Book of the Covenant" was indeed Deuteronomy or some portion thereof. Edward McGlynn Gaffney, "Of Covenants Ancient and New: The Influence Of Secular Law On Biblical Religion," *Journal of Religion and Law* II (1984), pp. 117-144. Gaffney refers to Wilhelm De Witte, *Dissertation Critico-Exegetica, Qua Deuteronomium A Prioritus Pentateuchi Libris Diversum, Alius Evivsdam Recentioris Auctoris Opus Esse Monstrator* (1805). On the basis of De Witte's work, Gaffney says, "Shorn of its nineteenth century rationalism, the suggestion of Wilhelm De Witte in 1805 that the law book referred to in these passages was a portion of *Deuteronomy* now enjoys the status of virtual consensus among contemporary biblical scholars" (p. 121). Gaffney then refers to a more contemporary scholar, confirming De Witte. Norbert Lohfink, "Zur Dekalogfassung von Deut. 5, 9" *Biblishe Zeitschrift* (1965), pp. 17-31.

I heard him. I will never forget a statement he made that has kept ringing in my ears for nearly the last twenty years. He said, "We are at the end of Christian civilization, and therefore, we are at the end of civilization."

Many would not agree with the premise of his comment, but how many would really contest that we are at the end of a culture? Most people sense it. Most Christians know it. Most secular intellectuals won't deny it. And I think the general populace would not hesitate to admit that the Christian mores that undergirded this culture for the last two hundred years are all but gone. No doubt many would applaud this decline. But Christians are left asking, "How do we recover our Biblical roots?"

Unfortunately, I don't hear a clear solution coming from any sector. Some say evangelism. Many say small groups. A few say liturgy. Others cry for political action. Certainly all of these have their proper place, but when are we going to look to the Bible for a model? When are we going to say, "Does the Bible tell of a time like ours, when Biblical influence was lost, and then recovered?" When are we going to look to see how *they*, the people in the Holy Scriptures, did it? I believe the Bible tells of a time such as that. The Bible really does have the answer, and the solution is right in front of our noses. It is the *covenant*, and Josiah's experience tells the story. Our forefathers knew the story. It's time we remember what they knew.

Our Biblical Heritage

We should never forget that *covenant* was the single most important theological idea in early America. Not only the Puritans, but virtually all Protestants came to the New World with this concept at the center of their theology and practice. Congregationalists, Presbyterians, Anglicans, Continental reformed groups, and independents were children of the Reformation. Federal theology, as covenant thinking had been called on the continent, had taken root at the time of the Middle Ages. In many ways, the dawning of the Reformation was a revival of this ancient theology. Slowly it seeped into European and British cultures, but not deep or fast enough.

When these diverse, yet similar, Protestant groups came to America, they implemented what many Europeans had wanted for centuries. Their rationale for applying the covenant was simple. The members of the Godhead related by *covenant*.[2] Since heaven is a

---

2. Edmund S. Morgan, *The Puritan Dilemma* (Boston: Little, Brown and Company, 1958), p. 93.

model for earth—as the Lord's Prayer says, "Thy kingdom come, Thy will be done, on earth *as it is in heaven*" (Matt. 6:10)—man is supposed to organize all of his life according to the same structure. People from England and the Continent were ready for this kind of society. They came to the New World because it offered what they had never been able to find in Europe: a society based not on "status but contract."[3] Their theology mandated it, and they acted on it.

The idea of a society based on the theology of the Reformation quickly spread through their literature. These were people with a religion of the *Book*, the Bible, and consequently they were heavily involved in the printed word. Because of this, the covenant idea probably became so pervasive. Two groups of note are the Puritans and the Anglicans.[4]

The Puritans produced thousands of sermons, books, and tracts.[5] The covenant theme occurs often. One of the first books ever published in America was a book on the covenant, the *Gospel-Covenant* by

---

3. Perry Miller, *The New England Mind: The Seventeenth Century* (Cambridge, Massachusetts: Harvard University Press, [1939] 1954), p. 399. Although Miller did "ground-breaking" work, he erroneously believed the "covenant" idea was original to the Puritans. George M. Marsden, "Perry Miller's Rehabilitation of the Puritans: A Critique," *Church History* 39, no. 1 (March 1970: 91-105), categorically proves that the Puritans derived the "covenant idea" from the teaching of John Calvin in Geneva.

Also, the Christian colonists did not believe in a social contract theory, because their view of covenant forced them to have a high view of authority. God establishes institutions through this authority, not the consent of the people. For example, those coming to the New World from England all sought *charters* from the king. They were not anarchists, striking out on their own without accountability.

4. Granted, the Puritans and Anglicans differed on their views of worship. Although the Puritans made some helpful contributions to American society, they were inconsistent with their view of covenant when it came to worship. They argued, "Do what the Old Testament teaches, unless the New Testament changes it." So they defended the right of magistrates to use the Old Testament civil laws as a guide. The Anglicans on the other hand used the same kind of argument regarding worship. They, too, held to the great reformational idea of the covenant. They, too, believed that the Old Testament should inform one's interpretations of the New Testament. *They looked at the Book of Revelation and saw that the form of worship was remarkably similar to the worship of the Old Testament. God had not done away with a basic "routine" around the throne of God. Thus, their worship was not plain and stark like the Puritans' worship.*

5. The Puritans also shaped culture through their high moral standards of living. Today, laws of the early Puritans against blasphemy, homosexuality, and adultery are still on many of the individual states' books, even though they are no longer taken seriously. And, Puritan family life is still studied to find out what made the interior of their lives so rich. Edmund S. Morgan, *The Puritan Family* (New York: Harper & Row, [1944] 1966), pp. 133-160.

Peter Bulkeley.[6] Other works basically reflected the same point of view, but maybe their greatest influence was expressed in their *creeds*.[7] In whole or in part, these statements of faith found their way to many different religious groups in America and England.[8] As covenant dominated their documents, the idea was able to cross denominational boundaries.[9]

The Anglicans were also quite influential in spreading covenant theology. Anyone who doubts the theological links between the Puritans and the Anglicans in seventeenth-century colonial America should consult Perry Miller's essay on "Religion and Society in the Early Literature of Virginia."[10] The Anglicans' commitment to good Christian literature was commensurate with their dedication to the thought of the Reformation.[11] In 1695, Thomas Bray wrote, *Proposals For Encouraging Learning and Religion In The Foreign Plantations*. What he really had in mind was books.[12] The result was the Society for Promoting Christian Knowledge (S.P.C.K.) in 1699. The king gave them their charter. One of the greatest movements in the history of the Church began. The S.P.C.K. disseminated a mountain of Christian literature in this part of the World. What kind of books? Mostly

---

6. Peter Bulkeley, *The Gospel-Covenant, or the Covenant of Grace Opened* (2nd ed., London, 1651). All future references to Bulkeley's work will be to this edition.

7. The most famous Puritan doctrinal standard is the *Westminster Confession of Faith*, 1640s. Even though it was produced in England, it spread to America to the New England Puritans. Presbyterian and Congregational groups quickly began to adopt it. The New England Puritans wrote the *Cambridge Platform*, very similar in many respects to the *Westminster Confession of Faith*.

8. The *Second London Baptist Confession of Faith 1677* is virtually a copy of the *Westminster Confession of Faith*, the major differences falling in the area of baptism, etc. Nevertheless, it is almost word for word the same. Most of the early Baptist groups used this modified version of the *Westminster Confession*. W. L. Lumpkin, *Baptist Confessions of Faith* (Valley Forge: Judson Press, [1964] 1979), pp. 235-296.

9. Benjamin Warfield, *The Westminster Assembly and Its Work* (New York: Oxford University Press, 1931), p. 56. One of its greatest interpreters, he says of the *Westminster Confession*, "The architectonic principle of the Westminster Confession is supplied by the schematization of the Federal [Covenantal] Theology."

10. Perry Miller, *Errand Into The Wilderness* (Cambridge, Massachusetts: Harvard University Press, [1956] 1970), ch. 4.

11. Charles and Katherine George, *The Protestant Mind of the English Reformation* (Princeton, New Jersey: Princeton University Press, 1961), pp. 50-55. Specific reference is made to such great Anglican thinkers as Bishop Ussher, who was firmly entrenched in covenant theology. For that matter, the *Thirty-Nine Articles*, the confessional standard of the Anglican Church, is remarkably similar to the *Westminster Confession of Faith*. Both are products of the same pool of theology.

12. Edwin Scott Gaustad, *A Religious History of America* (New York: Harper & Row, 1966), pp. 76-77.

the print coming out of and influenced by the Reformation. Thus, the Anglicans, like the Puritans, created a conduit through which Federal theology poured into the New World.

Christians in the West have forgotten this story. They have forgotten the covenant. Somehow, they must rediscover it. But what in particular about the covenant shaped society? There were five key concepts.

Key Covenant Concepts

First, the covenant taught a *transcendent* view of God. Not that He is distant but that He is *distinct* from His creation. This distinction meant God is Lord over everything. Men are not imbued with deity. Consequently, no one man or sphere (Family, Church, or State) is allowed to have absolute power. Europe had been dominated at times by clans, ecclesiocracies, and monarchical dictators. The application of God's transcendence did not allow any of these to have total control. It brought about a true separation of institutional powers, all ruled directly by God.

Second, the covenant taught a concept of authority, or *hierarchy*, based on *representation*. According to this system, people should be able to choose the kind of government over them. Once chosen, however, as long as the representatives met their duties, they were to be obeyed.

Third, covenant meant a society based on *ethics*, particularly the laws of the Bible.[13] "The covenant involved ethics in the very stuff of grace itself."[14] Peter Bulkeley said:

We must for our part assent unto the Covenant, not only accepting the promise of it, but also submit to the duty required in it; or else there is no Covenant established betwixt God and us; we must as well accept of the condition as of the promise, if we will be in Covenant with God.[15]

---

13. Harold J. Berman, *Law and Revolution* (Cambridge: Harvard University Press, 1983), a liberal Jew and professor at Harvard Law School, argues that Western culture is clearly based on Christian law and influence, a background so much the warp and woof of society that the American way of life cannot continue to function if this background is abandoned. Even writers who want to deny America's Christian roots cannot avoid the reality that "America was generally Christian in the structure of its law, its institutions, and its culture." Mark A. Noll, Nathan O. Hatch, George M. Marsden, *The Search For Christian America* (Westchester, Illinois: Crossway, 1983), p. 150.

14. Miller, *Errand*, p. 88.

15. Bulkeley, *The Gospel-Covenant*, p. 316; cited by Miller, p. 88; cf. part IV of *Gospel-Covenant*.

These colonial Christians did not believe in works salvation, rather in a salvation that works. Miller remarks that their view of ethics included more than "individual honesty and charity; it included participation in the corporate organization and the regulation of men in the body politic."[16] Men were judged, in other words, on the basis of behavior, no matter what their status. This gave "good" people a true chance to have upward mobility, something they could have never had as readily in the Old World.

Fourth, the covenant implemented a system of sanctions based on an *oath*. Once an oath was made, a man was expected to keep it. Any violation met serious sanctions. Perjury in the realm of the State was in many cases punishable by death. Adulteration of the marriage oath met the same end. Apostasy from the Church covenant resulted in banishment. The oath and the sanctions that enforced it were an effective stabilizing factor in American culture.

Fifth, the covenant implied a system of *continuity* based on something other than blood relations. The Puritans attempted to make experience the test for church membership. Also, a person had to be a member of the Church to be able to vote. Granted, these were misapplications. The first misapplication—experientialism—led to the Halfway Covenant, in which the grandchildren of church members were baptized, even though their parents had never joined the church formally. Though baptized, these "halfway covenant" children were not regarded as church members.[17] The other misapplication—political—corrupted the Church. Nevertheless, we do find hints of an extremely important aspect of a society rooted in contract and not in status. The mechanism of contract provided social continuity, and not blood or class. America, more than any other culture, had become a place of opportunity for the "little guy."

These seminal ideas of the covenant shaped American society. They created the strongest nation in the history of man. As they have diminished, so has every sphere: Family, Church, and State. A brief overview of these institutions in light of our five basic concepts demonstrates what the loss of covenant has done to modern society.

---

16. *Ibid.*, p. 89.

17. Edmund S. Morgan, *Visible Saints* (Ithaca, New York: Cornell University Press, [1963] 1968). Morgan argues that the "experiential" tests for church membership that they introduced in the early 1630s actually militated against their covenantal theology. Instead of having "objective" tests, they became overly subjective. They tried to do what only God can do, that is, *look into men's hearts*.

Family

First, God is *transcendent*. He directly relates to each sphere of society. Family, Church, and State are not stacked on top of each other. The Family does not have to go through the State, nor the Church, to get to God. This gives the Family institution a *sacred* character. No longer is the Family viewed this way. The State has crippled its God-given powers. A civil judge once said, "Whilst marriage is often termed by text writers and in decisions of courts a civil contract . . . *it is something more than a mere contract.* . . . *It is an institution.*"[18] By this he meant that the Family is a *covenant*. But the State does not believe this way any more. The Family is under attack from the State and society at large. Who can doubt the Family's loss of sacredness? Now other "gods" rule it.

Second, as for *authority*, most families are not sure "who's in charge." There was a time when the father was head of the house. Everyone knew it. Everyone acknowledged it. But the advent of the working mother has created a conflict. It's not the 1950s anymore. High inflation and debt have changed the economics of Western culture. A collapsing economy has forced the woman to go to the market place. When she does, she starts to bring in a sizeable portion of the family income, maybe as much or more than the husband. This threatens the relationship, and the wars begin. The rise of wife abuse statistics indicate the extent of the conflicts. War has been declared in the home. It remains to be seen whose authority will *take charge*.

Third, the covenant laid out a clear sense of right and wrong, *ethics*. The first colonists believed in the morality of the Bible, an objective standard. And every family was raised on this morality. Today, the family has lost this sense of right and wrong. Its children are indoctrinated with "values training" in public schools. The philosophical background for such training comes straight out of the *Humanist Manifesto I & II*. Students are taught, "We affirm that moral values derive their source from human experience. Ethics is autonomous and situational, needing no theological or ideological sanction."[19]

---

18. *Maynard v. Hill*, 1888. Cited in Ray R. Sutton, *Who Owns The Family: God or the State?* (Ft. Worth, Texas: Dominion Press, 1986), pp. 3-14. I devote the entire book to ten court cases that have changed American family life. In this particular chapter, "A Covenant, Not A Contract," I develop the *sacred* nature of the Family.

19. *Humanist Manifesto II* (1973), principle 3.

How frightening it is to think that the future leaders of our civilization will believe this way!

Fourth, it used to be that when a couple said their vows before God and man, their *oath* was taken seriously. Divorce was socially unacceptable. Our times tell us something about how people feel about their marriage *oath*. Thirty-eight percent of all first marriages in the United States fail. Seventy-nine percent of those people will remarry, and forty-four percent of these second marriages will fail.

The fifth area of the covenant is *continuity*. Most families cannot maintain the *bond* implied by this word. Indeed, studies indicate that "Christians" are not doing well at raising up a Godly "seed." They are losing their children to the government school system.[20] They are losing them to the humanists who write the screenplays for television shows. They are even losing them to the humanists who teach in Christian colleges.[21]

Also, the rapid death of the "family business" points to the loss of continuity. Each year a growing number of family businesses is terminated, not because there are no living heirs, but because *the heirs are not interested*. Some students of the "small business" believe this is one of the largest causes for the collapse of the "small business."[22]

At one time the family was understood as a covenantal unit. The loss of this idea has had staggering effects. The five foundational concepts of covenant have proven to be critical to the family's life or death, sickness or health. It seems that as the traditional marriage vows have been altered or destroyed—"In sickness and in health, for richer for poorer . . . till death do us part"—so has the entire institution. But the family is not the only institution that has lost its covenantal moorings.

The State

The New Deal, the Great Society, and all the other social innovations of our "progressive" society have failed.[23] Why? These

---

20. Robert L. Thoburn, *The Children Trap: The Biblical Blueprint for Education* (Ft. Worth, Texas: Dominion Press, 1986).

21. Gary North, "Foreword," to Ian Hodge, *Baptized Inflation: A Critique of "Christian" Keynesianism* (Tyler, Texas: Institute for Christian Economics, 1986).

22. Robert E. Levinson, "Problems in Managing A Family-Owned Business," *Management Aids No. 2004* (Washington, D.C.: Small Business Administration, 1981), p. 3. Leon Danco, *Inside the Family Business* (Cleveland: The University Press, Inc., 1980), pp. 248-250.

23. Charles Murray, *Losing Ground: American Social Policy 1950-1980* (New York: Basic Books, 1984).

programs are products of a government in violation of basic covenantal principles.

First, the State has attempted to become *transcendent*. This
assumption of the role of God has been the "Second American Revolution,"[24] title of John Whitehead's insightful work. Today's foremost
Christian Constitutional authority, lawyer, and author, his thesis is
clear: the judicial procedures of the last 100 years have so completely
re-interpreted the Constitution that the intent of the original 1776
American Revolution has been lost. He refers to a comment made in
1907 by Supreme Court Justice Charles Evans Hughes — "The Constitution is what the judges say it is"[25] — and compares it to one made
in 1936 by the Third Reich Commissar of Justice: "A decision of the
Fuhrer in the express form of a law or decree may not be scrutinized
by a judge. In addition, the judge is bound by any other decisions of
the Fuhrer, provided that they are clearly intended to declare law."[26]
Today, the Supreme Court has become our Fuhrer. We are left won-
dering, "Who really won World War II?"

Second, these quotes indicate confusion over *authority*. The representative concept was a covenantal idea, as we shall see in greater
detail later. The magistrate was to represent God and the people. It
could easily be argued, however, that we no longer have a functional
representative system. The Supreme Court, a group of appointed-
for-life officials, has the real power. The most recent example is the
infamous *Roe v. Wade* ruling (January, 1973). After the states failed to
pass pro-death amendments in the early 1970s, the Supreme Court
still made death the law of the land. Do we have a representative system? Where were our elected representatives? The Congress has the
right to overturn the future effects of any ruling by the Supreme
Court simply by withdrawing the Court's appellate jurisdiction.[27] By

---

24. John Whitehead, *The Second American Revolution* (Elgin, Illinois: David C.
Cook Publishing, 1982).

25. *Ibid*, p. 20, quoting David J. Danelski and Joseph S. Tulchin, eds., *The Auto-
biographical Notes of Charles Evans Hughes*, p. 143.

26. *Ibid*, p. 20, quoting Ernst von Hippel, "The Role of Natural Law in the Legal
Decisions of the Federal German Republic," p. 110.

27. Article III, Sect. 2, Clause 2. After the War Between the States, the Supreme
Court was anti-Reconstruction because its members had held their positions since
the 1840s. When a Southerner named McCardle filed against certain acts of the military rule of the South during Reconstruction, the court accepted the *jurisdiction*.
Congress, on the other hand, being pro-Reconstruction, voted to determine the *jurisdiction* of the court. President Johnson vetoed the bill, but Congress overrode his
veto. The Supreme Court thereupon withdrew from the case, declaring that the de-

removing the abortion question from the Federal courts and the Supreme Court, the issue would be returned to the states, where it began, and where all other capital penalties are enforced. (Abortion is murder; murder is a capital crime; therefore. . . .) So where were our elected representatives? Evidently, we have an authority crisis in our land!

Third, America was originally built on a clear sense of right and wrong. There was *fixity of law*, or *ethics*. Not so any longer. Whitehead explains this loss of "fixity of law and absolutes above men" in the following comment.

> Justice Hughes's statement [quoted above] was representative of a clear break with the American legal past. His view of law deviates from the American concept of constitutionalism — limited government under the rule of law.
>
> This concept was laid down in the colonial documents, including both the Declaration of Independence and the United States Constitution. But in its adoption of the English common law [which applied accepted biblical principles in judicial decisions], the Constitution was acknowledging that a system of *absolutes exists upon which government and law can be founded*. Moreover, under constitutionalism the people are governed by a written document embodying these principles and, therefore, not by the *arbitrary opinions to be found in the expressions of men*.[28]

Fourth, the concept of *oath* has been almost completely destroyed by attacks on the use of the Bible to administer it. If men do not swear by God, there is nothing transcendent to enforce the oath. There are no real sanctions. So we are left asking, "Where is social justice in our land?" Crime is up. On the one hand, the State is slow to respond to the fears of the average American. Crime is high on everyone's list of American crises. It seems that one has to commit a multiple killing before the ancient law, "an eye for an eye," is honored. On the other hand, some Americans are prepared to take matters into their own hands. More and more "vigilante" movies appear each year. Handgun sales are higher than ever. Self-defense courses are full. All sorts of protection devices are being installed. As one

cision of the Congress had removed its jurisdiction. The Court affirmed that Congress interprets the appellate jurisdiction of the Supreme Court. The case was *Ex Parte McCardle vs. Mississippi* (1869). See *The Constitution of the United States: Analysis and Interpretation*, Congressional Research Service, Library of Congress (Washington, D.C.: Government Printing Office, 1972), pp. 750-752.

28. Whitehead, *Second American Revolution*, pp. 20-21. Emphasis and brackets mine.

drives through the affluent, yet barred-windowed sections of cities, perhaps he asks himself, "Who's really in prison in this society?" No oath, no sanction, no justice. The innocent are captives to thugs in high places.

Fifth, the State faces a huge crisis over the *continuity* question. It has to do with *immigration* laws. I have already mentioned that the Puritans attempted to get around a blood basis of continuity by only giving the vote to church members, and that they were unsuccessful. Even though they failed, however, they had the right idea. The vote should not be on the basis of blood. Yet, the way the Constitution was written hindered what the Puritans wanted. If a person is *born* in America, he will be allowed to vote at age 18. Blood, not covenant, actually forms political continuity in the U.S. It is not a question of *citizenship*. Birth should entitle one to this status. But authority to vote should have some covenantal qualifications. Someone can be born in the country but be totally at odds with the American system, and yet have full voting privileges. This has always created a dilemma for preserving the ideals of the Founding Fathers.

Again, we see that the decline of covenant thinking has changed a major institution. The State today is not the same as it was when our nation was established. To become a truly Christian civilization, it must return to the covenant.

Church

Finally, the Church has also been influenced by the decline of covenant thinking.

God is *transcendent*. Not only should He be Lord over Family and State, but certainly He should be recognized as such in the Church. He is supposed to be Head of the Church. When He is not, the Church is left open to attack. The State becomes "Lord" of the Church. Anyone who doubts the State's "Lordship" should consider how many churches are 501 (c) (3) organizations. They have sought tax exemption, yet the law says such exemption is automatic for churches. In effect, they have gone to the State to ask for permission to exist. The implication: the Church no longer takes instructions from the true Head. It goes through an alternate "priesthood," the IRS.

The whole issue of *authority* has come into the Church. Do Church officers have any real authority? Does God hear them? Do the people hear them? I know of a church where it was discovered that one of the leaders was leading a double life. When he came to church he was a good husband and loving father. Meanwhile, he was leading the life of a gambler and adulterer across town. The pastor wanted to have the man removed. Members objected and instead removed the pastor.

How about *ethics* in the Church? Does the Church know the difference between right and wrong? Probably not. For decades a certain theology has taught that Christians are not supposed to obey the Ten Commandments. The thinking goes, "That's in the Old Testament. God was one way in the Old and another in the New. I'm not under law, but grace." Now after so many years of this kind of thinking and preaching, Christians do not know how to live. Take a look at the number of *large* churches in your town that are involved in the pro-life movement. This issue should be fairly clear cut. Killing babies is wrong! Right? I imagine that your town is like all the rest. The big churches are not interested in the pro-life issue. They will not take a stand because it is too controversial. They are not motivated to take a stand because they do not know right from wrong. They really do not believe abortion is murder. If they did, they would call for the death penalty for abortionists and abortion-seeking mothers. How else is murder to be treated in Old *and* New Testaments (Rom. 1:29-32)?

Now we come to the areas of *oath and sanction* in the Church. Church membership is serious. Most churches require some sort of membership commitment and/or vows. But the real test of the oath of allegiance to the Church is *discipline*. Just mention the word, and no one knows what you are talking about. Jesus taught that some may have to be put out of the Church (Matt. 18:15-18). When was the last time you heard of a church doing such a thing? Is this because everyone in the pew (or pulpit!) is so good? Hardly. Recently in Oklahoma, a woman was excommunicated for adultery—as a matter of fact she committed adultery with the *mayor* of the city. Her behavior scandalized the Gospel of Jesus Christ. She could have been forgiven, of course. But she did not want repentance. She wanted to live in open sin and have all the benefits of a member in good standing. The church cast her out. She sued the church and won. The State upheld her violation of a sacred oath to the Church!

Finally, *continuity* has also been a concern in the Church. The Church has faced the problem of maintaining continuity of belief in the midst of diverse religious opinions. Most churches give voting privileges to anyone who can commune. But since not everyone who communes believes the same way, yet all adult members have the power to vote, the church tends to drift toward the lowest common doctrinal denominator. I have heard of a church where a group of Masons joined. They brought in many of their friends. Eventually, they controlled the vote and voted to shut the church down. It was turned into a Masonic Lodge. Even if this is not true, it is certainly possible. The solution is to separate voting from communing privileges. Most churches, however, are not willing to take this kind of action.

So the Church, along with the other two institutions, has declined. The great concepts of the covenant have slowly been set aside. If they are to be redeemed, *covenant is the answer*. But if we do not know what it is and how it works, we will not be able to restore our world. Like King Josiah, we have to discover, understand, and implement it. And how we need to find the covenant! Just go to a Christian bookstore and ask for a book on the covenant. I dare say that you could probably find one sooner in a "secular" bookstore. We are a generation that has lost the covenant. We do not know what it is; we do not understand it; and we certainly do not know how it works. Ironically, this is the single most important Biblical concept in the history of our civilization. We have lost the most valuable information that has contributed to our national and personal success. This brings me to the main concern of *That You May Prosper*.

The Covenant's Structure

How do we discover the covenant? We have to be convinced that it is the central organizing principle of the Bible.[29] The only way to come to this conclusion is to understand the covenant itself. If we do not know what a covenant consists of, we will never be able to see it in all the segments of the Bible. Then, after we know the meaning of a covenant, we can consider how it works.

So, *That You May Prosper* has two parts: covenant and dominion. My primary purpose in the "covenant" section is to *define* the covenant. The Book of Deuteronomy is a model, a place where all of its

---

29. Walter Eichrodt, *Theology of the Old Testament*, 2 vols. (Philadelphia: Westminster Press, 1961). Eichrodt organizes the entire Old Testament in terms of the covenant. Gerhard von Rad, *Old Testament Theology*, I (1962), p. 178, states that although he does not believe in a consistent covenantal thread in the Old Testament, he has to admit, "The belief that Jahweh took Israel (by means of a covenant) as his own peculiar people is, of course, very old."

parts can clearly be seen. Deuteronomy is to the covenant what Romans is to systematic theology. But how do we know Deuteronomy is a covenant? Moses says, "He declared to you His *covenant* which He commanded you to perform, that is, the Ten Commandments [Words]" (Deut. 4:13). Deuteronomy is the *second* giving of the Ten Commandments, a "new" covenant so to speak. Moses says of the book as a whole, "Keep the words of *this covenant* to do them, that you may prosper in all that you do" (Deut. 29:9). Deuteronomy is definitely a covenant document.

Significantly, scholarship of the last few decades has uncovered the similarity between Deuteronomy and other ancient near-eastern covenant treaties, usually called *suzerainty treaties*: Hittite (sixteenth-thirteenth centuries B.C.) and Assyrian (eighth-seventh centuries B.C.). Suzerains were ancient kings who imposed their covenant treaties on lesser kings called vassals. The structure of these treaty documents is not identical to Deuteronomy, but close enough to help us better understand its structure. Suzerainty covenants had six parts.[30]

Suzerainty Covenants

1. *The Preamble*: Like an introduction, it declared who the suzerain (king) was as well as his great power.

2. *The Historical Prologue*: A historical summary of the suzerain's rule. In short, the one who controls history is lord and demands complete *submission*.

3. *Stipulations*: These were the specific laws of conquest to be observed, the stipulations being the very means of dominion. Also, they distinguished the servants of the suzerain from the other people of the world.

4. *Blessing and Cursing*: This section outlined the ceremony where an *oath* was taken, receiving sanctions in the form of blessing and cursing. The character of this oath was "self-

---

30. George E. Mendenhall, "Covenant," *Interpreter's Bible Dictionary* Vol. I (New York: Abingdon Press, 1962), pp. 714-723. It should be noted that Mendenhall's overview of the covenant in this article actually lists *seven* parts of the suzerain treaty: Preamble, historical prologue, stipulations, deposit arrangements, witnesses, blessing and cursing, and oath. But it is generally agreed that the suzerain covenants had six parts. See also, George E. Mendenhall, *Law and Covenant in Israel and the Near East* (Pittsburgh: Biblical Colloquium, 1955).

maledictory." The vassal swore his allegiance to the suzerain. It is called "self-maledictory" because the vassal condemned himself to death if he broke the covenant. In other words, if he was faithful, he was blessed. If unfaithful, he was cursed.

5. *Successional Arrangements*: The covenant document also specified successors to the suzerain so that the vassal could pledge his allegiance to them. Another feature is the enlisting of witnesses, often "heaven and earth," to the sealing of the covenant.

6. *Depository arrangements*: The covenant also stated how and where the covenant document would be stored and preserved. In the event there was a breach of covenant, this document could be produced to begin a process of prosecution against the offending vassal, usually called a *covenant lawsuit*.

The Biblical covenant in Deuteronomy has five parts.[31] It preceded the suzerainty treaties and was not a copy of them. The suzerains copied the Biblical pattern to form geo-political covenants. Deuteronomy, on the other hand, was the restatement and expansion of the *Ten Commandments*. Not only does Moses say as much (Deut. 4:13), but the parallel between the five-fold pattern in Deuteronomy and a *double* five-fold pattern in the Ten Commandments demonstrates the connection.[32] Nevertheless, studies in suzerain treaties have been helpful in understanding the basic structure of the Biblical covenant. I have used them in this regard, especially the work by Meredith G. Kline.[33] Therefore, let us briefly overview the five points of covenantalism.

The Deuteronomic Covenant

True Transcendence (Deut. 1:1-5). Kline and others point out that the covenant begins with a "preamble." But what does the Biblical preamble of Deuteronomy teach? Here we find that God declares *His* transcendence. True transcendence does not mean God is distant but that He is *distinct*.

---

31. Meredith G. Kline, *The Structure of Biblical Authority* (Grand Rapids: Eerdmans, 1972), pp. 131-153. Also, "Deuteronomy," Wycliffe Bible Commentary (Nashville: Southwestern Co., 1962), pp. 155-204.

32. See Appendix 1 for a development of how the Ten Commandments follow the covenant structure.

33. See Appendix 7: "Meredith Kline: Yes and No."

Hierarchy (Deut. 1:6-4:49). The second section of the covenant is called the "historical prologue." Suzerain treaty scholars point out that in this section of Deuteronomy, the author develops a brief history of God's Sovereign relationship to His people around an authority principle. What is it? And, what does it mean? Briefly, God established a *representative* system of government. These representatives were to mediate judgment to the nation. And the nation was to mediate judgment to the world.

Ethics (Deut. 5-26). The next section of the covenant is usually the longest. The stipulations are laid out. In Deuteronomy, this section is 22 chapters long (Deut. 5-26). The Ten Commandments are re-stated and developed. These stipulations are the way God's people defeat the enemy. By relating to God in terms of ethical obedience, the enemies fall before His children.

The principle is that law is at the heart of God's covenant. The primary idea is that God wants His people to see an *ethical* relationship between cause and effect: be faithful and prosper.

Sanctions (Deut. 27-30). The fourth part of Deuteronomy lists blessings and curses (Deut. 27-28). As in the suzerain treaty, Kline observes that this is the actual process of ratification. A "self-maledictory" oath is taken and the sanctions are ceremonially applied. The principle is that there are rewards and punishments attached to the covenant.

Continuity (Deut. 31-34). Continuity determines the true heirs. This continuity is established by ordination and faithfulness. It is historic and processional. The covenant is handed down from generation to generation. Only the one empowered by the Spirit can obey and take dominion. He is the one who *inherits*. The final principle of the covenant tells "who is in the covenant," or "who has continuity with it," and what the basis of this continuity will be.

These *five points of covenantalism* are the foundation of *That You May Prosper.* As I have said, it has two parts: covenant and dominion. In the "covenant section," I spend the first five chapters explaining the five points of covenantalism in detail.[34] In the next half, I move to their application.

---

34. We also have to answer, "Is this covenantal structure other places in the

Dominion

The subtitle of this book is *Dominion by Covenant*. After we have assessed the covenant, we need to ask, "How does it work?" It is my thesis that covenant is the *mechanism for dominion and success*. After all, Moses says, "Keep the words of this covenant to do them, that you may prosper in all that you do" (Deut. 29:9). If we really believe the Bible, then covenant is the key to daily living at every level.

In the "dominion section" I begin with a comparison of the *cultural mandate* (Gen. 1:28-30) and the *Great Commission* (Matt. 28:16-20). Some Christians do not understand their Commission from the Lord. It is a renewal of the cultural mandate; it has the covenantal structure; it means Christians are to take dominion by means of the covenant.

Having established that dominion is by covenant, we get down to specifics. I concentrate on the three institutions of Biblical society (Family, Church, and State), and I show how they were intended to function according to the covenant. Then I also point out historical examples from our own history. Someone might think that this covenant structure is overly *idealistic*. It is not; it has been tried before; it has been successful. The covenant is *practical*.

Finally, I conclude the book with a brief summary on how to apply the covenant to society-at-large. I call it "Little by Little." I don't want the reader to think we can impose this covenant concept on our culture by force, so I touch on the role of the witness: both in evangelism and in filing covenant lawsuits. After a short consideration of evangelism, seeing so much has already been written on this subject, I focus on the lawsuit. Very little has been said recently about this idea. I rely on the prophet *Hosea* as a guide, because his book follows the covenantal structure. But more importantly, the prophet shows us how he used the covenant to bring a *covenant lawsuit* against the

---

Bible? Or, is this just something unique to Deuteronomy and Moses? After all, we live in the New Covenant age. Maybe the same points are no longer valid. Can we find them in the New Testament?" As a matter of fact, once the five points of covenantalism are understood, we discover the pattern everywhere. In Appendixes one through six I show the covenant structure in several places in the Bible. Since Deuteronomy is actually the republishing of a previous covenant, we start with the Ten Commandments. We see the covenant structure twice, forming a twofold witness. Then we examine Psalms, Matthew, Romans, Revelation, and Hebrews 8. The five-fold pattern is a structure for both Old and New Testaments. Certainly there are differences, and we will consider them as well.

wicked. From this chapter, you will learn how to defeat the wicked when you are under-capitalized, out-classed, and under-manned.

So, *That You May Prosper* has two parts: covenant and dominion. When you finish, I hope you will see life differently. Perhaps covenant will have real, practical, life-changing meaning in your life! If our society could think and live this way, we could renew our forefathers' "errand in the wilderness" and change it into a *garden*. We could then see again the days of the new and final Josiah, a glorious rule by King Jesus!

1

TRUE TRANSCENDENCE
(Deuteronomy 1:1-5)

Just as King Josiah sat on his throne, another king also sat on a throne, a chair like a miniature mountain in the midst of a sea of ornate wealth. He had conquered all that could be conquered. He had built the greatest city in the world. Through his palace window, he could see the beautiful landscaped "hanging gardens" on the walls of the palace — gardens so legendary that they have been included among the seven wonders of the ancient world. Out of the corner of his eye, he caught a brief glimpse of a chariot darting by on the top of the wall surrounding the city, a wall so thick that it could handle six chariots riding side by side with room to spare. Who could break through such a fortress? Who could topple such a king?

He was to learn the answer soon: the God Who sits *above* men's fortresses.

His eyes then withdrew from the distance, distracted by the sun reflecting off the solid gold walls in the room where he was sitting. Old Babylon was truly one of the great wonders of the world, and this powerful king had been part of the creation of the empire. Then the old king began to think, "What's left for me? How can I rise above myself and history? How can I become immortally great?" Instantly, words popped into his head, seemingly from nowhere, but definitely from somewhere other than his own imagination.

> I will ascend to heaven;
> I will raise my throne above the stars of God,
> And I will sit on the mount of the assembly
> In the recesses of the North.
> I will ascend above the heights of the clouds;
> I will make myself like the Most High.[1]

---

1. These are statements made by a king of Babylon (Isa. 14:13-14). Some commentators attribute them to others, even Satan himself.

The words seemed right to him, yet they were horribly wrong. This king had been brought into covenant with God.[2] All of his greatness had come from God. Now the king had forgotten, and he desired to become more than man, even God Himself.

When God heard the king whisper these words in his heart, He said,

> You will be thrust down to Sheol,
> To the recesses of the pit.

God threw him down into hell because to attempt to be God was a denial of the covenant and specifically a denial of the first point of Biblical covenantalism, *true transcendence*. As we shall see, to err here was to break the entire covenant. Always.

That unnamed Babylonian king should have known better. He had the testimony of the greatest king of all before him: Nebuchadnezzar. We know from the life of Nebuchadnezzar what happens to men, especially great kings, when they elevate themselves in their own eyes to the very throne room of God. They are cast down by God. Adam learned this lesson in the garden of Eden when he was thrown out of it. Nebuchadnezzar learned it in the garden of Babylon, also when he was thrown out of it.

Nebuchadnezzar's Lesson

Nebuchadnezzar had a dream. He dreamed of a great tree that reached to the sky. The beasts of the field found shade under it. But the tree was cut down, and only the stump remained.

The tree was a man. The stump was a great man "cut down to size," so to speak. Seven periods of time passed over him. The dream informed the king:

> This sentence is by the decree of the angelic watches, and the decision is a command of the holy ones, in order that the living may know that the Most High is ruler over the realms of mankind, and bestows it [earthly sovereignty — R.S.] on whom He wishes, and sets over it the lowliest of men (Dan. 4:17).

---

2. The Bible does not say which of the Babylonian kings made this statement. Since the Babylonian leader, Nebuchadnezzar, was converted to Biblical religion but his family was not (Dan. 2:46-49), this would explain his descendants' familiarity with the covenant.

He asked Belteshazzar (Daniel) what the dream meant. It meant bad news for the king. The tree was the king himself. One of God's angels would cut him down. He would be driven into the fields, to eat grass with the beasts, for seven years. But there was hope in that vision, Daniel said, for "your kingdom will be assured to you after you recognize that it is Heaven that rules" (Dan. 4:26b).

Daniel then offered the king a way out of this prophecy. The way out is always the same for every person: *obey God.* "Therefore, O king, may my advice be pleasing to you: break away now from your sins by doing righteousness, and from your iniquities by showing mercy to the poor, in case there may be a prolonging of your prosperity" (Dan. 4:27).

The king forgot, as men so often do. A year later, he was walking on the roof of his royal palace. He saw himself as if he were God Almighty — a familiar sin in the history of man, from Adam to the present:

The king reflected and said, "Is this not Babylon the great, which I myself have built as a royal residence by the might of my power and for the glory of my majesty?" While the word was in the king's mouth, a voice came from heaven, saying, "King Nebuchadnezzar, to you it is declared: sovereignty has been removed from you, and you will be driven away from mankind, and your dwelling place will be with the beasts of the field. You will be given grass to eat like cattle, and seven periods of time will pass over you, until you recognize that the Most High is ruler over the realm of mankind, and bestows it [sovereignty] on whomever He wishes" (Dan. 4:30-32).

The dream's promised judgment came at last. But so did the restoration. After seven years, the king's sanity was restored to him by God, and he immediately praised God as the absolute Sovereign of the world: "For His dominion is an everlasting dominion, and His kingdom endures from generation to generation" (Dan. 4:34b). Then the king sat on his throne again: ". . . so I was reestablished in my sovereignty, and surpassing greatness was added to me. Now I Nebuchadnezzar praise, exalt, and honor the King of heaven, for all His works are true and His ways just, and He is able to humble those who walk in pride" (Dan. 3:36b-37).

But that was nothing compared to an even greater gift to that once-pagan Babylonian king. For what other king over a pagan empire ever had his own words recorded as the very Word of God to man? Not one. The fourth chapter of Daniel is the only chapter in the

Old Testament written by a non-Jew. Nebuchadnezzar's own words outlasted every kingdom of antiquity.

What was his theological lesson? First, he owed his position to God. Second, it is the essence of man's rebellion to think, speak, and act as though man is God. Third, God casts down those who seek to elevate themselves to the throne of God. In other words, man *falls* when he *seeks to rise* in his own power. Fourth, God offers restoration to man through man's grace-imposed humility and faithfulness to God's Word. A man who faithfully rules *under God* will rule *over the creation*.

God was above Nebuchadnezzar, yet He was also with Nebuchadnezzar. He could raise him up or pull him down. He is transcendent over mankind, yet close enough to know mankind's heart and to judge mankind perfectly. God, and God alone, is truly transcendent. The Biblical covenant starts with this point.

True Transcendence (Deut. 1:1-5)

The Deuteronomic covenant begins with a declaration of transcendence, when it says, "Moses spoke to the children of Israel according to all that the Lord commanded him to give to them" (Deut. 1:3). How does this statement indicate *transcendence*?

The Creator/Creature Distinction

Biblical transcendence means there is a fundamental distinction between the Creator's Being and the creature's being. The Deuteronomic covenant specifies such a distinction. Moses' words are differentiated from God's.[3] He speaks what God has given him. His words are not original. Thus, the covenant first declares God to be the Lord and Creator: the Creator of the covenant and everything else. Why Creator?

---

3. Kline, *Structure of Biblical Authority*, pp. 135-136. Kline makes note that the Hebrew *titles* of books are not the same as the titles in our English versions. They derived their titles from the Septuagint, the Greek translation of the Hebrew text (circa 200 B.C.). In the case of Deuteronomy, instead of receiving its name from Deuteronomy 17:18 ("A copy of this law," or "This second law" from the Greek, *to deuteronomion touto*), the Hebrew name of the text would actually be the first words, "These are the Words of." Since this phrase is clearly identical with the first lines of suzerain treaty covenants, Kline concludes that this way of *naming* the books of the Bible was a *covenantal* method of distinguishing the documents.

He also likens it to the phrase, "Thus saith the Lord." I find this observation to be extremely helpful because it means that the "thus saith the Lord formula" is the beginning of miniature covenants, and explains why it is constantly used.

The same fundamental distinction is basic to the creation of the world. God did not create the universe out of His own substance; He created it out of nothing. God says of His *creation covenant* of the world,[4] "In the beginning God created the heavens and the earth, and the earth was formless and void, and darkness was over the surface of the deep, and the Spirit of God was hovering over the surface of the waters" (Gen. 1:1-2). Space, time, matter, and history had a *beginning*. They are not eternal. Often God uses His transcendent creation of the world to make the point that He is Lord. Isaiah says,

I am the Lord, and there is no other; besides Me there is no God . . . The One forming light and creating darkness, causing well-being and calamity; I am the Lord who does all these (Isa. 45:5-7).

Paganism has always rejected this view of the origins of the universe. Pagans say that matter has always existed, whether they are primitive pagans ("the cosmic egg") or Greek pagans ("the co-eternity of matter and form") or modern scientific pagans ("the Big Bang"). They refuse to accept that God could *and did* create matter out of nothing. This would point to a God Who *presently sustains His creation personally*, which in turn points to the existence of a *God Who judges His creation continually*. Pagans seek above all else to escape God's judgment.

The Biblical idea of creation involves God's providential sustaining of creation throughout time and eternity. This is the meaning of providence. Because God *made* the world and personally *sustains* the world, He is present *with* the world, but is not part *of* the world. Because He is the Creator and Sustainer, He is also *present* (immanent) with us. This presence of God is equally an aspect of true transcendence. No other being is fully transcendent, so no other being is universally present. God alone is omnipresent (present everywhere).[5]

---

4. It is significant that God created the world with "ten words" in the repeated phrase, "And God said" (Gen. 1:3, 6, 9, 11, 14, 20, 24, 26, 27, 29), just as He *revealed* His covenant-law with "ten" words (Deut. 4:13). Also, Jeremiah refers to creation as a covenant (Jer. 33:19-26). Both in literary form and covenantal principle we see that the creation covenant begins with *true transcendence*, making creation itself another manner in which this principle is declared.

5. This becomes extremely important when we discuss the concept of hierarchy. Because Satan is not omnipresent, omnipotent, or omniscient, he must rely heavily on his covenantal hierarchy for information and power. God does not rely on His covenantal hierarchy; His people rely on it, but God does not. He voluntarily binds Himself to His creation by the terms of His covenant (Gen. 15), but He is not bound by any created hierarchy.

The following diagram (Figure 1)—one used by Cornelius Van Til, professor of apologetics at Westminster Theological Seminary (Philadelphia) for many years—pictures our definition of transcendence. The two separate circles show that each possesses a different "essence." God's Being is uncreated, and man's is created. God is original, and man is derivative, which explains why God's circle is bigger than man's. God is independent (aseity) and man is dependent. God is God, man is man, and the latter is never able to become God, although God did become man in Jesus Christ. Furthermore, God is also "near" by means of the covenant.

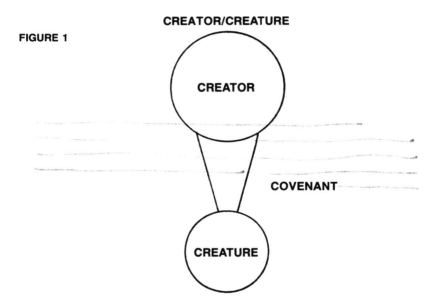

FIGURE 1

The covenant, as can be seen in the diagram, perfectly expresses a transcendent as well as an immanent view of God. Nothing but a Biblical covenant *could* adequately communicate both facets of transcendence. Such a covenant can be established only by a Creator God. Thus, at the heart of the Biblical doctrine of the covenant is the Biblical doctrine of creation.

The Fall as Covenant-Breaking

If man is not linked to God because of a commonly shared essence or being, then what is the link? Man is made in God's *image* (Gen. 1:26). He is under God *ethically*. He can understand God's

Word and obey God. In the state of perfection in the garden, Adam was assigned the task of dressing and keeping (guarding) the garden as God's agent. In other words, he was under a *covenant*.

But there is a huge problem with covenants: they can be broken. God says He will never break His, but that leaves man in a dangerous position. Break God's covenant, and God breaks you. A transcendent God lays down the law.

Man broke the law. He wanted to be as God, knowing (determining) good and evil (Gen. 3:5). That put man at the mercy of God. The personal relationship between Adam and God was broken, because all of God's *personal* relations with mankind are *covenantal* relations. They are not lawless relations. They are not random. They are personal because they are covenantal.

And Adam broke the covenant. He broke his personal relationship with God—a relationship of favor—and substituted a personal relationship of wrath. Understand, he did not move from a personal relationship with God to an impersonal relationship. God has no impersonal relationships with mankind. Man cannot escape the cosmic personalism of His Creator. Adam certainly could not escape. God returned to the garden, cross-examined Adam and Eve, and sentenced them. But He also offered them a promise of hope (Gen. 3:15), and then He clothed them before He cast them out.

Man's post-Fall relationship with God is therefore one of judgment, promise, and *preliminary* mercy: time to repent and then rebuild the covenantal relationship. What man needs is not some program to become God; that was his original sin. Instead, he needs restoration of a right relationship with God. He needs a *restoration inside the covenant*. This restoration is *judicial* (meaning legal), and it is *moral* (meaning ethical). God lays down the law, and we obey. God declares, and we respond. It is God's declaration which is fundamental. He judges, and we respond in terms of His holy judgments.

What fallen man needs, above all else, is a declaration from God, a declaration of "Not Guilty." Only a transcendent God can make such a declaration.

Covenant By Imputation

The same verse in the opening section of Deuteronomy is *declarative*, "Moses spoke all the Lord *commanded*" (Deut. 1:3). This tells us something foundational about the covenant. Transcendence means the covenant is created by a *legal declaration*. As a result of this declaration, a certain legal status is imputed to the relationship. We can call this the doctrine of *imputation*, a legal term meaning "to apply to the account of."

How does imputation work? God told Adam that the day that he ate of the tree of the knowledge of good and evil, he would die (Gen. 2:17). He ate, yet he did not *physically* die at the precise moment he ate the "apple." Then in what sense did he die? Some people try to explain his death as "spiritual." But the Bible does not speak this way. A better explanation is that *Adam's death was covenantal*, in that God imputed death to him. God *counted him as dead* because of the broken covenant. Then, as Adam experienced the burdens of history, he would draw closer and closer to physical and perhaps even eternal death. He would see the covenantal applications of death in history. Those manifestations of covenantal death would be all around him throughout his life. Imputation went from life to death: from Adam's physical life to Adam's eventual physical death.

Imputation worked the other way too: from death to life. How could Adam be allowed by God to live? How could he *legally* escape the immediate judgment of God? Because God looked forward in time to the death of Christ. Christ's death satisfied God's legal requirement that Adam be destroyed that very day, body and soul. Adam may or may not have been saved in the sense of eternal salvation, but he surely was saved from immediate physical death. God *imputed* earthly life to him — the life which Christ earned on the cross. He then gave Adam and Eve a promise concerning the future (Gen. 3:15). Christ's death had assured that future, and the promise spoke of Christ (the seed) crushing the head of the serpent.

We find this same concept of "applying to the account of" in the Biblical concept of redemption. What does it mean to redeem something? It means *to buy it back*. In the case of God's redemption of His people, He applies Christ's "account paid" certificate to each Christian's debt to Him. He imputes Christ's righteousness to us. And He could never impute redemption unless He is transcendent and possesses transcendent authority. This is why some of the Pharisees were so angry when Christ declared "Your sins are forgiven" to a man. They asked in their hearts, "Why does this man speak this way? He is blaspheming; who can forgive sins but God alone?" (Mark 2:7). They fully understood that He was claiming true transcendence for Himself.

Thus, covenant theology says that man's relationship with God is based on a transcendent declaration, that is, *a declaration which is both legal and ethical.* By this, God imputes a certain status to the relationship. Nothing is "infused" into man to change his being and thereby make him acceptable to God. God does not stand like a cosmic physician with a giant syringe filled with righteousness, to inject a dose of it into this or that person. He certainly does not inject a spark of divinity into anyone. Man is judged by God *as man,* not as "almost a devil" or "almost God." The Apostle Paul says that God *declares* us righteous:

> . . . being justified [legally declared right with God] as a gift by His grace through the redemption which is in Christ Jesus; whom God displayed publicly as a propitiation [payment] in His blood through faith. This was to demonstrate His righteousness, because in the forbearance of God He passed over the sins previously committed; for the demonstration, I say, of His righteousness at the present time, that He might be just and the justifier of the one who has faith in Jesus. Where is boasting? . . .The one who does not work, but believes in Him who justifies the ungodly, his faith is reckoned [imputed] as righteousness (Rom. 3:24-4:5).

When a man is saved, righteousness is laid to his account, and he is *declared* right, justified. This way, unrighteous men can have salvation. They do not have to become good before they can be saved. They *cannot become* good before they are saved. They are *objectively* saved because God *declares* them to be saved. They are objectively good because God declares them to be objectively good. He can do this in terms of His covenant because of Christ's objective work of salvation in history. That objective work is imputed to the redeemed person by God's grace. In theology, this is often described as the *objective* side of salvation. Always, *the objective forms the basis of the subjective.* Normally the term "objective" is applied to salvation, but this redemptive concept pulls over into all of life, making every relationship grounded in the legal or objective. That which is *declared legal* by God is therefore *objectively legal.*

We now have an answer to that old mind-twister: "Does God declare something good because it is objectively good, or is it objectively good because God declares it good." The covenantal answer is that something is objectively good because God declares it to be good, and He can do this because *God imputes Christ's objective, covenant-obeying goodness* to it. It meets God's objective standards of goodness because Christ met God's objective standards of goodness.

Understand, there is no conflict between objective and subjective in the mind of God. God's subjective evaluation of His subjective standards carries objective meaning. Something can be objectively true only because the whole universe is sustained and interpreted by a totally personal, totally subjective Creator. Christianity destroys the false dualism between subjective and objective, between personal and impersonal.

Man's covenant with God can only be declared by a transcendent legal act. All other covenants are formed on the same principle. Let us examine some cases in which this Biblical insight is the basis of social relationships.

Judicial Theology in Society

The principle is this: *transcendent declaration* is what officially creates or destroys a relationship; it imputes the status of covenant life or covenant death to the union.

Imputation of Covenant Death

Let's begin with covenant death. If you were talking to me, and I dropped dead on the spot, would you immediately bury me? I hope not! You would need to call a *coroner* and have me *declared legally dead*. Is this some unnecessary "legal fiction"? No. This principle of declaring someone legally dead is built on the first point of covenantalism. Who knows, you might "think" I am dead, when in reality I might be in a deep coma. I could be buried alive. (This "legal" way of thinking makes good *practical* sense.) So life and death are covenantal. They are not *primarily* physically determined.

It is true that I am not objectively dead because the coroner declares me to be dead. He has objective standards to apply. What we must say is that God establishes life and death, and He defines life and death, and progressively as men discipline themselves to God's covenantal standards, they can better apply these God-given standards in history. From a legal standpoint, however, society must delegate to someone the legal authority to declare someone dead. He may make a mistake, as men do, but he has the legal authority to make this mistake, for he has the legal authority to make the declaration. Without this delegated authority, a lot of murderers could escape earthly justice.

Is it possible for an institution to be covenantally dead, even though it still physically exists? Yes. Jesus says a *church* can become a "synagogue of Satan" (Rev. 3:9). The members are still physically alive, continue to meet, and go through all the motions of "churchiness," but the church body is *covenantally dead*. Its preaching, prayers, and worship are satanic. To God this death is more real than the physical. Is this church hopeless? No. To continue as a true church, members and officers would have to renew their *covenant* with God. That is, the particular local or denominational church would have to be resurrected.

Why can't we say this of other institutions? We can! They are also established on the basis of the covenant. If family governments and civil governments break it, they can covenantally cease to exist. And like the Church, to restore Biblical governmental authority to a family or a civil government, its members would have to *renew the covenant* and be *resurrected*. This would explain why Israel had to renew its national covenant before continuing as a nation (II Chron. 7:14; Neh. 8-9). This would also explain why nations are wiped off the face of the earth if they fail to renew their covenant after it is broken. Regarding the family unit, this would explain how marriages can be physically alive but covenantally dead. In fact, *covenantal death is the whole rationale for divorce and remarriage.*

Imputation of Covenant Life

Let us take another example of covenantal thinking. When is a marriage a marriage? Recently, a priest nullified a marriage between two quadriplegics. He reasoned that a marriage could not be a marriage unless it could be physically consummated. This implies that the physical relationship is the basis of marriage. But covenantal theology says that *God's legal, transcendent declaration forms a marital union.* The couple can be legally married and even have legal children through another aspect of imputation, adoption.[6]

Also, this transcendent and legal foundation of marriage makes it more than just a human institution. God establishes marriage, in addition to the other institutions of society (State and Church). Men

---

6. In the Old Testament, the father could legitimatize a relationship between his daughter and another man who fornicated with her before marriage (Deut. 22:28-29). The man paid a dowry price, and if the father accepted, the marriage was legitimate. A legal transaction created the marriage, not physical consummation, in other words.

do not autonomously (self-law) create marriages, nor should they destroy them. Marriage is sacred. Jesus says, "What God has joined together, a man should not put asunder" (Matt. 19:6). Only the covenantal principle of transcendence makes it possible to declare or impute such a status to marriage.

Thus, society's relationships are supposed to rest on what God declares to be legitimate (legal). They are formed and declared alive by covenantal transactions. As long as parties comply with the covenant, their relationship lives. Should they violate their covenantal arrangement, however, the declaration of life is challenged. Their relationship could be judged dead, and it would then come under a declaration of death. In either case, relationships are established and disestablished on the basis of some kind of legal declaration. The alternative is to base them on the physical (biological). Take the institution of marriage as an example. Sex, physical appearance, or even feelings (emotions) would be the basis of the relationship. They would also be the basis of its dissolution. Should one of the partners no longer be sexually appealling, the marriage could be dissolved. So, society's relationships are designed by God to be founded on a judicial proclamation, and not the physical.

To summarize: I have established two points in this chapter thus far. Transcendence (distinction of being) means God *creates* covenants. And second, He does so by means of *legal declaration*, what I have called *imputation*. Let us now change direction. Let us consider the counterfeits of Biblical transcendence.

Counterfeit Doctrines

Because of God's transcendent Being, man can relate to God only by *covenant*. This insight is the heart of Biblical religion. It has been neglected by Christians far too long. Christians have hardly bothered with such questions as transcendence and immanence. But anti-Christian religions have been quite aware of these issues. All rival worldviews have been forced to deal with the concepts of transcendence and immanence. But all anti-Christian worldviews deal with these issues in an anti-Biblical and therefore *anti-covenantal* way. They substitute a false doctrine of the relationship between God and man. They go right back to Adam's sin: the desire to be as God. They declare that *man and God are really of the same essence*. Nebuchadnezzar's lesson has been lost on them.

Fallen man wants either a transcendent god or an immanent god, but he does not want a *personal* God, for such a God is a *covenantal* God. Covenant means law, law means obedience, and disobedience means judgment. As I have said, fallen men above all want to escape God's judgment. Why? Because they are disobedient.

Fallen man wants a substitute. He does not want a substitute perfect man to serve as the sin-bearer of the world. This would point to fallen man's lack of divinity and his need of salvation. So instead of accepting Christ as man's legal substitute, the ethical rebel substitutes a false god who cannot execute legal judgment. The doctrine of substitution is inescapable: fallen man simply wants a substitute god of his own creation rather than a substitutionary atonement and God's imputation.

False Transcendence

Why do men want a transcendent God, but without a covenant bond linking such a God to man? Answer: to substitute a *distant* god of man's creation for the all-too-present God of the Bible. The idea of a god's transcendence in an anti-Biblical sense means distance, not God's absolute personal authority. Such a distant god is the god of deism. Such a god is said to have created the world. He "wound it up" long ago like the spring in a new clock. He then removed himself completely from his creation. He allows it to work its way down over time. He does not interfere with its activities. And, above all, he does not judge it. He is so transcendent that he just does not care what happens to it. In short, this god is *impersonal*. (By the way, hardly anyone has ever really believed in the purely deistic eighteenth-century god of the history books, since such a god is just too far removed to be of assistance when people get in a crisis. He does not hear prayers or answer them. He is just too useless to be saleable.)

Guess who becomes the god of this world if this creator god of deism is far, far away? You guessed it! Man does. Man becomes the substitute god. The creator god is "on vacation." He does not judge kings, kingdoms, or bureaucrats. When it comes to exercising judgment in history, he defaults. Man can speak; deism's god is silent. Man's word therefore substitutes for god's word. Man substitutes himself for this substitute god. Man becomes the god of the system, knowing (determining) good and evil.

So, without the transcendent, personal, *covenantal* God of the

Bible, man simply repeats the sin of Adam: to be as God.

The personal God of the Bible is too distinct for comfort. The impersonal god of deism is too distant to be taken seriously.

False Immanence

Virtually everyone has rejected such a deistic view of god. But what is the alternative? An *immanent* god. This is the god of pantheism, both Eastern and Western. This is the god who is immersed in his creation. He is the "true reality" of creation. In certain forms of Hinduism, he is the hidden unity that underlies the creation, and the creation is itself said to be an illusion, *maya*. But in all these pantheistic religions, man is endowed by a "spark of divinity," and man will ultimately experience union with god. This is the god of *monism*. God cannot be distinguished from the creation.

Guess who becomes the god of this world if pantheism's creation-immersed god is too, too close? You guessed it again! Man does. If god is immersed in the creation, then man becomes a substitute god. Man enjoys that spark of divinity. Man can also speak; pantheism's god is silent. Man's word therefore substitutes for god's word. Man becomes the god of the system, knowing (determining) good and evil.

So, without the transcendent, personal, *covenantal* God of the Bible, man simply repeats the sin of Adam: to be as God.

The personal God of the Bible is too close for comfort. The impersonal god of pantheism is too close to be taken seriously.

Shared Being

All non-covenantal views of transcendence and immanence have one thing in common. They teach union of *essence*. God's and man's "beings" run together in some way. The god of deism is so like the world that when he separates himself from it, he can have no influence over it. He just isn't transcendent enough to run the world system. Similarly, the god of pantheism is so like the world that when he immerses himself in it, he can have no influence over it. The key words for fallen mankind are *no influence*. So, when fallen man speaks of either transcendence or immanence, he means something completely different from what the Bible means. Cornelius Van Til's comments explain the difference.

It is not a sufficient description of Christian theism when we say that as Christians we believe in both the transcendence and the immanence of

God, while pantheistic systems believe only in the immanence of God and deistic systems believe only in the transcendence of God. The transcendence we believe in is not the transcendence of deism, and the immanence we believe in is not the immanence of pantheism. In the case of deism, transcendence virtually means separation, while in the case of pantheism immanence virtually means identification. *And if we add separation to identification, we do not have theism as a result.*[7]

False transcendence, defined as *distance*, totally removes God from any involvement with His creation, thereby making man his own "god." After all, whatever happens on earth is left up to man or fate. False immanence (pantheism) coalesces the nature of God and the nature of man, so that some kind of "spark of divinity in every man" results. Man again ends up being a god. Theologically and practically speaking, both of these false views lead to *man's deification* and *God's humanization*. The root of all heresy is found here. Van Til writes: "All forms of heresy, those of the early church and those of modern times, spring from this confusion of God with the world. All of them, in some manner and to some extent, substitute the idea of man's participation in God for that of his creation by God."[8]

Metaphysical Religion

There are only two theologies in the world: covenantal and metaphysical. Metaphysical religion means a union "beyond" (meta) the physical. It can also be called "chain of being" religion, or "monism."[9] The idea is that man and God are one essence, not two distinct essences joined by a legal covenant. This view is the archenemy of Christianity. This is the monistic monster that has many heads with one basic common denominator: *continuity of being.* Whenever men seek to discover the "underlying essence" of the uni-

---

7. Cornelius Van Til, *The Defense of the Faith* (Philadelphia: Presbyterian and Reformed Publishing Co., 1972), p. 11. Emphasis mine.

8. Van Til, *Theology of James Daane* (Philadelphia: Presbyterian and Reformed Publishing Co., 1959), pp. 122-123.

9. Arthur O. Lovejoy, *The Great Chain of Being* (Cambridge: Harvard University Press, [1936] 1964). This is difficult reading because his book was originally a series of lectures. But there is real "gold" in terms of insight. For a simpler but somewhat "heavy" presentation of "chain of being" religion is R. J. Rushdoony, *The One and The Many* (Nutley, New Jersey: Craig Press, 1971), pp. 36-62. Also see a more contemporary scholar, who attempts to define and extend Lovejoy, Francis Oakley, *Omnipotence, Covenant, & Order* (Ithaca: Cornell University Press, 1984), pp. 15-40, where he establishes that Lovejoy was cutting "against the stream" of the West. Lovejoy stood against the chain of being tendencies with covenant theology.

verse without reference to the Creator God of the universe, they have adopted a form of monism.

The Totem Pole

Perhaps this counterfeit of the Biblical covenant is best pictured by the familiar *totem pole* image, the organizing symbol of the American Indians, which is found in most religions of the world in some form or another. It graphically portrays society as beings on a continuum, either vertically or horizontally structured. Notice the contrast between the following diagrams and the covenantal picture in the first diagram (p. 26).

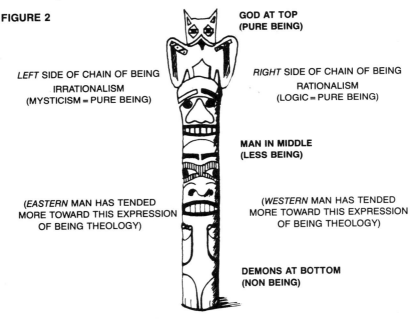

CHAIN OF BEING
(ALL LIFE OF SAME ESSENCE TO GREATER OR LESSER DEGREE)

FIGURE 2

GOD AT TOP
(PURE BEING)

LEFT SIDE OF CHAIN OF BEING
IRRATIONALISM
(MYSTICISM = PURE BEING)

RIGHT SIDE OF CHAIN OF BEING
RATIONALISM
(LOGIC = PURE BEING)

MAN IN MIDDLE
(LESS BEING)

(*EASTERN* MAN HAS TENDED
MORE TOWARD THIS EXPRESSION
OF BEING THEOLOGY)

(*WESTERN* MAN HAS TENDED
MORE TOWARD THIS EXPRESSION
OF BEING THEOLOGY)

DEMONS AT BOTTOM
(NON BEING)

FIGURE 3   **EVOLUTIONARY WORLDVIEW**
(BEING THEOLOGY ON ITS SIDE)

NON BEING   MAN   SPIRIT
PRE-EXISTENT MATTER   MORE BEING   PURE BEING
                                                            GOD

Continuity of being characterizes both diagrams. Life according to this system is a _continuum_. At the top is the purest form of deity. At the very bottom is the least pure. They only differ in _degree_, not in kind. God is a _part of_ creation. Man, who is somewhere in the middle of the continuum, is god in another "form." In other words, god is just a "super" man, and man is not a god . . . yet!

This kind of religion has expressed itself in many ways. The ancient Greeks, for example, officially worshipped Olympian gods who were nothing more than "larger-than-life" men. Such gods were not truly divine in the Biblical sense. They were not distinct from the creation. They married, committed adultery with other gods, came down to earth and committed more adultery with people, and so on. They were just an extension of man. This was the theology of legend and myth, and these myths were not taken very seriously by anybody in ancient Greece. The *real* religion of Greece was much worse: they worshipped the spirits of dead ancestors.[10] Families had to keep a ritual fire alive ("keep the home fires burning") and offer meat and meal sacrifices from time to time, in order to keep dead family spirits from haunting them.

The Greeks did not believe that every dead person would become either a wandering spirit or a local spirit that had to be placated by religious rites by his descendants. They believed that some men could become true gods after death. These people were called *heroes*. They were local athletes or warriors or political leaders who were publicly invested with divinity after death.[11]

A more modern example of this sort of thinking, and one very close to home, is *Mormonism*. Mormonism teaches that man can evolve into God.[12] In fact, Mormonism teaches that "good" Mormons die, change into gods, and live on other planets somewhere. This is the modern equivalent of Greece's hero worship.

Also, as for figure 2, there is a right and a left. Both sides express different methods of deification. The right side of metaphysical theology says "reason" is pure being: rationalism. Man becomes god through pure reason (logic). The left side holds that "mysticism" is

---

10. Fustel de Coulanges, *The Ancient City* (Glouchester, Massachusetts: Peter Smith, [1864] 1979).

11. Jane Harrison, *Prolegomena to the Study of Greek Religion*, 3rd ed. (New York: Meridian, [1922] 1955), ch. 7: "The Making of a God."

12. *Teachings of the Prophet Joseph Smith*, ed. Joseph Fielding Smith (Salt Lake City: Deseret Book Co., 1958), pp. 346-347.

pure being: irrationalism. Man becomes a god through experience. Sinful man tends to believe that he can know God through facts or feelings. He can "think" or "feel" his way to God. Although both forms of metaphysical religion appear in East and West, generally the West has drifted toward rationalism, and the East toward mysticism. Either expression of metaphysical theology and practice is pagan to the core. *All* ancient paganism holds to this diabolical theology: whether Ancient Egypt, Greece, or the Druids. The one common denominator is that *God and man are of the same essence*.

Figure 3

When we come to figure 3, we discover that it is figure 2 turned on its side. Science has called this religion "evolution." Matter is eternal. Man does not "mature" as is taught in the Bible; instead, he evolves in his very essence. Man becomes a new creature, not in the Bible's ethical sense, but rather through the generations, he literally becomes a new creature.

Ultimately, matter brings death and oblivion to mankind, for either the universe completely wears out over time (the "heat death" of the universe), or else it collapses and starts over again, wiping away all trace of mankind.[13] It goes forward into death, or else it oscillates and kills. Man is therefore like a parasite in a host that is dying, or else in a host whose actions will eventually kill him. Matter is therefore something to be escaped from, yet modern science knows of no way to provide an escape. But *in the meantime*, evolutionistic science affirms, things *can* change. Species can adapt to new environments. Life goes on. So, evolution is nothing more than the old ancient chain-of-being religion in disguise. Sociologist-historian Robert Nisbet has recognized this intellectual "missing link" between modern science and ancient religion and philosophy:

In the biological sciences also in the eighteenth century the ideas of the chain of being and plenitude prospered. In the writings of such notable biologists as Buffon, Cuvier, Maupertuis, Bonnet, and Erasmus Darwin, grandfather of Charles, the theory of biological evolution was first set forth lucidly and comprehensively. Although some held firmly to the separation of the species, envisaging evolution in the Aristotelian terms of intraspecies, others anticipated Charles Darwin in stressing the linkage of the

---

13. Gary North, *Is the World Running Down? Crisis in the Christian Worldview* (Tyler, Texas: Institute for Christian Economics, 1987), ch. 2.

species in time through the emergence of one from the other. The Platonic vision of perfect, uninterrupted, absolutely continuous nature and plentitudinous nature reigned widely, though it is doubtful that any of the evolutionists had the remotest notion of the origin of their visions of the past and present. Breaks in the chain were as obvious to the naturalists of the eighteenth century as they had been to Aristotle, but this merely intensified the search for "missing links."[14]

Modern man has fought hard to find biological "missing links." He is religious, yet he does not want to relate to God through His covenant. He finds a replacement in either form of chain-of-being religion: vertical or horizontal. Man seeks self-transcendence upward (mysticism) or forward (power). He chooses not to seek the restoration of the covenant, for this would place him in ethical bondage to a truly transcendent sovereign God forever.

Conclusion

The introductory story of the Babylonian king sums up everything in the first point of covenantalism. He claimed transcendence; he claimed to be *God*. And remember, he made this claim by *legal declaration*. He attempted to *impute* a certain status to himself. He *said*, "I will ascend . . ." (Isa. 14:13). He thus proposed a counterfeit form of transcendence.

There have been two parts to this chapter. First, I presented the concept of transcendence. It means *distinction of being*. Concerning Deuteronomy 1:1-5, I observed that God's words are distinguished from Moses'. Right off, God is presented as transcendent. I drew two corollaries from this observation. One, He is the creator of the covenant. His creation did not come from His Being, but separate from it, out of nothing. Creation is at the heart of the covenant. Two, God creates the covenant by legal declaration. After man's creation, he fell. He could only be restored by being *imputed a certain status of righteousness*, the doctrine of imputation. Adam did not immediately die as God had promised. His life was only sustained by the imputation of another life, Jesus'. God re-established covenant by imputation.

This led to a basic social application of the two points I made about transcendence. Transcendent declaration creates and de-creates relationships. It is supposed to be the basis of relationships.

---

14. Robert Nisbet, *Prejudices* (Cambridge, Massachusetts: Harvard University Press, 1982), p. 38.

A marriage, for example, is formed by God's declaration: "What God has joined, let no man put asunder." So this legal declaration — not sex, not romantic feelings — forms the covenant bond. This brought me to the end of the first half of the chapter.

Second, I presented the counterfeit doctrines of transcendence. God is a *personal* God because He is a *covenantal* God. When men seek to escape the covenant's bond, and therefore escape the judgment of God, they turn to concepts of God that are at bottom *impersonal*. An impersonal god always leaves man as the sovereign of the universe, by default. Man wants to be the sovereign of this world. This was Adam's sin. This was Nebuchadnezzar's sin.

True transcendence means there are only two systems of theology: covenant theology and chain-of-being theology. Since man is utterly distinct from God in his being, he must be united to God (and to other people) by a covenant. This union cannot be a union of "essence." Essential union is called *monism* or the *chain of being*. There are vertical and horizontal expressions of this theology. Ancient religion takes the form of the vertical, while modern religion has been called evolution. Both are essentially the same: man becomes god, either directly or by god's default.

In the second principle of covenantalism, we will turn our attention from transcendence to hierarchy, meaning the authority concept of the covenant. God is transcendent, and He establishes *legal representatives* who mediate life and death to earth. We will consider several questions. What is the authority structure of the covenant? What is the relationship between authority and history? Does God actually render judgment in history? What is the connection between what goes on among God's people and what happens in the world?

2

HIERARCHY
(Deuteronomy 1:6-4:49)

There was a time when God's people were very different from the rest of the world. Everybody else had a king, but they did not.

God's children did not like being "politically alienated." They complained. God heard them. He had planned for a king (Christ), but they wanted a king like the rest of the world's leaders. He gave them what they wanted, choosing the best looking, tallest, strongest young man He could find, Saul.

Saul started off well, but it was not long before he displeased God. Saul's basic problem was he could not follow *orders*, the fundamental requirement to be a soldier in God's army. God's prophet, Samuel, would tell him to do one thing, and he would do another.

One day, God sent Samuel to tell Saul to destroy the Amalekites. The specific instructions were,

Go and strike Amalek and utterly destroy all that he has, and do not spare him; but put to death both man and woman, child and infant, ox and sheep, camel and donkey (I Sam. 15:3).

Saul's orders were clear. With God on his side, he could not lose. The victory was swift. But Saul decided to take a short-cut to submission. He kept some of the sheep and other spoils of war, as well as the king, Agag. Samuel was extremely upset because he knew God would be angry with the whole nation for this insubordination.

When Samuel found Saul, the disobedient king tried to justify his behavior, saying he was going to use the sheep and spoils of war to offer sacrifice to God. He was even willing to use sacrifice as an excuse for not submitting to God's commandments.

Samuel said,

Has the Lord as much delight in burnt offerings and sacrifices
As in obeying the voice of the Lord?
Behold, to obey is better than sacrifice,
And to heed than the fat of rams.
For rebellion is as the sin of divination,
And insubordination is as iniquity and idolatry.
(I Sam. 15:22-23)

Saul had violated the Lord's *hierarchy*. Even though he was king, he was supposed to submit to the prophet Samuel. Why? The prophet was the embodiment of the Word of God, a hierarchy mediating life and death. To disobey the prophet was to disobey the covenantal system of authority.

Samuel's words — "Rebellion is as the sin of witchcraft" (divination) — summarize the relationship between authority and idolatry. Rebellion is a rejection of some sort of *representative* authority of God, who by definition represents God. It substitutes another hierarchy, in Saul's case, a medium. He started off rebelling against the authority structure God had placed over him, and ended up in witchcraft. Perhaps Saul thought that he, a covenantal man, would never stoop to such a thing. Eventually, however, he did exactly as Samuel had predicted; he began to consult a witch (I Sam. 28:3-7). He went to a foreign authority to have life mediated to him. At this point, he committed idolatry, since the medium *represented* another lord, Satan himself.

Idolatry and rebellion bring us to the logical connection between the first and second points of covenantalism. Saul's behavior links the two. Reject the truly transcendent God, attempt to find transcendence and immanence in the words of a medium, and the result is rebellion. How? If God is transcendent, the true Covenantal Suzerain, then He establishes His *authority* on earth. He makes His Lordship *visible* by establishing *representatives*, a hierarchy. He establishes *delegated* authorities, who work from the bottom up, not a bureaucracy, working from the top down. Saul wanted a manipulative bureaucracy in the form of mediums, instead of responsible obedience to the Word of God. When the king rejected the prophet's mediation, he was rejecting God's transcendent hierarchy and opting for a humanistic bureaucracy. Let us consider the second point of covenantalism to see how the Biblical hierarchy works.

Hierarchy: Visible Sovereignty

The second section of Deuteronomy begins with a brief statement of the hierarchy among God's people. Moses says,

How can I bear the load and burden of you and your strife? Choose wise and discerning and experienced men from your tribes, and I will appoint them as your heads. And you answered me and said, "The thing which you have said to do is good." So I took the heads of your tribes, wise and experienced men, and appointed them heads over you, leaders of thousands, and of hundreds, of fifties and of tens, and officers for your tribes. Then I charged your judges at that time, saying, "Hear the cases between your fellow countrymen, and judge righteously between a man and his fellow countryman, or the alien who is with him. You shall not show partiality in judgment; you shall hear the small and the great alike. You shall not fear man, for the judgment is God's. And the case that is too hard for you, you shall bring to me, and I will hear it" (Deut. 1:12-17).

It is really very simple. Biblical hierarchy is a series of courts with delegated authorities over each level. The procedure is from the bottom up. Since the Biblical system of authority is placed immediately after the transcendence section, it is the way in which God makes His transcendence known on earth. In the ancient suzerain covenants, a hierarchical and historical section (historical prologue) would always follow the preamble, what I have called the transcendence segment. The suzerain identified himself as Lord and then he proved it by setting up his authority in history.[1] To be precise, he made the newly conquered vassal a visible authority, one who represented him. This idea of "visible sovereignty" was copied from the archetype of all sovereignty, God.

The Biblical covenant has the same pattern. This progression of thought in Deuteronomy is very important. There is a movement from the declaration of transcendence to the temporal demonstration of transcendence, from the verbal to the visual, and from heaven to earth. This progression is the same all through the Bible. It is God's way.

---

1. Kline, *Structure of Biblical Authority*, pp. 114-115. Kline refers to the treaty of Mursilis and his vassal Duppi-Teshub of Amurru. He says, "Such treaties continued in an 'I-thou' style with an historical prologue surveying the great king's previous relations with, and especially his benefactions to, the vassal king." A translation of this treaty, along with many others, can be found in A. Goetze, *Ancient Near Eastern Texts*, ed. J. B. Pritchard (Princeton: Princeton University Press, 1950), pp. 203ff.

In the beginning, God created the world by His Word. What He declared was visualized. If God had declared light, and the light had not come into existence, then we could safely say that God could not declare light. The idea is that *what God says comes to pass*, and if it doesn't, then God is revealed as a liar.

Enter Satan. Six days after creation, Satan tried to make God a liar. His strategy was ingenious. He struck at God's hierarchy by taking the delegated authority given to Adam, and by actually convincing the first man to give it to *him*. He offered Adam divine authority in place of a delegated authority. He told man he would become like God, "knowing [determining] good and evil" (Gen. 3:5), if he ate the tree of the knowledge of good and evil. Yet, he was trying to convince Adam of something that was already true. Man was created in the "image" of God (Gen. 1:26). In this sense, he already was like God, a theomorphe. But the way to manifest God was not by "knowing" (determining) good and evil; rather, it was by ruling as a delegated authority. In the greatest deception of history, Satan had succeeded in robbing man of what he possessed by offering him what he could never have. By so doing, he effectively made the first man obey his authority, which in turn made him the vice regent[2] of the earth, and placed diabolical leaders in office. Adam's disobedience gave away God's visible sovereignty, as well as his own delegated authority, and made Satan, not man, appear to be God.

The implication was devastating. Remember the progression of the manifestation of sovereignty from verbal to visual and from declaration to temporal demonstration (history)? God speaks, and man obeys. God's authority is over man, and man's authority is over the creation. Man mediates between God and the creation. But Satan comes, disguised as a creature which was below man, and he also speaks. Whose voice is the true voice of authority? Man is tempted to respond to the creature and disobey the Creator. Man is still an intermediary. He mediates between the Creator and the creation. This is his inescapable role. It is never a question of mediation or no mediation; it is always a question of who is sovereign above man, and who is subordinate beneath him. Satan sought ethical authority (law-giver status) over man in order to manipulate God and God's plan for the ages. God had declared Adam as His image, yet man symbolically placed himself beneath the creation (a serpent) and

---

2. Sometimes written vice gerent.

over God. This was an act of rebellion. It was an attempt to reverse the order of creation by turning upside down God's hierarchy. God had specifically told Adam that man's rule over animals images God's rule over creation (Gen. 1:28). Now Adam listened to Satan as the supposed sovereign law-giver. He placed himself under a creature (a serpent), and a rebellious creature at that. Satan had reversed everything — covenantally, not metaphysically.

The rest of the Bible tells the story of how God re-established not His sovereignty — He never lost it because it can't be lost — but Adam's hierarchical rule over the world. God did this by sending a seed who represented Him better than Adam, Seth. But one by one each seed person fell, just like Adam, until the true Son, Jesus Christ. He was the only one who could truly manifest God's visible sovereignty. He died, rose again, and put a new delegated hierarchy on the earth again, the Church. The Apostle Paul describes this fact:

> He [God the Father] raised Him [Christ, God the Son] from the dead, and seated Him at His right hand in the heavenly places, far above all rule and authority and power and dominion, and every name that is named, not only in this age, but also in the one to come. And He put all things in *subjection* under His feet, and gave Him as head over all things *to the church*, which is His body, the fulness of Him who fills all in all (Eph. 1:20-23).

Notice the progression from transcendence to hierarchy in this passage. Christ is raised and seated in *heaven*, and then His authority is planted on *earth*. The Lord declares Christ's *transcendence*, and then establishes Christ's visible sovereignty through the rule of His people as His *authority*.

There is no escape from the principle of man's God-given mediatory authority. If God's authorities do not rule, neither does He, in the sense of a public manifestation of authority. He manifests visible sovereignty through the visible authority of those who are in visible covenant to Him. The Christian always affirms that God rules over His creation. God (*theos*) rules (*kratos*). We live in a theocracy. The entire universe is a theocracy. Every human institution is a theocracy — Church, State, Family, business, etc. There is no escape from theocracy. But Christians in every aspect of their daily lives are supposed to make manifest His rule *in every institution* (and not just the State).[3] This is why God is interested in having earthly authority.

---

3. This does *not* mean that the institutional Church is to control politics (ecclesiocracy). It means that Biblical principles are to govern the affairs of men.

This is why Paul encourages the Ephesian Church to take rule! Christ has conquered the powers and now He wants them out of office. It is time for Christians to take their place of authority! How is this done? First, we have to understand the central principle of hierarchy. Second, we can then analyze how God puts His people into positions of authority through accountability.

The Representative Principle

The second section of the covenant presents Israel as the Lord's *representative* on the earth. They were a priesthood, a hierarchy. They not only had an internal system of representation, they represented the rest of the nations. In the Old Testament, the priests of Israel during the feast of booths (trumpets) offered sacrifices for a week in the name of the gentile nations. This feast symbolized the ingathering of the nations. On day one, they offered 13 bulls, day two they offered 12, and so on, for seven days. On the seventh day, they offered seven bulls (Nu. 29:13-34). This totalled 70 bulls, corresponding to the 70 nations that represented all the nations of the earth (Gen. 10).[4]

The Church in New Testament times serves a similar function. The New Testament compares the Church's liturgy to the Old Testament's: ". . . golden bowls full of incense, which are the prayers of the saints" (Rev. 5:8; cf. 8:3). The same function of prayer was found in the Old Testament (Ps. 141:2). Instead of burning bulls on an altar, the Church offers prayers as sacrifices. Churches are supposed to pray "on behalf of all men" (I Tim. 2:1), and also for civil rulers, that we might experience peace (I Tim. 2:2). The key phrase, of course, is "on behalf of"—the *representative function.*

Representation is inescapable. Van Til observes, "The covenant idea is nothing but the expression of the *representative principle* consistently applied to all reality."[5] All of creation images God, especially man. And because of sin, man needs a representative to atone for him. Paul explains the representative principle when he says, "For if by the transgression of the one [Adam] the many died, much more did the grace of God and the gift by the grace of one Man, Jesus Christ, abound to many" (Rom. 5:15). Since mankind has no essen-

---

4. James B. Jordan, *The Law of the Covenant: An Exposition of Exodus 21-23* (Tyler, Texas: Institute for Christian Economics, 1984), p. 190.

5. Cornelius Van Til, *Survey of Christian Epistemology* (Grand Rapids: Den Dulk Christian Foundation, 1969), Vol. II, p. 96. Emphasis added.

2. It is here that the servant of God encounters certain other enemies whom he cannot defeat without submission to the hierarchy. Actually, they are usually "lesser" enemies. Israel's wilderness experience is a perfect example. Foreign powers were brought down on them. Until they repented (Deut. 1:41-46), the message was, "Paganism will dominate you when you rebel against the Lord's system of judgment." When Israel failed with the "big" enemy, Canaan, God withdrew them into a situation where they could practice before "smaller" enemies. The Lord riveted His point, as He often does in the Bible, through a series of instructive encounters. Some of the enemies God commanded Israel to pass by without conflict, as in the case of the "sons of Esau" (Deut. 2:8). Others God told them to fight and destroy, as in the case of the Amorites (Deut. 3:8). Why were they to fight some and not others? This leads us to point three.

3. Rebellion destroys unity among the brethren. God always directed Israel away from their closest "brothers," like the "sons of Esau" and the "Moabites" (Deut. 2:1-25). When Israel learned not to fight with the ones closest to them, they became more unified. And when they quit fighting among themselves, they were ready to fight the real enemies, the Amorites and even Canaan (Deut. 2:24).

4. Marching comes before fighting. Israel wandered for thirty-eight years (Deut. 2:14). They had to learn to march in military order before they would be able to fight in harmony.[6] God drilled them for over three decades. When they showed enough accountability to walk in formation, they were ready to begin to fight. The people of God have to learn how to submit when they walk, before they will be able to run.

5. Submission comes before privilege. After Israel absorbed the lessons of accountability, they were given a *covenant grant*. This was usually a grant given to a vassal who had demonstrated exceptional faithfulness. Israel's grant was Canaan (Deut. 3:12).

6. The ways of rebellion are removed slowly. God waited until the older, rebellious generation died (Deut. 1:35). This gave the younger generation an extended course in wilderness training. They had to submit to God and each other to survive. Individualists do not survive in the wilderness. Like Jesus in the wilderness, Israel was prepared for any challenge. If they could live in the wilderness, they could conquer in civilization.

---

6. James B. Jordan, *The Sociology of the Church: Essays in Reconstruction* (Tyler, Texas: Geneva Ministries, 1986), pp. 215-16.

7. The lack of accountability leads to idolatry. Moses makes the connection we saw in the life of Saul. Autonomous leaders and people end up worshipping the wrong god. Moses indicates this possibility in his last words, "So watch yourselves carefully . . . lest you act corruptly and make a graven image" (Deut. 4:15-16). Rebellion is as the sin of witchcraft (I Sam. 15:22-23)!

These are the fundamental principles of accountability. In time and through history, the representative principle became a way of life.

Appeals Court or Bureaucracy?

In Chapter One, I stressed the point that God is transcendent and immanent. He controls everything, but He knows everything personally. He is different from man, yet He is present with man, I said that this leads to a fundamental difference between the Biblical covenant structure and Satan's covenant structure.

Satan is not all-knowing, all-seeing, or all-anything. He is a creature. Thus, he is neither transcendent nor immanent in the way that God is. He has power, and he can move from place to place, but he cannot be everywhere at once.

This makes Satan highly dependent on his subordinates. His chain of command must get information to him from all over the globe. He must get information from his demonic subordinates, and he must exercise power through them. This limits him. Therefore, Satan's hierarchy is top down, whereas God's hierarchy is bottom up. God is in no way dependent on the creation, including His hierarchy, either angelic or human. Satan is dependent. So, in order to exercise his power, he must place great emphasis on his hierarchy. It is a classic bureaucracy. The being at the top exercises power through the chain of command as a military commander exercises power. It is a top-down chain of command.

The Church, like Christian institutions in general, is not structured along the lines of a top-down hierarchy. God knows all things, and He controls all things. Thus, He can safely delegate responsibility to subordinates, in a way that Satan dares not delegate power. Satan commands ethical rebels who threaten him; God commands everything, and no one can threaten Him. It is the very sovereignty of God that is the basis of the decentralized freedom of individuals in Christian society. It is the non-sovereignty of Satan that leads always to centralized power and bureaucracy. What Satan cannot achieve as a creature he attempts to achieve through centralized power and top-down bureaucracy.

This is the issue of omniscience. To exercise total authority the director needs perfect knowledge. In the Biblical social order, no institution needs such omniscience precisely because the Head, Jesus Christ, possesses it, and so does the Holy Spirit, who speaks to every covenantally faithful person. We have access to the Bible, and we have access to God in prayer. Thus, we can be left free to work out our salvation in fear and trembling (Phil. 2:12). Decentralization becomes possible in such a world.

YEAH!

Exodus 18 and Matthew 18

In Exodus 18, we have the story of Moses the judge. Every petty dispute is brought to him, for he has access to perfect judgment. God speaks to him. But the lines get too long. Justice is delayed. The people wear Moses out. So Jethro, his father-in-law, comes and tells him to allow the people to appoint righteous judges above them. The people need to get speedy justice, so they can get back to dominion. Better imperfect speedy justice in most cases than perfect justice after weeks or months of standing in line. Better dominion activities than standing in line.

What is the universal mark of all government bureaucracies? Standing in line. All over the Communist world, people stand in lines. They wait.

Moses set up an appeals court structure. Men were free to work out their salvation with fear and trembling. There was self-government under God. Only when there were disputes was the Biblical civil hierarchy invoked. This is even more true in New Testament times. Matthew 18:15-18 outlines the same sort of appeals court procedure for the Church—a hierarchy of bottom-up courts. The progression is from the private dispute to the public court of the church. Men need to get disputes settled properly, to reduce bickering and allow a return to the dominion activities of life. Things need to be settled if dominion is to proceed.

private → public

War

It is true that in wartime, civil governments adopt a top-down chain of command, *but only for military personnel*. To the extent that they try to run the economy by a bureaucratic system, production bottlenecks appear, and the economy becomes more irrational. The chain of command is supposed to be limited to warriors and battles.

We must recognize that military warfare is an exception to the normal activities of life. War is an extraordinary measure. In the Old Testament, the civil government numbered the people only before a military engagement. Each adult male twenty years old and older had to bring a heave offering of half a shekel of silver. This was a payment to make atonement (Ex. 30:12-16). When David numbered the people for the purpose of going to war, and he failed to make this atonement, God punished him by killing 70 thousand Israelites in a plague (II Sam. 24). He was acting like a pagan king, shedding blood without proper atonement.

It is true that we are in perpetual spiritual warfare in the New Covenant (Eph. 6). It is also true that they were in perpetual spiritual warfare in the old covenant. Spiritual warfare is ordinary; military warfare is extraordinary. This is why Christians are told to pray for civil peace (I Tim. 2:1-2). It is in peacetime that we can best do our work of dominion. A full-time military warfare State is an ungodly, satanic bureaucracy. In fact, war or the coming of war is used as the primary excuse to centralize the nation. Wars and rumors of wars are part of a fallen world, but we are not to indulge ourselves in perpetual war for perpetual peace.

The Biblical strategy for winning the spiritual war is self-government under God. Wars begin in the heart (James 4:1). The best means of keeping the peace is covenantal faithfulness (Deut. 28:1-14). Suppress the war of the heart, and the result is greater peace. The presence of the Biblical hierarchy helps men to face what is in their hearts. As we have already seen, Matthew's chapter on discipline outlines a bottom-up hierarchy similar to Moses' (Matt. 18:15ff.).

The priests of the Old Covenant did not operate a top-down bureaucracy. Why, then, should we, who have the Holy Spirit, seek to create a top-down bureaucratic hierarchy in any area of life except the military? We have the Bible — our marching orders — and we have prayer and therefore access to the throne room of God. There is no reason to imitate Satan's hierarchy, as if our Commander-in-Chief were not omnipotent, omniscient, and omnipresent. We should instead limit earthly hierarchies to appeals courts under God.

Redemptive History

History is covenantal.[7] It is the story of the application of the covenant in God's world. No covenant — no space, time, or history. The historical section of Deuteronomy is a miniature picture of this relationship between history and covenant. What happens in the second segment of Deuteronomy with God's representatives happens on a larger scale throughout the Bible. Consider the following overview: a hierarchy (Deut. 1:9-18), a fall of the hierarchy (Deut. 1:19-46), a series of tests (Deut. 2:1-3:29), judgments (4:1-24), and finally the transition from Moses to the new leadership of Joshua, a superior hierarchy (Deut. 4:25-49). All of these parts track Biblical history. As we saw earlier, Adam and Eve were God's hierarchy. Shortly after their creation, they fell. They faced a test and failed. Then God judged them and promised a new hierarchy in the form of a seed. This pattern repeats itself over and over again. We can say there is similarity. But, there is dissimilarity, as we see in the Bible that Adam's seed does not have the power to bring in a new hierarchy. God must send *His* Son in a miraculous way. Nevertheless, God summarizes Biblical history in this short segment of Deuteronomy.

Thus, we can posit two principles about the redemptive history of the Bible by comparing it to Deuteronomy (1:9-4:49).

First, just as there is *similarity* between Deuteronomy and the New Covenant that Jesus established, we can derive a principle of similarity in redemptive history. The similarity is in the *covenant* because the covenantal structure is repeated. Just as everything about a human being is encoded in those first cells of his existence, so the first beginnings of the covenant in Genesis are encoded in seed form. The following diagram pictures the growth of the covenant like a seed, containing everything from its first inception that it will eventually become in a much fuller sense.

---

7. R. G. Collingwood, *The Idea of History* (Oxford: Clarendon Press, 1946), p. 52. Collingwood said, "Any history written on Christian principles will be of necessity universal [transcendent], providential [hierarchical], apocalyptic [sanctions], and periodized [continuity]." I have added brackets to show how Collingwood's assessment of Christian interpretation of history easily fits the covenantal scheme I am presenting in this book. Gordon H. Clark, *Historiography: Secular and Religious* (Nutley, New Jersey: Craig Press, 1971), pp. 244-245, even refers to Collingwood's four points and adds a fifth: "revelation." This would fit the third point of covenantalism called "ethics," or law, being "special revelation" to man.

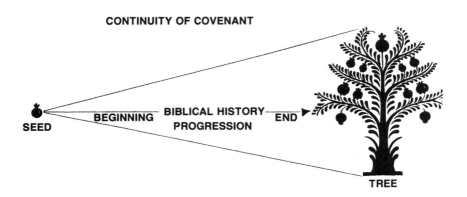

Second, just as there is dissimilarity in the progression from Moses to Joshua in Deuteronomy, there is a principle of *dissimilarity* in redemptive history because of its progress and development. God continues to reveal Who the true representative will be, and He brings about significant changes. So the representative principle helps us to understand history itself. When we come to the Bible, we should keep the similarity and dissimilarity concepts in mind. There will be the application of the covenant at every point, including a Mediator and mediators who follow Him. But there will also be progress as these representatives continue to fail.

Redemptive History, Old and New

The Bible describes a representative sacrificial and service system where some representatives are nearer to God than others. In Deuteronomy 1:9-18, Moses was at the top of the layers of representatives. In other words, there were degrees of closeness to God. James Jordan explains this elaborate hierarchy.

1. The High Priest acted as priest to the house of Aaron, the Levites, Israel, and the nations.

2. The house of Aaron, including preeminently the High Priest, acted as priests to the Levites, Israel, and the nations.

3. The Levites, including the house of Aaron and the High Priest, acted as priests to Israel and the nations.

4. Israel, including the Levites, the house of Aaron, and the High Priest, acted as priests to the other nations.[8]

All through the Old Covenant, we see that men stood between God and their fellow men. Progressively, however, there was movement to that one day when everything changed. This is implied in the shift from Moses to Jesus. When Jesus came, the principle of representation remained the same, but its *application* changed. Jordan explains this change.

With the coming of the New Covenant, these dualities were transformed. The New Covenant embodies the fulfillment of what the First [or Old] Covenant with Adam was supposed and designed to bring to pass, but never did. . . . There is no one Edenic earthly central sanctuary; rather, the sanctuary exists in heaven and wherever the sacramental Presence of Jesus Christ is manifest. The equivalent to being in the holy land is now to be in the Body of Christ.[9]

We still come to God by representation in Jesus Christ, but we have *direct* access to God. Through prayer, the Church has even greater access than the High Priest had in the Old Testament. He could only directly approach God *once* a year. We can come directly to God any time we want! The veil of the Temple was torn at Christ's death. The separation between the Holy of Holies and the sanctuary was removed.

The Old Testament believer could pray, but His prayer life was more restricted. The Holy Spirit has come in the New Testament, and He intercedes in a special way. "And in the same way the Spirit also helps our weakness; for we do not know how to pray as we should, but the Spirit Himself intercedes for us with groanings too deep for words; and He who searches the hearts knows what the mind of the Spirit is, because He intercedes for the saints according to the will of God" (Rom. 8:26-27). With the substitution of Jesus as the High Priest of God, who now sits at the right hand of God, the New Testament believer has a full-time intercessor or intermediary or *representative* in the throne room of God. The Spirit also can now intercede for us in a special way. The incarnation, death, resurrec-

---

8. James B. Jordan, *Sabbath Breaking and the Death Penalty* (Tyler, Texas: Geneva Ministries, 1986), p. 32.

9. *Ibid.*, p. 17.

tion, and ascension of Christ in history have made a fundamental difference in heaven.[10]

The effect of this shift in representation has brought about a *direct-access* view of government. The genius of Biblical representational government is that everyone in the Church has access to the "Man at the top." This leads to progress. There is less bureaucracy. In the Old Covenant, there was one man once a year who could approach God. Now there are thousands of men and *women* of every nationality and every race approaching God every moment of the day, twenty-four hours a day, every day of the year. This kind of communication from the bottom up creates greater activity, interest, and progress. God wants it this way because He designed the system!

Furthermore, the hierarchy and history of Deuteronomy 1:6-4:49 implies a *transformational* progression of history. Joshua implemented Moses' covenant. The ingredients of the covenant under Moses remained the same. The application was worked out through a *new* Head of the covenant. The change was not radical but transformational. In other words, the Old Covenant was not radically abolished; rather, it came under a new regime in history because of the incarnation, death, resurrection, and ascension of Christ. This seems to establish the proper sense in which the Old Covenant shifted to the New Covenant. Harvard legal historian Harold J. Berman states the change:

> In contrast to the other Indo-European peoples, including the Greeks, who believed that time moved in ever recurring cycles, the Hebrew people conceived of time as continuous, irreversible, and historical, leading to ultimate redemption at the end. They also believed, however, that time has periods within it. It is not cyclical but may be interrupted or accelerated. It develops. The Old Testament is a story not merely of change but of development, of growth, of movement toward the messianic age — very uneven [covenantal] movement, to be sure, with much backsliding [covenant unfaithfulness] but nevertheless a movement *toward. Christianity, however, added an important element to the Judaic concept of time: that of transformation of the old into the new. The Hebrew Bible became the Old Testament, its meaning transformed by its fulfillment in the New Testament. In the story of the Resurrection, death was transformed into a new beginning. The times were not only accelerated but regenerated. This introduced a new structure of history, in which there was a fundamental transformation of one age into another.*[11]

---

10. The Spirit takes the place of the cherubim. The mercy seat is Christ.
11. Berman, *Law and Revolution*, pp. 26-27. Emphasis added. On Berman's obser-

The effect of this transformational view of hierarchy means representation and accountability are still part of God's covenantal program. These ideas pull through to the Church. Granted, Christ is head of the covenant, and there is not the kind of elaborate hierarchy as is in the Old Testament. All men have access to God. Christ is the Mediator, capital *M*. But God still establishes representatives, elders (bishops and pastors), who pass judgment. They mediate with a small *m*. Thus, we can observe the same principles in the Church that we saw operative in Israel. Church members should obey Christ and His Word as well as its representatives as they attempt to apply the Bible.

Notice that the Book of Acts contains such an example. In the early Church, Ananias and Sapphira lied to the Holy Spirit, as He was represented by the Apostolic authority (Acts 5:1-7). The Spirit struck them dead. Even so, the following passages reveal that great persecution came on the Church (Acts 5:17-42). The implication is that the same thing happened to the Church that happened to Israel. When the Church rebelled, the enemies of the Church took them into captivity.

So there was change with the coming of the New Covenant, but the change was transformational, not radical. The change was total but not total obliteration of the covenant. The *covenant* shifted from Old to New.

Conclusion

God's hierarchy is established in history. A denial of Biblical authority and hierarchy is ultimately a denial of history. A rejection of history eventually gives up God's hierarchy. When Associate Professor of Bible and Religion at Emory University, Atlanta, Georgia, Thomas J. Altizer, wanted to reject the God of the Bible, he said, "God has died in our time, our history, our existence."[12]

---

vation about a "linear" view of time, it should be remembered that Augustine's *City of God* was a defense of a Christian interpretation of history. When the barbarians sacked Rome, some argued that Rome had been "cursed" because of the spread of Christianity and a betrayal of the "old" gods. Augustine countered by defending the idea of a "city of God," at war with the "city of the earth," which in my opinion was not to disregard completely the notion that Rome was "cursed" for its failure to embrace fully the Christian religion. For an interesting discussion of Augustine's linear view of time, as opposed to Basil's more cyclical interpretation, see Jean Danielou, *The Bible and the Liturgy* (Ann Arbor: Servant Books, [1956] 1979), pp. 262-286.

12. Thomas J. Altizer, *Mircea Eliade and the Dialectic of the Sacred* (Philadelphia: Westminster Press, 1963), p. 13.

The second principle of the covenant is the historical prologue, called the *hierarchical principle*. What have I attempted to do in this chapter? First, I presented the relationship between hierarchy and the first point of covenantalism. I said that hierarchy is the manifestation of God's transcendence. Hierarchy is visible sovereignty.

Second, I talked about the representative principle. God begins the historical section of Deuteronomy with a description of the court system in Israel. Everyone had a representative, and everyone was accountable. In this context, we saw seven principles of accountability.

Finally, I examined the relationship between hierarchy and history. In general, the historical section of Deuteronomy is a miniature picture of the whole redemptive process of Scripture. So there is similarity through all the parts of the Bible. They all grow out of a basic covenantal structure established in Genesis. Yet, there are dissimilarities due to the progression of revelation.

Next in the Biblical covenant we come to the principle of *ethics*. The *heart of man's bond to God is the fulfillment of righteousness*. In this section I will make the most important statement of the book. I will present the concept that there is an ethical relationship between cause and effect.

3

ETHICS
(Deuteronomy 5-26)

One of the classic contrasts of history took place at the giving of the Ten Commandments. Moses had gone up Mt. Sinai to receive the most succinct statement of God's ethical system ever codified: the Ten Words (Deut. 4:13).

Down below, at the foot of the mountain, the people waited for Moses to return. The Bible does not tell us how long Moses was on the mountain. The text only says that he "delayed" (Ex. 32:1). It did not take long, however, for trouble to begin to brew.

The people were anxious. Their commitment to a Biblical world was shaky. How ironic! The only world they had known was the "Gulag" of an Egyptian concentration camp. Their grandparents had handed down stories of the "way it used to be," but they had never seen the better side of Egyptian life. Still, it was all they had known, and Egypt continued to represent "home."

What did they miss? What was the first thing they asked for from Aaron, the man "tending the store" while Moses was gone? Strange as it may sound, they wanted an *idol*, a god they could see. They wanted a god they could manipulate through a golden mediator. Somehow they persuaded Aaron to join them. It was dreadful. A man of God, a leader, the High Priest, who had seen God defeat the mightiest nation in the world, without a single arrow fired, was cajoled to forsake everything he had known to be true about Biblical religion. The ordained mediator of God's hierarchical system built a dead, blind, metallic mediator for the people.

While Moses lay prostrate before his Creator, and as God etched eternal law into stone, Aaron and the people below built and worshipped a golden calf.

What is the contrast of this eventful day in history? It is the conflict between *ethical* and *magical* religions. Biblical religion is based on faithfulness to the Word of God (ethics). Pagan religion is always some form of manipulation through one means or another. The details are spelled out in the largest section of Deuteronomy (Deut. 5-26).

Ethics: The Cause/Effect Principle

The third section of every suzerain treaty consisted of special *terms*, or *laws*.[1] The treaty was ethical at its core. The suzerain and vassal(s) related to one another according to the *stipulations* laid out. If the vassal were to be consecrated to the suzerain, he had to comply with them.

In the ethics section of the Biblical covenant (Deut. 5-26), we find an expansion of the Ten Commandments (stipulations). The central idea: God establishes an *ethical relationship between cause and effect*. Since God and man do not have unity of being, God dictates the terms (commandments) under which man can have a relationship with Him. These terms are the standard of the covenant. Man is called to be *faithful* to God by submitting to them. If he submits (covenant-keeping), he is blessed. If he does not (covenant-breaking), he is cursed. (The specific results of blessing and cursing appear in point four of covenantalism, called *sanctions*). He is either a covenant-keeper or covenant-breaker. So, there is an ethical as opposed to a metaphysical relationship to God, and this relationship culminates in certain predictable effects. And, I might add, these effects are not just personal; they are cultural.

Everything in the universe is tied to man's covenant-keeping or covenant-breaking. This basic concept of ethics is presented in Deuteronomy 5-26. Moses summarizes the Ten Commandments saying, "You shall walk in all the way which the Lord your God has commanded you, that you may live, *that it may be well with you*" (Deut. 5:33). At another place, a passage from which the title of this book was taken, he says, "Keep the words of this covenant to do them that you may prosper in all that you do" (Deut. 29:9).

The ethical cause/effect principle is a *command/fulfillment* pattern. The books of Joshua and Judges are examples. The Book of Joshua follows the Book of Deuteronomy. It demonstrates that obedience (fulfillment) to the commandment results in blessing. How? Simple: Joshua obeyed Moses' commands, and the promise was fulfilled. He received the land. Even in the particulars we see the same pattern, like wheels within wheels. In the first chapter, God tells Joshua to enter the land and take it (Josh. 1:1-9). Then Joshua tells the officers of Israel precisely what God told him (Josh. 1:10-18). Finally, the people

---

1. Kline, *Structure of Biblical Authority*, pp. 115ff. See also, *Ancient Near Eastern Texts*, pp. 205ff.

do what God has told Joshua. God *commands*, Joshua *obeys*, and Israel *receives* what was promised. There is a cause/effect relationship between faithfulness to the commandment and the fulfillment of blessing.

The Book of Judges illustrates the other side of the ethical cause/effect principle: unfaithfulness resulting in death. The last verse of the book, "They did what was right in their own eyes," sums it up (Judg. 21:25). During the period after Joshua's great conquests, the people reverted to unfaithfulness. Judge after judge was raised up. Over and over again the people turned away from Moses' commandments. They learned the hard way that the ethical cause/effect relationship cannot be avoided. Break the commandments, and the curse of death will be fulfilled.

The ethics principle of the covenant is just this simple. All through the Bible, the command/fulfillment pattern repeats itself. Why? Man must relate to God by covenant. He either keeps or breaks the covenant; he is either faithful or unfaithful. Everything comes about according to this basic ethical cause/effect relationship.

Furthermore, the stipulations section of Deuteronomy specifies that only a certain kind of person can fulfill the commandments of God, a true *son* of the covenant. The ethics segment instructs the fathers to be true sons of God themselves by teaching their own sons the commandments (Deut. 6:1-26). The fathers imaged God by training their sons to image them. And when the sons followed their fathers in obedience to God, the second generation also imaged its Heavenly Father. In other words, a faithful son manifests his sonship by being a true image-bearer of his True Father, God (Gen. 5:1ff.) The faithful son in Genesis was to have demonstrated his sonship by carrying out three offices: prophet, priest, and king. So the motif of faithful sonship appears among the stipulations of Deuteronomy in the fulfillment of the same three offices. The kings apply God's law to the land (Deut. 16 & 17). The priests guard the sanctuary and law of God (Deut. 18:1-8). The prophets deliver messages from God's heavenly council (Deut. 18:9-22). Hence, the theme that only the true son can keep the commandments of God consistently surfaces in the ethics part of the covenant, and it comes to its ultimate fulfillment in Jesus Christ, the ultimate Son of the covenant.

Three Aspects of Biblical Ethics

When I speak of an ethical cause/effect relationship, am I just talking about an *external* obedience to the Ten Commandments? No. Following God's commandments involves proper *motivations, stand-*

ards, and *situational applications.*[2] To reduce Biblical ethics to any one of these elements distorts a covenantal understanding of man's relationship to God. One of the great doctrinal statements of the Church says, "Works done by unregenerate men, although for the matter of them they may be things which God commands; and of good use both to themselves and others: yet, because they proceed not from an *heart of faith*; nor are *done in the right manner, according to the Word*; nor to the *right end*, the glory of God, they are therefore sinful and cannot please God."[3] The statement refers to three parts of ethical compliance to God's commandments. The unregenerate man's attempts to please God are unacceptable precisely because they fail to have all three. The truly faithful (ethical) man has them all.

1. Motivation

First, the third section of Deuteronomy (5-26) indicates that God expects His commandments to be done from the proper *motivation*, from the *heart*. Moses says, "And you shall *love* the Lord your God with all your *heart* and with all your *soul* and with all your might. And these words, which I am commanding you today, shall be on your *heart*" (Deut. 6:5-6). Notice in Moses' comments that he makes the direct connection between heart and commandments. External compliance was not satisfactory. As Paul says, "Whatever is not of faith is *sin*" (Rom. 14:23). So someone like the Pharisees could keep the external commandments but be totally in sin. The Law was never intended to be kept without faith. Anyone who reads the Old Testament and thinks, "This was a system of works," has seriously misunderstood the Law itself. Works were to flow out of faith, not only in the Old Testament, but in the New as well.

Because there is generally so much confusion about the relationship between faith and works, however, a further word needs to be said about "works," or the fulfillment of righteousness.

First, the basis (ground) of the fulfillment of righteousness is sacrifice. Central to the third section of Deuteronomy is a discussion of the sacrificial system in Israel (Deut. 12:1-32), implying that the

---

2. Cornelius Van Til, *In Defense of the Faith: Christian Theistic Evidences*, Vol. III (Philadelphia: den Dulk Christian Foundation, 1974). See also John Frame's syllabus on "Ethics." It can be purchased from Westminster Seminary, P.O. Box 27009, Chestnut Hill, Philadelphia, PA 19118. In many ways, Frame has fleshed out Van Til. He is clearer and simpler to understand.

3. *Westminster Confession of Faith*, XVI.7. Emphasis added.

fulfillment of righteousness begins in God's sanctuary of sacrifice. The only thing that can offset man's sin is a blood atonement. In the Old Testament the sacrifice is temporary, and Christ becomes the permanent blood sacrifice in the New Testament (Hebrews 9:25-28). So, fulfillment of righteousness is never intended to be to the exclusion of the finished work of Christ.

Two, the instrument of the fulfillment of righteousness is a faith that works. Faith is holistic. The Bible distinguishes between works that are outside of faith and works that are part of faith. Paul says, "For by grace you have been saved through faith; and that not of yourselves, it is the gift of God; not as a result of works, that no one should boast. For we are His workmanship, created in Christ Jesus for *good works*, which God prepared beforehand, that we should *walk in them*" (Eph. 2:8-10). See the distinction in Paul between "bad" works — works prior to faith — and "good" works — faith and its works? It is faith *and its works* that lay hold of Christ. Faith is more than just mental assent. It involves the total man. For this very reason, James says, "Show me your faith without works, and I will show you my faith by my works" (James 2:18).

Therefore, the fulfillment of righteousness requires sacrifice and faithfulness. Moses did not teach "salvation by works." The Biblically consistent man would never have considered this possibility. Habakkuk 2:4 says, "The righteous shall live by his faith." Works of *faith* should never be separated from true faith. For without true faith, there can not be true works of righteousness. Indeed, faith without works is nothing less than works salvation.

2. Standard

Second, the ethics section of the covenant teaches that faith is not a *standardless* faith. Good motivations are not enough. After all, Moses says the *commandments* are to be on the heart (Deut. 6:5-6). Faith has a standard of righteousness so that the Church knows how faith is supposed to act. Objectively speaking, the Ten Commandments are a summary of God's ethical standard. Deuteronomy 5-26 follows the outline of the commandments, only in greater detail.

I. Overview of the Ten Commandments (Deut. 5:1-33)

II. The Ten Words

   1st Word (6:1-11:32): Not to forget transcendent God

2nd Word (12:1-13:18): Hierarchy of the Sanctuary
3rd Word (14:1-29): Consecration of God's Presence
4th Word (15:1-16:17): Sabbath rest
5th Word (16:18-18:22): Fathers of covenant community
6th Word (19:1-22:12): Laws of killing God's transcendent image bearer
7th Word (22:13-23:14): Laws of submission
8th Word (23:15-24:22): Laws against various forms of manipulation
9th Word (25:1-19): Justice
10th Word (26:1-19): Firstfruits

As one reads through the list of the Ten Commandments, expounded in detail, perhaps he notices that they follow the five points of covenantalism, repeating them twice (5 and 5). I will go into this structure at length in a later chapter where the Ten Commandments are used as support of the five-fold covenantal concept. But even with this short summary of the third section of the covenant, the *objective* character of God's ethics stands out. He has categorized His requirements.

Have they changed? Although aspects of the commandments themselves have been altered, the ten summary categories have not. Listen to what Jesus says when He was asked about the "greatest commandment."

He said to them, " 'You shall love the Lord your God with all your heart, and with all your soul, and with all your mind.' This is the great and foremost commandment. The second is like it, 'You shall love your neighbor as yourself.' On these two commandments depend the whole Law and the Prophets" (Matt. 22:37-40).

Do these words sound familiar? They should. They are direct quotations from Deuteronomy, particularly the section to which we just referred above (6:5). When Jesus was asked about the greatest commandments, He quoted the Law. Thus, God's standard of righteousness does not change.

His standard, for that matter, reflects His character. If His character does not change, neither can He. Several years ago, I remember that I took the New Testament and started to list all of the *commands*. To my surprise, they could all be grouped in the categories of the Ten Commandments. All of them were there. So, God's standard is the same because He is the same.

The difference between the Old and New Covenant is how they
are *fulfilled*. It is the special way in which the commandments are
kept in the New Covenant that accounts for change. The Old Covenant man was expected to fulfill the standard of righteousness by
faith. But he was never able to. He lacked complete atonement for
his sin. He was required to look forward in history in faith to a covenantal representative's act of atonement (Isa. 53). In the New Covenant, *Christ* became the fulfillment of righteousness. He perfectly
obeyed; He perfectly fulfilled the Law; He incarnated the Law of
God in His person, meaning the fulfillment of the righteousness of
Deuteronomy 5-26 ultimately came through Him. The ethics categories do not change. They pull through Christ. There is still an ethical cause/effect relationship. The standard is kept in Christ, and anyone who trusts in Him will therefore keep His standard. John says,
"The one who says, 'I have come to know Him,' and does not keep His
commandments, is a liar, and the truth is not in him" (I John 2:4).

We have therefore seen that the ethical cause/effect principle has
motivations and an objective *standard*. There is one final aspect.

3. Situational Application

Having the right motivation and standard is not enough. These
should be properly applied in different situations. Very simply, people with good motivations can misapply God's law. How so? During
World War II, there were Christians who believed that a person
should never "lie." One day, the Germans came to their house and
asked if they were hiding out any Jews. The Christians thought, "I
cannot tell a lie. The Bible says lying is wrong. We must tell the Germans that we are hiding out Jews in our basement." So the Christians told the Germans. The Nazis went into the house, captured the
Jews, marched them out front, and killed every one of them in the
presence of their betrayers.

These Christians had good motivations. They wanted to help the
Jews. They wanted to please God. They had double-good motivations! What went wrong? They misapplied the law.

Ironically, the Bible has a similar situation. When the Jews prepared to attack Jericho, spies were sent in ahead (Josh. 2:1). A prostitute named Rahab hid them out. When the soldiers of Jericho asked if
she had seen any of the Jewish spies, she *lied* to them (Josh. 2:6).
Moreover, James calls attention to the lie, stating it was an act of jus-

tification. He says, "And in the same way was not Rahab the harlot also justified by works, when she received the messengers and sent them out by another way?" (James 2:25). Commentators have gone out of their way to twist the plain sense of these Scriptures. Only a few in recent years have allowed the Bible to speak for itself.[4] *Rahab was justified for lying to the enemy*! How? The answer concerns the Biblical concept of truth. Truth does not simply mean faithfulness to the "facts." This is the Greek view. Biblical truth is faithfulness to the covenant, meaning faithfulness to God and His people.[5]

More to the point, certain situations affect the *application* of the Law of God. In Joshua, the nation was at war. There was a place to lie to the enemy and not violate the truth. During WWII, there was a similar situation, a situation that affected the use of the Bible. The Bible did not change, only the situation. Is this the same as "situational ethics"? No. Situational ethics says that the situation totally determines truth, so truth changes from situation to situation. Biblical ethics says the truth always remains the *same*: the Word of God. Only the *application* of the truth changes.

The situational side of Biblical ethics is important. As we saw above, it can mean a matter of life or death. It is not enough to have the right motives and just keep the commandments. They have to be kept in the right way.

Thus, the ethical cause/effect principle is not some mechanical obedience to the Bible. Biblical ethics consists of faithfulness in varying circumstances from a heart of faith. Given this understanding, the man of God should see the cause/effect relationship between faithfulness and what happens.

Dominion: The Proper Effect

Dominion over the enemies of God is explicitly stated as the proper effect of obedience in the ethics section of Deuteronomy. It is placed here because God wants His people to associate faithfulness and conquest. This reality of victory is expressed in the form of a fulfilled promise given to Shem, the son of Noah (Deut. 7:1-26). What

---

4. R. J. Rushdoony, *Institutes of Biblical Law* (Nutley, New Jersey: Craig Press, 1973), pp. 542-49. See also in the same volume, Gary North, "In Defense of Biblical Bribery," pp. 838-39.

5. B. Holwerda, *Jozua en Richteren* (Kampen, 1971), p. 13. Referred to in Don Sinnema, *Reclaiming the Land* (Toronto, Canada: Joy in Learning Curriculum Development and Training Centre, 1977), p. 19.

was it? Noah promised his *covenant-keeping son*, Shem, that "Canaan would be his servant" (Gen. 9:26). Moses then tells Israel how the promise will come to pass.

When the LORD your God shall bring you into the land where you are entering to possess it, and shall clear away many nations before you, . . . the Canaanites. . . . Know therefore that the LORD your God, He is God, the faithful God, who keeps His covenant and His lovingkindness to a thousandth generation with those who love Him and keep His command-ments; but repays those who hate Him to their faces, to destroy them; He will not delay with him who hates Him, He will repay him to his face. There-fore, you shall keep the commandment and the statutes and the judgments which I am commanding you today, to do them. Then it shall come about, because you listen to these judgments and keep and do them, that the LORD your God will keep with you His covenant and His lovingkindness which He swore to your forefathers. And He will love you and bless you and multiply you. . . . And the LORD will remove from you all sickness; and He will not put on you any of the harmful diseases of Egypt which you have known, but He will lay them on all who hate you. And you shall consume all the peoples whom the LORD your God will deliver to you (Deut. 7:1-16).

The formula for victory is simple: keep the covenant and domin-ion will be the proper effect. The key to success is not a secret in the Bible. It is revealed, and it is illustrated time and again.

There is no greater example of the fulfillment of what Moses said than in the battle of Jericho. Instead of instructing Israel to fight with weapons, God commanded them to march around the city, symbolically circumcising it (Josh. 6), since circumcision is the ini-tial application of the *covenant* (Gen. 17). God commanded them to begin with Jericho in the same way they had been commanded to be-gin with their personal lives. And through this ritual of faithfulness at Jericho, God surrounded the city as He had surrounded the lives of the Israelites. He then provided a living example of what happens when the enemies are encircled by God through the faithfulness of His people. On the seventh day, the day of judgment in the Bible, God caused the walls to fall down. Israel kept God's Word, and God kept His Word to Israel by defeating their enemies.

At a time when the Church has a horrible self-image, because it has wrongly been told that it will have to be raptured out of its own unavoidable defeat, the lesson of Jericho needs to be taught. Jesus is as emphatically clear as Moses and Joshua that the gates of hell will not prevail against the Church (Matt. 16:18). The enemies will be defeated, and the Church will have dominion and blessing, if it will keep God's covenant!

Job: A Fly in the Ointment?

There is one apparent exception, one that caused the Puritans a great deal of consternation: the life of Job. I have spent considerable space developing the relationship between how man responds to God and what happens in life: the ethical cause/effect principle. Does this concept break down in the story of Job? No.

Job's life only breaks down cause and effect in that from all outward appearances he is *temporarily* stripped of all blessing. He lost his children, possessions, health, and friends. His friends, moreover, continue throughout the main body of the book to use the cause/effect principle to persuade Job that he is guilty. Yet, Job does not yield. He argues that he is justified before God. In many ways, the entire book is an exposition of the great doctrine of justification. Finally, he is exonerated by God. In the end, Job does receive the blessing of the covenant. Not in another life but in *this* life.[6]

So, there are times when it seems like there is no connection between ethics and effects. Indeed, there are moments in history where it appears that the wicked are "blessed," and the righteous are "cursed." Why? Sometimes, the people of God as a covenantal whole are being disciplined. In His discipline, God restricts and even takes away blessing from individuals. This in itself confirms the ethical cause/effect principle. At other times, God's people — martyrs and others who have to undergo unusual suffering — receive delayed portions of the blessing. Their blessing comes in the form of internal and even greater amounts of blessing when they reach heaven. Finally, God sometimes tests His people to see if they will live by faith (James 1:1-2). The test is the apparent reversal of the cause/effect principle to strengthen the righteous' faith. Job is the classic example. In the short term, he was "cursed" for being righteous. In the long term, he was blessed *doubly*, receiving multiples of his original blessings (Job 42:10-17). Job is not a "fly in the ointment." His life reinforces the ethics principle of the covenant.

The very center of the covenant is *ethics*. Man is called upon to view the world through the eye of faith. He is to believe that everything going on around him is tied to the covenant. If he does not understand life's events in these terms, he will resort to other cause/effect explanations.

---

6. Jesus confirms the promise of "this life" blessing when He says, "There is not one who has left house or wife or brothers or parents or children, for the sake of the kingdom of God, who shall not receive many times as much at this time and in the age to come, inherit eternal life" (Luke 18:29-30). In the New Covenant, everyone gets to be like Job!

False Cause/Effect Explanations

Fallen man does not want to live according to faithfulness. He does not even want to admit that his unfaithfulness to God is related to anything that happens in his life, culture, government, marriage, and especially not his life in the hereafter. He wants to achieve and live according to other false cause/effect notions. There are three: mechanical, manipulative, and magical. They are similar in that they are all sinful and false explanations of cause and effect in the universe. Yet, each reflects a different variation of fallen logic.

1. Mechanical Cause/Effect

First, the mechanical explanation of cause/effect. As the term implies, some "impersonal" force brings about cause and effect, like "natural law." Once man begins to view natural laws as impersonal autonomous acts, however, they become a replacement for the real law that governs the universe, Biblical law. The world is then understood in terms of a mechanical cause/effect relationship, and additionally, a view having serious social and political ramifications. We return to the time of the Enlightenment, a time when natural law supposedly reigned supreme, to see an example of a mechanical explanation of cause and effect in the universe.

Louis Bredvold observes in *The Brave New World of the Enlightenment* an important nuance of natural law that was lost during the Enlightenment.[7] He argues that prior to this time (second half of the Middle Ages), natural law was broken into two categories: ethics and physical phenomena. There were laws for humans and laws for things. The Enlightenment threw out this distinction, and made the law for things the basis of ethics. In the words of Descartes, "All philosophy is like a tree, of which Metaphysics is the root, Physics the trunk, and all other sciences the branches that grow out of this trunk, which are reduced to three principal, namely, Medicine, Mechanics, and Ethics."[8]

Mathematics became the basis of life. A "universal science" became the foundation out of which everything sprang. It is not that men such as Descartes, Spinoza, and Liebnitz did not talk about ethics. As a matter of fact, they wrote important treatises on the subject. The innovation, however, concerned the basis for ethics. The

---

7. Louis I. Bredvold, *The Brave New World of the Enlightenment* (Ann Arbor: University of Michigan Press, 1962), pp. 4-7.
8. René Descartes, *The Method, Meditations, and Selections from the Principles*, tr. by John Veitch (6th ed.; 1879), p. 184.

seventeenth-century social philosopher Thomas Hobbes, for example, discovered Euclid's *Geometry* at the mid-point of his life. He was not a mathematician, but when he read Euclid, he was impressed. "Here was the first and only book he had ever found in which every proposition was incontrovertible. Why were there no other books like it? And why not write a philosophy of man and society, that troublesome subject of controversy in all past ages, in a similar style of step by step demonstration? This project Hobbes decided to make his own."[9] He produced a mathematical explanation of the universe. In the Epistle Dedicatory to *De Cive* he writes,

> Truly the Geometricians have very admirably performed their part. . . . If the moral philosophers had as happily discharged their duty, I know not what could have been added by human industry to the completion of that happiness, which is consistent with human life. For were the nature of quantity in geometrical figures, the strength of avarice and ambition, which is sustained by the erroneous opinions of the vulgar, as touching the nature of right and wrong, would presently faint and languish; and mankind should enjoy such an immortal peach that [unless it were for habitation, on supposition that the earth should grow too narrow for her inhabitants] there would hardly be left any pretence for war.[10]

This statement is revealing. Hobbes moves from a mechanical view of cause and effect to *utopianism*, summarizing the effects of the Enlightenment on the twentieth century. The mechanical view of cause and effect led to a collectivist concept of government, as do all utopian theories. One commentator on Bredvold makes this very point:

> As heirs of the Enlightenment, many social theorists in the West are unaware of how deeply they share with Communism a faith in materialism and the methods of physical science as applied to man. Many in the West hold a Rousseauist belief in the natural goodness of man, combined with the materialist principle of the omnipotence of environment [mechanical cause/effect]. These principles are fundamental. . . . To the extent that the philosophy of the Enlightenment has permeated Western Thought, our statesmen are disqualified or at a disadvantage in waging an ideological war with Marxian tyranny on moral grounds. The West cannot endure half positivist and half Christian.[11]

---

9. Bredvold, p. 31.
10. Cited in Bredvold, p. 32.
11. Peter Stanlis, "The Dark Ages of the Enlightenment," *University Bookman* (Autumn 1962), p. 14. Brackets added.

So, we begin with a mechanical explanation of cause and effect, and end in collectivism. The Biblical covenant stands in stark contrast. God is personal. He created the world. He also created mathematics. A formula may explain what happens in a physical sense, but not *why*. The water cycle can be studied, for example, but this does not explain why famines occur. God sends famines as a curse. *Everything that happens is the result of covenant-keeping or covenant-breaking.* Life is not mechanical.

2. *Manipulative Cause/Effect*

I call this false explanation of cause and effect "manipulative" because *force* is often viewed as the basis of life. Brute power creates cause and effect. The manipulation can be in the form of personal theft or injury to another, or it can come in the shape of *national* theft or murder. The conflict is always the same: right vs. might. Theories of power believe that might creates cause and effect. When they are implemented, as Shakespeare said through Ulysses in *Troilus and Cressida,*

> Then right and wrong
> Should lose their names, and so should justice too,
> Then everything includes itself in power,
> Power into will, will into appetite,
> And appetite, a universal wolf,
> So doubly seconded with will and power,
> Must make perforce a universal prey,
> And last eat up itself.

Interestingly, Shakespeare observed that "right and wrong" disappear when "power" rules. Man is not ruled by an ethical standard; instead, he is left to the whims of a *power-State*.

The struggle of "right vs. might" is one of the basic movements of the Bible. Fallen man tends *to replace the covenant with force*. But we can rest assured that "right" prevails—that there is always an ethical cause/effect relationship—because the Bible also tells the story of the re-establishment of rule by covenant. The plan of redemption, therefore, constantly clashes with the power-State. Finally, redemption wins out!

Consider Cain. He was driven to the east of Eden. The Biblical text calls attention to the kind of society he established. The descendant of Cain says, "I have killed a man for wounding me; and a boy for striking me; if Cain is avenged sevenfold, then Lamech seventy-sevenfold" (Gen. 4:23-24). The sons of Cain were destroyed, however, by the Flood. Seth's sons prevailed through Noah's family (Gen. 6:1-8:22).

Consider Pharaoh. The conflict between Moses and Pharaoh was one of "right vs. might." Pharaoh had built a civilization based on manipulation. He was the most powerful manipulator in the world. He met his match in Moses. The account of the conflict emphasizes that Moses defeated Pharaoh with God's ethical means: the "rod" (Exod. 14:15-20), the law, and Passover (Exod. 12:1-51). God so devastated Pharaoh, as a matter of fact, that Pharaoh asked Israel to leave.

Consider Daniel. The story of Daniel tells how the power-States of the world culminate in one final defeat by the kingdom of God. Taken into exile, Daniel and his people overcome the greatest leader in the world by *revelation*, the Word of God. It comes to Nebuchadnezzar in the form of a dream (Dan. 2:1-3). The dream terrorizes the king of Babylon. He sees a huge man being toppled by a stone.[12] Daniel is the only one able to interpret. The giant man represents four great empires: Babylon, Medo-Persia, Greece, and Rome (Dan. 2:36-45). A true empire in the Bible is one that dominates the whole world. These ancient idolatrous empires represented humanity's attempt to rule the world by power. The final kingdom of stone, a common metaphor for the Lord's kingdom (Matt. 16:18), crushes the Roman Empire. Thus, the last true empire was the Roman Empire. There have been other "great" kingdoms, but none have been "world" empires in the true, Biblical sense.

Consider Christ. The movement of history reaches the apex of conflict at the cross. The power-State nations of the world crucify their Savior. Their weapon of destruction (the cross), however, becomes that which brings them to ruin. Power States were brought under the covenant. Since the death of Christ, the same conflict has been waged. The early Church found its message hostile to Caesar worship. The modern Church has been bitterly opposed by the "isms" of Communism and Fascism.

Always the manipulative approach to cause and effect proves out what C. S. Lewis said.

There neither is nor can be any simple increase of power on Man's side. Each new power won *by* man is a power *over* man as well. Each advance leaves him weaker as well as stronger. In every victory, besides being the general who triumphs, he is also the prisoner who follows the triumphal car.[13]

12. The story of David and Goliath presents the same image (I Sam. 17:1-58). David threw a stone and "struck" the giant. The same language is used (cf. Dan. 2:35 and I Sam. 17:50).
13. C. S. Lewis, *The Abolition of Man* (New York: Macmillan, [1947] 1965), p. 71.

How the dictators of history illustrate Lewis's words. Every time they rule by force, they end up trapped by their own power. Their constituencies wait to use the same power to conquer them. The Biblical story of redemption also illustrates. Man's attempts to manipulate resulted in the death of Christ. Man was conquered by his display of power. The Apostle Peter argued at Pentecost that Jesus' Death and Resurrection established Christ as Lord, the true power (Acts 2:22-36). Right prevailed over might.

3. Magical Cause/Effect

E. M. Butler begins her book *Ritual Magic* (1949) with this observation: "The fundamental aim of all magic is to impose the human will on nature, on man or on the supernatural world in order to master them." Once again, the issue is cause and effect. Magic is also power-oriented, like the manipulative approach to cause/effect. Instead of appealing to God, it seeks the demonic to manipulate God and His world. All power religions have one basic weakness. Gary North builds on Lewis's observation mentioned earlier and says,

The problem with power is always the same: the user is simultaneously subjected to it. The man who wields the scientific power of the modern world must have a theory of the transmission of power. If causes have effects, then by becoming an intermediary cause a man must admit that his decisions are also effects of prior causes. If he denies that he is necessarily determined, then he must also deny his own power to determine certain effects. Similarly, if a magician uses the power of an ally or demon to produce certain effects, he inevitably places himself under the power of the ally. At the very least, he is subjected to a rigorous series of rituals that must be used when calling forth occult power. To command power — any power — is to acknowledge the sovereignty of the source of that power, whether God, demons, natural law, random variation, or whatever. Men will serve that which they believe to be sovereign.[14]

The quest for power enslaves. Power religion turns on the user. The New Testament tells the story of Jewish exorcists who tried to use Jesus' name to manipulate demons (Acts 19:8-20). They had seen the power of Jesus' name. To them, it was the perfect *formula*. They called on the demons. The demons responded to the exorcists,

---

14. Gary North, *Unholy Spirits* (Ft. Worth, Texas: Dominion Press, 1986), p. 142.

"We know Jesus and Paul but who are you?" With that, the evil spirits viciously attacked the men. To these exorcists, power was in an *equation*, in this case the name of Jesus. They discovered that Jesus cannot be maneuvered by any formula. The exorcist's use of a *formula* also explains why science so easily slips into magic. Both tend to reduce life to an equation. Atheistic science seeks to manipulate the universe through an *equation*, and magic uses an incantational *formula*.

Ethics, not elitist formulas, is the key to Biblical religion. David says, "Thou dost not delight in sacrifice . . . with burnt offering. The sacrifices of God are a broken heart" (Ps. 51:16). Then David continues on the ethical note, "By Thy favor *do good* to Zion, *Build the walls* of Jerusalem, then Thou wilt delight in *righteous* sacrifices . . . in whole burnt offering" (Ps. 51:18-19). Biblical religion has "ritual," or perhaps a better word would be "routine."[15] But the ritual of the Bible follows the covenant. David calls for covenantal faithfulness to make the routines of offering sacrifices legitimate. Without faithfulness, the sacrifices were useless.

Mediation By Magic

The problem of mediation is basic to the question of cause and effect. Man cannot escape his position as God's subordinate over the world. Man calls on God's power to assist him in his dominion tasks. The question is: How does he call on God? The Biblical answer is that man calls on God as the covenant God who enforces the terms of His covenant in history. But the magician, like the humanist, cannot admit this. That places too much emphasis on the terms of the covenant: ethics. So he seeks other ways of calling on God.

The heart of the humanist Renaissance was magic. It was a self-conscious attempt to revive pagan humanism, including classical magic. The fundamental assumption of magic is the chain of being idea: "As above, so below." God and the heavens are essentially like man and his environment. So there must be a search for the appropriate means of *intermediating* between heaven and earth. This is the magician's quest. Frances Yates describes this rival worldview:

> For the All was One, united by an infinitely complex system of relationships. The magician was the one who knew how to enter into the system,

---

15. *Ibid.*, p. 136. North discusses how Protestantism created a superior work ethic by emphasizing *routine*.

and use it, by knowing the links of the chains of influences descending vertically from above, and establishing for himself a chain of ascending links by correct use of the occult sympathies in terrestrial things, of celestial images, of invocations and names, and the like.[16]

As above, so below. Manipulate the creation, and the forces of the heavens can be mastered, directed toward the magician's goals. Here is the vision of man as God, the one who directs the forces of nature and the supernatural as a craftsman.

In Biblical religion, what is above (God) is fundamentally different from that which is below (the creation). Man's position as intermediary is God-given. Man must exercise dominion as God's covenantal agent, not as an autonomous master of the cosmos. The link between heaven and earth is therefore covenantal. It is governed by the terms of the covenant. For man to get his way, he must choose God's way for him. Keeping the law of God is not a way to manipulate (MAN-ipulate) God; it is man's way of conforming himself ethically to God. The Biblical character who failed to understand this was Simon the magician, who sought to buy the power of God from Simon Peter. Peter consigned him to hell. He called on him to repent (Acts 8:14-24).

Magical, mechanical, and manipulative explanations are all false. They define life's problems as metaphysical, not covenantal. According to them, man lacks something in his being; maybe he is racially inferior; maybe he lacks the right spell; maybe he is not saying the spell the right way; maybe he does not know enough. In every case, the problem is a flaw in his being and not his ethics. The third section of the covenant, however, calls for submission to God in terms of His stipulations.

Conclusion

Law is at the heart of God's covenant, building on the principles of transcendence and hierarchy. The temptation of the people of God is to resort to magic. As it was in the days when Moses received the law, so it is in our day. The conflict is still between ethics and magic.

In this chapter, I have sought to accomplish one main thing: to establish the ethical connection between cause and effect. First, I presented the principle. It can also be called command/fulfillment.

---

16. Frances A. Yates, *Giordano Bruno and the Hermetic Tradition* (New York: Vintage, [1964] 1969), p. 45.

Covenant-keeping results in blessing. Covenant-breaking ends in cursing. The principle of the third section of Deuteronomy is just this simple.

Second, we considered that faithfulness is not mere external conformity to the Ten Commandments. Although the ethics segment expounds them, they are to be kept from the proper motives and applied properly from situation to situation. This kind of ethical faithfulness acquires dominion and influence.

The Book of Job was raised as a possible exception to this principle. We found that Job is an example of how God tests His people with temporary "cursing." The purpose is to strengthen their faith. Actually, the testing results in greater blessing.

Third, there are false explanations of cause and effect. The mechanical explanation tries to reduce the universe to natural laws and formulae. The manipulative approach explains cause and effect according to brute force. The magical theory combines the first two, using a formula to manipulate nature. All three are wrong and misleading.

This completes the third step in the covenantal process. In the next chapter, the fourth principle is considered. It has to do with how the covenant was entered through the reception of sanctions. We will examine such issues as why the sanctions symbolize and seal judgment to a person. Is the covenant conditional or unconditional? Can a person lose his salvation?

D. Fourth Point of Covenantalism

4

SANCTIONS
(Deuteronomy 27-30)

One night God came to Abraham. It was time to cut a covenant.

Many years before this interrupted evening, God had promised him that he would be the father of many nations (Gen. 12:1-3). But so far, he had only wandered around the known world finding out how great the other rulers were!

This evening was different though. God came to him and told him to look into the heavens and count the number of stars (Gen. 15:5). Why? God wanted Abraham to see how large a number of descendants he would have. To many men, this exercise would have seemed futile, since his wife was much too old to bear children. But he was not just any man.

He believed the Lord (Gen. 15:6).

Faith, however, does not rule out the possibility of questions. Abraham asked God how he could know that he would really be given the land promised to him. God answered his question by cutting a covenant (Gen. 15:18). To form this covenantal alliance, a standard procedure was used.

Abraham was instructed to bring five different types of animals: a three-year-old heifer, a three-year-old female goat, a three-year-old ram, a turtledove, and a young pigeon. They were cut in half, and the halves being separated, were placed in front of Abraham. Normally, Abraham would have passed between the animals, and burned them with fire to seal the covenant. By this time, however, a day had gone by and the sun was about to set. God made Abraham fall asleep, and *He* passed between the animals, burning them with fire.[1] He takes an oath, sanctioning *Himself* for Abraham's benefit.

---

1. Jesus did the same thing in the Garden of Gethsemane (Luke 22:39-46). The disciples fell asleep. He sweated drops of *blood* for them. God the Son received a maledictory oath on Himself, becoming a substitute.

Here are the ingredients of the next principle of covenantalism, the actual process of ratification. To cut a covenant, three elements are necessary: sanctions, oath, and witnesses.

All of these elements are present in the fourth section of Deuteronomy (27-30). Israel accepted the sanctions of blessing and cursing by dividing into two groups on Mt. Gerizim (blessing) and Mt. Ebal (cursing). They received the sanctions by sacred oath, saying "amen" to the curses of the covenant. Finally, the witnesses of "heaven and earth" verified the authenticity of the ceremony. This momentous occasion was the actual ratification of the covenant.

Let us consider each aspect of this process, beginning with sanctions.

I. Sanctions (Deut. 27-30)

First, the sanctions are blessing and cursing. Blessing always has to do with the reception of *inheritance* (Gen. 48:1-22). This inheritance is personal and cultural, everything from holiness to financial and civilizational prosperity (Deut. 28:1-14). The most common image of blessing is a *garden*. The Bible begins and ends in one. Jesus was taken by the authorities in a garden. Cursing, on the other hand, concerns *death*. It too has personal and cultural dimensions. The same list of blessings in Deuteronomy is followed by an even more extensive list of cursings such as sickness, famine, war, and bankruptcy (Deut. 28:15-68). The metaphors of cursing are the sea (chaos) and the desert (desolation). These are pictures of what the world becomes when man breaks covenant, places where the devil and demons live.

Second, the sanctions of blessing and cursing are actually *promises*. This promissory idea goes back to the garden. Two original promises were made to Adam. God promised the blessing of rest on the Sabbath Day (Gen. 2:1-3), and He promised the curse of death if the tree of the knowledge of good and evil were eaten (Gen. 2:15-17). Because the sanctions were issued beforehand, they were promissory in character. Heads of households did the same. Before they died, they called the first-born, laid on hands, blessed the first-born, and thereby transferred the inheritance. In some cases, the father even issued a curse to an unfaithful son (Gen. 49:4). In short, all sanctions are *prophetic*.

Third, the sanctions are judicial, involving a judgment before blessing. Adam was to have received blessing first. Cursing was not supposed to have been involved in the Sabbath Day experience at all. Sin disrupted the day of blessing, however, and cursing ended up coming first. From that moment on, blessing could only come through cursing. God said to the serpent, "I will put enmity between your seed and her seed; He shall bruise you on the head, and you shall bruise Him on the heel" (Gen. 3:15). In the midst of declaring the curse, God promised the blessing of a seed who would destroy the serpent. We know that this is the first giving of the Gospel. Through the Seed's death, none other than Jesus Christ's Crucifixion, blessing came to the world. *Blessing comes through cursing.* Thus, the covenant is always ratified through the curse. It has been this way ever since Adam sinned. Abraham's animals had to be severed and burned with fire. The Deuteronomic covenant was cut by receiving twelve curses on Mt. Ebal (Deut. 27:15-26).

A very critical point about the covenant now emerges. Blessing, reward, and inheritance come through *judgment* and its counterparts: discipline and suffering. The way of the covenant is: judgment first, and success later. *Nothing is instant.* If you want to build a mud hut, it takes a day. If you want to build a cathedral, it takes a century. If you want to build a civilization, it takes generations. The kingdom is built one brick at a time. Judgment comes before blessing. God's true people do not despise judgment. They are willing to meet judgment up front in life. They confront Christ's death while alive, rather than wait until Judgment Day. Moreover, all other phases of the Biblical faith that also involve meeting judgment take on clearer meaning: discipline, suffering, or receiving correction and rebuke. Christians are willing to face these, because they understand that life comes through judgment. People who are willing to implement these sanctions capture a civilization. They will rear better children, because they will be willing to discipline them. They will make better employees, since every *occupation* requires judgment and discipline. They will make better leaders, due to the fact that leaders have to make critical judgment calls. Thus, the covenant engages one in judgment, and judgment transforms him and his world.

Fourth, dual sanctions imply that there is *one* covenant with two sanctions of blessing and cursing. Both are applied, not just one. And, because there are two sanctions, it is possible to break the covenant. Students of the covenant, however, have often tried to avoid this conclusion by creating two covenants: law and promise.[2] Law is understood to be conditional, and promise is interpreted to be un-

---

2. Robert D. Brinsmead, *Covenant* (Fallbrook, California: Verdict Publications, 1979), pp. 85-99.

conditional and everlasting. Some have even gone so far as to say that law covenants are "works" oriented, and promise covenants are characterized by "grace."[3] None of these approaches does justice to the plain sense of the Bible. "Promissory" covenants have conditions, and so-called conditional covenants are built on promises.

Conditional or Unconditional?

Promissory covenants. Take the New Covenant as an example, a covenant which no one disputes is promissory. Paul says,

> In the case of those who have once been enlightened and have tasted of the heavenly gift and have been made partakers of the Holy Spirit, and have tasted of the good Word of God and the powers of the age to come, and then have *fallen away*, it is impossible to renew them again unto repentance, since they again crucify to themselves the Son of God, and put Him to open shame (Heb. 6:4-6).

I am aware of the fact that some commentators have tried to use the grammar involved to remove the real possibility of departing from the covenant. In other words, there is no *real* potential for "falling away." The warning is only *hypothetical*. This is nonsense. A nonconditional covenant would nullify Paul's warning. There would be no real *warning*. If I should say, "If you don't move out of the street a car will hit you," when there is no possibility whatsoever that a car would ever hit you while you stand in the middle of the street, what is the sense of the warning? Why even give it? The fact is that the promissory New Covenant is conditional, and the *traditional* interpretations of Hebrews 6 reflect just such a conditional sense.[4] Promissory covenants always have conditions.

Law covenants. Just as promissory covenants have conditions, so-called law covenants always have promises. Moses says, "And now, O Israel, listen to the statutes and the judgments which I am teaching you to perform, in order that you may live and go in and take possession of the land which the Lord, the God of your fathers, is

---

3. C. I. Scofield, editor, *The Scofield Reference Bible* (New York: Oxford University Press, 1909). See especially the notes on Galatians. Note that the *New Scofield Reference Bible* has removed the idea that Old Testament saints were saved by "works."

4. John Owen, *Hebrews* (Marshallton, Delaware: The National Foundation For Christian Education, [1668] 1970), Vol. III, pp. 3-144.

giving you" (Deut. 4:1). This statement refers back to the promises of seed and land given to Abraham (one of the "fathers") (Gen. 12:1-3). Their obedience was based on the promise. Yet, the promise is not actualized without obedience. The false dichotomy between grace and law just will not work. Grace and law are not in conflict.[5] As one man says, "There is no grace without law or law without grace."[6]

Every covenant with the exception of Christ's on the cross was unconditional. Even the first covenant with Adam was unconditional. Adam had done nothing to be created or to earn the garden. The terms of not eating the tree of the knowledge of good and evil were in the context of the unconditionality of creation. We can call them the *terms of unconditionality.* The only person who entered a purely conditional covenant was Christ. But once He met its terms and died on the Cross, it became unconditional to everyone who received it. God the Father will never revoke His declaration that Christ perfectly met the terms of the covenant. The unconditionality of the covenant is assured eternally. As long as one lives in Christ, he is under an unconditional covenant.

This does not mean people in the covenant cannot apostatize. We enter an unconditional covenant, but there are terms of unconditionality. James speaks this way when he says, "Show me your faith without the works, and I will show you my faith by my works" (James 2:18). If the terms of unconditionality are not lived out, faith and its works, then the covenant becomes a *works-oriented* system. It then becomes *conditional.* Thus, the covenant-breaker turns the covenant into a conditional system as it applies to him. He refuses to accept Christ's perfect work in place of his own feeble efforts to placate God's wrath.

"Not Guilty" or "On Probation"?

Apostasy is real. People can fall away. Question: Fall away from what? They fall from the *visible covenant.* If they never come back and repent, then they were never truly converted to begin with. From the *human* point of view, however, we can only live by the visible cove-

---

5. Thomas McComiskey, *The Covenants of Promise* (Grand Rapids: Baker, 1985), pp. 59-93. Arthur W. Pink, *The Divine Covenants* (Grand Rapids: Baker, 1975), pp. 139-202.

6. Ernest Kevan, *The Grace of Law* (Grand Rapids: Baker Book House, [1966] 1983), pp. 208-209.

nant. We cannot read hearts and say infallibly that a person *really and truly* is a Christian. We do not have to view every believer in a skeptical manner either. If a person "says" he believes, is baptized, and shows basic outward evidence of being a Christian, he should be treated as a believer.

Should he fall away from the faith, his assurance is lost. The easiest way to understand the apostate's position is to compare it to a judge's granting of a suspended sentence with probation. He does not declare them "Not Guilty." He gives them a suspended sentence with probation to see what they can do with their freedom. He reserves the right to put them back into prison at any time.

Matthew 18 is a major New Testament passage dealing with Church discipline (sanctions). Jesus gave a parable about a man who owed a fortune to a lender. When the lender calls in the debt, the man pleads that he cannot repay the debt yet. The lender graciously gives the man time to pay the debt. But the man then goes out and hounds a poor man to pay him what is owed — money that cannot possibly go very far to repay the huge debt he owes. The original debtor has him thrown into prison. He had not forgiven the debt; he had only suspended the collection day. Because the debtor refused to show mercy, the creditor decided that he was no longer entitled to mercy (Matt. 18:23-35).

But what of the terms of the covenant? Disobedience requires death, from Adam to the present. On what basis does the heavenly Judge extend time to the sinner? On what *legal* basis can a suspended sentence with probation be handed down? Only on the basis of Christ's death and resurrection. God does not have to extend anyone time, but He does so. Even so, some apostatize like the original debtor in the parable. Such a person dies as an unrepentant sinner. In this account, the story applies in particular to Israel. Their lives built up more wrath for themselves (Rom. 12:20).

Thus, the doctrines of Sovereign Grace and predestination are "covenantally qualified." From the moment a person begins his walk with God, he does so by faith. Then he is baptized and enters life as a covenant-keeper. All of these things are covenantal qualifications that he knows the Lord. No one has the ability to look into the decree of God to see what was written before the foundation of the world. Man's assurance can only be in terms of the covenant. Jesus points to the covenantal response of faith to make this clear. He says, "He who believes on Me has eternal life" (John 6:47). So anyone who has believed in Christ should have this assurance. Why? Because faith is a covenantal response. Faith informs a person that the Holy Spirit has indeed worked in his heart.

What if this covenantal response of faith stops? What if a person *says* he has faith in his heart, is baptized, and then leaves the faith? If he never comes back to covenantal faithfulness, it indicates that he was never truly one of God's elect, and that he had been a tare in the congregation. The covenant does not consist of *perfect* but persevering people. Everyone sins, but the test of faith is whether one recognizes, confesses, and moves on in the faith. It is possible, however, to have members of the Church who are in the process of covenant-breaking and falling away. The Church is not like the name of a certain church in my town that is called *True Vine Church*. Think of the implications of this name. It means this church believes that only "true" believers are members. This sounds so "spiritual," but it is impossible. I know for a fact that there are members who professed faith, were baptized, and then fell away. And, I also know for a fact that this is true of every church and every denomination that has ever existed. The covenant is not inviolate.

To say God deals without dual sanctions, therefore, is to weaken the covenant. The ratification of the covenant is nothing more than a "fire insurance policy" against hell. A person lives any way he wants without the consequences of being cursed. But, the sanctions do not work this way. They consist of blessing and cursing; they are promissory; they are judicial; and they are both part of one covenant. Now that we have seen what they consist of, let us address how they were actually received.

II. By Oath Consigned (Deut. 27:1-30:20)

The sanctions of blessing and cursing were received by an *oath*, a self-maledictory ("to speak evil on oneself") oath. The suzerain entered the covenant by pledging and calling down evil on himself from his deities, in the event that he failed to honor his word. The vassal also entered the covenant by taking a self-maledictory oath. Perhaps it could be argued that "secular" covenant-cutting involved *two oaths*. It seems, however, that the vassal actually received the suzerain's oath. What the suzerain called down on himself would hit the vassal, should the latter violate his agreement. So, there was essentially *one* oath by the suzerain *consigned* to the vassal.

Even if this were not the situation in secular oath-taking, the Bib-

lical covenant was by *consignment*. When the Abrahamic covenant
was first established, God took the maledictory oath. God passed
through the dismembered bodies of the animals (Gen. 15). Then,
Abraham received the same oath through the rite of circumcision, a
bloody symbol of death (Gen. 17:1-27). It ultimately pointed to
Christ's death: God's own self-maledictory oath. It was a sign and
seal of what God did to Himself through Jesus Christ. Paul records,
"In Him [Christ] you were also circumcised with a circumcision
made without hands, in the removal of the body of the flesh by
Christ" (Col. 2:11). Thus, *the covenant was received by taking hold of God's
own self-maledictory oath*. Specifically, the Deuteronomic congregation
said "amen" to the "curses" of the covenant (Deut. 27:15-26), or what
Von Rad has called the "dodecalogue."[7] Twelve times they responded
with "amen" on Mt. Ebal, the mount of "cursing."[8]

Man enters the covenant by saying "amen" to God's self-maledictory oath.
In other words, "amen" means, "May God render to *me* the curse
that He has been willing to take on Himself, should I renege on the
covenant." What exactly does this mean? Going back to the Abrahamic example again — where animals were cut in half and burned
with fire — the one who enters covenant with God is saying that that
would literally happen to *him*; *he* would be torn in half; the birds
would come and devour *him*; *he* would be utterly burned with fire.
Saying "amen" should not be taken lightly!

The Sacrificial System

Apparently the congregation's amen was also focused in the
offering up of sacrifices. The fourth segment of the covenant says,
"You shall build there an altar of the Lord your God of uncut stones;
and you shall offer on it burnt offerings to the Lord your God; and
you shall sacrifice peace offerings to the Lord your God" (Deut.
27:6-7). Then the description of the list of amens follows. This structuring of the chapter indicates that amen was said in relation to a
sacrifice.

How did this work? Remember that two sanctions were received
by a consigned maledictory oath. The sanction of cursing fell on God
Himself, so that the sanction of blessing could be received by the one
in covenant with God. In other words, God pledged that covenant-

---

7. Gerhard Von Rad, *Deuteronomy: A Commentary* (Philadelphia: Westminster
Press, 1966), p. 167.
    8. *Wycliffe Bible Commentary*, p. 192.

breaking would result in death. But the presence of sin meant that the maledictory oath would hit the person in covenant with God. To avoid this judgment he needed a sacrifice, or *substitute*. In the example at the beginning of this chapter, the animals served as objects of malediction, preventing Abraham's being burnt with fire. Through them, Abraham ratified and said "amen" to the covenant.

The sacrificial system was at the heart of covenant ratification. It expressed the need of atonement. It pointed to an oath that was made in terms of an object that took the place of man. It was directly linked to the covenant itself. As a matter of fact, there were *five* sacrifices, matching the five points of the covenant.

First, there was the *reparation* offering.[9] The introductory formula to this offering parallels the transcendence point of the covenant, "When a person acts unfaithfully against the *Lord*, and deceives his companion . . . . He shall make restitution [reparation] in full, and add to it one-fifth more. He shall give it to the one to whom it belongs on the day he presents his guilt [sin] offering" (Lev. 6:2).[10] So the transcendence of the *Lord* was acknowledged first by paying a form of restitution as an offering. This also was a show of good faith that the guilty party believed God was immanent.

Second, the *sin* (purification) offering was a way of *confessing* actual sin. This offering provided a process of *mediation*. Hands were laid on the head of the purification offering, thereby transferring the guilt of the sinner to the animal (Lev. 4:33). This is the representational principle we discussed in the hierarchical point of covenantalism. The animal represented the man.

Third, a *whole-burnt* offering was made. Stress was placed on a "perfect male animal" (Lev. 1:3, 10). Why? This offering atoned for all of the breaking of the law so that the individual could completely offer himself up to God.[11] It had specifically to do with the *breaking of the commandments*.[12] The ethical section of the covenant comes to mind.

---

9. Gordon Wenham, *The Book of Leviticus: New International Commentary on the Old Testament* (Grand Rapids: Eerdmans, 1979), pp. 106-112. This offering is also called a "trespass" sacrifice. Wenham correctly prefers to call it a reparation offering.

10. Note by the way that the sacrifices are arranged *theologically* in the first chapters of Leviticus. Their *liturgical* order, the actual order in which they would be offered, is specified in Leviticus six and nine, and Numbers six in reference to the Nazirite.

11. Wenham points out that the other sacrifices "atone," but that the whole-burnt offering "atones in a more general sense" p. 57.

12. *Ibid.*

Fourth, a *cereal* offering was made. This was a *tribute* made by a mixture of grain and *salt* (Lev. 2:13). *Salt* is a symbol of judgment. "The cereal offering then was a gift by the worshipper to God. It normally followed the burnt offering. God having granted forgiveness of sins through the burnt offering, the worshipper responded by giving to God some of the produce of his hands in cereal offering."[13] Thus, the sanctions point of the covenant surfaces. I have pointed out above that blessing comes through *judgment*.

Fifth, the *peace* offering was offered last (Num. 6:17). This was a communion meal between the priest and the guilty party's family. As we shall see in the final point of the covenant, it has to do with the reception of confirmation in the context of a *meal*.

These five sacrifices match the five points of covenantalism. They were obviously a way of saying amen and renewing the covenant. But there is another interesting twist. Animal sacrifices were only temporary means of averting the malediction of God. Why? Remember, God took the malediction on *Himself*. Because of *His* pledge, He promised His own eventual judgment. God did not have to make this pledge, but He did. This is grace! The animals protected man, and because God took a *Self*-maledictory oath, they also held in abeyance a judgment that He *Himself* would have to incur.

This brings us to the Cross and the New Covenant. Due to man's sin, the self-maledictory oath was received unto the Son of *God*. The sanction of cursing, accepted by the consignment of a self-maledictory oath, fell on Jesus. Thus, the sanctions segment of the covenant necessarily involves substitutionary atonement. Faith receives the payment for a broken maledictory oath.

Now we are prepared to see in Deuteronomy that this faith is expressed through symbols, and that the sanctions are applied to households.

1. Symbols

The oath is made by faith but not to the exclusion of certain symbols of faith. The recipient of the covenant says "amen" to God's oath by means of specific *symbols*. Whether Old or New Testament, these symbols declare the *sanctions* of blessing and cursing in a visible form. The covenant with Abraham was cut by means of severed animals and fire. The fire indicated judgment sanction. Then, Abra-

---

13. *Ibid.*, p. 71.

ham's personal reception was the rite of *circumcision*. Of course, circumcision was a "bloody" ordeal that also denotes cursing sanction in symbolic form. In the New Covenant, the symbols of the sanctions become baptism and communion. They too imply blessing and cursing. In *Appendixes 8 and 9*, I discuss the sanctions of the Old and New Covenants in detail. For now, however, it is important to understand that all of these symbols manifest both sanctions. For example, the Lord's Supper is a visual manifestation of the finished work of Christ, which mediates life and death. It communicates life and death. If partaken wrongly, it kills the recipient (I Cor. 11:27-34).

In each case, the covenant is actually received by use of some symbol. In Deuteronomy, perhaps the most obvious symbol involved in renewing the covenant is the use of the "large stones," coated with lime and etched with the actual covenant (Deut. 27:2-4). The covenant was actually *written* on them. So they did more than symbolize, they *sealed* the people and the land to Yahweh. But the logical question is "Are these symbols *real?*" And, "What is the relationship between the symbols and their meaning?" The questions being raised are one of the connection between "sign and thing signified." There are only three views: nominalism, realism, and covenantalism.

Nominalism says there is no connection between the symbol and what it means. There is no relationship between cause and effect. The judicial ceremonies that Israel engaged in have nothing to do with reality. The signs and seals of the covenant really do not mean anything. Using an analogy that David Chilton applies, "A kiss is just a kiss." When a nominalist sees a woman kiss a man, he says, "That doesn't mean anything. What they're doing is only symbolic." The kiss does not mean love, affection, or necessarily anything. The absurdity of this is that if the nominalist is right, a man could just as easily "slap" the woman with a glove — that is, if "symbolic gestures" do not really mean anything.

The Bible disagrees. While man's symbols may at times have no meaning, *God's* symbols have power because His word is behind them. When He says He will bless those who are faithful to the covenant sign, His word is true. When He says cursing will fall on the one who violates the symbol of the covenant, that too will happen. So, God's special covenant signs *really* seal a person to God: *incorporation*. The word comes from the Latin, meaning "one body." *Incorporation* is automatic upon the reception of the covenantal sign, but *not* automatic *salvation*. Remember, there are *dual sanctions*, precisely what the nominalist fails to realize.

The other extreme is called *realism*. Realism says that a covenant is established through some kind of "substantial" contact between the persons. Whether it is legal is not important. What really counts is *substance* or *material contact*. This is the theology of the Roman Catholic Church. As mentioned in Chapter One, a Roman Catholic Archbishop cancelled out a marriage involving a paraplegic. His reasoning: Since the marriage could not be "physically" consummated, it was not *legitimate*. The substantial, physical, sexual contact of the persons was supposedly the basis of marriage, not the covenant bond itself.

The third approach to the relationship between sign and thing signified is *covenantalism*. The connection is covenantal, meaning *representative*. The reception of the covenantal symbol represents something greater than itself. What thing? Symbols of the covenant stand for *God's self-maledictory oath*. Thus, Jesus commands His disciples to baptize in the "*Name* of the Father and the Son and the Holy Spirit" (Matt. 28:19). The power of the symbol of baptism is in the *Name of God*.

The nominalist says there is no power in the symbol. Just because one is baptized does not mean he is in covenant with God. The realist, on the other hand, would say there is power in the *substance*, the water itself. Both views *deny the covenant*. The covenantalist says the symbol has meaning because it represents God's oath on Himself. Since it represents something *God* has done, it is a *real symbol*; it is not empty. Anyone baptized has God's *Name* on him. He is claimed by God and should ordinarily be counted as a believer. But, because the symbol has no power in and of itself, covenantalism requires *faithfulness*. Thus, if one lives in contradiction to the covenantal symbol, he should be warned that apostasy is a real possibility. There are dual sanctions to the covenant. If he does not repent, God's curse will fall on him because *His Name* is at stake.

The covenantalist argues that God's *Trinitarian* Name helps to explain properly the relationship between symbol and reality. In the Trinity, the members of the Godhead are "distinct but not separated." So, since the Church is baptized in this Trinitarian Name (Matt. 28:19ff.), the relationship between symbol and reality is "distinct but not separate." Faith is distinguished from the rite (baptism), meaning there is no power in the sacramental elements themselves to convey salvation, but neither is faith to be separated from the sacraments. The latter clarifies why baptism is so closely associated with salvation (Acts 22:16).[14]

Only the covenantalist can adequately present the connection between symbol and reality. The nominalist does away with reality, and the realist loses the symbolic.[15] God's *covenantal* symbols are powerful. They are the God-appointed means of saying "amen" to God's self-maledictory oath. They picture blessing through curse. The sanctions are *really* conveyed through symbol.

2. By Households

The consignment of God's oath-sanctions is applied to *households*, not just individuals. When Adam and Eve fell, their family fell with them. What happened to them happened to their descendants by legal *representation*. "In Adam's fall we sinned all," as the Puritans' primer for children began. But, by the grace of God, we are not all left in this state of condemnation. Indeed, the Bible is the story of how God brings salvation to the world. But, as Van Til says, "The redemptive revelation of God had to be as *comprehensive* as the sweep of sin."[16] Thus, since sin destroyed the family, we must conclude that redemption saves it, unless "grace is *not* greater than all our sin." As a matter of fact, the redemption of Adam and Eve is also the redemption of the *family*, demonstrated by the constant emphasis on bringing the whole *household* into the faith.

The same principle of representation holds true in salvation of a family unit. Many cases of household salvation by representation can be cited. Noah's family, not just "adult" believers, is brought into the ark. Abraham's family is given salvation through the circumcision of the males: males represent females. And, in the sanctions section of Deuteronomy, we read of the various categories of people to whom the sanctions are applied. Moses says,

---

14. If a person should be providentially hindered from baptism in this life, like the thief on the cross next to Jesus, he still passes through God's baptismal "sea" around His throne (Rev. 4:6).

15. Indeed, this is precisely how the reformers argued against the Roman Catholic view of the sacrament. If the elements changed, then they ceased being *real symbols*. They became the *reality*! B. A. Gerrish, "John Calvin and Reformed Doctrine of the Lord's Supper," *Una Sancta* (Pentecost 1968), pp. 85ff.

16. Cornelius Van Til, *An Introduction to Systematic Theology* (Nutley, New Jersey: Presbyterian and Reformed, 1974), Vol. V, p. 133.

You stand today, all of you, before the Lord your God; your chiefs, your tribes, your elders and your officers, even all the men of Israel, your *little ones*, your wives, and the alien who is within your camps, from the one who chops your wood to the one who draws your water, that you may enter into the covenant with the Lord your God, and into His oath which the Lord your God is making with you today (Deut. 29:10-12).

Notice how Moses first lists the covenantal "heads" of the nation. Then he includes the children and even the alien. We know from other passages in the Old Testament that the alien was not circumcised, but he was required to live in the general sphere of the covenant (Ex. 29:33).[17] Regarding children, however, how can the Bible include them in the covenant? Parents *represent* their children. If they are in the faith, then their children are claimed for the faith as well.

Is this just an Old Testament principle? Even in the New Testament, salvation by household continued to be a practice. Once when Jesus' disciples were keeping parents from bringing their children to Christ, He rebuked them saying,

And they were bringing even their babies to Him so that He might touch them, but when the disciples saw it, they began rebuking them. But Jesus called for them, saying, "Permit the children to come to Me, and do not hinder them, for the kingdom of God *belongs to such as these*. Truly I say to you, whoever does not receive the kingdom of God like a child shall not enter it at all" (Luke 18:15-17).

Mark makes it clear that Jesus was laying His hands on the children to "bless them" (Mark 10:16). Remember, to bless someone is to impose a sanction. So, Jesus was placing the sanction of the covenant on these children and including them in the household of faith. The only basis for doing so was that their *parents* were in the covenant.

Finally, when one comes to Acts, he discovers that households are being saved by the same principle of representation. In one chapter where households are mentioned, Luke speaks of their being brought into the kingdom and being baptized without stopping to explain why. He says "Lydia and her household were baptized" (Acts 16:15). Of the Philippian jailer, Luke says, "He [the jailer] took them that very hour of the night and washed their wounds, and immedi-

---

17. The "stranger" is forbidden in the Exodus passage to eat sacrificial food because it is "holy." Circumcision entitled an Israelite to eat this food (Lev. 1-5), so the stranger obviously was not circumcised.

ately he was baptized, he and all his household" (Acts 16:33).

Luke does not have to stop, because the New Testament builds on the Old. God redeems the family, as well as individuals, by placing them under the sanctions. Remember, the covenant has *terms of unconditionality.* The children may grow up and deny the covenant. They may fall away. But of course, this is a possibility for adults. *The sanctions are familial.* Cut off the children, and one effectively destroys the future!

We come to the end of our discussion on the second aspect of cutting a covenant, and we come to the third and final element.

III. Witnesses

The last but not least important aspect of cutting a covenant is the role of the witness. Notice that Moses calls two witnesses to verify the ratification of the covenant. He says, "I call *heaven and earth* to witness against you today, that I have set before you life and death, the blessing and the curse. So choose life in order that you may live, you and your descendants [seed]" (Deut. 30:19). *Witnesses make the ratification official.* They testify to the fact that a covenant was actually made, whether the recipients were serious or not. I add the last statement because the attitude of the recipient when the covenant is ratified is not of primary importance. *God's disposition* is of main concern. Even though someone might not take his entrance into the covenant very seriously, God does! *He* will make sure the sanctions of the covenant are carried out one way or the other. These witnesses testify to the fact that *God's oath has been consigned to the candidate.* As a matter of fact, should the covenant be broken, the witnesses are called forward to prosecute the one who has actually broken the covenant, called a *covenant lawsuit.*

The "officialness" of entering the covenant raises an important question. When is a person considered a Christian? When he says he is a Christian *or* when he is baptized (ratifying the covenant by sanction, oath, and witnesses)? Notice that the question is not "When *is* a person a Christian?", but when is he *considered* a Christian? This distinction is quite important.

For one, certainly belief in Christ is the basis of personal salvation, but any professing believer who will not be baptized and come under the accountability of a local church is probably not a true Christian. He is like a man and woman who say they love each other but will not make their love "official" in a marriage ceremony. Most people would not take their love very seriously. Love involves commitment, and committed people should have no difficultly making their commitments *legal*.

Two, man can only live by a "visible" covenant. He cannot look into the soul of his fellow man. Sinful man cannot be trusted with such power. Anyone who says he can do this should be considered demon-possessed. Moreover, just because a person *says* he is a Christian does not necessarily mean that indeed he really is. One is not a Christian because he *says* he is, but because *God* says he is. God initially makes this declaration at the reception of the signs and seals. They, and only they, make the covenant official. One might be a Christian before they are applied, but there is no official way of knowing so. The normal *covenantal* place of transferring from the kingdom of darkness into the kingdom of light is at baptism.

The temptation of the Church through the ages has been to elevate other indicators of salvation above baptism and communion, like experience and knowledge. Granted, they have their place of importance, but the covenant is damaged when salvation is determined by them. The New England Puritans destroyed the theological foundation of their entire culture when they created experiential tests of conversion in the 1630s, producing the infamous "Halfway Covenant."[18] Nowhere does God make experience the basis of salvation. It grows out of salvation. The covenantal signs, however, symbolize the heavenly witnesses, the most important testimony. They demonstrate that God's Name is at stake.

The result of covenantal theology is that more weight is given to the sacraments. Anyone who is baptized should be counted as and treated as a believer unless he is apostatizing. But even in this case, he would be approached as an apostate, and not an unbeliever. The check and balance against the violation of the covenant is always dis-

---

18. E. Brooks Holifield, *The Covenant Sealed* (New Haven: Yale, 1974), pp. 169-186, 193. Church leaders in Puritan New England decided to alleviate the visible/invisible tension in their churches. They started requiring conversion experiences of their children. Even if children were baptized, but could not produce a "credible" profession, they were not permitted to be part of the church. Then came the grandchildren. They had not owned the covenant. What should be done with them? Their parents had the sign of baptism but were not allowed to come to the Table. The grandchildren did not even have the sign. The solution was to proceed with the baptism of the grandchildren, but view them as only "halfway" in. The "Halfway Covenant" was born. Children were in the covenant but not really considered believers.

cipline. Groups that emphasize the sacraments should not be criticized for their sacramental theology so much as they should be condemned for not applying church discipline. Nevertheless, experience and knowledge have not proven to be superior checks and balances against "leakage" from the covenant. All the experiential and intellectual groups have had just as difficult a time with apostasy. The best prevention of covenantal leakage is the last point of covenantalism: continuity. Before we consider it, one final application should be made in reference to the ratification process.

The Doctrine of Adoption

The cutting of a covenant—involving sanctions, oath, and witnesses—creates a transfer. The member of the covenant receives a new *name*, or a name change which amounts to the same. Abram received a new name (Abraham) when the covenant was ratified (Gen. 17:5). Jacob became Israel. The New Covenant sign of baptism places God's name directly on the baptizand (Matt. 28:19-20). Historically, the Church has added a Christian name at baptism to be placed in front of the surname, indicating that the covenantal tie supersedes the blood bond. Most churches' language still reflects this: "What is your Christian name?" is a traditional expression for "What is your first name?" This change in name means the covenant member has been transferred into a new family. It is called adoption.

Adoption is covenantal. It enables someone outside the family line to become an heir. Since the Fall, man has been outside God's family. His parents are "dead." He lost them when Adam sinned. And along with his parents' death, he even lost his inheritance. *Covenantally, man is an orphan.* The only way that God can become his parent and he can become God's son is through adoption. He is not, never was, nor will he ever be part of God's essence. He cannot go rummaging through lost archives to prove that he is a *legitimate* heir by natural descent.

Children of believers are to receive the covenantal sign for this reason. They are born covenantally *dead* (Psa. 51:5). Death is associated with the womb (Lev. 12:1-8). After birth, the parents are supposed to bring the child to the leaders of the church to receive the sign of the covenant. When the child receives the sign, he (or she) thereby is declared covenantally alive and given back to the parents, a gesture indicating that *sin takes our children away but the covenant gives them back.* This is an adoption process. The covenant teaches that all of our children are actually to be adopted. They are entrusted to parents by the covenant.

The doctrine of adoption is totally contrary to blood-religion, not to be confused with the Biblical requirement of blood sacrifice. Non-covenantal religions sometimes advocate salvation by *bloodline*, instead of blood sacrifice. Bloodline religion is racist. One race is supposedly purer, or better equipped, than all the others, whether the Arian race as advocated by the Fascists, or the Jews as proposed by the Zionists. All racists are the same. They believe their race or even their nation is special because of its ethnic distinction. Faithfulness to God's covenant has nothing to do with salvation, only faithfulness to the race. This inevitably leads to war, because impure races have to be destroyed. They are a threat to the pure race.

The Jews had forgotten the covenant. They thought their race was superior. If they had believed in the covenant, however, they would have known there was nothing special about their blood. It was like all the other bloodlines. Their greatness had been due to covenant. And they were certainly not part of the covenant because of their bloodline. Jesus reminded them of this fact when He said, "But as many as received Him, to them He gave the right to become children of God, even to those who believe in His name, who were born *not* of blood, nor of the will of the flesh, nor of the will of man, but of *God*" (John 1:12-13). They were adopted sons. Thus, if the Biblical covenant is rejected, man easily becomes a racist!

Conclusion

This concludes our analysis of the fourth principle of the covenant, *sanctions*. The covenant is established by the reception of these sanctions through an oath before witnesses. First, the oath has *dual sanctions*, blessing and cursing, giving the covenant terms of unconditionality. When the Bible speaks of faith, it means *faithfulness*. Man is required to persevere! If he fails to do so, the oath that God takes on Himself will hit the participant in the form of a curse. Along with the terms of unconditionality, the covenant is both promissory and legal. Grace and law are not in conflict.

Second, the oath is received through the consignment of a self-maledictory oath. God pledges Himself to the participants, attaching blessings and cursings. When man places his "amen" on the covenant, he receives what God has done. He says "amen" through certain symbols, and has them applied to his household.

Finally, *witnesses* are required for the ratification of the covenant. The witnesses are heavenly and earthly when the covenant is cut. They verify that an actual covenant has been created. Without them, the covenant is not official.

This ratification process creates a transfer of name, called the doctrine of adoption. Covenant cutting adopts the initiate into the kingdom of God. He receives a new name and inheritance.

The next chapter advances the study to the last principle of the covenant, *continuity*. In this chapter, we will focus more on *inheritance*. The ratification of the covenant creates a new inheritance, but a constant process of covenant renewal has to occur before the inheritance is actualized. Several questions will be answered. What is the point of continuity in the covenant: blood-bond, or something else? What is the inheritance of God's people? Is it spiritual or physical?

5

CONTINUITY
(Deuteronomy 31-34)

Nobody wants to start from scratch. Actually, no man can ever start totally from scratch, for we are creatures living in history. Only God can start from scratch historically (Gen. 1:1). The Biblical man, especially, recognizes that he can move forward only on the basis of a legacy bequeathed to him by his righteous predecessors.

There is a story in the Old Testament that deals with a man who knew that he was in a position of having to start almost from scratch, and he took steps to overcome his predicament. His name was Joseph.

Joseph had to start almost from scratch several times. His brothers tossed him in a pit — clearly a symbol of hell — to keep him until they could kill him.[1] Judah spoke up for him, and wisely suggested that they sell him, something his greedy and short-sighted brothers immediately agreed to. So Joseph was carried down to Egypt by foreign traders. He was sold into bondage. But to sell him, they had to pull him out of the pit — resurrection.

He was sold to Potiphar. He then built up the household wealth of Potiphar. He used Potiphar's capital, of course, but he multiplied it. Then Potiphar's wife lied about his integrity, and Potiphar had him thrown into prison — right back in the pit! But this time, it was a bigger pit.

So he started over again. Before long, he had taken over the

---

1. This took place in Dothan (Gen. 37:17). Dothan was the place of the pit, an historical symbol of hell for Israel. The Hebrew root word for Dothan is the same as the root for Dathan. Dathan and his family revolted against Moses, "and the earth opened its mouth and swallowed them up, and their households, and all the men who belonged to Korah with their possessions. So they and all that belonged to them went down alive to Sheol, and the earth closed over them, and they perished from the midst of the assembly" (Nu. 16:32-33).

administration of the prison, under the authority of the captain of the prison. He also prophesied concerning the dreams of the Pharaoh's baker and cup-bearer (probably second in command, or at least a very high official).[2] But the cup-bearer forgot about Joseph after he was released, as Joseph had prophesied, so Joseph remained a captive for several more years. At age 30, however, his fortunes changed (Gen. 41:46).

When the Pharaoh had a dream that he could not interpret, the cup-bearer remembered Joseph, and told the Pharaoh of Joseph's skills of prophecy and dream interpretation. The king brought him out of prison — resurrection.

The rest of the story is familiar. He interprets the dream, prophesies, and recommends that the king choose a man to administer the grain storage program. The Pharaoh believes Joseph, and therefore believes God's Word. He wisely chooses Joseph as the administrator.

Then he does something extremely important. He places the robe of office, a chain of authority, and the ring of authority on Joseph (Gen. 41:42). He was also given a chariot. As we have seen in Chapter Two, *there is no authority without subordination.* There is no power without bondage. We must wear someone's yoke. Pharaoh places Joseph under the overall authority of Egypt. Egyptian theology taught that the Pharaoh was a divine figure, the link between the realm of the gods and man.

Pharaoh did what Laban had tried to do with Jacob and Nebuchadnezzar later tried to do with the Hebrew youths: bring God's power and blessings under the authority of a foreign power system. Potiphar and the captain of the prison had done the same thing. This story is repeated throughout the Bible. Daniel under Nebuchadnezzar, Belshazar, and Darius is an example of this same process. Mordecai was also given a robe, crown (chain for the head), and a ring by Ahasuerus. Mordecai also was given access to the king's chariot (Esther 8-9). But Ahasuerus was at least married to Mordecai's niece, and may himself have been a converted man. He was not trying to manipulate God in the way that Laban tried.

What pagan kings wanted to do was to *imprison God* through imprisoning God's servant. They were using God's men as magical talismans, or manipulative implements that command supernatural power. This even applied to Nebuchadnezzar, for he was not really

---

2. Baker and cup-bearer: bread and wine.

converted until after his time in the fields (wilderness).

Joseph ruled as the king's delegated sovereign agent. He gave Joseph a wife: the daughter of the priest of On, the holy city. Her name? Asenath, the daughter of Potiphera (Gen. 41:45). He therefore became a son of the priest. He went from the house of Potiphar to the house of Potiphera. In effect, Joseph was brought under a new covenant. Covenantally, Joseph no longer was under Jacob's authority. Jacob believed him to be dead. Joseph also thought he was covenantally dead. We should remember that he saw everything in terms of the covenant, and particularly the covenant made to Abraham. God had promised the first patriarch *seed* and *land* (Gen. 12:1-3). Joseph had been cut off from both. He had been disinherited by his brothers, and he had been sold into slavery. He was in Egypt, the Biblical symbol of hell (the pit), where even Jesus as an infant was carried to. *Covenantally, Joseph appeared to be dead.* He could not inherit from Jacob. His inheritance would come from Egypt. It would be a large inheritance, but it was nevertheless Egyptian. His only hope was for some kind of resurrection. More to the point, *his two sons needed resurrection.* He could not give them covenantal life. He was now a covenantal son of Egypt, not a covenantal son of Israel.

So alienated from the past had Joseph become that he named his two sons with pro-Egyptian names:

And Joseph named the first-born Manasseh [making to forget—R.S.], "For," he said, "God has made me forget all my trouble and all my father's household." And he named the second Ephraim [fruitfulness—R.S.], "For," he said, "God has made me fruitful in the land of my affliction" (Gen. 41:51-52).

He named his sons as though he had forgotten two things. First, he had forgotten the dream that promised that his brothers and father would bow down to him. Second, he had forgotten God's prophecy to Abraham, that before the Israelites could take the land of Canaan, they would be enslaved and oppressed—afflicted—for four generations (Gen. 15:13-16). God was not finished with him covenantally yet. He was therefore not finished with Joseph's sons. There had to be a transfer of the inheritance.

The Inheritance

Eventually, Jacob and his family came to Egypt. Joseph's father and his brothers were forced to bow down to him, even as he had foretold when interpreting the dream that had gotten him sold into bondage (Gen. 37:7-11). They were to dwell in the land of Egypt, as God had prophesied.

With the arrival of Jacob in the land, Joseph knew that he was back in the family covenant. But his two sons had been born in Egypt while Joseph was outside the family, and outside his father's authority. In effect, they were Egyptians, and their names testified to Joseph's Egyptian covenant. Would they inherit? Could they? Wouldn't their inheritance be subject to some future challenge by his brothers or their descendants, as Egyptians?

One day Joseph heard that his father was sick (Gen. 48:1). Joseph could not wait any longer, just as Jacob could not wait when *his* father Isaac was about to give the family blessing to his brother Esau. If Jacob died before his inheritance could be transferred to Joseph's heirs, they could not be included in the covenant. They were sons of Egypt. Joseph had to act immediately. His oldest son needed to receive the special blessing from his grandfather. Without it, he had no inheritance with the people of Israel.

But how could they be given the inheritance if they were sons of Egypt? There was only one way: *they had to be adopted by the dying old man.* If he refused, there was no hope. Joseph's line would be cut off. Joseph had "died" in order to save the people of Israel. He could not pass the inheritance to his own sons by himself. The blessing had to skip generations.

Jacob understood what had to be done, and he did it. To help us to understand exactly what he did, I have emphasized some neglected key words:

And now your two sons, who were born to you in the land of Egypt *before I came* to you in Egypt, *are mine*; Ephraim and Manasseh shall be mine, as Reuben and Simeon are [the first two sons of Jacob by Leah] (Gen. 48:5).

The boys were born *in Egypt* before Jacob arrived. They had been born outside the land, and therefore outside Jacob's familial authority. They were outside the hierarchy of covenantal authority. Their father was a covenantal agent of Pharaoh, not Jacob. How could they inherit? Jacob adopted the two boys as his own sons, equal in authority to the two sons by Leah. This placed them back inside the covenant.

Joseph had two sons who needed to inherit. Joseph therefore transferred to them the double portion of the family's inheritance that he was entitled to as the son who was feeding his father. In making the transfer of his inheritance, Joseph was claiming the double portion, as Jacob recognized: "And I give you one portion more than your brothers" (Gen. 48:22a). In short, *Joseph transferred his birthright to his sons.* Unlike his present-oriented uncle Esau, who had transferred his birthright to Jacob because Jacob promised to feed him, Joseph acted as a future-oriented man.

There is no doubt concerning Joseph's forfeiture of his birthright. Jacob made it plain that other children born out of Joseph's loins and the womb of the Egyptian could come into covenant only by joining the tribes of Ephraim or Manasseh. By handing over the double portion to the "Egyptian" sons, Joseph had nothing left of the Hebrew inheritance to transfer to his other children who had been born (or would be born) under the biological family covenant, since Jacob and the family were now reunited to Joseph's household. The sons who would be considered sons of the covenant by birth would participate in the covenant only through their older Egyptian brothers. The two boys had to be adopted by Jacob, and any other children had to be adopted by the two boys. The other children could become sons of the covenant only through adoption, just as Ephraim and Manasseh were adopted.

> But your offspring that have been born after them shall be yours; they shall be called by the names of their brothers in their inheritance (Gen. 48:6).

Why should they be called by the names of their brothers? Because they could not be called by the name of their father. Their father had no family inheritance in Israel. He was clearly outside the covenant.

This points directly to the Jews' need for adoption in Christ's day. Christ left His birthright to those who would affirm Him as their brothers. The gentiles would inherit, and the Jews could claim their birthright only by being adopted by the gentile Christian believers. Only in the covenant of the dead testator's gentile heirs is there salvation, deliverance, and resurrection.

Joseph knew exactly what he was doing when he brought only the two older sons and not the others, who were obviously alive at the time. He brought in his first-born son and his second-born son. The theme of the first-born and second-born sons is one which is basic to the book of Genesis, and to the Gospel: Adam and Christ.

First-born and Second-born

The two boys entered Jacob's presence. They could now tell that their grandfather was blind. They stood there and stared. They could see him, but he couldn't see them. Their father pushed them forward in a special arrangement. To make sure the inheritance went to the first-born, Joseph placed Manasseh (the first-born) opposite Jacob's right hand and Ephraim in front of the left. There could be no mistake. All Jacob had to do was stick out his right hand and touch the boy in front of him.

To everyone's surprise, Jacob stretched his hand in a diagonal direction and put it on Ephraim, the second-born. Joseph was in dismay. He said to his father, "Stop, Manasseh is the first-born." Jacob answered, "I know, he will be a great tribe too, but the younger one will be greater" (Gen. 48:1-22). Once again, the second-born son would inherit the double portion instead of the first-born, which is God's normal pattern of inheritance (Deut. 21:15-17). Sin disrupts the normal pattern, and God's grace intervenes to re-establish legitimate inheritance on ethical and covenantal lines. Jacob inherited, not Esau; Ephraim inherited, not Manasseh—Jacob's reminder to Joseph of the source of *his* inheritance: a God-established break with the normal pattern, God's sign of special grace.

Who received the double portion in the family of Jacob? No one did. The land later was distributed by family size (Nu. 26:54), and no family received a double portion. Normally, with twelve sons, the inheritance would have been divided into thirteenths, with the eldest son inheriting a double portion. But with respect to the land, two sons received no land, Levi (which became the priestly tribe) and Joseph (who was covenantally dead). Ephraim and Manasseh replaced them.

Joseph's heirs did receive a double portion, however. Ordinarily, all Joseph's sons would have divided his single portion. But the adoption of Manasseh and Ephraim as Jacob's sons gave them two portions to share equally. The real winner was Ephraim, for had he been simply an heir of Joseph rather than Jacob, all of Joseph's sons would have inherited equal portions of Joseph's portion, with Manasseh receiving the double portion. But Ephraim received a full portion as an adopted son of Jacob, not simply a partial portion of Joseph's inheritance. However, his name, *fruitful*, proved accurate. But the Biblical rule prevailed: greater blessings bring greater responsibility. Joshua, an Ephraimite (Nu. 13:8,16), led them into the

Promised Land. Joshua becomes Israel's deliverer. In a symbolic sense, Joshua is Joseph resurrected, and he carries Joseph's bones up to the Promised Land.

Joseph should have received the double portion, for it was he who protected his father in the father's old age. Joseph was Israel's savior. But to offer this protection, Joseph had to die covenantally. Thus, his two sons inherited the equivalent of his double portion, but only by their adoption into the family of Joseph's father. This sealed their inheritance. It could never be challenged by Jacob's other sons or by their heirs. No better example can be found in the Old Testament concerning the basis of the inheritance of the Church. The Church inherits the double portion that belongs by right to Christ, but only because of the death of the Savior-Testator does the Father in heaven adopt the Church.

It is worth mentioning that Jesus was the son of another Joseph, who was himself faithful to the word of the angel, and who did not put Mary away, but married her and reared her son Jesus as his own. He therefore adopted Jesus, making Him covenantally legitimate in terms of Hebrew law. This act of adoption by Joseph established Christ's legal birthright. Like Joshua, after whom Jesus is named, the Deliverer came through adoption.

It is also worth mentioning that the only two men of Moses' generation who were totally faithful (Nu. 14:5-6), and who therefore were allowed by God to cross into the Promised Land (Nu. 32:12) had been adopted into the covenant. Joshua was the descendant of Ephraim, who was adopted in, and Caleb, who was a Kennezite (Nu. 32:12), and the Kennezites were a tribe that dwelt in Canaan, and which had been marked out for destruction by God in His original covenant with Abraham (Gen. 15:19).

False Inheritance

The one who feeds his father is the true first-born son and the one who deserves the double portion. Joseph fed the Pharaoh, too. Joseph said to his brothers, after they had come to be fed in Egypt,

God sent me before you to preserve for you a remnant in the earth, and to keep you alive by a great deliverance. Now, therefore, it was not you who sent me here, but God; and He has made me a father to Pharaoh and lord of all his household and ruler over all the land of Egypt (Gen. 45:7-8).

He had fed the Pharoah and his people; he had delivered them, too. He was therefore the true first-born son of Pharaoh, the covenantally legitimate heir of the Pharaoh's double portion. Pharaoh understood this. He gave Joseph the double portion in Egypt, the land of Goshen, the best of Egypt (Gen. 47:6). But the Egyptians did what he had feared that his brothers and their descendents might do: deny the legitimacy of his birthright. The Egyptians hated Egypt's true first-born son, the family that had fed Egypt and saved it: the Hebrews. The Book of Exodus speaks of another Pharaoh who arose who did not remember Joseph—did not acknowledge the lawful inheritance that Joseph and his family had been given. The later Pharaoh stole the inheritance by placing the Hebrews in slavery, just as Jacob's sons had done to Joseph in Dothan. Egypt once again proved itself to be a pit, a place of bondage, just as God had told Abraham it would. There can be no salvation in Egypt.

What was God's response? He killed the first-born sons of Egypt as His final plague, and the Egyptians let them go free. The Egyptian kidnappers of the Hebrews died, just as the kidnapping brothers of Joseph would have died of starvation, had not God through Joseph showed them grace. We need to be fed by the true first-born son, or else we die.

Legitimacy

I call what happens in this story the principle of *continuity*. What is it? Continuity is the confirmation of the legitimate heir, thereby transferring the inheritance to him. First, the inheritance is confirmed by the *laying on of hands*.[3] The ratification process of circumcision normally would have entitled Joseph's sons to their inheritance. But they were probably uncircumcised because they were the sons of a covenantally dead man. Probably, they would have been circumcised in connection with the process of adoption, though the Bible

---

3. An inheritance of seed and land is passed from Israel (Jacob) to Ephraim. God calls it a "blessing" to Abraham (Gen. 12:2). This fact connects it with the original blessing promised to man in the garden. In the last chapter we called it "rest" (Gen. 2:1-3). But now we should expand our understanding of blessing. It is a person and an environment. The person is the Seed-Man, the Messianic line and eventually none other than Jesus Christ (Gal. 3:16). The environment is the Promised Land in the Old Testament, which becomes the whole world in the New Testament (cf. Exod. 20:12; Eph. 6:3; Note the shift from "land" to "earth"). When Christ saves the world, Paul describes this as the coming of true "rest" (Heb. 4:1-11). His argument is that Christ's First Advent brought this rest, so the Church is supposed to enter into it by applying the Word of God to the world.

does not say. They were nevertheless sons *by declaration*, and the laying on of hands was a judicial act that simply declared who the heirs were, symbolizing a transfer from one generation to the next.

What happens to Joseph's sons does not disrupt the covenantal progression from ratification to continuity that we see in Deuteronomy. Nor should the Joseph situation confuse in the reader's mind ratification and the last step of covenantalism. The Deuteronomic covenant places ratification before the final stage of covenantalism; most of the time ratification and continuity are simultaneous to one another, which may explain the Joseph account. At any rate, ratification does provide an element of continuity. It (circumcision in the Old Covenant and baptism in the New Covenant) *initially* establishes continuity. Ratification places legal claim on the recipient by means of the "first" sacrament. It entitles him to an inheritance. It officially guarantees a legacy even to the household, as we learned in the last chapter. So it is obvious that the fourth and fifth points of the covenant are inseparably bound. But the final point of the covenant, what I am calling "continuity," is a *continuation* of ratification. It is the means whereby the claim is actually extended. It is a confirmation process that usually involves the second sacrament (passover in the Old Covenant and communion in the New Covenant) as we shall see. In Deuteronomy, the continuity section begins with the laying on of hands (via a sacred meal), and then it moves to a second element that we also see in the Joseph account.

Second, the covenant transfer is confirmed by the *actual conquest of the land*. After Joseph's second-born becomes the heir, Jacob describes how God will bring the nation to the Promised Land again (Gen. 48:19-22). If there is no actual conquest of the land, Jacob's transfer is invalidated. This would mean his heirs are not the true heirs, and he would not get to come back to the land. To the victors go, not the spoils, but in this case, the inheritance.

Third, the inheritance is *not* confirmed on the basis of *natural descent*. Man's fallen nature disrupted the natural flow of things. Normally, the first-born would have been the recipient of the double portion of the blessing, but the Fall of man morally disabled him. In the Bible, the first-born is covenantally unable to obtain the inheritance: Adam, Cain, Esau, Ishmael, Reuben, and so forth. The constant failure of the first-born goes back to Adam, and the constant success of the second-born points forward to Jesus, the second Adam and true first-born.

This brief introduction takes us directly to the fifth point of covenantalism in Deuteronomy (31-34). The obvious connection is that

Joshua is a descendent of Joseph. But more importantly, we see how a process of confirmation follows ratification, forming continuity from one generation to another.[4]

Confirmation (Deut. 31-34)

Continuity is a process of confirmation. Ratification, the fourth point, was only the beginning. It brought a person under the covenant, but he also needed confirmation. He needed to receive the *full benefits* of being a covenant member. This inheritance did not come all at once but in stages. The confirmation of Deuteronomy is three-fold.

1. Covenant Renewal

Moses first engaged Joshua and the congregation in *covenant renewal*. This was done by means of a large worship service (Deut. 31-32). The service was covenantal. The Song of Moses part of worship followed the outline of the covenant (Deut. 32).[5] From this we should learn that the church's formal worship service is not a time of entertainment, but simply a renewal of God's covenant. Furthermore, worship is the logical step after the covenant has been cut. If for some reason a person cuts the covenant, and then never attends or even drops out of worship, his ratification of the covenant is not confirmed, meaning he never truly covenanted with God. On this basis, his inheritance in the covenant is forfeited (Heb. 10:22-25).

A meal is often associated with worship. Why? It is a way of confirming a covenant that has previously been cut.[6] In the suzerain covenants, the soon-to-die suzerain would gather all of his followers together at a special ceremony involving a sacred meal. He would require them to pledge an oath of allegiance to his successor. Then, after he died, the successor would have another ceremony and meal.

---

4. *Wycliffe Bible Commentary*, p. 197. Kline says, "This final section of the covenant document has as its unifying theme the perpetuation of the covenant relationship. Of special importance is the subject of royal succession. . . . This succession is provided for by the appointment and commissioning of Joshua as the dynamic heir to Moses in the office of mediatorial representative of the Lord (ch. 31). The testamentary assignment of kingdom inheritance to the several tribes of Israel (ch. 33) reckons with the status of all God's people as royal heirs. Included also are two other standard elements in the international (Ancient Near Eastern) treaties. One is the invocation of covenant witnesses, here represented chiefly by the Song of Witness (ch. 32). The other is the directions for the disposition of the treaty document after the ceremony (31:9-13). By way of notarizing the document, an account of the death of Moses is affixed at the end (ch. 34)."

5. *Wycliffe Bible Commentary*, p. 199-201.

6. Still today, a meal often follows a business agreement, or other important meetings. In China it is the same way.

The followers would again pledge an oath and renew their covenant to seal legally and ritually the transfer of power.[7] In Deuteronomy and Joshua the same process takes place. Israel is confirmed in its allegiance to Joshua with Moses. After the death of Moses, they have other ceremonies and meals to renew their covenant with their new leader (Josh. 5:10; 8:30-35). The *confirmation of communion* is supposed to be an *ongoing process*.

These events were, in the ancient world, a combination of civil and ecclesiastical. Today, we separate the two governments more clearly, but similar rituals still exist. Many churches ordain pastors, elders, and deacons by the practice of the laying on of hands. Existing elders touch the shoulders of kneeling men who have been ordained but not yet confirmed. This is the act of confirmation. Sometimes they celebrate communion immediately after the laying on of hands. In civil government, there must also be confirmation and some variant of the laying on of hands. In this context, Moses laid hands on Joshua (Deut. 34:9). This was a judicial act. It was not magical. Nothing of substance flowed from Moses to Joshua. But this legal act symbolized that Joshua was in continuity with the historic covenant. Historic continuity is extremely important. To cut oneself off from history results in fighting the same battles of the past. It is a common saying that those who do not understand history are condemned to repeat the mistakes of the past.

For example, the modern Church generally reacts to the creeds of the early Church. The liberals want to change them, and the evangelicals want to curse them: "No creed but Christ," and so forth. What happens? The Church finds its old enemies creeping back into history. It fights Arian theology of the third and fourth centuries in the form of the Jehovah's Witnesses. It fights gnostic theology in the form of the New Age movement. So, essentially, it becomes difficult for the Church to make progress without the confirmation process of the historic Church.[8]

We should always maintain that the basis of continuity is the Word

---

7. Don Sinnema, *Reclaiming the Land* (Toronto, Canada: Joy in Learning Curriculum Development and Training Center, 1977), pp. 45-46.

8. This bears on the "Apostolic Succession" question. Some would argue that only the ordination of a "certain" church is to be recognized. East and West have been divided on this matter. But recently, there have been Catholic and Orthodox scholars who see the succession question in a more "processional" sense, meaning the succession is in the body "politic," and not just in the bishop. See Alexander Schmemann, *The Historical Road of Eastern Orthodoxy* (Crestwood, New York: St. Vladimir's Seminary, 1977), p. 45.

of God. The Bible does not change. Secondarily, the creeds of the Church serve as sources of continuity, though they can and must be changed as major Biblical insights are discovered, and as crucial historic issues arise that the Church must address. (Abortion in our day is one such issue; yet the historic creeds do not specifically refer to it.) Continuity is provided to the Church by the Bible; continuity is then provided by the Church through preaching, sacraments, and discipline — its unique marks.

There must be a link between heaven and earth. Christ is that link. His Church continues institutionally and covenantally the link that Christ established. But there must be an absolute confirmation which supports the historic confirmations of the Church. Without this, the confirmations of the Church would become relative. This raises the question of "binding and loosing."

I will give you the keys of the kingdom of heaven; and whatever you shall bind on earth shall be bound in heaven, and whatever you loose on earth shall be loosed in heaven (Matt. 16:19).
Truly I say unto you, whatever you shall bind on earth shall be bound in heaven; and whatever you loose on earth shall be loosed in heaven (Matt. 18:18).

Like prayers that God promises to honor, so are the disciplinary and confirmatory actions of the Church: they must be. As always, the Bible is the standard, not the mouth of man. But when the lawfully ordained man speaks God's Word appropriately to the historical situation, God promises to confirm that word.

2. Conquest

Moses says their confirmation comes through the actual conquest of the land: "Then Moses called to Joshua and said to him in the sight of all Israel, 'Be strong and courageous, for you shall go with this people into the land which the Lord has sworn to their fathers [historic continuity] to give them, and you shall give it to them as an inheritance . . . .which you are about to cross the Jordan to *possess*'" (Deut. 31:7). The requirement of possessing the land is restated by God, when He speaks to Joshua, saying, "To *possess* the land which the Lord your God is giving to you, to *possess* it" (Josh. 1:11). The Hebrew word for "possess" (*yarash*) conveys the way Israel was to conquer. One commentator says:

The verb *yarash* has three meanings when used in relation to land. The first is to receive the land as a gift [Lev. 20:24; *RSV* "inherit"].

The second is to occupy and organize the land according to God's teaching. . . . again and again they [the Scriptures] say that the commandments are to be applied "in the land to which you are going over, to possess it. . . . that it may go well with you . . ." [Deut. 6:1-3, etc.]. Conversely, failure to observe the conditions of faithful tenants will mean that the rights of tenancy of "possession" will be taken away [Deut. 4:26; 28:63]. The tenants will be "dispossessed" [Num. 14:12].

The third meaning derives from the first two. Receiving the right of tenancy [possessing in the sense of inheriting] and living on the land [possessing in the sense of a proper ordering of society on the land] can be effected only if there is actual control. . . . The causative form of the verb *yarash* means to cause a change in the power structure on the land . . . so that a new social order may be set up.[9]

Under the guidance of the Holy Spirit (Deut. 34:9), Joshua was called to "possess" the land in this threefold sense. He was to lead Israel to take what was theirs—not by "natural right," but because they were "covenantal tenants." They were to apply the covenant, and they were to set up a new social order under the Word of God. They were to conquer the land by *obedience to the law.*

The conquest in this regard was rather unique. We see an example at Jericho. Israel marched around the city, symbolically circumcising it, and performing a divine liturgy against the enemy. Israel obeyed God's word. The walls of paganism could not collapse by brute power. God defeated the Canaanites through obedience to the covenant. As the words of the title of this book go, "So *keep* the words of this covenant to *do them* that you may prosper in all that you do" (Deut. 29:9). Covenant renewal by worship and the laying on of hands was not enough. The confirmation of one's inheritance started there, but it could not end there. Covenant renewal is supposed to move out from around the throne of God and into civilization. If it doesn't, the inheritance is lost. Churches that are only caught up in their liturgies forfeit society, and consequently forfeit everything. Liturgy should translate into life. When it does, the inheritance is fully realized.

---

9. E. John Hamlin, *Joshua: Inheriting the Land* (Grand Rapids: Eerdmans, 1983), pp. 9-10.

3. Discipleship

Moses addresses a third aspect of confirmation. He tells them to read the law every seven years at the "remission of debts" (Deut. 31:10). It was for "their children, who have not known" the ways of the Lord (Deut. 31:13). He had established continuity with the past and confirmed them with the obligation of conquest in the present. Now he prepares them for the future with the requirement of perpetual instruction in the law. The children and everyone were to be educated in the Lord. I call this process *discipleship*.

Civilization cannot be maintained by force. Societies are preserved by God's power, self-discipline, and the day-to-day disciplining of the three institutional covenants: Family, Church, and State. People need to be instructed and disciplined in the ways of righteousness. Their habits have to be changed. This takes time. The Biblical way requires constant evangelization, missions, and grassroots discipleship. Recognition of the past and the present are not enough. Discipleship extends historically what has happened in the past and is happening in the present. Without discipleship, the next generation will simply lose everything worth having. Without raising up the next generation, there can be no real dominion.

Overcoming Illegitimacy

In Israel, anyone could become a king within ten generations. The law said that the Moabite and the Ammonite had to wait ten generations before they could enter the presence of the Lord (Deut. 23:3). Why did it take that long, when it took an Egyptian, the oppressor state, only three generations to become a ruler (Deut. 23:8)? Because Moab and Ammon were bastards, the sons of the incestuous relationship between Lot and his daughters. The rule applied to Moab and Ammon that applied to bastards in general: ten generations of circumcised sons or faithful daughters before a descendent could become a full citizen — a ruler (Deut. 23:2).

David was the descendent of Tamar, who committed adultery with Judah. He was the tenth generation after Judah and Tamar's son, Perez (Ruth 4:18-22), which represents approximately six hundred years, or about half a millennium. This indicates that it takes time to change civilization and secure the inheritance of the Lord. David represented ten generations of discipleship and future-oriented preparation. It took those generations of parents a long time, but consider the effects. He began a Davidic millennium that lasted until the time of Christ.

It is interesting that Jacob's blessing for Judah included this promise: "The scepter shall not depart from Judah, nor the ruler's staff from between his feet, until Shiloh comes. And to Him shall be the obedience of peoples" (Gen. 49:10). Yet this promise was conditional. From Perez to David, no one in Judah's line could rule. Yet the promise came true because each father circumcised his sons. Each looked forward ritually to the fulfillment of Jacob's promise. Then, with David, came the most powerful king in Israel's history. This was a typical fulfillment: from darkness to the highest blessing. We see it in Joseph's life, in Job's life, and in Nebuchadnezzar's after his years in the fields. The resurrection is greater than a person's position before his fall.

Overcoming Debt

Moses also ties the process of instruction in the law to the "debt cancellation laws" (Deut. 31:10). Every seventh year the debts were cancelled. Every seventh year the Bible was read to the people. Every seventh sabbatic cycle, the land was returned to its owners, the year of Jubilee. The principle: *debt could not extend beyond the preaching of the law.* If it did, the civilization became debt-oriented and lost its inheritance. If it did, they would have two gods: God and Mammon. Debt-oriented societies are polytheistic cultures that simply cannot hang on to their inheritance. They are not future-oriented because they end up inflating their way out. This is nothing else but theft. The present cannot be conquered by stealing from the future.

Moses knew Israel was receiving covenant renewal and was willing to possess the land. He also knew they would fall in the future if the present generation was not discipled. They would end up with a great past and a semi-great present, but no future. Any society that is not discipled for the future becomes a culture of death and debt.

This is the process of transferring inheritance. Continuity is created through confirmation. It consists of covenant renewal, conquest by obedience, and discipleship.

Discontinuity

Discontinuity is the opposite of continuity. Just as heirs are transferred their inheritance by confirmation, so are the false heirs disinherited.

Dissolubility of the Covenant

The covenant can be terminated, or dissolved. The continuity of all the covenants — God to God, God to man, and man to man — is in fact *dissoluble*.[10]

The "primary" covenant — God to God — could be broken upon covenantal death. Even though Jesus perfectly obeyed God, the Cross is a picture of God the Father forsaking God the Son.[11] Jesus said, "My God, My God, Why hast thou forsaken Me" (Matt. 27:46). This is truly a great mystery, but Jesus was covenantally cut off from the "land of the living."[12] A kind of "covenantal death" occurred prior to physical death.

The secondary level of covenant — God to man — can be broken upon covenantal separation. The writer to the Hebrews warns the believers not to forsake their covenant. He urges them to "press on to maturity" (Heb. 6:1), the implication being that they were thinking of departing from their covenant with God. Again, we take notice of the following sobering words:

For in the case of those who have once been enlightened and have tasted of the heavenly gift and have been made partakers of the Holy Spirit, and have tasted the good word of God and the powers of the age to come, and then have fallen away, *it is impossible to renew them again to repentance*, since they again crucify to themselves the Son of God, and put Him to open shame (Heb. 6:4-6).

---

10. There are three levels of covenants in the Bible. The *primary* level of covenants is the God-to-God-covenant. This is the covenant among the Godhead, illustrated in the Abrahamic covenant where God took a covenantal "oath" to Himself and used the other members of the Godhead to "witness" (Gen. 15:1-21). The *secondary* level is from God to man. When one is converted, he enters this covenant. Finally, there is the *tertiary* level of covenants from man to man, falling into two categories: Self-maledictory covenants which are binding until the "death" of those involved, and contracts which should not be accompanied by "self-maledictory" oaths, oaths that call down death to the one who breaks the covenant.

11. Klaas Schilder, *Christ Crucified* (Grand Rapids: Baker, [1940] 1979), pp. 371-426. As indicated by one of Schilder's sermon titles, "Christ Thrust Away But Not Separated," Christ's death did not do "violence" to the Godhead. Nevertheless, the covenant was fractured such that God the Son incurred the full fury of the wrath of God the Father.

12. Here, by the way, is a classic example of how physical death is based on "covenantal" separation. The physical death of one's spouse causes the covenantal death of the marriage, but only because all physical death is the result of the covenantal violation of Adam and Eve (Rom. 5:11-12).

Notice that the writer makes the connection between the cutting off of Christ at the crucifixion, and apostasy. I pointed out above that Christ's death was actually a covenantal separation. So, the point about covenantal death is extended to the God-to-man level.

The third level of covenants — man to man — can also be terminated by covenantal death. At this level we find the three institutions of society: Family, Church, and State. Although they are covenants among men, they all have a special relationship to God, yet not indissoluble. Take marriage as an example. Jesus says, "What God has brought together, let no man separate" (Mark 10:9). This is an imperative (ethical requirement), not a declaration. He does not say, "No man *can* separate." There is quite a difference between a "negative" command and the assertion that the bond cannot be broken. The Apostle Paul argues that, indeed, covenantal as well as physical death can break the marriage bond (Rom. 7:1-4).

The context of this death is covenantal. The verse immediately preceding this section is Romans 6:23, "For the wages of sin is *death*, but the gift of God is eternal life through Jesus Christ." Furthermore, the context directly following is a discussion about *death to the law*. So, it is clear that *covenantal death* is in view regarding the marriage covenant, implying that the marriage bond can be severed, "covenantally" as well as physically. The point is that even at the tertiary level of covenants, the same principle of termination appears. This is only one example of how the man-to-man covenant can be destroyed through covenantal death. But it proves that the "indissolubility doctrine" is unbiblical.

The fact that covenants can be dissolved is certain. Let us now consider how covenantal discontinuity comes about. It is the opposite of the confirmation process.

1. Covenant Denial

The covenant should be continually renewed. Renewal leads to the laying on of hands, a confirmation of the true heir. If the covenant is *denied*, however, the blessing is lost. The heir becomes a bastard son. One clear example of this is Esau. He was the first-born son, entitled to be the heir of the double portion, the one through whom the seed would come. But Esau was a man of war. The text calls attention to the fact that he was a hunter (Gen. 27:3). His name literally means "hairy" (Gen. 27:11). His name compares him to an animal, a beast. He is also called "Edom," meaning "red," probably referring to blood (Gen. 36:8). He had a "taste for game." He liked the taste of blood. Esau believed in power religion. Force was the means of acquiring and sustaining the inheritance. And his warring nature turned against him.

Esau was not a man of the covenant. His power-oriented way is contrasted to Jacob's "peace-loving" ways (Gen. 25:27). This means that Jacob dealt with people according to the covenant. Esau was the opposite. He dealt according to power, blood, and the desires of his own stomach. He was not past-oriented or future-oriented. One day he went into the field to hunt. He came back and found Jacob cooking a "red stew" (Gen. 25:30). Again the red is probably a reference to "blood." Esau was hungry and wanted something to eat immediately. The fact that it was a "blood" stew made him desperate. Of course the stew was not a blood dish. It was a lentil stew (Gen. 25:34). I believe Jacob knew his brother was a bloody man and would be reminded of blood when he saw it.

Jacob took advantage of the situation. He was a man of the covenant. He knew and respected the covenantal transfer of inheritance. He had to have the laying on of hands. But since he was not a power-oriented person, he wanted to acquire the legal right of the first-born by Esau's choice. He told Esau that he could have some food if he would give up his birthright. Esau agreed. The way Esau so quickly agreed, as a matter of fact, proves that Esau did not regard his birthright very highly. He probably thought this covenantal oath to his brother was worthless. He believed in power, and he perceived that he could hang on to his inheritance by power and blood.

The conflict between Esau and Jacob does not stop here. Even after Jacob lawfully obtained the birthright, Esau still wanted to have the blessing of his father. He wanted to be a man of blood and also have the benediction of the covenant. The two do not mix. Rebekah and Jacob knew it. They also knew that Jacob needed more than Esau's oath. Jacob had to have his father's confirmation. So a plan was devised to obtain the blessing (Gen. 27:6-17). Jacob dressed up like Esau and went into his father. He served a meal. (Remember the covenant renewal process involves a meal.) But Isaac was blind. He smelled and touched Jacob. He was not able to tell the difference. Jacob received the blessing.

Esau was cursed. His father told him he would always be a man of war (Gen. 27:40). As Jacob had been communicated, Esau was excommunicated from his father's table of blessings. From that point forward, Esau sought to destroy Jacob.[13] This conflict runs all the way through the Bible, coming to a head in Jesus' day. The Herodian kings, who sought to kill the baby Jesus through genocide, and who eventually crucified Him, were Edomites. Like their original ancestor, the Herodians did not want to inherit by covenant renewal. They wanted inheritance through the power-state. They wanted covenant denial with all the benefits of the covenant. For this they lost the inheritance in 70 A.D.

2. Defeat

The second phase of covenant transferral is *conquest* by faithfulness. The Biblical man is confirmed in his inheritance when he takes dominion over what belongs to him. Yet, his dominion mandate must be carried out according to the Word of God. He must trust and obey. So the second aspect of discontinuity is *defeat by disobedience*. This is covenant renewal *without* dominion. The connection with the past is made, but it is not pulled into the present.

There is an example of this when Israel entered the Promised Land. Israel had had its greatest victory at Jericho. But God had told them not to take anything from the city. Everything was to be placed totally under the "ban," that is, totally devoted to God. They were to build their new civilization on devotion and covenant renewal, not the corruption of a decadent society. One man named Achan disobeyed. How did they find out? After Jericho, Israel discovered that it could not defeat the smallest of enemies (Josh. 7:2-5).

Joshua was alarmed. He thought as a covenant man. He knew something was wrong. He sought God and was told that there was "sin in the camp"! Achan had disobeyed and brought defeat on everyone. Because of Achan's sin, thirty-six men lost their lives, a graphic illustration of the doctrine of representation (Josh. 7:5). Joshua understood what had to be done. Achan and his entire family were judged covenantally.

Covenantal Judgment

Defeat through disobedience is a sign of judgment. Also, God judges disobedience and defeat *covenantally*. This is a foreign idea to a world lost in "hyper-individualism." Let us consider briefly several points about covenantal discontinuity.

---

13. The greatest enemies of the kingdom of God are *always* its former members!

First, there is no such thing as a "natural" catastrophe. Nature is not neutral. Nothing takes place in nature by chance. God governs all things. Not even a bird falls to the ground that God does not control (Matt. 10:29). What happens in nature happens as a result of God's involvement with the physical universe. Catastrophes are included. Although we may not know the exact sin being judged, what occurs results from God. Often, God may send a series of natural judgments to warn a whole civilization that it is about to be judged in greater finality. It is remarkable throughout the history of man how such things come about shortly before the fall of a great empire. Many of those are happening in the West today: herpes, the AIDS plague, cancer, soil erosion, drought, and so on. Perhaps God is warning that a more comprehensive judgment approaches.

Second, God uses a *lex talionis* system of judgment. *Lex talionis* means an "eye for eye" and "tooth for tooth." He always secures His restitution. When the evil Haman tried to have Mordecai hanged, God punished Haman by having him hanged from his own gallows (Esther 7:1-10). God judges in kind. If millions of babies are murdered before they are born, I think we can expect God to render *lex talionis*. One provision should be made, however. God gets His restitution through *conversion* as well as destruction. When one is converted, he dies in Christ (Rom. 6:2-7). Conversion has a killing-unto-life effect. Therefore, the West is either standing on the edge of the greatest revival or the greatest disaster of its history. Perhaps it will be both: disaster followed by revival. The Reformation began in 1517, just 24 years after Columbus' crew brought back syphilis and began a massive, deadly infection of Europe.

Third, most modern Christians only think of judgment in terms of the individual. But God destroys *groups* as well as individuals. Moses emphasizes covenantal judgment when he says, "I will heap misfortunes on *them*; I will use My arrows on *them*. *They* shall be wasted by famine, and consumed by plague and bitter destruction" (Deut. 32:23-24). The third person plural pronoun indicates that God judges the *group*. Judgment of entire *households* serves as a recurring Biblical example. God judged the households of Korah, Dathan, and Abiram for rebelling against Moses' leadership (Nu. 16:32).[14]

---

14. Korah was also involved with Dathan and Abiram. But God often gives the family members an opportunity to distance themselves from the sins of the one bringing judgment on the whole family. Evidently, some of Korah's children did not stand with him. They did not die (Nu. 26:9-11). Moreover, later in the Bible their descendents stand and "praise the Lord" (II Chron. 20:19).

Achan's family was destroyed. The entire household of Haman was destroyed for his sin against Mordecai and the people of God (Esther 9:1-19). Many other examples could be given. God imposes covenantal discontinuity on households, and not just on individuals.

In view of the third point, it should be added that the innocent sometimes die along with the wicked. If they are in the proximity of a covenantal judgment, they will also be destroyed. When Elijah brought famine on the land through his prayers, many of the righteous were affected by this judgment (James 5:17). Often God makes a way of escape, but certainly many Christians have died in history as a result of covenantal disasters. Of course, the faithful immediately go to be with the Lord. But they may have to suffer with the wicked. It is quite possible that many innocent will die from the AIDS plague in our own day, not because of any immorality but because they are in the sphere of an overall judgment on the land.

Just as blessing comes according to the covenant, so does judgment. As the wicked benefit from living near the righteous, so the people of God suffer from sin in the land. Continuity and discontinuity are covenantal transmissions of the inheritance of God. Obedience leads to continuity. Disobedience results in discontinuity.

3. Permissiveness

Discipleship, education, and missions are necessary for the perpetuation of inheritance. The future is lost without them. Neglect in these areas is devastating.

Lot's life is a case in point. He started out so well. He was given the choice of his inheritance, something God rarely gives anyone. He was confirmed by Abraham. He even experienced conquest in the land (Gen. 14:1-16). But Lot ended up being disinherited. Why? He chose Sodom as a place to live, an evil and corrupt environment (Gen. 13:13).[15] He selected a city where his children could not be discipled and educated properly in the Bible. He wanted to live in the luxury of a corrupt society with a wicked educational system, instead of wandering around in a bunch of tents with Abraham. Lot was a man who only lived for the present.

The long-term price was great. Lot ended up living in a cave, a symbol of death (Gen. 19:30). More importantly, he lost his *children*.

---

15. The Book of Proverbs begins with the concept of *moral environment*. Obviously the author of wisdom wants covenantal parents to see that next to the "fear of the Lord," moral environment is the most important issue (Prov. 1:8-19).

The city of Sodom had been destroyed, but its educational influence was still left on the children. Under the influence of Sodom, they became spiritual sodomites. One day his two daughters caused their father to get drunk, and then they seduced him. This incestuous relationship eventually produced children: Moab and Ammon (Gen. 19:37-38). The covenantal way of expansion was inverted. The original marital covenant said the children were supposed to "leave father and mother" (Gen. 2:24). With their inheritance they were supposed to take their new marital covenant and expand. Incest turns back into the family and mutates expansion.[16] In the case of Moab and Ammon, they were never able to have part of the inheritance. Their land was always just outside of the Promised Land. Lot did not disciple the future, and he *and his children* were disinherited.

Dispossession is a variation of disinheritance. Sometimes, when enough of the people of God do not disciple their children in the covenant, God brings a foreign power to dispossess and place them in captivity. This slavery becomes the very instrument by God to restore the covenant. But note: *this can only happen when there is a faithful remnant.* It is the show of good faith that God should preserve the whole group for the sake of the righteous.

For example, Daniel and his three friends were taken into Babylon with the rest of Israel. Nebuchadnezzar and Belshazzar wanted them to become talismans to force God to bless their kingdom. But God forced their hand. He spared Daniel and his friends from the fiery furnace and the lion's den. And eventually, Cyrus was raised up to take them back to their inheritance. The nation had been prepared by captivity and imprisonment to receive its legacy. Yet even in this situation, someone had discipled Daniel and his friends (Dan. 1:8-21). Our point stands. Without discipleship, education, and missions there is no future.

Conclusion

We began the chapter with the story of Jacob's transfer of his inheritance to Joseph's son Ephraim. This introduced us to the final point of covenantalism: continuity. I defined it as a confirmation of the true heirs that transfers inheritance. This confirmation has three parts. First, there must be *covenant renewal*. Normally, this is some kind of worship service where laying on of hands judicially transfers

---

16. The biological results of incest are often some kind of deformity.

the inheritance. A meal is often part of this ceremony, sealing the benefits of the covenant. Second, there should also be *conquest by obedience*. There must be a connection with the present as well. Third, the future generation should be *discipled*. If not, they will lose everything given to them. The inheritance will be lost.

Discontinuity or disinheritance results if the covenant is not confirmed. The covenant is dissoluble. It can be broken. And it can be killed. There are three aspects of discontinuity. First, *covenant denial*: the covenant can be denied and consequently the inheritance will be forfeited. Second, due to disobedience, the inheritance can be lost through *defeat*. Finally, *permissiveness*: lack of discipleship results in disinheritance. The wicked end up providing their wealth for the righteous (Prov. 13:22b).

This concludes our introduction to the five points of covenantalism. Can you remember all five of the points? Can you summarize them? In case you have forgotten, the next chapter will briefly summarize. Then we want to consider *how they work*. They are the mechanism for *dominion*.

6

FIVE POINTS OF COVENANTALISM

At this point it is good to stop and summarize what we have
done. Essentially, I have attempted to define the covenant by using
Deuteronomy as a model.

Perhaps the reader notices that I have not resorted to any particular "etymological" or word study. I agree with O. Palmer Robertson's conclusions, former professor of Old Testament at Westminster
Theological Seminary, when he says, "Extensive investigations into
the etymology of the Old Testament terms for 'covenant' (berith)
have been proven inconclusive in determining the meaning of the
word."[1] Trying to "word study" one's way to a conclusive understanding of the covenant is, as Delbert Hillers has pointed out, "Not
the case of six blind men and the elephant, but of a group of learned
paleontologists creating different monsters from the fossils of six separate species."[2] In short, this is "dry bones" scholarship!

Even so, we are not left in the dark about this basic concept. I
have used a broader and more contextual approach. Deuteronomy is
so systematic that it has been the basis of my conclusions. Five principles have been isolated by comparing Deuteronomy with suzerain
treaties and reflecting on the details of the Biblical text itself.

---

1. O. Palmer Robertson, *The Christ of the Covenants* (Grand Rapids: Baker, 1980),
p. 5. Robertson has an excellent summary of various etymological findings in such
sources as Moshe Weinfeld, *Theologisches Worterbuch zum Alten Testament* (Stuttgart,
1973), p. 73; Leon Morris, *The Apostolic Preaching of the Cross* (London, 1955), pp.
62ff.; Martin Noth, "Old Testament Covenant-Making in the Light of a Text from
Mari" in *The Laws in the Pentateuch and Other Essays* (Edinburgh, 1966), p. 122; E.
Kutch, "Gottes Zuspruch und Anhspruch. *Berit* in der alttestamentlichen
Theologie," in *Questions disputees d'Ancien Testament* (Gembloux, 1974), pp. 71ff.;
Kutch simply revives the basic idea of one of the earliest covenant studies by Johannes Cocceius. See study by Charles Sherwood McCoy, *The Covenant Theology of
Johannes Cocceius* (New Haven, 1965), p. 166. Anyone wishing to see the various
views that have been taken on the basis of pure etymology can consult these sources.
2. Delbert R. Hillers, *Covenant: The History of a Biblical Idea* (Baltimore, 1969), p. 7.

119

Summary

A. First Point of Covenantalism: True Transcendence

All covenants begin with a statement of Lordship by distinguishing God from man one of three ways: creation, redemption, and revelation. The key statement of Lordship in this section is, "Moses spoke . . . all that the Lord had commanded him to give to them" (Deut. 1:3). The covenant declares God's Lordship by distinguishing God's words from Moses'. True transcendence lies in this *distinction* of essence. At the same time, the proper view of transcendence leads to immanence: God is present. True transcendence is *personal*.

This covenantal *declaration* at the beginning also establishes a *legal* basis for forming a covenant, called the doctrine of *imputation*. All covenant arrangements are rooted in the legal. Man cannot connect with God in His "essence." If God and man are not joined in their essence, then they have to relate covenantally and ethically. Christianity is not like a totem pole religion with false oaths, rites of passage, and secret societies. This first point of the covenant lays out the parameters to understand the covenant.

B. Second Point of Covenantalism: Hierarchy

Biblical hierarchy is the *representative principle* (Deut. 1:6-4:49). God and man are distinct. Therefore, God makes His transcendence known through *visible authorities*. They mediate His judgments. To reject them is to reject God's judgment. But this authoritative structure is not a complete top-down bureaucracy. There are *accountability* principles for everyone. Each person is responsible to submit to someone. At the same time, this submission is not absolute. God creates an appeals system to handle disagreements.

All of this has historical consequences. The second section weaves history and authority together (Deut. 1:6-4:49). The world turns according to man's response to God's *mediated system of judgment* manifested in His appointed authorities. History is the outworking of this redemptive program. God's Revelation has similarities. He always works by means of His covenant. Yet, there are dissimilarities. The *progressive* nature of God's Revelation brings about change, due to the historic shift from *wrath to grace* at the cross. Everything that happens relates directly to this program of redemption. If God's people rebel, they are judged by the world. If they submit, the covenant community passes judgment on the world and converts it. History is covenantal. Events are not random, nor are they disconnected from what happens in the covenant. Everything transpires according to God's redemptive purposes.

C. Third Point of Covenantalism: Ethics

There is an *ethical cause and effect relationship*. Things do not happen mechanically, manipulatively, or magically. Covenant-keeping leads to blessing. Covenant-breaking results in cursing. Fulfillment of righteousness is the ethical core of the covenant. Deuteronomy 5-26 summarizes the Ten Commandments, sometimes called the "stipulations" section (Deut. 5-26). This ethical relationship is not just external compliance. God expects proper *motivations (faith), standards, and situational applications*.

D. Fourth Point of Covenantalism: Sanctions

The covenant is ratified through the reception of the sanctions of blessing and cursing by means of a *self-maledictory oath*. God takes an oath by His own Trinitarian name. He pledges to fulfill the covenant on Himself. This form of covenant-cutting expresses that God fulfills His own standard of righteousness, but it also states that the participant is expected to live consistently with the covenantal stipulations. Should he fail to do so, one of the dual sanctions take force: cursing. Thus, the covenant is unconditional, but there are *terms of unconditionality*.

Symbols are part of this process of entrance by oath. They are real symbols. They are not nominal, having only symbolic value. They are not realistic, infusing grace. They are *covenantal claims of God*. Their meaning and power are in His name who stands behind them. They claim a person to life or death, depending on whether he lives according to the terms of unconditionality. Because these symbols represent God's Trinitarian name, which is One and Many, they are applied to individuals and households, which are one and many.

Finally, the ratification process is actually an *adoption*. A change of name occurs. God becomes the true Father by covenant. Man ceases to be a covenantal orphan.

E. Fifth Point of Covenantalism: Continuity

After ratification, the true heirs should be confirmed. Normally this legitimization takes place in three stages. First, the heirs are confirmed by covenant renewal, the laying on of hands at a meal.

Second, the heirs are confirmed when they take possession of their inheritance by obedience to the covenant. Third, the *future* heirs have to sustain the inheritance through the discipleship of the next generation.

A breakdown in confirmation leads to discontinuity. First, if the covenant is denied, or not confirmed, there is no succession from the historic past. Second, failure to obey leads to defeat. Third, permissiveness toward the future accounts for the loss of inheritance in the *next* generation.

This is the covenant, and this is the model we shall be using throughout the book. Perhaps, however, the reader might wonder, "Is there any way of evaluating this model to see if it is an 'exceptional' case? On what basis can I conclude that this structure of the covenant holds true for the rest of the Bible?" The only way is to check and cross-check with other Scripture. One of the checks is "covenants within covenants."

Covenants Within Covenants

The Bible is a covenant document. We have only looked at one expression. But at the outset, it should be understood that "covenant" is so much a part of the warp and woof of man and God's world that there are covenantal patterns within the various parts of the covenant. In the covenant model of Deuteronomy, the same five-fold structure is within the individual points on a much smaller scale, confirming the larger model.

For example, in the *continuity* section, we find the basic overall covenantal pattern. Moses' "Song of Witness" follows the five points of covenantalism: Preamble (32:4-6), historical prologue (32:7-14), rebellion to stipulations (32:15-18), sanctions (32:19-43), and transfer of the covenant to Joshua (32:44ff.).

Also, although the covenant can be broken down into five parts, it is not unusual to see elements of each one under one of the main points of the covenant. Deuteronomy chapter five falls in the *ethical* section. But it mentions some of the sanctions of the covenant. Does this mean our selection of principles is arbitrary? No, the overall *context* of Deuteronomy five is in the ethical category.

Moreover, using the ethical point of covenantalism as an example, we could say that each part of the covenant is ethical. It is not as though only the third point is ethical. How do I make distinctions then? Again, the key is *context*. Even though we might find an aspect of one of the points of covenantalism out of place, or see each point in every category, the broader context follows the five-fold pattern of Deuteronomy. Furthermore, the repeated use of the five points of covenantalism becomes a *cross-check* on itself.[3]

Conclusion

Deuteronomy has been used as the model of covenantalism, because it is the most systematic presentation in Scripture. It is to the covenant what Romans is to doctrine. But is this structure *practical*? How does it shape our view of the world? I have tried to show in these brief introductory chapters how the covenant relates to other parts of the Bible. Now I want to shift our focus to *how the covenant works in society.* I believe it is *the* model for how the Christian is to live in and evangelize society. Let us begin with a brief introduction to this idea. Let us start with perhaps the most basic *commission* given to the Christian, the *Great Commission.* In the next chapter we will see that our Lord presents it in the very covenantal framework we have been studying. This means the mandate of Christ is really *dominion by covenant.*

---

3. See appendixes one through six for a complete study of other passages that serve to *cross-check* my study of Deuteronomy.

7

DOMINION BY COVENANT

How is the covenant applied to society? Unfortunately, most recent scholarship concerning the covenant has failed to ask this question. There are only a handful of studies that even consider the social ramifications, Edmund S. Morgan's brilliant research on the Puritan family being one of them.[1] Studies on the covenant suffer on two counts: lack of basic Biblical work that pushes out into critical theological matters, and failure to consider the historical and social outworkings of its theology. My book is divided into two halves. Up to this point, I have concentrated on the Biblical meaning of the term. Now we should turn our attention to its *application*. To begin with, covenant has enabled Christians, when they have been successful, to dominate the earth. It is *the* model for dominion. Why? The dominion mandates of both testaments are structured according to the covenant: the cultural mandate in Genesis, and the Great Commission in the Gospel.

The Cultural Mandate

The first dominion mandate is often called the "cultural mandate" given to Adam and Eve on the sixth day of creation.

And God blessed them; and God said to them, "Be fruitful and multiply, and fill the earth, and subdue it; and rule over the fish of the sea and over the birds of the sky, and over every living thing that moves on the earth." Then God said, "Behold, I have given you every plant yielding seed that is on the surface of all the earth, and every tree which has fruit yielding seed; it shall be food for you; and to every beast of the earth and to every bird of the sky and to every thing that moves on the earth which has life, I have given every green plant for food"; and it was so (Gen. 1:28-30).

1. Edmund S. Morgan, *The Puritan Family* (New York: Harper & Row, [1944] 1966).

124

Francis Nigel Lee, in his helpful work, *The Central Significance of Culture*, calls this segment of Scripture the "dominion charter."[2] Definitely, the tone of dominion rings throughout the passage, and the Christian Church has generally understood these words to mean that man is to dominate culture and society for the glory of God.[3] There are no sacred/profane categories inherent in creation. The original garden had zones that were nearer to and farther away from God, but everywhere was sacred. Corporate man, male and female, was to spread "culture" (from *cult*ural mandate). What is "culture"? "Culture" comes from "cultus," meaning *worship*.[4] Thus, the task of dominion was to transform the world into a place of worship, and thereby create true culture. No worship, in other words, means no culture. Dominion is not secularized work. It is *sanctified labor* involved in making society into a proper place to worship God. In Adam's case, he was to take the raw materials on the ground and fashion a society, not just a cathedral, in concert with God's presence. In our case, it consists of transforming the unethical debris of society into the glorious praise of God.

Specifically, this is done by means of the application of the covenant. The original mandate falls in the context of a *covenantal order*. The creation account of Genesis 1 says ten times, "Then God said" (Gen. 1:3, 6, 9, 11, 14, 20, 24, 26, 28, 29). With "ten words" God creates the world, just as He speaks the law (covenant) with ten words (Deut. 4:13). Could the parallel be any more obvious? To be clear, however, let us look at the ten words of creation to see where the cultural mandate falls.

First Five

1. "Let there be light" (1:3): *Transcendence*. Light conveys God's

---

2. Francis Nigel Lee, *The Central Significance of Culture* (Nutley, New Jersey: Presbyterian and Reformed, 1976), p. 10.

3. Of course many have rejected the notion that this mandate still applies in the New Covenant age. Leo Tolstoy was militantly opposed to "culture" altogether, believing that Old Testament Law had been entirely done away with. See the book by the theological liberal, H. Richard Niebuhr, *Christ and Culture* (New York: Harper & Row, 1951), pp. 45-82. Niebuhr, himself sympathetic to the non-transformation of culture, refers to "conversionists" of Church history who believed in only changing men "subjectively," but not the transformation of the world "objectively" (pp. 190ff.).

4. Of course, there are other views of culture, stripped of this "liturgical" orientation. Nigel Lee refers to them as "materialistic and idealistic" views of the cultural mandate: *Central Significance of Culture*, pp. 1-20. For an excellent presentation of a Christian view of culture, see Klaas Schilder, *Christ and Culture* (Winnipeg: Premier, [1947] 1977).

glory, probably the strongest image of transcendence in the Bible.

2. "Let there be an expanse in the midst of the waters, and let it separate the waters from the waters" (1:6): *Hierarchy*. Waters are arranged from the waters above to the waters below. The Noachic Flood indicated that the waters above had primary importance, representing *God's* judgment.

3. "Let the waters below the heavens be gathered into one place, and let the dry land appear" (1:9): *Ethics*. The land in the Old Testament had a central cause/effect relationship to everything else. For example, when a murder is committed, a man's blood "cries out from the land" (Gen. 4:10). Point three also involves ethical and geographical *boundaries*.

4. "Let the earth sprout vegetations, plants yielding *seed*" (1:11): *Sanctions*. This *seed-bearing* process is specifically mentioned in the sanctions section of Deuteronomy (Deut. 28:38-40).

5. "Let there be lights in the expanse of the heavens to separate the day from the night, and let them be for signs, and for seasons, and for days and years . . . and to *govern* the day and the night" (1:14): *Continuity*. The great lights are the instruments of continuity from one day to the next — continuity made visible by discontinuity.

Second Five

1. "Let the waters teem . . . let the birds fly . . . . And God blessed them, saying, 'Be fruitful and multiply' " (1:20-22): *Transcendence*. Creatures of special transcendent glory are mentioned: the birds that fly *above*, and the great sea monsters (Leviathan, cf. Job 3:8; 41:1; Psa. 74:14; 104:26).

2. "Let the earth bring forth living creatures" (1:24): *Hierarchy*. Animals are part of the specific hierarchy of the earth. They are used to *represent* man as sacrifices (Gen. 3:21).

3. "Let Us make man in Our image . . . and let him rule" (1:26): *Ethics*. Man rules over the animals by carrying out this dominion commandment. Dominion and ethics are inseparable.

4. "Be fruitful, subdue, and rule" (1:28): *Sanctions*. All things are to be brought under and ratified in a covenant relationship.

5. "I have given every plant . . . and every tree" (1:29): *Continuity*. Man is given a specific inheritance of *food*, the meal. Through this nourishment, man is able to lay hold of his inheritance.

The "ten words" of creation have the same double witness of the covenant, as do the Ten Commandments. This being the case, the "cultural mandate" falls on the fourth word of the second series (Gen.

1:28), in other words, the *sanction* point of the covenant. As it so happens, just before the mandate, we read, "God *blessed* them," a sanction concept (blessing). Therefore, it would seem that the cultural mandate was intended to be a process whereby the world was shaped into a "cultus" by *covenant ratification*. But also notice that the fourth creation word (second series) is a virtual repetition of the one before it, "Let them rule." Why? I have stressed throughout the book that *ethics*, or faithfulness to the covenant, establishes dominion. The slight variation in Genesis, however, means the stipulations must be *ratified* before the full dominion process is completed. Indeed, this is the first thing Adam does with the woman. He brings her under the stipulations by a special oath, "This is now bone of my bones" (Gen. 2:23).

The covenantal design of the cultural mandate is unmistakable. Had Adam obeyed, he would have completed his covenantal commission. But the Fall interrupted everything. The seventh day, the day of special *blessing*, again a sanction word, was turned into a day of cursing. The Day of the Lord became a day of judgment. Ironically, as we have already seen, "curse" not only judged the world's rebellion to God's first covenantal mandate, it also provided a means for redemption to emerge, ultimately of course in the death of Christ. His death accomplished the original cultural mandate by receiving the curse-sanction, and introduced the blessing-sanction back into the world. This appears in a special way at a final meal He conducts, just before His *ascension*. It is here that He gives a new cultural mandate, the Great Commission.

The Great Commission

The Great Commission is a covenant within a covenant. Looking at the life of Jesus, it falls within the *continuity* section. Jesus gathered His disciples to a communion meal, and prepared them for His final *blessing* (Luke 24:41-51). In this context, He gave the blessing in the form of a new commission, just like Moses had done with the nation. Jesus had reached the point of giving the adopted heirs their new inheritance. What was it? The content of the Great Commission tells us. The disciples were given the "nations" of the world to bring to Christ, just as Israel of old had been given the land of Palestine and surrounding territories. The New Covenant people were given the *world*. How? Their dominion mandate was specifically laid out in the form of the five points of covenantalism.

The Covenantal Structure of the Great Commission

True Transcendence: Matthew 28:16
Hierarchy: Matthew 28:17-18
Ethics: Matthew 28:19a
Sanctions: Matthew 28:19b
Continuity: Matthew 28:20

1. True Transcendence (Matt. 28:16)

The Great Commission Covenant starts, "But the eleven disciples proceeded to Galilee, to the *mountain* which Jesus had designated" (Matt. 28:16). Many of the covenants begin on God's mountain. The Adamic covenant had a mountain in Eden from which the
four rivers flowed.[5] Moses received the covenant on top of Mt.
Sinai. The mountain concept implied God's transcendence and immanence. Its shape and height pointed to a Being outside of man
(transcendence). This was consistently a place where God made
Himself known (immanence). The mountain became a symbol of
the true Church, God's dwelling place: "Great is the Lord, and greatly
to be praised, in the city of our God, His holy mountain" (Ps. 48:1).

The Book of Hebrews speaks of God's revealing Himself on two
mountains, Mt. Sinai as a symbol of the Old Covenant, and Mt.
Zion as an image of Christ and the Church. The first mountain was
a place where God was present and had all the characteristics of God
Himself. If an animal even touched the mountain, it had to be put to
death. Why? The "beast" had violated God's presence.

> For you have not come to a *mountain* that may be [1] touched and [2] to
> a blazing fire, and [3] to darkness and [4] gloom and [5] whirlwind, and
> [6] to the blast of a trumpet and [7] the sound of words which sound was
> such that those who heard begged that no further word should be spoken to
> them for they could not bear the command, "If even a beast touches the
> *mountain*, it will be stoned." And so terrible was the sight, that Moses said, "I
> am full of fear and trembling" (Heb. 12:18-21).

This mountain had seven characteristics, numbered above. The
"sabbath," seventh day, was a sign of the Old Covenant, a symbol
that everything ended in *judgment*. It was on that day that Adam,

---

5. We know Eden was on a mountain because there were rivers flowing off it, and
water does not flow uphill (Gen. 2:9ff.)!

Eve, and the serpent were judged. Just as the introduction to the suzerain treaties invoked fear when the suzerain was identified, so the mountain of God with its transcendent/immanent qualities drew out the same response.

The Hebrews passage goes on to speak of another mountain. It begins with the word of contrast, "but." Its characteristics speak of a mountain that is more transcendent and immanent through the person of Christ; it is *heavenly*, yet present with the Church on *earth*.

> But you have come to [1] Mount Zion and [2] to a city of the living God, the heavenly Jerusalem, and [3] to myriads of angels in festal assembly, [4] and to the church of the first-born who are enrolled in heaven and [5] to God, the Judge of all, and [6] to the spirits of righteous men made perfect, and [7] to Jesus, the mediator of a new covenant, and [8] to the sprinkled blood, which speaks better than the blood of Abel (Heb. 12:22-24).

This mountain has *eight characteristics* because the New Covenant was begun on the eighth day of history, the day after the Old Covenant sabbath, the day of the resurrection. It is explained from outside in, working its way to the center where the ark of the covenant would have been in the Temple. Although it is similar to Mt. Sinai, it is dramatically different. Mt. Sinai's mountain was *earthly* with a *heavenly* presence, meaning the presence of God was limited in scope to Mt. Sinai and other special manifestations. The New Covenant mountain is *heavenly* with an *earthly* presence, meaning its immanence is broader and comprehensively covers the whole earth.

So, when Christ begins the Great Commission by taking His disciples to a *mountain*, He symbolizes that the New Covenant starts from a transcendent and immanent point, none other than Jesus Christ Himself. The Church is to go to this new mountain, receive Him, walk off of it with Him, and go into the world to shape it into a new "cultus."

2. Hierarchy (Matt. 28:17-18)

After coming to the mountain, "When they [the disciples] saw Him, they worshipped Him; but some were doubtful. And Jesus came up and spoke to them saying, 'All *authority* has been given to Me in heaven and on earth'" (Matt. 28:17-18). The citation of "authority" follows the covenant pattern: hierarchy. Moses had final authority in the Deuteronomic covenant. Christ replaces him. Moses made the connection between worship and authority, when he warned Israel at the end of the hierarchical section not to bow down to idols (Deut. 4:15-24). The structure of the Ten Commandments confirms this pattern. The second commandment forbids idolatry.[6]

This Christological hierarchy has an important ramification for the Church and the world. When Christ says, "All *authority* has been given to Me," He means *now*; He has it in heaven and *on earth*; there is no delay! This authority is not make-believe. It is not some exclusively spiritual power, for He calls on His disciples to go out and bring the nations under this authority. Nations are real, historical entities. They are not subdued by make-believe power in some make-believe, non-historical world.

Christ's authority is not limited to heaven. He has it on earth. He said so, *on earth*. He said so *before His Ascension*. And His Ascension accentuates His full heavenly and earthly authority even more so. It served to activate this power because it was here that He sat down at the right hand of God the Father to *rule*. As the familiar verse of the most popular eschatological Psalm quoted in the New Testament says, "The Lord said to My Lord, sit Thou at My right hand *until* I make Thine enemies a footstool under Thy feet" (Ps. 110:1). Think of the implications of this statement. We know that Jesus is the "My Lord" of this statement. He sat down at the "Lord's" right hand at the Ascension (Col. 3:1). Thus, He cannot move from the right hand of God the Father, not even to rapture the Church, *until* all the enemies are defeated. Christ has and does exercise full authority because of His Resurrection. He has ascended on high where His triumphant heavenly reign now establishes His earthly rule!

3. Ethics (Matt. 28:19a)

The new covenantal mandate continues next with a *stipulation*, "Go and make disciples of the nations" (Matt. 28:19). Christ's command logically grows out of the previous statements on authority. A "disciple" is primarily one who is under Christ's authority. He goes where Christ goes and does what Christ does. He did not say, "Have an experience and join the rest of us who have had a mystical experience." Nor did He say, "learn a catechism and bask with us in the knowledge of this new catechism." No, Christ defined discipleship in terms of authority and obedience.

---

6. See Appendix 1.

Jesus' commission has *stipulations*. He said, "teaching them to observe all that I *commanded* you" (v. 20). What were Christ's "commandments"? At one point He summarized them for us. A lawyer asked Him, "Teacher, which is the great commandment in the Law?" (Matt. 22:36). He said to him, " 'You shall love the Lord your God with all your heart, and with all your soul, and with all your mind.' This is the great and foremost commandment. The second is like it, 'You shall love your neighbor as yourself.' On these two hang *all* the Law and the Prophets" (v. 36-40). Christ did not initiate any "novel" idea of law, but these two laws summarized *all* law. So when given an opportunity to outline His commandments, He affirmed the old ones. He even said He did not come to destroy them (Matt. 5:17ff.).

But what about the "new commandment" which Christ gave, "to love one another, as I have loved you" (John 13:34)? What was "new" about it? It was not new in the sense that this commandment had not been around before. We just noted that the Old Testament commanded men to love their neighbors as themselves (Matt. 22:36ff.). "Loving one another" is not a new command. "Loving one another as *Christ has loved the Church*" is new. The newness is in terms of Christ, so the new commandment is actually a *renewed* commandment, a commandment that has died and been resurrected through the death of Jesus. These are the stipulations. They are the laws of the Old Covenant renewed through Christ. The program of conquest is still a process of covenanting with God.

The "Nations"

Christ further stipulates that these commandments are to be applied to the "nations." The scope of the Great Commission is not to be confined to the "church." Rather it reaches out by definition to "nations," to the *political* arena. And not just one nation or political scheme. It is multi-national. Every magistrate in every land is supposed to apply the stipulations of Christ, the Word of God (Rom. 13:1ff.). Every missionary in every land should be striving to apply the Great Commission commandments.

The idea of missionaries going into other countries and deliberately trying to avoid "affecting culture" is utterly absurd. Significantly, the same theory was used by the Jesuits in the seventeenth century in China. Barraclough's observation is telling.

The Jesuit missionaries to China in the 17th century, far from attempting to impose a European pattern of Christianity, did all they could to assimilate Christianity to Chinese patterns of civilization. They were careful to dress in the robes of Chinese mandarins, and their object was to show that Christian doctrine and Confucianism were compatible and supplemented each other. . . . Their efforts, after some initial success, were brought to nothing, not by Chinese hostility, but by the opposition of Christians in Europe.[7]

Eventually, the missionaries were brought home because they were converting to Confucianism — the Chinese brand of situational ethics! This type of approach has been taken in the Third World for a long time. For 150 years there has been intense missionary activity in the Third World. Today, the Marxists are kicking out the Church. How have they gained such power? Because missionaries have not evangelized, or have not been able to evangelize, with a complete Biblical world-and-life view. They have brought a gospel without law, and this "lawless gospel" has not changed the world. If anything, the resistance to Christianity has been made worse, not better. The missions and churches have allied themselves to a now-collapsing humanist status quo. The Marxists are overthrowing the status quo, and they are steadily removing the churches. They are systematically teaching the West that culture is not neutral. Although there will be *distinctives* of each land, and Biblical law is necessarily cast in many forms, Biblical culture is a culture based on the Word of God.

For example, clothing may be decorated differently, but there is clothing! Representative government may have a "parliament" instead of a "congress," but there is government by representation. Homosexuality is homosexuality in any land, and its unrepentant practitioners deserve the death penalty (Rom. 1:18-32; cf. "worthy of death" in v. 32). AIDS is AIDS in any land, and it threatens whole populations. Christ says the "nations" are to be discipled by His law. The skill of the missionary is in seeing God's law asserted over the nation he is evangelizing. This has many expressions, but *it is expressed!*

This is the third section of the Great Commission Covenant. Notice that there is an overlap in this part of the covenant. The specific way to disciple the "nations" is through baptism and instruction (vv. 19-20a). Making a disciple begins at baptism, which is receiving the symbolic, yet covenantally real, sanctions of Christ. Then the

---

7. Geoffrey Barraclough, ed., *The Christian World: A Social and Cultural History* (New York: Harry N. Abrams Publishers, 1981), p. 29. Barraclough's view of history is Marxist — class struggle etc. — but he does have some interesting insights.

"commandments" are taught (v. 20). Why does the Great Commission Covenant overlap the ethical and the judicial? *Teaching the law of God both precedes and follows baptism.* Also, Christ is instructing the disciples and at the same time telling them "how to." The "dovetailing" of these concepts, however, makes for a perfect connection to the next section of the covenant, the *sanctions.*

4. Sanctions (Matt. 28:19b)

Christ commissions the disciples to sanction the nations by "baptizing them in the Name of the Father and of the Son and of the Holy Spirit" (Matt. 28:19). Like the Deuteronomic sanctions, baptism is a symbol of God's self-maledictory oath. Jesus says of His own death, "Are you able to drink the cup that I drink, or to be *baptized* with the *baptism* with which I am *baptized*?" (Mark 10:39). In other words, the death of Christ is a baptism. *Through Christ, God fulfills His own maledictory oath to save man.* When the covenant is entered by baptism, God's oath fulfilled in Christ is consigned to the recipient.

For this reason baptism has dual sanctions. Because baptism is a symbol of Christ's death, it represents *life and death.* Paul says, "Therefore we have been buried with Him through *baptism* into death, in order that as Christ was raised from the dead through the glory of the Father, so we too might walk in newness of life" (Rom. 6:4). Baptism applies life and death to the baptizand. If he perseveres, then he has life. If he falls away, he eventually dries up like a branch, is cut off, and is thrown into the fire (John 15:6).

Baptism is a *real symbol.* The Trinitarian formula for baptism explains the relationship between symbol and reality. God the Father, Son, and Holy Spirit are *distinct but not separate.* To refresh our memory: This Trinitarian guide means baptism is neither an "empty" symbol, nor is it more than a symbol, meaning the substance of water has the power to save. So, faith is not to be separated from baptism, but distinguished from it. The New Testament tells people to be baptized to be saved, while at the same time it distinguishes faith. Ananias commands Paul, "Arise and be baptized and wash away your sins, calling on His name" (Acts 22:16). Baptism is God's claim on man and man's entrance into the covenant. But where is *faith?* Baptism is the normal way of professing faith. Thus, Acts 22:16 adds, "*Calling* on His name." Only this interpretation does justice to the very language of the New Testament and preserves evangelical faith at the same time.

Finally, Jesus' language in the Great Commission says the nations are to be baptized *household by household*. How do we know households (infants) are to be baptized? Jesus says, "Disciple the *nations* (neuter gender), baptizing *them* (masculine gender)" (Matt. 28:19). "Nations" is the antecedent of the personal pronoun "them." Why the discrepancy between the pronoun and its antecedent? The "nations" are not to be baptized all at once. The "nations" are to be baptized *household by household*. This interpretation is confirmed by the actual conversion and baptism of whole households (Acts 16). The conversion of the family, and not just the individual, is the key to the fulfillment of the Great Commission.

The spread of the Gospel is not a top-down operation. Salvation comes from above, in that it is applied through the work of the Holy Spirit. But normally, the spread of the Gospel should be from household to household, "leavening." This is certainly what we see in the Book of Acts. The Gospel begins in the menial households of the Roman Empire, and it spreads to the greatest family, Caesar's household, when Paul is taken captive and converts Caesar's own bodyguards.

Representative Priests

The household concept also reinforces the concept of the *priesthood of all believers*. Protestants say that they believe in this idea, but the way they baptize people does not always reflect this faith. If the head of a family accepts Christ as Savior, and therefore places himself or herself under the covenant sign of baptism, with its dual sanctions of blessing and cursing, then what about those who are under his or her authority? Do they remain outside this covenant administration? The head of the household is the *representative* in that household for all those under his or her authority. He or she becomes a *priestly representative of Christ in the household*. But Protestants radically individualize the covenant. They regard it as being no more than a symbol for the individual who is baptized. The priesthood of all believers becomes the priesthood of no believers, for the necessarily representative character of God's priesthood is denied.

Not to baptize household units is a failure to be consistent with the Trinity, which is one and *many*. It is also inconsistent with the hierarchical principle of priestly representation. Just like the Deuteronomic covenant, therefore, the Great Commission has all of the aspects of sanctions' principle. The Trinitarian Name of God is the key which unlocks all the problems surrounding baptism. God's Name—attached through the sanction of baptism—is so powerful that it brings life to covenant-keepers and death to covenant-breakers.

5. Continuity (Matt. 28:20)

The Great Commission Covenant closes with "Lo, I am with you always, even to the end of the age" (Matt. 28:20). Christ's presence was the new inheritance. Deuteronomy establishes that inheritance is received at the throne of God—where He is *present*. It is this unique throne-room presence that Christ promises. Moreover, in our study of continuity in Deuteronomy we have learned that man receives ordination (commission), food (sacred meal of communion), and anointing. If we keep the Great Commission in context, it is apparent that all of the features are here. The Great Commission is given on the eve of the arrival of the *Holy Spirit*, in the midst of a sacred meal.

Fifty days after Passover was the time of Pentecost, a great *feast*, symbolizing the coming of the harvest. It also referred to the *time of the Jubilee*. The year of Jubilee was every fiftieth year. During this year, the land returned to the families of the *original owners*. Dominion was given back to the rightful heirs. Putting these ideas together, we see that the coming of God's Presence was the true harvest of the world. The earth started to be given back to the *true owners*. The movement from *God's throne to the edge of the world* begins. What Jesus willed at the Sermon on the Mount—"The meek shall inherit the earth" (Matt. 5:5), meaning *meek before God*—actually transpires.

But first Christ had to depart in order to sit at the right hand of God. After He gives the Great Commission, He ascends into heaven. His presence is left behind through the Holy Spirit and the Lord's Supper. The Spirit is especially present at this meal. Life, health, and healing are tied to it. If taken unlawfully, sickness and death result. Paul says, "For this reason many among you are weak and sick, and a number sleep [die]" (I Cor. 11:30).

The meal itself *represents* the whole inheritance. What is the New Covenant inheritance? The whole world. Jesus redeemed the world, and the meal is the Church's first claim on what rightfully belongs to it. Feeding on Christ, God's people lay hold of the One who owns all things. As his "younger brother" (Christ being the true "first-born") the Church receives what He has. Here, *continuity* is established. Paul argues that Christ lays *everything* up for His Church:

> He made known to us the mystery of His will, according to His kind intention which He purposed in Him with a view to an administration suitable to the fullness of the times, that is, the summing up of all things in Christ, things in heaven and on *earth.* In Him also we have obtained an inheritance, having been predestinated according to His purpose Who works all things after the counsel of His will. . . . And He put all things in subjection under His feet, and gave Him as head over all things *to the Church,* which is His body, the fullness of Him Who fills all in all (Eph. 1:9-23).

So, the Church first encounters its inheritance at the meal of inheritance. The Church needs the food of Christ. It should eat it weekly (Acts 20:7-12). Communion should not be viewed as some insignificant ritual tacked onto the Christian faith. Jesus' meal is the place where the Church receives its inheritance and strength to continue on. As long as the meal is taken in faith, the Church will grow and strengthen. Taken in unbelief, it will die. Why? Because Christ is really present (although not physically)! He is present *everywhere* in the New Covenant, but His presence is special in the meal of inheritance. Because He is everywhere, however, all of the illegitimate sons (bastards) of the earth will eventually be driven off, or else *adopted* into the covenant.

Conclusion

The Church dominates the world by means of this covenantal mandate, extending the first dominion mandate forward. Dominion began as a covenantal application. Christ stipulates that *dominion is still by covenant.* But now it is time to be even more specific. It would seem that if the general dominion mandate is covenantal, then the particulars will be too. How about the main institutions of society? We have already seen that the Great Commission involves nations and families: the Church goes out and conquers family by family until the Gospel reaches the upper political echelons of society.

In the next chapter, I will begin this covenantal application with the family, showing how it plays a vital role in the over-all dominion of the world. Some of the questions I will be answering are: What is a family? How does the covenantal model resolve the divorce question? How has the covenantal model been used in history to create strong family ties?

I begin first by showing that the covenant is the *Biblical* model by which the family is to be run.

8

THE BIBLICAL FAMILY COVENANT

A couple of years ago, I participated in a seminar on the family. Its purpose: to draft a statement on the family from a Christian perspective that would be sent to politicians, showing them that a "traditional" view of the family exists in the consensus of our society. I remember the members of the group well: there were housewives; there was a theological professor with admitted family problems who was participating for his own sake; there was a family therapist; there was the head of a leading family organization. I was the minister.

For two days, we sat in a small room, trying to hammer out a statement on the family, seeming to make little progress. What was the problem? No one could answer the question: "What is the family?"

There were basically three options presented. One, the family is a *blood-bond*, involving all those related by blood. Of course, this raises the issue of "extended" vs. "nuclear" family. If the family is related by "blood-bond," then the family consists of all those near and distant relatives who have any of the "clan's" blood running through their veins. The group was inclined to reject this view, but on the other hand, it wanted to adopt it.

Second, the resident "family therapist" vehemently objected to the "blood-bond" definition, submitting the idea that marriage was a *social contract*, along the lines laid down by Rousseau. Some were immediately pulled this direction, thinking it was the solution to our dilemma. But then, one of the "down-to-earth" housewives said, "Wait a minute. If marriage is simply arranged among various parties by social agreement, what would stop someone from calling a social organization of homosexuals a 'family'"? She was correct, because homosexual couples do call themselves a "family."

Finally, after hours of listening to this fruitless debate, another housewife — the housewives seemed to have more sense than anyone

137

else in the meeting — suggested that we turn to the Bible for a definition. They turned to me, the resident minister, and said, "Does the
Bible define the family anywhere?" I took them to the Old Testament, and this became the third and accepted definition.

Malachi says,

The Lord has been a witness between you and the wife of your youth,
against whom you have dealt treacherously, though she is your companion
and your wife by *covenant* (Mal. 2:14).

The Bible defines the family as a *covenant*, the same Hebrew word
(*berith*) being used in Malachi that is used elsewhere for the God-to-
man covenant (Gen. 6:18). Once this definition is accepted, however, it affects how one views the family. It is the missing concept
that has not been addressed. Consequently, most Christians have a
defective view, and only see the family as a series of isolated "principles" concerning "how to communicate," "child-rearing techniques,"
and so forth, but they do not have the faintest idea how all these concepts relate. In other words, they lack the *integrating concept* that properly outlines *what the family is*.

To take dominion over the family, we should begin here. Let us
analyze the first *family covenant*.

Then the Lord God said, "It is not good for the man to be alone; I will
make him a helper suitable for him." And out of the ground the Lord God
formed every beast of the field and every bird of the sky, and brought them
to the man to see what he would call them; and whatever the man called a
living creature, that was its name. And the man gave names to all the cattle, and to the birds of the sky, and to every beast of the field, but for Adam
there was not found a helper suitable for him. So the Lord God caused a
deep sleep to fall upon the man, and he slept; then He took one of his ribs,
and closed up the flesh at the place. And the Lord God fashioned into a
woman the rib which He had taken from the man, and brought her to the
man. And the man said, "This is now bone of my bones and flesh of my
flesh; She shall be called Woman, because she was taken out of Man." For
this cause a man shall leave his father and his mother, and shall cleave to his
wife; and they shall become one flesh. And the man and his wife were both
naked and were not ashamed (Gen. 2:18-25).

How do we know that this passage refers to a covenant? In the
previous chapter, we saw that the creation days were structured according to the covenant, creation being called into existence with *ten*

words. This account of the creation of woman and the first marriage falls within such a covenantal context. The following introduces briefly the first model of the family. It too follows the five-fold pattern.

True Transcendence (Gen. 2:18)

The section begins with a certain "revelatory" character, similar to the Deuteronomic covenant: "Then the Lord God *said*" (Gen. 2:18). God creates the first marriage and immediately *distinguishes* marriage from creation, distancing Biblical religion from all ancient pagan religions. Pre-Christian pagan religious cosmologies generally involve creation itself with the first marital union. For example, the marriage of one "god" to another "god," or even to man, produces offspring that populate the earth. Consequently, to worship "god," or the "gods," is bound up in the family ancestory. The result is that the worship of god is worship of the family!

Since God is transcendent, the family is not absolute, nor is it the *center* of society. How ironic. Modern Christian writers frequently insist that the "family" is the most important institution of society, making it transcendent and absolute. They simply ignore the covenantal aspect of Biblical religion, and they return to pre-Christian pagan concepts of the family. Is it any wonder that we cannot tell much difference from Christian and non-Christian teachers on the subject? A covenantal view of the family begins here, distinguishing God from the family, thereby placing Lordship in God and putting the family in the proper role.

Carle Zimmerman gives modern man the best analysis of the history of the family, being a creationist and rejecting all traditional "evolutionary theories" of its development.[1] His evaluation classifies the family's history into three categories: trustee (clan), domestic, and atomistic. He explains that the family tracks these three "phases" in every major period of history, particularly in the West, although he summarizes the same tendencies in the East.

For our purposes, however, he reminds us that the spread of

---

1. Carle C. Zimmerman, *Family and Civilization* (New York: Harper & Row, 1947). Although Zimmerman was a Harvard University professor and one of the leading experts on the family, he was ignored, and still remains ignored, because he was a *creationist*. His works are mammoth and monumental, but very few take note of him simply because he was a devout Catholic who believed strongly in creation and rejected, particularly at the time he lived, the standard Marxist and evolutionary interpretations of history.

Christianity had to counter a "clan," or what he calls the "trustee," view of the family. The clans were the final authority about everything, even to the point of executing one of its own members should he be found guilty of some "capital," or rather "familial" offense. The Church attacked this clan view, and taught that the Church is the means of change.[2] It taught that the family can only draw true life from the Family of God. Build God's Family, and God will save man's family.

The true transcendence of God, therefore, keeps the family from being "absolutized." On the other hand, with God as the Creator of the family, He becomes the source of salvation and hope for it.

Hierarchy (Gen. 2:19-22)

The second section of the family covenant describes the creation of woman: how God showed man his need and made the special provision. Herein are all the facets of the principle of *hierarchy.*

God actually created a hierarchy by which the first dominion mandate could be accomplished. He, through the headship of the male and submission of the female, uses couples to perform His work. God first shows Adam his need by involving him in naming the animals. The Lord causes the man to see that man cannot carry out his mandate alone. A hierarchy of checks and balances is required.

It is important, however, that the Biblical hierarchy of the family be theoretically and historically distinguished from the pagan patriarchal or clan family system. Such pagan family structures have persisted in Central and Eastern Europe, but they invariably collapse within one or two generations when these families arrive in the West, especially in countries with a Protestant background. The clan family simply cannot compete with the Biblical covenantal family. The Biblical family order is supposed to replace clans and patriarchs.

Abraham, Isaac, and Jacob are frequently referred to as patriarchs. Biblical patriarchs, yes; patriarchs of a clan system, no. When Abraham sent Ishmael away, he broke from Ishmael legally. Ishmael no longer had to take orders from Abraham, although he showed filial honor by joining Isaac at his father's burial (Gen. 25:9). Similarly, after Abraham passed the inheritance to Isaac — a transfer symbolized by his transfer of Sarah's tent to Isaac — so that he and Rebekah could

---

2. *Ibid*, pp. 462-495.

begin their life together in it (Gen. 24:67), he left the region. He remarried, journeyed east, and disappeared from covenantal history until his death (Gen. 25:1-9). He was father of many nations: Ishmaelites, Semites, Midianites, and so forth. But he wisely and faithfully ceased to meddle in the lives of those sons who had gone their own way.

The patriarchs in the Bible were not patriarchs in the sense of men who ruled a single pyramid of families beneath them. The sons and daughters-in-law were not expected to live in their father's house, or even nearby. The familiar "in-law problem," reflected culturally by the "mother-in-law joke," is the product of sin: unbiblical interference by would-be patriarchs and matriarchs, and smoldering resentment and outright rebellion by resentful sons and daughters-in-law. If men understood and honored the covenant basis of the Biblical family model, such problems would be drastically reduced. To put it bluntly, the in-laws' authority stops long before and far outside the heirs' bedroom door, not because of biology, but because of *a legal declaration of a new unit of government* that is created by marriage.

The creation of Eve out of Adam adds another dimension to the Biblical hierarchy. Her creation is analogous to man's. As Adam was created by God, she is created by God. Unlike Adam, however, she comes into existence through the male's own being (rib), making her distinct from God, but forever *dependent* on the male for life. Not until the Fall does woman appear in a totally "autonomous" and independent role. So, the man needs the woman, and the woman needs the man.

The hierarchy of authority places the male in the position of *representing* God to the woman. Although she is man's "vice-president," and top advisor, she is created to submit to man (Eph. 5:22). The Apostle Paul uses her creation as an argument explaining why women should not be allowed to exercise authority over men in the Church.

But I do not allow a woman to teach or exercise authority over a man, but to remain quiet. For it was Adam who was first created, and then Eve. And it was not Adam who was deceived, but the woman being quite deceived, fell into transgression (I Tim. 2:11-14).

The Biblical chain of command runs from the man outward and then downward to the rest of the family. Although modern man, in all of his rebellion to the God Who created him, tries to escape this reality, the Biblical authority structure is a major ingredient missing from American homelife. A. C. R. Skynner speaks of the need to have a *set hierarchy*, as opposed to an "equalitarian," everyone-is-equal approach.

The parts of the group, like the parts of the individual, are not all on one level but require to be arranged in a certain *hierarchical* order if they are to function effectively. No one disputes this in the organization of the central nervous system, where lower centers are under the dominance of higher. . . . But groups and families also have an optimum type of organization which must involve a form of *dominance hierarchy* and while there is again a range of possibilities of varying effectiveness, it appears that breakdown of the authority structure — whether through the loss of control of a nation by its government, abdication of responsibility by a father, or destruction of the cortex through birth injury — *leads to uncoordinated release of tendencies which can be damaging to the whole system*, however valuable these may be within proper bounds and in their proper place.[3]

The second covenantal principle for the family is a set hierarchy around the male (under Christ's authority). What about a day when there are so many "one-parent" families? The institutional Church is the Biblical solution until the woman remarries. Women can find the "true Groom" Jesus Christ to be an immense comfort. The male will discover that the Bride of Christ, the Church, can offset his deficiencies. Nevertheless, the problems do not negate the Biblical reality of *hierarchy*.

Ethics (Gen. 2:23)

After God creates the woman, Adam *names* her (Gen. 2:23). "Naming" was part of the cultural mandate and original *command* given to man. Not only was Adam told to name everything, but thereby to have dominion. So, this function is in compliance with an *ethical stipulation*. Biblical dominion is ethical and not manipulative, designed according to the Ten Commandments.

The law of the family is supposed to be the Ten Commandments of God, with fathers teaching their sons how the commandments are applied. Moses tells Israel's fathers,

And these words [Covenant of Ten Commandments] which I am commanding you today, shall be on your heart; and you shall teach them dili-

---

3. A. C. R. Skynner, *Social Work Today* (July 15, 1971), p. 5.

gently to your sons and shall talk of them when you sit in your house and when you walk by the way and when you lie down and when you rise up. And you shall bind them as a sign on your hand and they shall be as frontals on your foreheads. And you shall write them on the doorposts of your house and on your gates (Deut. 6:6-9).

I do not believe Moses intended these verses to be taken according to the Talmudic Jewish tradition, writing the Ten Commandments on little pieces of paper and nailing them in special boxes to the doorposts of one's house. The family was to be taught the law of God: what it was, and how it applied.

Solomon reiterates this message to families, devoting the entire book of Proverbs to "wisdom" (*hocmah*). What is wisdom? It is the ability to think and apply God's *Law*. In Proverbs, Solomon tells sons to listen to their father's instruction in the "commandments" of God.

My son, if you will receive my sayings, and treasure my *commandments* within you, make your ear attentive to wisdom, incline your heart to understanding; For if you cry for discernment, lift your voice for understanding; If you seek her as silver, and search for her as for hidden treasures; Then you will discern the fear of the Lord, and discover the knowledge of God (Prov. 2:1-5).

The ethics of the family is the covenantal commandments of God. Throughout this book, we have seen the relationship between the covenant and ethics, the Ten Commandments. Solomon says that God's ethics should be so internalized that one's "natural" response is obedience to His Law. This is the task of the family and parents.

Sanctions (Gen. 2:24)

Next in Genesis 2 the text says, "For this cause a man shall leave his father and mother and cleave to his wife, and they shall become one flesh" (v. 24). Moses adds his own editorial comment (under the inspiration of God), which is judicial in character. All of the language here implies some kind of legal process of oath-taking to establish a marriage union.

"Leaving" (*'azab*) implies the termination of a covenant bond, the same Hebrew word being used of apostasy from the covenant (Deut. 28:30; Judges 10:10; Jer. 1:16). The covenant being ended is the parental bond. A new covenant or bond is formed by "cleaving" (*dabaq*).

The parental relationship is temporary and the marital covenant is permanent.

Even the "one flesh" language is primarily legal and covenantal, not primarily "physical." The word for "cling," or "cleave" (*dabaq*) is the key to understanding the full sense of "one flesh." *Dabaq* is a technical term, often used in covenant contexts like Deuteronomy (Deut. 10:20; 11:22; 13:4; 30:20; Josh. 22:5, 23:8). The parallel words to this concept are "serve, love, fear, obey, swear by His name, walk in His ways, and keep his commandments," all of which is covenantal language for receiving God's sanctions.[4] Of particular interest is the use of this word in the *sanctions* context of Deuteronomy. The covenant is bonded to by "clinging" to it in love and obedience (Deut. 30:20).

The language of Genesis 2:24, therefore, implies a *legal* process whereby God's sanctions are received for the marriage covenant. In essence, the traditional marriage ceremony even to this day reflects the covenantal influence on marriage, "Till death do us part." Most people do not realize that they are taking an "oath" before God, witnessed by the minister (Church), the relatives (Family), and civil authorities via the marriage certificate (State). All three institutions testify that an oath was taken, sealing the two together until one or the other *dies*. The consequences for breaking the oath is the judgment of God (Mal. 2:14ff.).

The point of all this, though, is that marriage is a *covenant*, creating a *new family unit*. The old family covenants that used to govern the newly married partners are broken, and a new covenant is formed. Marriage means that family ties are not by *blood* — father to sons, and to the daughters-in-law through their husbands, as in pagan Greek and Roman families[5] — but by covenant. Although children have responsibilities to aid their parents, the parental covenant and authority cease at the point of marriage. The "new" husband is head of his house, and neither his nor his wife's father is the covenantal head. Thus, the terms "nuclear" (autonomous) and "extended" (patriarchal) miss the true description of the Biblical family. It is covenantal, being created through a legal process of receiving *sanctions*.

---

4. E. Kalland, "*Dabaq,*" in *Theological Wordbook of the Old Testament*, ed. R. L. Harris; 2 vols., (Chicago: Moody, 1980), 1:178. Also, see Walter Brueggeman, "Of the Same Flesh and Bone (Gen. 2:23a)," *Catholic Biblical Quarterly* 32 (1970), p. 540.

5. Fustel de Coulanges, *The Ancient City* (New York: Doubleday Anchor, [1864] 1955), Book Second, ch. II.

Continuity (Gen. 2:25)

Finally, the family covenant consists of *continuity*, the fifth point of covenantalism. Moses says, "And the man and his wife were both naked and not ashamed" (Gen. 2:25). Why would Moses add such a statement?

Following upon the "one flesh" comment of verse 24, Moses describes the marital bliss of Adam and Eve. His words, however, are not in terms of physical union—none is mentioned—rather, there was no "shame." They needed no clothing because before the Fall they were *clothed by God's covenant.* More to the point, the covenant bond of Genesis 2:24 had created perfect continuity. Their union was complete. It was confirmed by the absence of shame. The Bible expresses their continuity this way so as to create a contrast with the following chapter in Genesis. Satan destroys their absence of shame by provoking the Fall. They become guilty, and their shame becomes a reminder of their complete *loss of inheritance.* In an ironic sort of way, as long as they had no shame, they had inheritance. When their shame was removed, ultimately in Christ, their inheritance was returned (Matt. 5:5). Only people who have their sin forgiven are able to lay hold of the inheritance.

Continuity is in the covenant, and it is very important to the being and well-being of the family. In our house, for example, we teach our children that if they really love us, then they will love the God that we love. They are warned that if they ever leave the covenant into which they have been baptized, then they will be cut out of their inheritance. In a Christian home, "blood is not thicker than (baptismal) water!"

Is this cruel? No. This is precisely how God treats us, and how the families of the Bible treated their children. When a son left the covenant, he was removed from the family inheritance. When Cain killed his brother and deserted God's covenant, he was cast out (Gen. 4:9-15). Of course, to apply this concept of marriage and family, one must love the covenant more than he loves his children. Family continuity should be built on the covenant. Children should be taught to see the connection between covenant faithfulness and inheritance, both spiritual and material. Christians are not to subsidize evil, which is what unconditional inheritance does in a world of sin and covenant-breaking.

Conclusion

The family is a covenant. In this chapter, I have used the first marriage to demonstrate its covenantal nature. To review, first we saw that God is transcendent over the family, meaning the family is not the center of society. Second, God set up a hierarchy around the male, not denigrating but subjugating the woman and children to him. Third, man carried out God's commandments by naming the woman, making the covenant ethical. Fourth, the family is created by the application of sanctions (oath and legal declaration), meaning the family tie is covenantal and not primarily of blood. Fifth, the continuity of the family is in compliance to the covenant of God.

This is the Biblical model, but do we find that it has been adopted anywhere in history? Is this ideal unobtainable, in other words? No, as a matter of fact, Edmund Morgan says that the covenant was the most important family concept in early Puritan America.[6] In the next chapter, therefore, let us take a more historical look at the family covenant.

---

6. Morgan, *The Puritan Family*, pp. 26ff.

9

THE HISTORICAL FAMILY COVENANT

In our society, there are three basic spheres of life: Family, Church, and State. All three are covenants: legal institutions formed by self-maledictory oaths. Their importance is obvious. In this chapter I want to *apply* what we learned about the Biblical covenant to history.[1]

Modern man tends to forget that marriage is a covenant. It used to be that two people did not get marriage *licenses*. Rather, they drew up marriage contracts, and filed them at the city courthouse. Why don't people do this today? The answer is simple. *Contracts make it too hard to secure a divorce.* A contract (covenant) is much more binding than a license. In the following, I have reproduced an old marriage contract from 1664/1665.[2]

Marriage Contract
January 20, 1664/65
Plymouth, Massachusetts

This writing witnesses, between Thomas Clarke, late of Plymouth, yeoman, and Alice Nicholls of Boston, widow, that, whereas there is an intent of marriage between the said parties, the Lord succeeding their intentions in convenient time; the agreement, therefore, is that the housing and land now in the possession of the said Alice Nicholls shall be reserved as a

---

1. Edward McGlynn Gaffney, "The Interaction of Biblical Religion and American Constitutional Law," *The Bible in American Law, Politics, and Political Rhetoric*, ed. James Turner Johnson (Philadelpha: Fortress Press, 1985), pp. 81-106. Gaffney's thesis is that the *suzerain form of the covenant* was influential on Constitutional law in this country.

2. The reason why there are two years listed is that prior to the late 1700s, the new year came in mid-March. This is still reflected in the names for several months: SEPTember, OCTober, NOVember, and DECember — seven, eight, nine, and ten — when today they are the ninth, tenth, eleventh, and twelfth months. The second year listed is the year we reckon it in retrospect, according to our calendar.

stock for her son, John Nicholls, for him to enjoy and possess at the age of twenty and one years, in the meantime to be improved by the parents towards his education. Also, that what estate of hers the said Alice shall be found and committed to the said Mr. Clarke, if it should so please the Lord to take the said Alice out of this life before the said Thomas Clarke, he shall then have the power to dispose of all the said estate sometimes hers so as it seems good to him. Moreover, if it shall please the Lord to take away the said Thomas Clarke by death before the said Alice, she surviving, then the said Alice shall have and enjoy her own estate she brought with her, or the value thereof, and two hundred pounds added thereto of the estate left by the said Thomas Clarke. All which the said Thomas Clarke does hereby promise and bind himself to allow of and perform as a *covenant* upon their marriage. In witness of all which, the said Thomas Clarke has signed and sealed this present writing to Peter Oliver and William Bartholmew of Boston, for the use and behoof of the said Alice Nicholls. Dated this twentieth day of January 1664.

per me,   Thomas Clarke[3]

This historical document is quite revealing. It contains or implies all the features of the Biblical covenant. In the following, let us use the Biblical grid of the last chapter, to evaluate this application.

True Transcendence

The contract has a *transcendent* character to it. It makes reference to "the Lord" three times. The parties agreed that "the Lord" establishes marriage and the covenant between them. Obviously they presupposed that God had created the institution of marriage, and He had brought them together in "holy" (set apart) matrimony. We know from the history of New England that they were a people who believed this theocentric (God-centered) worldview. They went out of their way to mention the "Lord." When was the last time you saw any contractual statement that spoke this way?

Marriage is a Divine institution. It is created by *lawful representatives* of God as a Divinely sanctioned institution. Transcendence is not in the marriage itself. If transcendence shifts to the marriage, then the family becomes a "god"; it is *idolized* and put on a *pedestal*. This only further destroys it. Marriage and family cannot take that kind of pressure.

---

3. *Foundations of Colonial America: A Documentary History*, Ed. W. Keith Kavenagh, Vol. I, Part 2 (New York: Confucian Press, 1980), p. 667. Emphasis added.

A "well-intentioned" Christian couple sets out to have the "perfect" marriage. In the process, they elevate marriage to an idolatrous position, make it transcendent, and expect too much out of the marriage. Then they have those "normal" problems adjusting. But because they have an almost "deified" view of marriage, they become disillusioned. Sometimes they end up getting a divorce.

How ironic! Modern society, in desperation, creates all kinds of ways — TV shows, books, "marriage encounters," etc. — to revive the family institution. Even though these techniques might not be bad in and of themselves, in the process, the family is placed in the position of God. The family itself is worshipped. Maybe the spouse or even the children end up at the center of some well-intentioned person's worldview. In either case, Biblical transcendence is lost. The family itself becomes "god." The contract above rejects such a notion. It projects a high view of marriage and the family, but not so high that it shatters the Creator/creature distinction.

Hierarchy

That what estate of hers the said Alice shall be found and committed to the said Mr. Clarke, if it should so please the Lord to take the said Alice out of this life before the said Thomas Clarke, he shall then have the power to dispose of all the said estate sometimes hers so as it seems good to him. . . .

A Biblical covenant has representatives. The 1665 marriage does something that might tend to go unnoticed, but is quite revealing about the representative character of the relationship between these two parties. The covenant is in the name of the *man*. Why? He represents both parties. According to the original language of the New Testament (Greek), the very word for "family" is derived from the word for "father." Paul says, "For this reason I bow my knees to the *Father* [*Pater*], from whom every *family* [*Patria*] in heaven and on earth derives its name" (Eph. 3:14-15). Both Greek words come from the same root. This representation of God by the father originated with the first marriage between Adam and Eve. Adam "named" Eve and declared her to be his wife. Moses says for this reason a "man shall leave his father and mother and cleave to his wife" (Gen. 2:24). To "name" something is to set up authority over it. Since the man was given this responsibility, he represented God in a special way. So the emphasis of the Bible is that the man is God's representative in the household.

In the event that the man dies, leaves, or divorces his wife, she can become the representative. In the Old Testament, as we shall see toward the end of this chapter, the woman became the husband's "sister" through a process of adoption. She was both wife and sister so that she could be a "co-heir" with the husband. This way, when left without a husband, the woman can lawfully be the family's representative. An example of a woman who is head of her household is Lydia of the New Testament (Acts 16:11-15).

Whether the man or the woman is head of the household, however, the family has *representatives*. They represent the Lord.

This brings us to the government of the household. Since the covenant is in the man's name, he is *head* of the household. We can assume that the woman takes his name because she is under his authority. The idea of changing names grows out of the Biblical passage where Adam gave Eve her name (Gen. 2:23). More than anything else it meant that Eve was under the authority of Adam. The Bible is very clear that the *governmental* structure of the household is that man is the head. He is the provider and has the final say in the decision making process. Actually, he is a *manager*. He can delegate responsibilities, but the "buck stops with him."

The role of the wife in this hierarchy is that she is the husband's top *advisor*. The contract mentions certain provisions for the wife's child from a previous marriage. Probably she advised the new father regarding these stipulations. Is this Biblical? Definitely. In the ancient city of Hur — the city from which Abraham was called — archaeologists have discovered copies of "Hurrian marriage contracts." These contracts stipulate that the wife also becomes the *sister* of the husband. In addition, it was customary to make the sons *brothers* to the father.

> In Hurrian society the bonds of marriage were strongest and most solemn when the wife had simultaneously the juridical status of a sister, regardless of actual blood ties. This is why a man would sometimes marry a girl and adopt her at the same time as his sister, in two separate steps recorded in independent legal documents. Violations of such sistership arrangements were punished more severely that breaches of marriage contracts. The practice was apparently a reflection of the underlying fratriarchal system, and it gave the adoptive brother greater authority than was granted the husband. By the same token, the adopted sister enjoyed correspondingly greater protection and higher social status.[4]

---

4. E. A. Spiser, *Genesis* (Garden City, New York: Doubleday, 1964), p. 92. See also by the same author, "Wife-Sister Motif in the Patriarchal Narratives," *Biblical and Other Studies* (Harvard University Press, 1963), pp. 15-28.

More than likely, the same type of contract was practiced in the Bible (Gen. 24:1-67; Song of Solomon). This sheds much light on the passages in Genesis where Abraham told Abimelech, the King of Egypt, that Sarah (his wife) was his sister (Gen. 20:1ff.). Abraham was not lying to Abimelech. He had *legally adopted* Sarah as his sister. Why? The bride was the top advisor of the husband. She shared in the inheritance, and could rule in the father's absence.

The role of advisor is powerful. The advisor usually wields more *influence* than the person in authority. Consider, for example, who has more power: The President of the United States or his advisory cabinet? It is the latter. The President almost never goes against his advisors. They are the primary source of the information that flows to him, on which he will base his decisions, in counsel with them. They are the people to whom the bureaucratic hierarchies report. The Bible presents the woman as having this kind of influence over the husband. The positive Biblical example is Esther, the Jewish Queen of the Persian Emperor, Ahasuerus (Xerxes). When Haman, a vicious member of the king's court, plotted against her people and relative, Mordecai, she used her advisory power to get him hanged (Esth. 4:1ff.; 7:10). This is ultimately a picture of how God's Bride, the Church, advises the kings of the world to get the wicked hanged from their own gallows. But at a very basic level, it is a Biblical view of the power of the role of the wife. It is the role which God has ordained for her.

The contract above also mentions that the woman was bringing with her a sizeable estate. This may have been what was left from the previous marriage. Maybe it was her inheritance or gift from her father. In either case, we see the ability of the woman to *deal in business matters*. The Puritan woman was often left to run the household and even bring in extra income while the husband was away. This too is a Biblical idea. The woman of Proverbs 31 was a shrewd business woman, quite familiar with the ways of the *market place*. There is nothing wrong with a woman's working, as long as it does not jeopardize her domestic responsibilities.

The hierarchy of the Puritan covenant is clear. God is the transcendent authority, and the father represents Him to the family. The wife stands with the father as his top advisor. She has delegated authority and the children must submit to her because she represents the father.

Ethics

All which the said Thomas Clarke does hereby promise and *bind* himself to all of and perform as a *covenant* upon their marriage.

The marriage covenant between Clarke and Nicholls is *ethical*. Both parties are responsible to provide certain tangible items. But again it should be underscored that the Lord was the final authority of this covenant. They were living according to some sort of transcendent *law*. Recalling what we said about the ethical character of the covenant in the last chapter, ethical stands in contrast to magical. We can work our way into the significance of this distinction with our "totem pole" analogy.

Mormonism is a classic example of a modern religion that has a magical view of authority, since it believes that man evolves and becomes a "god" on other planets.[5] Lorenzo Snow, former president of the Mormon Church, said, "As man is, God once was: as God is, man may become."[6] This is a totem-pole religion. It has a "chain of being" view of life and the world. This means the family plays an important role, and specifically the father. The following diagram is somewhat like the totem-pole analogy used earlier. This time we will not draw a totem pole, just a column representing the static, vertical, continuum of life.

CHAIN OF BEING VIEW OF FAMILY

GOD	
FATHER (HIS SEED POSSESSES BEING OF GOD)	FAMILY VIEWED AS CENTRAL INSTITUTION
STATE	OTHER INSTITUTIONS HAVE LESS BEING. THEY MUST GO THROUGH THE "PATRIARCH" TO GET TO GOD.
CHURCH NON BEING (NO FAMILY)	

---

5. *Teachings of the Prophet Joseph Smith*, ed. Joseph Fielding Smith (Salt Lake City: Deseret Book Co., 1958), pp. 346-47.

6. Walter Martin, *The Kingdom of the Cults* (Minneapolis, Minnesota: Bethany Fellowship, 1965), p. 178.

In the diagram, the reader should notice that the father is the "link" between god and the rest of the family. Remember that since god is in time and part of creation, the father is a *physical* extension. He contains within him the "stuff" out of which god is made. When he impregnates his wife, he is passing the spark of the "divine" into her womb. The pantheon of the gods is being extended. As one Mormon leader said, "The only men who become Gods, even the Sons of God, are those who enter into polygamy."[7] Brigham Young even said,

How much unbelief exists in the minds of the Latter-day Saints in regard to one particular doctrine which I revealed to them, and which God revealed unto me — namely that Adam is our father and our *God* . . .
"Well," says one, "Why was Adam called Adam?" He was the first man on the earth, and its framer and maker. He with the help of his brethren, brought it into existence. Then he said, "I want my children who are in the spirit world to come and live here. I once dwelt upon an earth something like this, in a mortal state. I was faithful, I received my crown and exaltation."[8]

This is a magical, perverse view of the family. Adam is "God," as well as man. Each male is infused with Adamic deity. His children are "spirit babies," brought into existence by procreation, and so sex deifies humanity.

There are many ramifications, but the governmental and ethical ones are of particular interest. If the father is deity in the home, then the way to god is through the father. Ultimately, the way to god is through sexual union with the male. The hope of the female is to find a man who can impregnate her with the very "being" of god. This is one of the reasons that Mormons have so many children. They are literally putting, according to their theology, little Mormon "gods" on the earth.

Also, since the father is the divine connection between heaven and earth, his authority is *absolute*. It cannot be contradicted. For example, Mormon books on the role of father and mother, like *Man of Steel and Velvet* and *Fascinating Womanhood*, give the father *absolute* authority.

Biblical authority is not this way. The authority of the home is

---

7. *Journal of Discourses*, vol. 11, p. 269.
8. *Deseret News*, June 18, 1873, p. 308. Cited in *Kingdom of the Cults*, p. 179. Emphasis added.

God, not the father. Whatever the father has is delegated to him. He is a *representative* of God, not an extension of Him. There are *checks and balances*. He *might sin*, and ask his family to do the wrong thing. So, there is a time to disobey the father. The Biblical example is the story of Ananias and Sapphira (Acts 5:1ff.). Ananias lied to the Holy Spirit, and asked his wife to follow him in his disobedience. Because she obeyed her husband, she was executed by God.

The Biblical picture of authority is perhaps best illustrated with a triangle. God is at the top of the pyramid. Father, mother, and children have access to and are directly responsible to God. The father is the legal representative as opposed to magical leader. The father has certain limits and checks and balances on him.

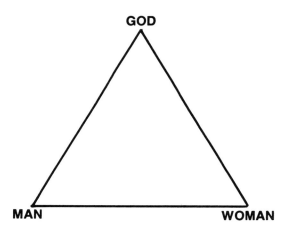

The clearest check and balance is that the family can appeal the decisions of the father. Where? In the Church court (I Cor. 6:1ff.), and if civil matters are involved, in the State. Take the Biblical example of Ananias and Sapphira. Because Sapphira had an opportunity to contradict her husband in front of the officers of the Church, this means the Church is a higher court, an appeals court for the family. Significantly, this legal structure broke up the old clan system of Europe. When Christianity began its trek across this barbaric part of the world, there was a constant "Hatfield vs. McCoy" type of feuding. The family had absolute power to convict and even execute its own members. The Church broke down the clans through its court system. It argued that the father does not have absolute authority. The check and balance on his power is the court of the Church.

Such a system developed because the marriage covenant is ethical. The historical marriage covenant, by the fact that there is a set contract, limits the powers of the father, and the mother for that matter. They could not do anything they wanted with each other, or with their children. There were ethical boundaries that defined the limits of their power.

Unfortunately, there are Christians in places of great influence today who continue to teach a clan view of the family, a kind of "almost Mormonism." They do not acknowledge the Protestant principle of *multiple authorities*. They teach that the father's word is law, that a pagan father can, for example, keep a Christian son from marrying a Christian woman, no matter what the girl's parents say, or the son's and girl's church courts say. This simply transfers to the father the kind of authority which the Roman Catholic Church officially invests in the Pope. A father becomes a final court of earthly appeal, one who can veto a marriage. This is radically anti-Biblical. There are always multiple human courts that are established by God to speak in God's name, and no single earthly governmental authority has a monopoly on speaking God's covenantal word, and therefore absolute authority to create or dissolve a marriage.

Sanctions

In witness of all which, the said Thomas Clarke has signed and sealed this present writing to Peter Oliver and William Bartholmew of Boston, for the use and behoof of the said Alice Nicholls. Dated this twentieth day of January 1664.

"Signing and sealing" is a process of sanctioning. Both parties of this early American marriage covenant are taking a solemn *oath*. The example being used is similar to other documents of that era. There was some sort of ceremony; there was the actual "cutting" of the covenant, just as we have already seen in Deuteronomy. It is still today called a *wedding ceremony*. In our society, all three institutions participate in it. The minister officiates at the ceremony because the Church is the "guardian" of marriage. The families draw up the contract. The State is a witness because marriage is an institution of *society* as well. In the event there is a divorce, or the settlement of the family's estate, the State may be drawn into the legal process. So marriage does not belong exclusively to any of these institutions.

The covenant has *terms of unconditionality*. To say that marriage has no terms means there is no possibility of divorce. When this view prevails, the innocent are victimized. As in God's covenant, people sometimes apostatize. The Biblical view of marriage is able to cope with such a possibility, even though some modern evangelical views are not. Marriage often ends up being absolutised. It is taught that there are no justifications for divorce. Of course, I have never seen a "no reason for divorce" position that did not have to create some kind of doctrine of *annulment*, an escape-valve. It points out the reality that on "this side of heaven," there are no perfect people and therefore no perfect covenants. If God has a legal right to break sinners, then victims of sinners have a legal right to break covenants.

Marriage is a covenant. The Apostle Paul argues that "death" is the basis of the dissolution of a marriage bond (Rom. 7:1-4). But from the context immediately before and after this passage, "death" is referred to in "covenantal" terms. For example, just before the "death" passage of chapter seven, the last verse of chapter six reads, "For the wages of sin is *death*, but the gift of God is life eternal" (Rom. 6:23).

Clearly the "death" here is more than just *physical*. Death is understood in terms of the Biblical covenant. To be separated from God, to break the covenant, is to be dead. This means that when the spouse does things to violate the marriage covenant, the marriage dies, and the innocent partner is free to divorce and remarry. What are the things that kill the marriage? One will have to read the *entire* Bible. They are capital offense crimes like murder, homosexuality, apostasy, idolatry, witchcraft, bestiality, and adultery.[9]

The pastor who refuses to counsel divorce to someone whose spouse is involved in bestiality is thereby sanctioning evil. (By the way, it should be pointed out that bestiality is nowhere mentioned in the New Testament, which creates a difficult exegetical problem for pastors who operate under the presupposition that all Old Testament laws are abolished unless specifically re-sanctioned in the New Testament.) There can be no neutrality. But the pastor who cannot find a Bible-based reason to sanction the divorce is in a weak position as a marital counselor.

If the Church is not able to deal with these kinds of sins, and the reality that "Christian" marriages are today plagued by such sins,

9. Ray R. Sutton, *Death Did Us Part: A Defense of the Innocent Partner.* Scheduled for 1987.

then the Church will lose its ministry. Divorce rates among church members continue to rise. The sad fact is that the innocent are being victimized. If the Church's view of divorce accomodates victimization of the innocent, it will never be able to speak believably to the world. There is an effective way to deal with the issue of divorce. The answer lies in the covenant and its terms of unconditionality.

Continuity

The agreement, therefore, is that the housing and land now in the possession of the said Alice Nicholls shall be reserved as a stock for her son, John Nicholls . . . .

Finally, the marriage covenant between Clarke and Nicholls is *legitimate*. It formed a real bond between them. This fact made their children legitimate heirs of the inheritance. The contract details some of this, and even specifies who should execute the will in the event one or the other dies. The covenant transfers specific blessings.

It is no secret that income taxes and inheritance taxes were designed by envy-ridden legislators who represented envy-driven voters. Such taxes have been designed to inhibit the economic growth of highly successful families. Interestingly, these laws were instituted around the time great industrial development of natural resources were making families wealthy and powerful. The result has been that government has tried to use "family" wealth to intervene in the market and create monopolies. The rich families all escaped this by setting up huge charitable foundations—Carnegie, Rockefeller, Ford, Mellon, etc.—that have kept this wealth intact. Thus, the real inheritors have been the foundation bureaucrats who operate the great foundations. But officially, the State itself has virtually become the new "family" (Big Brother) of our world.[10]

The question is, "Who is the legitimate heir?" The Bible says the children and those specified in the covenant are the legitimate heirs. No one else has the right to take the inheritance away. In the event there are no heirs, the Church should receive the inheritance, but *never* the State.

---

10. Gary North, *The Sinai Strategy: Economics and the Ten Commandments* (Tyler, Texas: Institute for Christian Economics, 1986), pp. 103-14.

Conclusion

This concludes our application of the covenant to the family. An old marriage covenant has been used. I freely admit that not all marriage contracts follow the Biblical outline. That is not my point. This one did, and I think we can see in history that such a view of marriage produced the seed-bed out of which our entire culture has sprung. At no other time in American history has the family been so strong.

But what about the Church? Is it structured according to the covenant? And are there any historical examples? In the next chapter we examine the *Biblical Church Covenant*.

10

THE BIBLICAL CHURCH COVENANT

To demonstrate the covenantal character of the Church, let us turn to a section of Scripture that follows the five-fold structure, Revelation.[1] In the "letters" segment (Rev. 2-3), we see that even this *sub-section* is drafted in a covenant format. Each letter is outlined according to the five-point model. The first Church, Ephesus, is an example.

To the angel of the church in Ephesus write: The One Who holds the seven stars in His right hand, the One who walks among the seven golden lampstands, says this: "I know your deeds and your toil and perseverance, and that you cannot endure evil men, and you put to the test those who call themselves apostles, and they are not, and you found them to be false; and you have perseverance and have endured for My name's sake, and have not grown weary. But I have this against you, that you have left your first love. Remember therefore from where you have fallen, and repent and do the deeds you did at first; or else I am coming to you, and will remove your lampstand out of its place—unless you repent. Yet this you do have, that you hate the deeds of the Nicolaitans, which I also hate. He who has an ear, let him hear what the Spirit says to the churches. To him who overcomes, I will grant to eat of the tree of life, which is in the Paradise of God" (Rev. 2:1-7).

True Transcendence (Rev. 2:1)

The covenant always begins by distinguishing God from man. The preamble to this letter tells us that the words come from God, "The One Who holds the seven stars." In the previous chapter, we are told Who this is.

And when I saw Him, I fell at His feet as a dead man. And He laid His right hand upon me, saying, "Do not be afraid; I am the first and the last, and the living One; and I was dead, and behold, I am alive forevermore, and I have the keys of death and of Hades. Write therefore the things which

---

1. See Appendix 5.

159

you have seen, and the things that are, and the things which shall take place after these things. As for the mystery of the *seven stars in My right hand, and the seven golden lampstands*: the seven stars are the angels of the seven churches, and the seven lampstands are the seven churches" (Rev. 1:17-20).

Christ is the One who sends the letters to the churches. His opening statement in the first one is careful to make this point, and He thereby distinguishes Himself from the Church. Both His "authorship" and distinction make two critical statements.

First, Christ is *Head of the Church*. The Church is created by God, and so it is a "Divine" institution, not some kind of ecclesiastical "social contract."[2] The Lord builds the Church; it is His body; it is not of man, nor does it belong to him. To attack the Church is to attack God. He is the truly transcendent Lord of the Church.

Second, even though the Church is a "Divine" institution, it should be distinguished from God. The Word of God and the preaching of the Church are supposed to be the same, but the distinction should be kept at all times. When the words of the Church are "equivalent to" Scripture, the ecclesiastical institution is viewed as infallible. Calvin at Geneva negotiated around the dilemma by teaching that the *Word of God* is supposed to be the center of society.[3] Granted, the Church spreads the "Good News," making it in some sense the center of society. But still, the critical distinction between God and man should be maintained, unless the Church becomes an "absolutized" organization, creating the worst form of "ecclesiastical tyranny."

The first covenantal issue, transcendence, gives the Church true power, but not too much power. God is transcendent, leaving mankind in the role of glorious humanity, and never allowing it to cross the Creator/creature line that He has created.

---

2. James Bannerman, *The Church of Christ* (Edinburgh: Banner of Truth Trust, [1869] 1974), I:423.

3. R. J. Rushdoony, *Politics of Guilt and Pity* (Nutley, New Jersey: Craig Press, [1970] 1978), pp. 263-290. In this brilliant essay, Rushdoony properly notes that Calvin believed the Word of God, and not any human institution in a "governmental" sense should be the center of society. Rushdoony, however, misses the mark by failing to distinguish between the "governmental" and "sacramental" roles. The Church is given the *keys of the kingdom of God* (Matt. 16:19), manifested in the Preaching of the Word, the sacraments, and discipline. When Rushdoony says, "No social distinction between the redeemed and the reprobate is possible" (p. 281), he inadvertently undermines the unique place of the Church. It is "sacramentally" the center of society. The Tree of Life appears both in the form of the Word of God (written) and the Sacraments (visible), given only to the Church. Only this institution can use them to apply discipline: not the State, and certainly not the family!

Hierarchy (Rev. 2:2-4)

Christ commends the Ephesian Church because they "put to test those who call themselves apostles . . . and found them to be false" (Rev. 2:2). There is the presence of authority; there is the presence of a mediated system of judgment. How? The Church metes out judgment through a process of "testing." Probably, this involved a judicial setting similar to the Jerusalem Council (Acts 15). When the Church assembles to settle a dispute about whether or not it is necessary to be circumcised, the apostles and elders must settle it.

And the apostles and the elders came together to look into this matter. And after there had been much debate, Peter stood up and said to them, "Brethren, you know that in the early days God made a choice among you, that by my mouth the Gentiles should hear the word of the gospel and believe. And God, who knows the heart, bore witness to them, giving them the Holy Spirit, just as He also did to us; and He made no distinction between us and them, cleansing their hearts by faith. Now therefore why do you put God to the test by placing upon the neck of the disciples a yoke which neither our fathers nor we have been able to bear?" (Acts 15:6-10).

Shortly thereafter the dispute ended. Notice, however, that Peter uses a *question* to draw his point home. Perhaps this is how the Ephesian Church arrived at its decision about the false teachers. At any rate, the same relationship between judgment and history is made that has previously been seen in the other covenants. Ephesus proves its loyalty *in history* by mediating judgment.

Ethics (Rev. 2:5a)

Jesus tells the Ephesians to "do the deeds you did at first" (Rev. 2:5a). What are these "deeds"? John says in one of his epistles, "The one who says, 'I have come to know Him' and does not keep His commandments, is a liar, and the truth is not in him" (I John 2:4). These commandments are the ethical stipulations of the covenant. The Church covenant is Biblically required to include a commitment to the Law of God.

The application of Biblical law prevents the "tyranny of the minority." In every church there seem to be people who are easily offended. To paraphrase the pastor who gave parting words to the Pilgrims shortly before they left England, "Watch out for people who

are easily offended because they will be the first to give offense."[4]
Nevertheless, tyranny of the minority surfaces when certain members of the congregation do not like the fact that others do not see
things the way they do. Then these "offended" ones usually try to
manipulate people with verses of the Bible wrenched out of context.
Usually, these verses are drawn from passages that talk about "denying oneself" certain things because others are "stumbling" (I Cor.
8:13; Rom. 14-15).

Perhaps the favorite verse used by the tyrannical minority is
"Therefore, if food causes my brother to stumble, I will never eat
meat again, that I might not cause my brother to stumble" (I Cor.
8:13). I know of a church where people left because "coffee cake" was
being used that did not meet the health food requirements of the
tyrannical minority. (These people eventually stopped going to any
church.) Does this verse apply to coffee cake or similar foods? No.
The word "stumble" means to *sin*. The point is that if a Christian is
doing something to cause his *weaker* brother to *sin*, then he should
give it up. What we find, on the contrary, is that Christians are
asked to refrain from doing something allowed by the Bible. The
passage is not talking about something another person does not ap-
prove of or like.

Biblical law should rescue a true covenantal church from a
myraid of these kinds of problems. God's ethical standard provides
objective requirements that prevent the manipulative techniques of
those "saints" who have strong convictions about certain foods or
drinks that are not explicitly condemned in Scripture.

Sanctions (Rev. 2:5b)

Christ warns that if the Ephesians will not repent, then He will
remove their lampstand (Rev. 2:5b). When sin is not dealt with in a
church, God directly applies the sanctions of the covenant. That is,
if the church fails to discipline its own members, implementing the
sanctions, then God will do it for them. It may take many years for
the discipline of God to work its way out. But He will render *lex
talionis* ("eye for eye"). The process of Church discipline is explained
by Christ.

---

4. Cotton Mather, *The Great Works of Christ in America: Magnalia Christi Americana*
(London: Banner of Truth Trust, [1702] 1979), Vol. I, p. 50.

And if your brother sins, go and reprove him in private; if he listens to you, you have won your brother. But if he does not listen to you, take one or two more with you, so that by the mouth of two or three witnesses every fact may be confirmed. And if he refuses to listen to them, tell it to the church; and if he refuses to listen even to the church, let him be to you as a Gentile and a tax-gatherer. Truly I say to you, whatever you shall bind on earth shall be bound in heaven; and whatever you loose on earth shall be loosed in heaven (Matthew 18:15-18).

Notice there are three steps. First, each Christian has a responsibility to "reprove" a brother if he sins. Church discipline is always *restorative*, never punitive. The brother is to be restored if at all possible.

Second, if the brother will not listen, then witnesses are to be taken that "every fact may be confirmed" (v. 16). These witnesses are not necessarily witnesses to the initial sin. Rather, they witness that the second phase of discipline has been carried out.

Third, the sin is told to the whole church. How would this be done? The process presumes that the officers have been involved at this point. The tendency on the part of people is to run to the leaders when they see or hear of someone committing a sin. Officers should resist the temptation to take matters into their own hands too soon. Nevertheless, when the third stage is arrived at, the accused may deny that he has committed any such sin — adultery, for example. In this case, a trial will have to be held.

Finally, in the event that the accused is found guilty and still does not repent, he is to be put out of the church and *declared excommunicate*. Notice that I say "declared." The Church's power is judicial, "declarative," not having the actual power to condemn a person's soul to hell. Even so, if the Church binds on earth "what has already been bound in heaven," meaning it acts in accordance with Scripture, then God will uphold the discipline of His people.

Jesus, however, says to the Ephesians that if they do not repent and discipline themselves, then He will deal with them Himself, removing their church, "lampstand." The covenant is real. God honors it whether His people do or not. If they neglect discipline and the use of Biblical sanctions, then He will do what they have failed to do: sanction.

Continuity (Rev. 2:7)

Continuity is in Christ's statement, "He who has an ear, let him hear what the Spirit says to the churches. To him who overcomes, I will grant . . . the paradise of God" (Rev. 2:7). Covenantal continuity is in "listening." "Hearing" seems so simple, yet both in Proverbs, and the discipline account we just examined, "listening" is the key to persevering in the Kingdom of God (Prov. 4:1, Matthew 18:15, 16, 17).

Observe that in all three steps of the discipline process, each stage advances if the accused does not "listen." Eventually, it means that the brother is excommunicated. All Church discipline, therefore, is based on the sin of *contumacy*. Jay Adams makes the same point when he says,

> Excommunication never takes place for committing the sin that occasioned the process in the beginning. Excommunication always occurs when one rejects the authority of the church of Christ; he is excommunicated for contumacy. One is excommunicated then, not for adultery, but for failure to repent and be reconciled. The sin that occasioned discipline may have been relatively "small" in its effects, but to *that* sin is added the *enormously* significant sin of the rejection of Christ Himself as He demands repentance through His representatives.[5]

Jesus tells His disciples essentially that the "sin" shifts from the particular to the sin of "unrepentance," or contumacy. In this regard, Jesus echoed what Moses told the children of Israel, meeting contumacy with harsh discipline.

> If any case is too difficult for you to decide . . . so you shall come to the Levitical priest or the judge who is in office in those days, and you shall inquire of them, and they will declare to you the verdict in the case. . . . And the man who acts presumptuously by not *listening* to the priest who stands there to serve the Lord your God, nor to the judge, that man shall die; thus you shall purge the evil from Israel. Then all the people will *hear* and be afraid, and will not act presumptuously (Deut. 17:8-13).

In the civil realm, such as this situation, the death penalty was applied. In the sphere of the Church, officers are not allowed to use this penalty, only excommunication. Yet, in both cases, the individual who does not "listen," and is contumate or contemptuous, receives the severest form of discipline.

Jesus gives a second requirement for continuity in the Biblical Church covenant. He says, "To him who overcomes" (Rev. 2:7). "Overcome" is a word indicating dominion. The covenant is never

---

5. Jay Adams, *The Christian Counselor's Manual* (Grand Rapids: Baker, 1973), p. 54.

static: It is always either growing or dying. I have found that the biggest trouble-makers in the Church are those who *never do anything constructive*. They are not taking dominion. Consequently, they end up out-of-sorts with the whole congregation, and either leave or find themselves being disciplined. One either dominates for Christ, or he is dominated.

The Two Tables

There is no neutrality, no safety zone between dominion and being dominated. The Apostle Paul summarizes continuity in terms of two tables. He says,

> You cannot drink the cup of the Lord and the cup of demons; you cannot partake of the table of the Lord and the table of demons (I Cor. 10:21).

There are only two tables in the world. Man either eats Christ's meal or he eats Satan's. Christ's meal is a covenant of life. Satan's is a covenant of death. Christ's meal is focused in the Lord's Supper. This table, as we have said time and again, is not magical. Grace is not infused by the elements themselves. The *act itself* of eating communion with God's people is covenant renewal.

But what of the other table, the table of demons? Where is it? Paul leads us to believe that man *inescapably* eats with the devil if he does not eat with Christ. Everything he does becomes a rite of covenant renewal with the devil: politics, science, education, athletics, and so forth. Every activity of the unbeliever, or perhaps the professed believer who never communes, takes on a satanic sacramental character. Yes, the devil's table becomes a life apart from Christ.

Self-conscious pagans speak of their work in a sacramental way. Poltics, art, economics, or whatever are viewed as somehow infusing the world with life. They become "sacraments." If Christ's table is not the answer, something else is perceived as the source of life. Often, a meal is connected with it. Consider a simple example: modern athletics. Remember, athletics in the ancient world, particularly the Olympic Games, became a way of determining who was a god. Today, there is almost always a superstitious ritual before the game. Athletes, who don't go to church on Sunday, have their last special meal before the big game. This is not satanic in and of itself. But it merely points to the fact that man has to find a substitute communion. If the last meal with the athletes is a substitute for Christ's table, it is demonic. If anything is a substitute sacrament, it is demonic.

There are only two tables in the world. One leads to life and the other to death. There is no neutrality. *No man can keep a chair at both tables.* Judas was a man who tried to have a chair at both tables. He was disinherited and cast out. The modern Church needs to learn from Judas. Its covenant binds it to Christ. Yet, it is possible to lose the "lampstand." It can only be lost by trying to eat at two tables at the same time! When this happens, the legitimate become the illegitimate.

Conclusion

The Biblical Church covenant has all five of the parts of the Deuteronomic covenant. Only by applying them can real dominion be taken inside the Church. It almost sounds preposterous to speak of taking dominion in the Church. Most churches, however, are struggling with their own internal battles. "Judgment begins at the house of God" (I Pet. 4:17). Whatever happens in civilization-at-large is only a reflection of what is going on in the Church. Dominion begins at home. Dominion begins in the Church. Until it does, it will never happen in the State!

11

THE HISTORICAL CHURCH COVENANT

Like the family, the Church has a covenantal character to it. Church covenants are expressed in many forms. Most of them are too long to be reproduced in this chapter. But there is one place to find the essence of a Church covenant: in *membership and baptismal vows*.

The following sample is from the baptismal vows of the Episcopalian Church and dates back several centuries, parts of it all the way back to the early Church. They date from a period in which the Episcopalian Church was more orthodox than at present, although much renewal is presently in progress in various Episcopal Church spin-off congregations and movements. These vows represent an excellent summary of a Church covenant. They are the baptismal vows taken at the point of Church membership.

Church Covenant
Baptismal and Membership Vows

Minister: Dost thou renounce the devil and all his works, the vain pomp and glory of the world, with all covetous desires of the same, and the sinful desires of the flesh, so that thou wilt not follow, nor be led by them?

Answer: I renounce them all; and, by God's help, will endeavor not to follow, nor be led by them.

Minister: Dost thou believe in Jesus Christ, the Son of the Living God?

Answer: I do.

Minister: Dost thou accept him, and desire to follow him as thy Savior and Lord?

Answer: I do.

Minister: Dost thou believe all the Articles of the Christian Faith, as contained in the Apostles' Creed?

Answer: I do.

Minister: Wilt thou be baptized in this Faith?

Answer: That is my desire.

Minister: Wilt thou then obediently keep God's holy will and commandments, and walk in the same all the days of thy life?

Answer: I will, by God's help.

In this chapter, I want to use the same five-fold structure of the covenant. The basic themes are found.

True Transcendence

Dost thou accept him, and desire to follow him as thy Savior and Lord?

The church covenant is *transcendent*. The candidate confesses Christ as Savior and *Lord*. God's sovereignty is part of confessing Christ. In Peter's famous sermon at Pentecost, he said, "Therefore let all the house of Israel know for certain that God has made Him both Lord and Christ—this Jesus Whom you crucified" (Acts 2:36). The word "Lord" means Sovereign. There is no "chance" or "contingency" in God's program. If God is not sovereign, then man or something else is. If He is not 100% sovereign, then God is not God. And this is the whole point. To confess Christ as God means Christ is sovereign, the controller of all things.

The transcendent character of the Church covenant means the Church is not infallible. This was Martin Luther's great point. He argued that the Bible is the "depository of truth." The Roman Catholic Church had held that the *Church itself* is the depository. What is the difference? If the Church is the depository of truth, then its interpretations of the Bible are infallible and cannot be contradicted. This places man above the Bible and confuses revelation with interpretation. It also creates a monopoly of interpretation.

The covenant also has an *immanent* sense. God is not only transcendent, but He is also present: at baptism. These vows are simultaneously an entrance into the Kingdom of God and the Church. Christ made this kind of association when he spoke to Peter. He said,

And I also say to you that you are Peter, and upon this rock [Christ] I will build My Church; and the gates of Hades shall not overpower it. I will give you the keys of the kingdom of heaven; and whatever you shall bind on earth shall be bound in heaven, and whatever you shall loose on earth shall be loosed in heaven (Matt. 16:18-19).

Christ's words give unusual authority to the Church. He brings together His presence and this particular institution (Matt. 28:18). Christ is *with* the Church. To go against the Church is to go against Christ. Saul of Tarsus found this out when he persecuted the Church. Christ stopped him on the road to Damascus, and He said, "Saul, Saul, why are you persecuting *Me*" (Acts 9:4). So, we must make a distinction between Christ and the Church, but we must also be careful not to separate Christ's presence from it. The Church is Christ's priesthood that represents Him on earth.

Hierarchy

Wilt thou be baptized in this faith?

The church is the agent that baptizes "into the faith." As such, the church is by definition a hierarchy, meaning authority. There can be no law without some kind of institutional authority to apply it. Holiness cannot take place in a vacuum. It can only come about in the context of a lawfully constituted authority. To say one is committed to Christ, therefore, and not be a member of a local Church, is a contradiction to his baptism. It is a contradiction to the Christian faith.

Why? Everyone should be accountable. If one does not have real accountability to the Body of Christ, then he is symbolically and covenantally *autonomous*. Not only is this extremely dangerous to one's spiritual health, but it implicitly destroys the Church. To be accountable means to be in submission to the Church, and this means that one can be pursued in a process of discipline, as in Matthew 18:15. If one is not a member of a Church, then he cannot be disciplined. He cannot be *excommunicated*. How can a person be excommunicated from something that he is not a member of?

Here is the real practical value of a church *roll*. There is a Church roll in *heaven* (Rev. 13:8; 17:8). If the Church has power to bind and loose on earth, and if this implements what has already been established in heaven, then a church roll is a picture of the roll in heaven. Jesus' words quoted above indicate this. A church roll is a simple way to maintain accountability. Just because churches abuse their rolls does not remove the fact that a roll is necessary to accomplish true discipline. *The abuse does not negate the use.*

Not only should the members be accountable, but so should the officers. The Biblical system is that *everyone* is accountable. Although it takes more to bring a charge against an elder, he should still be accountable to a system of discipline. No one should be above the law.

I began this section saying that members are to obey their leaders. Does this mean the leaders can tell members to do "anything"? This brings us to the next section.

Ethics

Wilt thou then obediently keep God's holy will and commandments?

The covenant is *ethical*. The baptismal candidate commits to the Lord's "will and commandments." These are the stipulations and laws of the Bible. The elders and/or officers may not ask the people to do anything and everything. They may only command what is stated in the Bible. An elder, for example, may not tell his congregation that it may not ride bicycles. He does not have authority to do so because the Bible does not forbid such activity. His power is limited to the ethical, and only the ethics expressed in the Bible. When it comes to the commandments of the Bible, however, the officers have special authority to apply them.

The Church covenant is *ethical* in character. It is not magical. The will of God is expressly laid out in the Bible. Any time the will of the Lord is sought, the ethical character of the covenant should be kept in mind. We use our same "totem pole" diagram.

CHAIN OF BEING VIEW OF CHURCH

GOD

PRIEST
(POSSESSES BEING OF
GOD IN HIS PERSON)

CHURCH VIEWED AS
CENTER OF SOCIETY

FAMILY

OTHER INSTITUTIONS
HAVE LESS BEING. THEY
MUST GO THROUGH
THE PRIEST TO
GET TO GOD.

STATE
NON BEING
(OUTSIDE OF CHURCH
AND ITS REPRESENTATIVE
PRIESTS)

In this particular diagram, I have placed the elder, or officer, in the "middle" position. Actually, this is a picture of the Roman Catholic Church. Its officers are believed to be "infused" with the special "being" of God. There is a connection between the "Being" of God and the "being" of man. It is not based on an ethical relationship, the covenant. The "bond" is *magical*. In the Roman Catholic Church, it is believed that this "being" of God is transferred to communion. It even physically changes the substance of the bread and the wine into Jesus (*transubstantiation*).

The Bible teaches that the officers do represent and even speak for the people. They speak for God to the people. But they do not have part of God in them. They are distinct from Him. Consequently, they do not have a "mysterious" relationship to God. Every believer has direct access to Him because every believer shares in the *same* covenant. The members also have a covenantal bond to their leaders. They are responsible to obey them, but these men have limits on their powers and abilities because they are not God. If a leader is connected to God in his "being," then he shares in Divinity. This makes him the *same as* God! He can speak as God! Only the Word of God, the Bible, speaks in this authoritative manner. The "words" of the preacher are different. The Word of God should be distinguished from his "personal" opinions.

These are some of the matters effected by an ethical understanding of the covenant. It places authority and leadership in the proper light. It gives leadership a high place of authority, but not so high that it becomes "Godlike."

Sanctions

Dost thou renounce the devil?

The candidate passes judgment on the devil. As he judges, however, so is he judged. Should he ever leave the covenant, all that he has judged will judge him. Satan, the world, and the flesh always wait for the candidate to fall, so that they can return the judgment by killing him.

Also, the questions preceded *baptism*. Christian baptism identifies one with Christ's baptism. The Gospel of Mark asks us:

"Are you able to drink the cup that I drink, or to be baptized with the baptism with which I am baptized?" And they said to Him, "We are able." And Jesus said to them, "The cup that I drink you shall drink; and you shall be baptized with the baptism with which I am baptized" (Mark 10:38-39).

The "cup" and "baptism" that belonged to Christ were manifested in His death on the Cross. Baptism unites a person with this death so that *the recipient enters a symbolic death*. This death is not merely a symbol, however; it is covenantal. In saving a person, God legally declares the "old man" dead; He legally declares the regenerate person a new creature. Baptism is the Church's institutional *ratification of what God has declared*. This places a seal on the man's faith, bringing him under the covenant's sanctions of cursing and blessing. This is judgment. It begins the Christian walk. Judgment is a way of life for a church member.

Christians do not normally think of the Church as a place of *judgment*. In fact, some "Christians" pride themselves in telling other Christians not "to judge one another." But the Apostle Paul says Christians are the "judges" of the world (I Cor. 6:2-3). Christians are supposed to judge. They judge because they have met judgment in Christ and are part of bringing that judgment to the rest of the world.

What the "judge not" passage in Matthew 7:1 says is that we are not to judge with judgment that we do not want to receive.

> Do not judge lest you be judged. For in the way you judge, you will be judged; and by your standard of measure, it will be measured to you (Matt. 7:1-2).

This means that we *are* supposed to judge with the judgment we *want* to receive: God's righteous judgment. Thus, if we want to be judged fairly, we must judge fairly. If we choose not to judge, then we will be judged by some other judgment. There is no neutrality possible: not giving judgment is the same as providing a sanction for what is going on. When the old woman is mugged by some hoodlum and has her purse stolen, the jury must decide: Is the hoodlum guilty or innocent? The jury *must* judge. To seek to avoid making a judgment grants the hoodlum the purse. To say nothing in the face of evil is to *condone* evil institutionally. This is precisely what the "judge not" antinomians are doing: condoning evil in every area of life.

Since there are *dual sanctions* to the covenant, blessing and cursing, there are two kinds of judgment that God brings. There is judgment unto life and judgment unto death. Christians are judged to *life*. But they are still *judged*. Christians are not afraid to face judgment. The whole point of facing Christ is that there is no fear in facing other judgments. What "other" judgments can be worse than facing Christ? "And do not fear those who kill the body, but are unable to kill the soul; but rather fear Him who is able to destroy both soul and body in hell" (Matt. 10:28). When the new member answered the questions above, he was entering the judgment of Christ. It was believed that resurrection would occur. This was only the beginning.

During his life, the church member will face the judgment of the Word of God many times over, each time to be resurrected to newer life. And, in the end, he will pass through God's fiery Judgment Day to the final Resurrection. This is a Church covenant that is *judicial*.

Continuity

Dost thou believe in the Articles of the Christian faith, as contained in the Apostles' Creed?

Perhaps the reader notices that one of the questions is, "Dost thou believe in the Articles of the Christian faith, as contained in the Apostles' Creed?" This question concerns *legitimacy*. The Apostles' Creed is made part of the church covenant because it legitimatizes church membership.

The Apostles' Creed

I believe in God the Father Almighty, maker of heaven and earth;

And in Jesus Christ, his only Son, our Lord, who was conceived by the Holy Ghost, born of the Virgin Mary, suffered under Pontius Pilate, was crucified, dead, and buried: he descended into hell; the third day he rose again from the dead; he ascended into heaven, and sitteth on the right hand of God the Father Almighty, from thence he shall come to judge the quick and the dead.

I believe in the Holy Ghost; the holy catholic (universal) church; the communion of saints; the forgiveness of sins; the resurrection of the body; and the life everlasting. Amen.

The Apostles' Creed is one of the earliest confessions of the historic Christian Church. It is a *creed*. A creed is simply what the Church believes. It should be based on the Bible. If the statement is true to Scripture, it is a confession of *faith*. The issue is not whether a person has a creed — everyone does — but "Does the creed conform to the Word of God?"

Creeds are inescapable. There is no such thing as a "creedless" person or church. The word itself comes from the Latin "credo" and means "I believe." Everyone has an interpretation of the Bible, and every church has a creed. Creeds can be found in such places as doctrinal statements, hymns, sunday school material, and the preacher's sermons. A church may not actually say, "This is where our creed is located," but these are the places where one finds out what a church "believes."

When a church professes to have no creed, it has opened itself up to both tyranny and liberalism. Tyranny, because the preacher or controlling group can say whatever he or they want, interpreting the Bible any way that furthers the interests of the controllers. It becomes difficult for anyone outside the inner circle to dislodge them. The struggles for control over the Church become power struggles, and liberals (who profess no creeds) are usually better at political infighting than orthodox Christians are. The liberal's religion is power religion: salvation by power, salvation by law. He lives by politics and Roberts Rules of Order; the Christian lives by the Bible and the Holy Spirit. Creedless churches, if they are systematic in their confession of creedlessness, have opened themselves to those who profess the error of relativism and who exercise authoritarian power.

Why is this ancient confession important today? It is *the* statement of the faith of the historic Church. All of the basic "fundamentals" are expressed: the Trinity, Creation, the Deity of Christ, the historic death and resurrection of Christ, His bodily return and judgment of the world, baptism, forgiveness, and the Church. If a person does not believe these, he is not a Christian. If a church is not willing to confess these points, it is not part of the historic faith.

So what? What is so important about being part of the historic church? The Church is bigger than any one local church, and bigger than the present. It grows out of the past and into the future. It had a Founder; it has members; it will have *heirs*. The legitimate ones are those who profess the "true" Christian faith. Paul says:

If anyone advocates a different *doctrine*, and does not agree with *sound words*, those of our Lord Jesus Christ, and with the *doctrine* conforming to all godliness, he is conceited and understands nothing (I Tim. 6:3-4).

To submit to the historic confessions of the Church is to submit to the "doctrine." Here is how the early Church defeated the cults. The battle the modern Church is facing cannot be won without *sound doctrine*. The modern Church will have to regain a sense of history, particularly its own. It will have to be legitimatized by joining the confession of the Church of *all ages*. The very point of joining the *Church* is to join not just a *local* church, but the Church that has gone on for centuries. So, the Church covenant reflects a statement of who qualifies to be a legitimate heir of the faith.

This is the final aspect of covenant. For a covenant to be transferred, the heirs have to be legitimate. The true covenant does not get handed down to "bastards." To legitimatize the faith on the basis of doctrine and practice means there must be some kind of *discipline*. It is not enough to just join the Church, and then live like "hell." Take the modernist churches as an example. They no longer believe in the fundamentals of the faith; they have denied their confession. So, their confession *condemns* them. There is no escape from the covenant: blessing or cursing. Any church that professes a Christian creed which its members in fact do not believe has become a spiritual bastard. So has any denomination that denies the *faith* that has been handed down from the Apostles.

But we should make one final point about legitimacy. Although the "mainline" churches have all but collapsed theologically, they have survived institutionally for centuries. How? It is the issue of legitimacy. If one is a legitimate heir of the Christian faith, then he will perpetuate the faith one more generation. Here is where confessionalism comes in. If people do not know what it is they are supposed to transfer to the next generation, then the faith will be lost in that particular church.

This is why the confessional churches have been the biggest, strongest, and most influential churches in history. To be sure, some of them are falling by the wayside, because they have illegitimated themselves by denying the historic faith. So it is fine to criticize an apostate church. But the critic needs to ask, "Am I producing a church that will even rise to the heights of influence of the church I'm criticizing?" Any church that wants to perpetuate itself over the ages, and even climb to the former glory of such churches as the Episcopalian Church, will have to be confessional.

Conclusion

We have examined a church covenant. There is no doubt that it is a *covenant*. It fits the qualifications: true transcendence, hierarchy, ethics, sanctions, and continuity. Not all church covenants are this complete. I have tried to take the "best" example that I could find. But even a defective covenant would prove my point. What is it? All arrangements between groups of people are based on some sort of covenantal model: contracts, etc. To the extent their covenant conforms to the prototype of all covenants, the Biblical covenant, the bond they established will be successful. So, even a bad covenant proves the covenantal nature of man's dealings.

Family and Church follow the pattern of the covenant. What about the State? Is there a Biblical guide to determine whether it, too, should be organized by the covenant? Are there any historic examples? Let us begin with the Biblical and then make our way to the historical.

12

THE BIBLICAL STATE COVENANT

Everything belongs to Christ and should be governed by His Word. The State is no exception, for it is one of God's three institutional monopolies, governed by covenant. To modern ears, this may sound like a strange note. We should keep in mind at the outset of this chapter, however, one very fundamental presupposition of the Bible. *There is no freedom apart from Jesus Christ.* Jesus said, "The *Son* shall make you *free*" (John 8:36). There is no freedom in the family apart from Christ. There is no freedom in the Church apart from Christ. There is no freedom in the *State* apart from Christ. If we believe in Christ, this must be our basic presupposition. There cannot be freedom outside of the Lord of lords. Unless there is a *Christocracy*, society ends up in some kind of bondage.

Modern man, to the contrary, has attempted to define liberty without the Son of God. Secularized freedom has become the grand political delusion, foisted on the people of the West by a demonized public educational system. This has become the system's overarching (should I say, "under-arching") purpose: to indoctrinate a civilization founded on a *sacred* view of liberty to believe the lie that a *secular* view has been the key to its success. This is a great deception. This will be the ruin of every liberty as we know it. Why? *Freedom apart from Christ is impossible.*

Beginning with this presupposition, so basic to the Christian faith, let us turn our attention to the final sphere of society, and examine how to take dominion. Again we shall see that the State belongs to God, and it too is a covenant.

Let every person be in subjection to the governing authorities. For there is no authority except from God, and those which exist are established by God. Therefore he who resists authority has opposed the ordinance of God; and they who have opposed will receive condemnation upon themselves. For rulers are not a cause of fear for good behavior, but for evil. Do you want to have no fear of authority? Do what is good, and you will have

177

praise from the same; for it is a minister of God to you for good. But if you do what is evil, be afraid; for it does not bear the sword for nothing; for it is a minister of God, an avenger who brings wrath upon the one who practices evil. Wherefore it is necessary to be in subjection, not only because of wrath, but also for conscience' sake. For because of this you also pay taxes, for rulers are servants of God, devoting themselves to this very thing. Render to all what is due them: tax to whom tax is due; custom to whom custom; fear to whom fear; honor to whom honor (Rom. 13:1-7).

True Transcendence

Paul argues that magistrates are "ministers of God" (Rom. 13:4). In the realm of the State, we find the same emphasis that we did in the Church. The transcendent character of the covenant in the civil realm is God, not the State itself. The State is created by God; it is a "Divine" institution. But, it is carefully distinguished from God by the designation, "minister." If one ignores either, he falls off a dangerous precipice on the right or left side of the truth.

The State should not be allowed to become "divinized" or a new "god." The Puritans believed that if transcendence is placed in the State, then this sphere becomes "absolutized": the new "priesthood." All through history, pagan cultures have tended to be statist, believing in some kind of political salvation. One of many examples in the Bible is Darius, King of Babylon. He set up "Emperor worship," asking everyone in the land to bow down and worship him (Dan. 6:7). Daniel would not, and was thrown into the "lion's den" (Dan. 6:16-24).

On the other hand, the State is created by God, and thus, as an "institution," cannot be the enemy of the Church (Rom. 13:1). Does this contradict what I just said? No. We should be careful to distinguish "evil men" who hold office from the "institution" itself. Paul was reminding Christians of this fact at a time when Nero was Caesar of Rome. If Christians think the enemy is the State, they end up involved in "anarchical" activity that is thwarted by God, because they are opposing the institution that He made.

The anarchist argues along the lines of *nominalism*. He says that the State does not really exist; what we *call* the State is simply groups of people acting as individuals for certain purposes. It is not responsible to God as a collective entity, for it has no separate reality. It is not a true representative of the citizens; rather, certain people speak on behalf of the citizens, despite the fact that citizens cannot delegate power to any independent organization.

The statist argues along the lines of *realism*. He says the State has an existence totally independent of the people who participate in it. No one has individual rights (legal immunities) from the State, for the State is all-encompassing.

The Biblical answer is the only alternative to both nominalism (anarchism) and realism (statism). The State is a representative collective that can and is judged by God in history. The kingdoms of this world are judged by God throughout history. Kings are responsible before God, not just as individuals, but as lawful civil representatives of whole populations.

Thus, the State is not a "deity" but a "Divine institution" set up by God. The Lord's transcendence makes magistrates His "ministers" of justice. If they do not act as His representatives, then *He* will bring them down.

Hierarchy

Paul says, "He who resists authority has opposed the ordinance of God" (Rom. 13:2). The original Greek has an interesting play on words. The words for "resist" and "ordinance" have the same Greek root word (*tasso*), meaning "order." So, we could paraphrase the verse: "The one who stands against the *order* of authority has opposed the *order* of God." The State is therefore part of *God's* hierarchy, and is not a "social contract" formulated by *men*.

Biblical hierarchy draws the connection between God's judgment and history. In Deuteronomy and the other covenants, God sets up human authorities to represent Himself. The Lord *mediates His judgment* through these appointed officers. Romans 13 clearly establishes the same relationship. The civil "ministers of God" wield *His* "sword"; His judgment is carried out through them. They are not to act on their own. Moreover, because magistrates minister God's judgment, society sees visible Divine consequences to evil acts when the civil servants carry out the Lord's justice. Thus, civil magistrates are "authorities" set up by God. To oppose them is to oppose God!

Does this mean, however, that there is never a place for opposing evil and corruption in the State? No. Paul says, "Submit to the governing *authorities*" (Rom. 13:1). Notice that the "authorities" are plural, meaning there is always more than one lawful authority in the State, and more than one lawful civil government in society as a whole. There are also rival governments: Family and Church. This opens the possibility that when one State authority does wrong, a person should be able to appeal this decision, thereby gaining lawful support in opposing him, and still be in submission to other State authorities, thereby enabling him to "resist" the State without "resisting" God's authority.

Historically, this has been called the doctrine of the "lesser magistrate."[1] It is also sometimes called the doctrine of *interposition*. George Washington was a good example. He was troubled over the Romans 13:1ff. passage, when asked to lead the army of the Continental Congress against England. How could he have been involved in a "revolution" and still obey Romans 13? The first American Revolution was not a revolt of "individuals." "Lesser magistrates" (Continental Congress) were raised up, asserting that they were the true representatives of God and the people. So, when Washington accepted the call, he was not opposing the State so much as he was obeying the true State.

This view of hierarchy avoids rebellion, yet it protects the hierarchy of God's chain of command, thereby allowing God's people to oppose wickedness among its leaders without becoming rebellious in heart. The State is not absolutized, nor is it undermined. It can be called into question for unrighteousness.

Ethics

The ethics section of the covenant speaks of the fulfillment of righteousness. How is righteousness fulfilled in the State? What is its standard? I have already hinted at several points that *natural law* is the unbiblical statist measure of righteousness. We shall consider this standard in greater detail in a moment. But Paul says that "magistrates" are "ministers of *God*," "avenging" *Him* (Rom. 13:4).

Magistrates are to rule by "God's Law." If they are to "avenge" His wrath, by what other law could they rule? But Paul's use in Romans of the "wrath of God" (*orgē theou*) makes a key connection between the Deuteronomic "ethics" section and New Testament civil law. Since this is what the magistrate "avenges" (13:4), by studying it in Romans we can arrive at an answer to the question, "By what law should the magistrates rule?"

Early in the book, Paul says, "For the *wrath of God* (*orgē theou*) is

---

1. Samuel Rutherford, *Lex, Rex* (The Law and The Prince) (Harrisonburg, Virginia: Sprinkle Press, 1980). This valuable reprint of Rutherford's 1584 "classic" outlines the doctrine of the "lesser magistrate."

revealed from heaven against all ungodliness and unrighteousness of men" (Rom. 1:18). Paul then proceeds to elaborate on what the "wrath of God is revealed against." He concludes the passage, lest there be any doubt in the reader's mind, that "those who practice such things [homosexuality, murder, etc., 1:21ff.] are *worthy of death*" (Rom. 1:32). Paul's use of "worthy of death" is helpful because this is an identical phrase that comes out of the Hebrew and Septuagint translations of Deuteronomy (Deut. 17:6, 19:6, 21:22, 22:23). Here is the vital connection between the phrase "avenger of God's wrath" and the Law of God. *All* magistrates' standards should be God's law.

What about *unbelieving* magistrates over unbelieving nations? Should they rule and be ruled by God's law? Yes, they should. Nero was Caesar at the time of the writing of Romans — as evil a ruler who ever lived, at least until the twentieth century's totalitarian tyrants. Furthermore, Paul does not make the believing — non-believing distinction in Romans 13. He says, "There is no authority except from God" (Rom. 13:1). All men are bound by God's covenantal standard. Is not this Paul's point in Romans 1:18ff.?

His argument is simple. All men have sinned before God's righteous standard. Since all men are accountable, all need a Savior. If they are not accountable, then they don't need a Savior! Someone who wants to argue that the "unbeliever" is not bound by God's covenantal standard ultimately has no basis for presenting the Gospel to the unbeliever. If he is not accountable in the area of civil rule, then he has found a loophole in the gospel, an area of neutrality, a "King's X" from God. He therefore does not need the Christ of the Bible.

The New Testament clearly teaches that civil authorities are supposed to rule by the Bible. Their purpose is ethical. If their function is not ethical, then it becomes manipulative. For example, the Bible makes no provision for "prisons," with the exception of holding cells and cities of refuge for cases of manslaughter (Nu. 35:9-15). In modern society, many of those who would be put to death under Biblical law not only go unpunished but are fed and housed by the taxes of those on the "outside." The innocent pay for the crimes of the guilty.

Neutral Natural Law

The concept of natural law was first developed by the Stoic philosophers of the late classical Greek period. The Greek city-states had collapsed. Alexander the Great had created an empire, but in 322 B.C., he died. His empire then fragmented into four sections shortly thereafter. What was to become of Greek culture? It was a State-worshipping culture. Salvation and social order were exclusively political. But without a coherent political order, what would become of classical culture?

The Stoics created an answer: the doctrine of natural law. They argued that there is a universal law structure, and that all rational men can apprehend it. This universal law was said to be the basis of universal humanity, and therefore the basis of a universal culture. The only trouble was (and is), they could provide no evidence that such a universal legal order exists, or that rational minds will universally agree about what this legal order is. In fact, self-proclaimed rational men have argued ever since about reason, "right" reason, and natural law "properly understood." Roman philosophers later adopted Stoic philosophy and used the idea of natural law to justify the Roman Empire.

What was fundamental to Stoic theology was its denial of the Creator/creature distinction. The Stoics held to a humanistic theory of a common ground between man and God. The Roman philosopher Epictetus had been a student of Seneca's, who also taught the Emperor Nero. Nero rewarded Seneca by having him executed in A.D. 65. Epictetus wrote:

> When a man has learnt to understand the government of the universe and has realized that there is nothing so great or sovereign or all-inclusive as this frame of things wherein *man and God are united* . . . why should he not call himself a *citizen of the universe* and a *son of God*?[2]

It was the collapse of classical religion, and the attendant collapse of classical philosophy, which led to the collapse of the Roman Empire, which in turn opened the door historically to the triumph of Christian religion and philosophy.[3] Any attempt to save Western civilization by means of a revival of classical philosophy is suicidal. It is interesting that the last great Stoic philosopher, the Emperor Marcus Aurelius, was a persecutor of the Church. Justin Martyr died under his reign.

---

2. Epictetus, *Discourses*, I, ix (trans. P. E. Matheson; cited by Sheldon Wolin, *Politics and Vision: Continuity and Innovation in Western Political Thought*) (Boston: Little, Brown, 1960), p. 80. Emphasis added.

3. Charles Norris Cochrane, *Christianity and Classical Culture: A Study in Thought and Action from Augustus to Augustine* (New York: Oxford University Press, [1944] 1957).

The Bible denies the theological foundation of Stoicism. God and man are distinct, for God is transcendent. Men are created, and they share a common humanity, but they do not share common ethical principles after the Fall of man. The Bible teaches that all men know the *work* of God's law, but not the law itself. Paul, a contemporary of Seneca and Epictetus, writes to the Church at Rome:

> For when Gentiles who do not have the Law do instinctively the things of the Law, these, not having the Law, are a law to themselves, in that they show the *work* of the Law written in their hearts, their conscience bearing witness, and their thoughts alternatively accusing or else defending them (Rom. 2:14-15).

The problem for a theory of universal natural law is this: there is no assurance that unbelievers will *obey* the work of the law written in their hearts. Paul had just argued that all men have the testimony of nature before them that God created it, yet they refuse to worship God, but instead worship creeping things. Covenant-breakers "suppress the truth in unrighteousness" (Rom. 1:18b). Therefore, God gives them over to the lusts of their hearts (Rom. 1:24). They become perverse (Rom. 1:26-28). They are then

> filled with all unrighteousness, wickedness, greed, evil; full of envy, murder, strife, deceit, malice; they are gossips, slanderers, haters of God, insolent, arrogant, boastful, inventors of evil, disobedient to parents, *without understanding*, untrustworthy, unloving, unmerciful; and, although they know the ordinance of God, that those who practice such things are worthy of death, they not only do the same, but also give hearty approval to those who practice them (Rom. 1:29-32).

In short, the work of the law in their hearts only serves to condemn them. It cannot be relied on as a way to save them socially or politically. Classical Greek philosophers believed a lie: that man's ethical problem is essentially a lack of knowledge. Paul's warning is clear: *evil men know what is morally right, and they deliberately commit evil.* God then takes away their understanding. So, the fact that men have the work of the law in their hearts guarantees nothing socially, politically, or any other way. Reason does not save men; God saves men. Reason does not heal a political order; God heals it. Natural law theory serves temporarily as a believable political philosophy only when there is a common religious agreement beforehand. Shatter that religious agreement, and natural law theory becomes useless. Thus, it

never served as an agreed-upon philosophy in politically disintegrat-
ing Greece and religiously polytheistic Rome; it began to be taken
seriously only after Rome had fallen to Christ, when Christianity
provided religious order to Western culture. But the amalgamation
between "Jerusalem" and "Athens" has never successfully overcome
the inherent errors of natural law theory, and in the late-eighteenth
century the alliance began to disintegrate, and after Darwin, natural
law theory collapsed,[4] never to be taken seriously again except by a
handful of conservative humanists and a few Christian intellectuals.

Let us not be misled: natural law theory rests on a self-conscious
belief in the possibility of judicial neutrality. Civil law must be neutral — ethically, politically, and religiously. Civil law must permit
equal time for Satan. There are Christians who believe in neutrality;
they send their children to public schools that rest legally on a doctrine of educational neutrality. There are also Christians who think
abortion should be legal. This belief rests on the belief that killing a
baby and not killing a baby are morally equivalent acts; God is neutral regarding the killing of babies. That such Christians should also
adopt a theory of judicial and political neutrality is understandable.
But what is not easily understandable is that Christians who recognize the absurdity of the myth of neutrality in education and abortion cling to just this doctrine in the area of civil law and politics.
This is a form of what Rushdoony calls intellectual schizophrenia.

It is only the Christian who has the law of God itself written in
his heart, what the author of Hebrews calls a new covenant — the internalization of the old covenant (Heb. 8:7-13). For a Christian to
appeal to a hypothetical universally shared reason with fallen humanity is to argue that the Fall of man did not radically affect man's
mind, including his logic. It is to argue that this unaffected common
logic can overcome the effects of sin. Anyone who believes this needs
to read the works of Cornelius Van Til and R. J. Rushdoony.

The appeal to natural law theory is pagan to the core. It is in
some cases a self-conscious revival of pagan Greek philosophy.[5]
Natural law theory is totally opposed to God's law.[6] Sadly, we find

---

4. R. J. Rushdoony, *The Biblical Philosophy of History* (Nutley, New Jersey: Presbyterian & Reformed, 1969), p. 7. Cf. Gary North, *The Dominion Covenant: Genesis*
(Tyler, Texas: Institute for Christian Economics, 1982), Appendix A.

5. Archie P. Jones, "Apologists of Classical Tyranny: An Introductory Critique of
Straussianism," *Journal of Christian Reconstruction*, V (Summer, 1978); Jones, "Natural
Law and Christian Resistance to Tyranny," *Christianity and Civilization*, 2 (1983).

6. Rex Downie, "Natural Law and God's Law: An Antithesis," *Journal of Christian
Reconstruction*, V (Summer, 1978).

throughout Western history that compromised though well-intentioned Christian philosophers have appealed to this Stoic concept of
natural law in support of some "neutral" system of social and political
order. Thomas Aquinas is the most famous of these scholars, but the
same mistake is common today. Roger Williams appealed to natural
law as the basis of the creation of a supposedly religiously neutral
civil government in the 1630s in New England. This is the appeal of
just about every Christian who refuses to accept Biblical law as the
legal foundation of political order and civil righteousness. The only
alternative to "one law"—whether "natural" or Biblical—is judicial
pluralism, a constant shifting from principle to principle, the rule of
expediency. It is the political theory of polytheism.

Pluralism

When I speak of the Biblical principle of plural authorities,
meaning plural governments, I am not speaking of what the modern
world calls pluralism. What the modern world calls pluralism is antinomianism and relativism: *many moralities*. This ultimately means:
many gods. The Bible calls such a view polytheism or idolatry.

First, the effects of pluralism have been devastating to the Christian faith. Man is a religious creature, meaning he is covenantal.
The word "religion" comes from the Latin *"religo,"* meaning "to bind."
This implies the idea of "covenant." Nigel Lee says, "Religion is the
binding tendency in every man to dedicate himself with his whole
heart either to the true God or to an idol. In this sense all men are religious, for every man dedicates his powers to some or other object of
worship, either consciously or unconsciously."[7] Technically speaking, "religion" is a covenantal "bond"! Man is a "religious" creature in
that he is made of a "covenantal" fabric (Gen. 1:1ff.). Everything he
attempts—spending money, doing scientific research, writing a
book, as well as going to church—is religious in nature. As a matter
of fact, if a person is a non-Christian, his so-called "secular" activity
is just as religious as going to church, because he worships another
"god" through his endeavors, and thereby rejects the Christian Faith.
There is no "neutral" zone.

Thus, "pluralism" is a misnomer and a myth. Pluralism allows all
positions except the Biblical one. This is what we see in our society

---

7. *The Central Significance of Culture*, pp. 121ff. Also, see Henry Van Til, *Calvinistic
Concept of Culture* (Grand Rapids: Baker, 1959).

today. In the name of pluralism, the Church is being suppressed. Advocates of pluralism know continuity of Christian faith will destroy their idolatrous society. So they have implemented a humanistic "theocracy" in the name of pluralism.

Theocracy is inescapable (*theos* = God; *kratos* = rule). All men have a view of God and their view always determines how they run society. As David Chilton says,

> The fact is that all law is "religious." All law is based on some ultimate standard of morality and ethics. Every system is founded on the ultimate value of that system, and that ultimate value is the god of that system. The source of law for society is the god of that society. This means that a *theocracy is inescapable*. All societies are theocracies. The difference is that a society that is not explicitly Christian is a theocracy of a false god.[8]

Consider the ramifications of this one failure to comply with the "ethics" section of the Biblical covenant. In the non-Biblical society there is more incentive to be a criminal. There are no real visible consequences to breaking God's revealed law. Moreover, those who commit crime are rewarded, being subsidized by the innocent. So, the victims have to pay higher and higher taxes as the entire society steadily becomes a civilization of criminals. Eventually, everyone is on the dole: virtually the situation in every modern society. Biblical law, however, determines the specific guide for civil authorities: even the penal sanctions.

Sanctions

Paul says that the magistrate is given the instrument with which to *sanction*: the "sword" (Rom. 13:4). But the power of the sword implies a fundamental Deuteronomic element in the application of God's sanctions: *the self-maledictory oath*. How? Paul says God's wrath is to be brought by the sword on the one who "practices evil" (Rom. 13:4). A man's actions have to be "proven" evil. Hence, he is innocent until proven guilty. What does this process have to do with the self-maledictory oath? Everything.

The self-maledictory oath is the basis of all government. When a person takes the witness stand, he swears by God that he will tell the whole truth. In the United States, he generally swears with his hand on the Bible. In other words, he *covenants*. If he does not tell the

---

8. David Chilton, *Paradise Restored* (Ft. Worth, Texas: Dominion Press, 1985), p. 219.

truth, the self-maledictory oath takes effect. He calls the wrath of God down upon his head. In some cases of perjury, the death penalty could be rendered. At any rate, the oath becomes the *foundation of all judicial processes*. The presumption is that God renders judgment on the witnesses. They are not just testifying before men but the judge of all men. It is not men who even render the judgment but only carry out God's judgment through these witnesses sworn to His allegiance. Thus, if there is no oath, a conviction becomes merely the "common consent" of a group of individuals who want to do another man in. Atheism leads to chaos in the courts and the worst kinds of injustice.

Christianity has always seen the relationship between *oath and judgment*. Justice is lost without the Biblical oath. In 1675, John Taylor, yeoman from Guildford in Surrey, uttered these blasphemous words:

Christ is a whore-master, and religion [Christianity] is a cheat, and profession [of Christianity] is a cloak, and they are both cheats, and all the earth is mine, and I am a king's son, my father sent me hither, and made me a fisherman to take vipers, and I neither fear God, devil, nor man, and I am a younger brother to Christ, an angel of God and no man fears God but an hypocrite, Christ is a bastard, god damn and confound all your gods, Christ is the whore's master.[9]

He was charged with "blasphemy" and taken to the House of Lords for trial. After considerable deliberation, he was then handed over to the common-law courts. Never before had they been given jurisdiction over blasphemy. In 1676, however, Taylor was taken before the greatest jurist of the day, Chief Justice Matthew Hale. Hale found him guilty and said,

And . . . such kind of wicked blasphemous words were not only an offence to God and religion, but a crime against the laws, State and Government, and therefore punishable in this Court. For to say, religion is a cheat, is to dissolve all those obligations whereby the civil societies are preserved, and that Christianity is parcel of the laws of England; and therefore to reproach the Christian religion is to speak in subversion of the law.[10]

---

9. *Journals of the House of Lords*, XII, 688, May 11, 1675; 691, May 14; and 700-1, May 20. Cited in Leonard W. Levy, *Treason Against God* (New York: Schocken, 1981), pp. 312-314.

10. *Ibid.*, Rex v. Taylor, 3 Keble 607, 621.

Abuse of God's name destroys any notion of true justice. It destroys the whole covenantal fabric of civilization. Here is the importance of the oath. So, without explicitly mentioning the oath, Paul draws greater attention to its necessity. His comments imply the maledictory oath in determining guilt. Then the application of the sword becomes part of the process of creating continuity and discontinuity.

The magistrate is involved in the removal of those who practice evil by means of the sword. The wicked are supposed to experience discontinuity in their lives. The righteous maintain social continuity. But what are the "evil practices" in the New Covenant Age for which a person can receive the sword? The rationale for answering this question is the same as the "ethics" section. By examining what the "wrath of God" is poured out against in Romans 1:18ff., we can begin to see what the magistrate "avenges" in Romans 13:1ff.

Paul's list at the end of Romans 1 is very similar to the capital offenses of the Old Testament. His summary includes idolatry, homosexuality, murder, and teenage incorrigibility to name only a few (Rom. 1:29-31). All of these offenses are capital crimes in the Old Testament. Of course, even in the Old Testament the death penalty is the *maximum and not necessarily the mandatory* penalty.[11] The exception is murder because the only appropriate restitution would be to render a "life for a life." The "maximum, not mandatory" principle would also apply in the New Testament.

As we shall see below, Paul includes several "less significant" offenses in the "worthy of death" category: untrustworthy, unloving, deceitful, boastful. Thus, the New Covenant view of the State is not to the end that every nation would become another "Hebrew Republic." There are New Testament similarities and dissimilarities between Old and New Testament sanctions that should be noted.

Old and New Testaments

First, Paul's Romans 1:18-32 language indicates that New Testament penal sanctions are *similar to the Old Testament*. The vast major-

---

11. Jordan, *The Law of the Covenant*, pp. 148ff. Rev. Jordan makes the point that adultery did not always require the death penalty by referring to Joseph and Mary. He quotes the Bible text, "Joseph, being a *just* man . . . was minded to put her [Mary] away privately" (Matt. 1:19). Joseph could privately put away (divorce) Mary since she was pregnant and "apparently" had committed adultery. Due to the fact that this option was open to Joseph, Jordan concludes that the death penalty was "maximum but not mandatory." This could also explain why David was not put to death after his sin with Bathsheba.

ity of Old Testament penalties should still be instituted. As earlier sections of this book indicate, the proper hermeneutic for determining what carries over into the New Testament is the principle: continue what is not changed in the New Testament. This would apply to the penal sanctions of the Old Testament. The death penalty offenses that should be extended into the New Testament are witchcraft (Deut. 18:10-11), idolatry (Deut. 13:10), murder (Gen. 9:6), blasphemy (Lev. 24:11-23), homosexuality (Lev. 18:22-29), bestiality (Lev. 18:23), rape (Deut. 22:25-27), adultery (Lev. 20:10), incest (Lev. 20:14), incorrigibility of teenagers (Deut. 21:18-20), kidnapping (Exod. 21:16), and some instances of perjury (Deut. 19:19-20).

Second, the New Testament penal sanctions are *dissimilar to the Old Testament*. In some instances they can be more lenient. After the shift from wrath to grace in history, "reformability" has greater possibility. In the Old Covenant, before redemption comes in history, the negative influence of wickedness is so great that it cannot be overcome. It would seem that virtually all of the "bad elements" of society would have had to be killed for this reason. But in the New Covenant, the kingdom of God has a positive effect on wickedness. Some of the wicked—indeed many more than could have been in the Old Covenant—can be restored. We discover that former homosexuals, for example, are in the Church of Corinth (I Cor. 6:11). No death penalty is called for. Thus, we see how Paul can speak of the similarity of Old Testament sanctions in Romans 1, and yet maintain the possibility that not every convicted homosexual would have to be put to death according to I Corinthians 6. In the New Covenant Age, only the "unreformable" element would be put to death.

In some instances, however, the New Covenant sanctions are stricter than the Old Testament. Paul allows in Romans 1:30-31 for other offenses that can draw the death penalty: arrogance, unmerciful, strife and others. Why does the New Testament speak this way? Some of these offenses have historical precedent. For example, God put Korah and family to death because they caused "strife" (cf. Rom. 1:29 & Nu. 16:1-50). But at first glance, it might not seem possible to commit an offense tied to "arrogance" (Rom. 1:30). Modern society, however, presents some situations where the death penalty would be appropriate. For example, as recently as Hitler's reign of terror, we find people committing horrible atrocities in the name of "Super-race doctrine." Their racial "arrogance" involved such things as frontal lobotomies on Jews. According to Paul's language, therefore, a doctor who performs surgery for such purposes could be put to death.

Therefore, the New Covenant application of penal sanctions is both similar and dissimilar to the Old Testament. The historic shift from wrath to grace in Jesus Christ allows for a much fuller and powerful application, guaranteeing a truer continuity and discontinuity with the covenant.

Continuity

Paul argues that continuity in society should be on the basis of God's law (Rom. 13:3a). What about idolatry? Should the magistrate put idolaters to death? How should this be handled? A variety of explanations have been suggested. In the Massachusetts Bay Colony in the 1630s, Roger Williams proposed that the magistrate should only sanction the last six commandments, avoiding the ones having to do with worship and sabbath keeping. [12] The long-term effect has created a multi-religious society: polytheism. Has this been good, and if it is wrong, how could a Christian civilization be legislated?

To the question, "What have been the long-term effects of Roger Williams' position?" the answer is not encouraging for those serious about the Christian faith. The modern Church lives in the age of a religious cold war. A State that has not formally declared war on the Church "unofficially" strives to put it to death!

---

12. Henry Martyn Dexter, *As to Roger Williams, and his "Banishment" from the Massachusetts Plantation; with a few further words concerning the Baptists, Quakers, and Religious Liberty: A Monograph* (Boston: Congregational Publishing Society, 1876). Roger Williams believed the magistrate was only supposed to enforce the last six commandments and not the first four, avoiding the crime of idolatry. For this, he has been recognized in textbooks as the "Father of Religious Liberty." In *Roger Williams and the Massachusetts Magistrates*, ed. Theodore Greene (Lexington, Massachusetts: D. C. Heath and Co., 1964), pp. 1-21, however, from many of the actual accounts we see that the Puritans, John Cotton of note, believed that Williams's views would eventually lead to religious and political chaos, since politics is always an expression of the religion of the land. Furthermore, Romans 13 does not allow for Williams's position, which allowed some capital offenses and not others. On what basis can such "arbitrary" decisions be made?

For an excellent summary and re-publication of select passages from Dexter, see *Failure of the American Baptist Culture*, ed. James Jordan (Tyler, Texas: Geneva Divinity School Press, 1982), pp. 233-243. The reader will discover that Dexter "demythologizes the many fantasies surrounding the relationship between Williams and the Puritans of Massachusetts Bay. His 146 pages demonstrate thoroughly, for instance, that Williams was not a Baptist when he was in Massachusetts, and thus was not disciplined for being a Baptist by the Puritans; that Williams's views concerning religious liberty were not at issue when he was dealt with by the Puritans; and that Williams was never banished into the wintry wilderness, but chose to leave of his own accord rather than accept comfortable accommodations back to England or move to another colony" (p. 233).

The second question to be considered is: "How could a modern Christian civilization be legislated?" The answer is: *Christian civilization cannot be legislated*. To argue that it can would be a return to the humanist heresy of salvation by law. A civilization reflects its god; its laws reflect that god. We therefore need to ask: "How should the legislation of a State reflect the requirements of the Bible?" How is the State to serve as God's covenantal representative? Can it do so, and also serve as the covenantal representative of Satan?

The classic practical problem concerns the issue of cults. They are obviously detrimental to society, but how can the State deal with them? To do so, it would have to define a "church." To do that would involve distinguishing a true from a false one. To do that would ban whatever has been declared false: hence the end of pluralism. But how could the State even begin to define the true Church? Easy. The Apostles' Creed to which I referred in the last chapter on the Church already has defined it. Any "church" that denies it is a cult. Any "church" that will not confess it is a cult. Any "church" that violates it has become a cult. The great advantage of the Apostles' Creed is that it would allow for a *multi-denominational* society, but not a polytheistic society.

Of course, within this discussion, it should be kept in mind that Biblical religion is the only one that truly allows for religious freedom. The reader may think that the position on pluralism that has been taken in this book would not allow for religious diversity. Actually, Biblical Law allows for "private worship," in this sense a "limited" freedom of religion. The basis is the Old Testament "stranger in the land" concept. As long as he obeys the commandments of God that are legitimately enforceable by civil government, he enjoys the benefits of a Biblical society.

During the Reformation, this concept was used to solve the problem of how Protestant countries should deal with Catholicism. In the Netherlands, for example, post-Reformation Catholics were allowed to continue to hold worship but not to conduct processions down the street. But the Netherlands is one simple example to show how religious diversity could be tolerated. Perhaps in a multi-denominational society, the Apostles' Creed could be used as a minimum standard of orthodoxy.

If the West does not return to some kind of Christian theocracy, the price will be its very civilization. Already in England there are more members of Islam than the Methodist Church. Already in

America, Eastern religions and cults are taking over the thinking of large segments of the public school-educated youth. The outcome will be a complete change of society and governmental structure.

Law as Covenant

As we have seen already in this chapter, oath and covenant form the basis of politics. Civil law reflects civilization, and it can also be used to change people's actions, thereby influencing their thinking. To change the law in any area of life is a *covenantal act*. To take away Christian laws of blasphemy is to point to a change in civilization, and to accelerate this change. The whole judicial system changes, reflecting a change in the god of the civilization. Change the judicial system, and the whole civilization experiences parallel changes.

Humanists know this, but very few Christians have even begun to think about it. Rest assured, however, that modern civil government knows it. At present, civil government in the West wants liberty without the Gospel, morality without Christ, affluence without covenant. It is willing to do anything, including the forfeiture of its own lands to Mohammedans, except submit its nation to Christ. Civil leadership is even willing to subsidize polytheism.

False Continuity

More than one scholar has described the American public (government) school system as the nation's only established church. It has a self-certified priesthood, and graduation from its various hierarchical levels (high school, college, graduate school, professional school) is one of the most important means of an individual's social and economic advancement.

The humanists have successfully used the public schools to overturn Christian civilization. By establishing a substitute priesthood, which in turn replaces the true family in the field of education, the humanists have been able to reshape the first principles of students, generation after generation. This has all been done in the name of religious neutrality. But public schools are not religiously neutral. Nothing is religiously neutral. People are asked throughout their lives: "Choose this day which God you will serve."

So, in the name of neutrality, the God-hating humanists have stolen the hearts and minds of generations of public school students. This process of legalized kidnapping has only begun to be recognized by Christian parents since the 1960s. The rise of the Christian school movement has been the product of this new awareness.

But Christian parents need to ask themselves: "If there is no neutrality in the abortion room between life and death, and no neutrality in the classroom between God and humanism, how can there be neutrality in the courtroom or legislature between God and humanism?" This question is only beginning to be asked. When Christian voters at last make the obvious conclusion—"There is no difference; there is no neutrality!"—then a political transformation will take place. The humanist kidnappers will be removed from positions of influence. They will be removed from places where they can tax Christians in order to promote humanist religion.

The Christians' educational goal is therefore not to recapture the public schools for Jesus. The public schools are innately immoral; they are substitute churches and substitute families. The Christian goal is to replace the public schools with private Christian schools. This will re-establish parental authority over children. If the humanists want humanist schools for their children, let them teach their children at home, as the "strangers within the gates" would have done in the Old Testament. Let no one's tax money be used to finance public education; there is no religiously neutral curriculum.

As long as any tax-financed school remains open, other than military academies or other schools that train public officials, Christians have not recaptured their children from the kidnappers.[13] They will still be fighting for the future of Christian civilization. There is no neutrality. As long as Christians act as though there is, they will not have taken steps to reclaim the future.

Conclusion

The humanist political leaders know what they are doing. As long as the civil government subsidizes and educates a society toward polytheism in the name of pluralism through its own educational systems, Christianity will not be allowed a free-market opportunity to change the culture. We desperately need a resurgence of covenantally minded Christians to forge the way! Why "covenantally minded Christians"? The covenant is the model to inform the Church how to return to its original mandate: "discipling the *nations*" (Matt. 28:19). How can a "nation" be discipled if there is confusion over the "master plan"?

---

13. Robert L. Thoburn, *The Children Trap: The Biblical Blueprint for Education* (Ft. Worth, Texas: Dominion Press, 1986).

As in the two other institutions of society, the State should be structured according to the Biblical covenant. All five parts of the Deuteronomic covenant are outlined in Romans. The New Testament did not change the standard by which nations are to be ruled.

American society, perhaps more than any other in the history of man, was extremely self-conscious about the Biblical concept of covenant. In its early history, one of the first documents was clearly arranged according to the Deuteronomic covenant. In the next chapter, we shall examine the *Mayflower Compact*. Was it truly a covenantal document? Aside from the indication in the name, "compact," it was most definitely a historic covenantal document.

13

THE HISTORICAL STATE COVENANT

Both Family and Church are historically based on the covenant. But what about the history of the State? In this chapter, we will see that the original model we began with applies to the civil realm as well. It also is a covenant. The historical example I have chosen is perhaps one of the oldest covenants of our society, the Mayflower Compact. From the word "compact," which means "covenant," it is apparent what kind of document this is. But watch for the actual use of the word *covenant* in the body of the document.

The Mayflower Compact
1620

In the name of God, Amen. We whose names are underwritten, the loyal subjects of our dread soveraigne Lord, King James, by the grace of God, of Great Britaine, Franc, & Ireland king, defender of the faith, &c., haveing undertaken, for the glorie of God, and advancemente of the Christian faith, and honour of our king & countrie, a voyage to plant the first colonie in the Northerne parts of Virginia, do by these presents solemnly & mutually in the presence of God, and one of another, *covenant* & combine our selves togeather into a civill body politick, for our better ordering & preservation & furtherance of the ends aforesaid; and by vertue hearof to enacte, constitute, and frame such just & equall lawes, ordinances, acts, constitutions, & offices, from time to time, as shall be thought most meete & convenient for the generall good of the Colonie, unto which we promise all due submission and obedience. In witness whereof we have hereunder subscribed our names at Cap-Codd ye 11. of November, in the year of the raigne of our soveraigne lord, King James, of England, France, & Ireland the eighteenth, and of Scotland the fiftie fourth.
Ano:Dom.   1620.

These colonists brought from England a basic understanding of life. When given the opportunity to form their own nation, their documents reflected their theological world-and-life view. At the very heart of their theology was the word "covenant." It is stated in this document. One of the first civil documents in America is a *covenant*. Again we see present the five parts of the Biblical covenant.

True Transcendence

In the name of God. Amen.

From the first line of the Mayflower Compact there is no question of its nature. It starts off, "In the name of God. Amen." Although this was the establishment of a new civilization, it was recognized by these people that the God of the Bible is the Creator and "Soveraigne" of all life. By using this language, they set up the fundamental Creator/creature distinction. They knew the difference between God's Word and man's words.

The early colonists of this land did not believe in an "anarchical" kind of democracy.[1] Fisher Ames (1758-1808), member of Congress and orator, expressed the early Pilgrims' and Puritans' views about democracy: "This French mania is the bane of our politics. . . . Democracy [French] will kindle its own hell."[2] They did not believe in tyranny.

This covenant was not a "social contract." It was a covenant structured according to a Divine standard. They wanted a Christian government. They believed in *Christocracy*. The colony they settled was designed to be run by Christ.

They believed that God was *present* in everything that they did. He was *immanent*. They did not believe in a separation of "religion and politics." It is like the comment by George Santayana: "It should be observed that, if a systematic religion is true at all, intrusion on its part into politics is not only legitimate, but is the very work it comes into the world to do. Being by hypothesis enlightened supernaturally, it is able to survey the conditions and consequences of any kind of action much better than the wisest legislator . . . so that the spheres of systematic religion and politics—far from being independent—are in principle identical." The writers of the Mayflower Compact believed that God is present in politics, economics, and everything else. Therefore, all of these matters should be governed by His Word.

---

1. R. J. Rushdoony, *The Nature of the American System* (Fairfax, Virginia: Thoburn Press, [1965] 1978), pp. 24-31.

2. *Works of Fisher Ames, with a Selection from His Speeches and Correspondence*, ed. Seth Ames, Vol. I, p.139ff., 367. Cited in *The Nature of the American System*, pp. 25-26.

Civil representatives do not just represent man to God. They also represent God to man. Their position is given to them by God (Rom. 13:1ff.). They are to rule for "good" and be a "terror to evil." Modern government has lost this sense of transcendence and immanence. It puts transcendence in man. Man has become "God" in his own eyes. He has re-made God into his own image. There is no doubt that the Mayflower Compact takes issue with such views.

Hierarchy

Subjects of our dread soveraigne Lord, King James.

This civil document has a *hierarchy*. The parties involved must *submit* to authority. Revolution is not the proper way of establishing government. It was not the method that they had used. Notice that at the beginning and the end of the document, it acknowledges the King of England to be their "Soveraigne." Revolution was not "lawful" for the Christian.

The Mayflower Compact created a Biblical hierarchy. These colonists were in submission to God, and they expected future members of society to do the same. Their right to form this government did not come from themselves; it came from God. They believed that God worked through His hierarchy so they had to acquire permission from King James to come to America. Once here, they established a hierarchy based on the Bible. Since England had been influenced by the same authority—the King of England is the "defender of the faith"—we can see the same heritage in England. But in America, these people were able to create a much more consistently *Biblical* government.

Ethics

. . . And frame such just and equal laws.

The Mayflower Compact is an ethical covenant. The fact that these Pilgrims were covenanting to build a society based on "law" indicates how well they understood the covenant. Since the Biblical covenant is ethical, we can see the connection. They wanted a society that was "ethical." It was not based on the "Divine right of kings." This was significantly different from England.

At the same time in England, the Puritans were just a few years away from doing something that had never been done before. Led by Oliver Cromwell, the Puritans, just a little under thirty years after the writing of the Mayflower Compact, beheaded the King of England, Charles I. The reason was that the king had committed high treason and had violated the law of the land and of God. Such violations were to be punished by death, even the death of the king. Such an action was a historical precedent.

What was the issue? Up to this time, it was believed that the King had "Divine right" to the throne. This meant that he was above the civil law. But with the influence of the Reformation, Western Civilization adopted an ethical basis of rule. The king's authority was given by a covenant. Again we use our "totem pole" analogy to explain. In the following diagram we see that this time it is not the "father" or "church leader" placed on a continuum with God. It is instead the "king." If the king is "infused" or "injected" with deity, then to oppose him is to oppose God.

CHAIN OF BEING VIEW OF STATE

GOD	
MAGISTRATE (POSSESES BEING OF GOD IN HIS PERSON)	STATE IS VIEWED AS CENTER OF SOCIETY
FAMILY	OTHER INSTITUTIONS HAVE LESS BEING. THEY MUST GO THROUGH
CHURCH NON BEING (OUTSIDE OF MAGISTRATE'S DISTRICT)	THE STATE TO GET TO GOD.

The Biblical view, however, is that the King, his other "lesser" rulers, and the people are all *bound in an ethical covenant with God*. When the king breaks that covenant, the people have a basis to *sue* the king, without at the same time suing God. According to the other view, to oppose the king was to oppose God. The king could and did, many times, do anything he wanted. But the king and God are distinct, the Puritans insisted. God is God, and the king is part of creation. When the ethical bond between them, or between the king and the people is broken, there is a legal way to deal with the king. According to an ethical covenant, *all* men are under law.

This was the position of the Mayflower Compact. Although these people were in submission to the King of England, they made a covenant directly with God. The document reads, "Doe by these presents solemnly and mutually in ye presence of God, and one of another, covenant & combine ourselves togeather in a civill body politick." This was a covenant that they, the people, entered into along with the king. They realized that what was happening was a break with the system they had known in the past. Eventually, this kind of covenantal politics would stir up England, in the situation between Charles I and the Puritans to which I referred earlier.

Sanctions

Dread Soveraigne Lord.

The Mayflower Compact is a *judicial* covenant. The signers of this compact knew they were under God's judgment; they were under a *self-maledictory oath*. The opening statement reads, "We whose names are underwritten, the loyall subjects of our *dread* soveraigne Lord." Their belief was that the God of the Bible is a God of judgment. They knew that if they violated the covenant, God would judge them. We know from history that the early colonists set up a society based on judgment. They re-established the sanctions of Biblical law. We know from John Cotton's Abstract of the Laws of New England (1641) that crimes such as homosexuality, adultery, witchcraft, bestiality, and murder were all punishable by death.[3] This was a society of judgment.

Yet it was not a repressive society. Only someone who regards living under God's revealed laws as repressive would call Puritan society repressive. Their mistakes with respect to human freedom were nothing compared to modern humanism's calculated policies in the name of freedom. One has only to read the diaries of those early Puritan children. They were a people who wrote diaries. They wanted to write down all that God was doing in their lives. These diaries make it apparent that Pilgrim and Puritan children were extremely happy. Why? Because they were taught to face judgment by believing in Christ. When people deal with judgment the proper way, they can be "happy."

The Mayflower Compact is a sample of a judicial document that reflected a certain view of God. This is the whole point. People who believe in a God who judges can create a society founded on law and judgment. *Capital punishment is one of the best evangelistic tools of a society.*

---

3. "Abstract of the Laws of New England"; reprinted in *Journal of Christian Reconstruction*, V (Winter, 1978-79), pp. 82-94.

It was in the Old Testament, too. It reinforces the truth to the psyche
of man in a profound and dramatic way. Paul says that the magistrate is an "avenger of the wrath of God" (Rom. 13:4). When a civilization sees evil-doers judged by God, it brings home the reality that
men are accountable for their actions. There is judgment, and there
is hell. Men do not convert if they do not believe in eternal judgment. When the people of a society see *visible* judgment, they have
an incentive to convert. This is the doctrine of a *judicial covenant*.

Continuity

Covenant and combine ourselves together into a civill body politick.

Finally, the Mayflower Compact is a *legitimate* covenant. The
signers of this document were bound by it. It was a *real* covenant.
This raises an important issue: *legitimacy was determined by a constitutional document.* As I said earlier, up to this point in history, legitimacy
had been determined by "natural" right. When the Reformation
resurrected covenantal theology, Europe began to change. Kings no
longer had absolute power over their subjects. The people wanted
their countries to be run by a *constitution.*

We see the effects of this today in that there are virtually no more
true kings in the world. It is as one deposed mid-eastern "king"
(Farouk) once said, "There are only five kings left in the world: the
King of England, the king of hearts, the king of diamonds, the king
of clubs, and the king of spades." His point is well made. There is
really only one true king left. All other countries are either communist, which pretend to have constitutions—even the heathen must
pretend to Christian principles to have legitimacy—or they are run
by *covenants* called constitutions. Covenant theology has had that
much influence on the world.

It is worth noting briefly that the United States Constitution has
this five-point covenant structure, though not in the same order. It
begins with a statement of sovereignty (point one): "We the People of
the United States. . . ." It has a section on hierarchy (point two):
Article III, the judicial power.[4] It has a section on law (point three:

---

4. It took a generation after the ratification of the Constitution for Supreme
Court Justice John Marshall to hammer out the position of the Supreme Court as
the pinnacle of the authority structure. Because the Court can declare what the law
is, it is at the top. This was not understood by the Founding Fathers, however, who
paid comparatively little attention to the courts, as reflected in the debates. The Executive has become the enforcer of the law declared by the Court; thus, I have
placed the Executive under point four. But the positions of the Court and Executive

ethics): Article I, the legislative powers. It has a section on sanctions (point four): Article II, the executive power. It has a section on continuity (point five): Article V: amending the Constitution.

Conclusion

Society is designed to run according to covenantal arrangements. Early American history is an excellent example of what can happen when politics is built on the Word of God. As we have seen with all the other spheres, the Mayflower Compact is a covenant document that was used to govern the sphere of the State. It is a true image of the Biblical covenant. This concludes not only our study of the State, but an application of the covenant to the spheres of society.

We have one last application of the covenant. How do we take what we have learned in this book and re-establish a covenantal society? There is a positive and a negative approach. We want to answer such questions as, "What do Christians do when they meet opposition? Do they revolt? Do they give up? Are they defenseless and helpless?" No, God has provided a powerful application of the covenant. In the next chapter, we shall learn how to take society *little by little*.

---

might have been reversed historically, with the Executive at the pinnacle, had events happened differently, or had the brilliant Marshall not been appointed Chief Justice. In some sense, this battle for Constitutional supremacy is still in progress, although in our day, the Court has retained its position at the top of the hierarchy. The great irony here is that the Founding Fathers probably believed that the Legislative branch would be the dominant force. This is why most of the debates centered on the legislature.

14

CONCLUSION: LITTLE BY LITTLE

"I will drive them out before you little by little, until you become fruitful and possess the land" (Exod. 23:30).

We come to the end of our study of the covenant. The final question to be answered is, "How do we establish a society based on the concepts presented in this book?" I raise it because I do not want there to be any confusion about how a Christian society is created. I do not want the reader to leave this book thinking a covenantal culture comes from the *top down*, meaning by some "theocratic elite" forcing everyone to be a Christian, or believe a certain way. Nothing could be farther from the truth.

God told the Israelites that their Biblical culture would come "little by little." It did not come *suddenly*, or overnight. It came gradually. The covenantal society that I have proposed can only come the same way. That is, if it is to survive, it must come about from the *bottom up*. Sure, the reader can implement the covenant structure in his home and can seek to establish it in his church. But its fulfillment in society-at-large will be much more difficult. It can only successfully come about (and stick), if it takes hold at a *grass-roots level* through *evangelism*.

The expansion of the Gospel from Jerusalem to Rome serves as an example. Jesus says at the beginning of Acts, "You shall receive My power when the Holy Spirit has come upon you; and you shall be My witnesses both in Jerusalem, and in all Judea and Samaria, and even to the remotest part of the earth" (Acts 1:8). This verse summarizes the spread of the Gospel from one part of the world to the rest. It began in Jerusalem, and ended up in Rome. The method was *little-by-little evangelism*, just like the land of Canaan.

Yes, Acts parallels the Book of Joshua. Joshua is the account of the conquest of the land; Acts is the story of the conquest of the world.

But there is one striking contrast. Joshua took the land by use of the *sword*, even though it played a secondary role. None of the Apostles used the sword to spread the Gospel. Why the difference? Joshua, although a type of Jesus Christ, was under the Old Covenant. The Old Covenant was a covenant of the *flesh*, graphically portrayed in the sacrament of circumcision.[1] And, if anything, the Old Testament teaches that the kingdom of God could not be established in the flesh, meaning by the sword. The garden of Eden was sealed off by a "flaming sword" (Gen. 3:24), prohibiting *re-entrance*. Man could not return to that particular garden by a carnal weapon because his sword could not stand against God's. Even David, a great man of God, was unsuccessful in creating God's kingdom. He was a man of war, so he was not allowed to build the Temple (I Kgs. 5:3). When the disciples asked Jesus, "Lord, is it at this time that You are restoring the kingdom to Israel?" (Acts 1:6), they were expressing their confusion about the nature of the kingdom of God. They still thought it would be a political order, that is, a kingdom established by the sword.

They were wrong. The next verses in Acts speak of a new regime. The New Covenant kingdom is created by the Spirit. God had conquered Jericho by His might, to be sure. But the Holy Spirit had not come in all of His historical fulness. Christ had not yet come in history. Israel needed to use the sword, but Israel ultimately failed. The Church succeeded. In Acts, the Spirit of God went forth and created the beginnings of a Christian world from the *bottom up*.

The instrument the Spirit used was *evangelism*, witnessing. The role of the witness is twofold. Positively, he stands before men and the courts of the world, and he testifies of the Resurrected and Living Christ. Peter, John, Stephen, and Paul all became witnesses in the courts of man. Indeed, Acts tells how God sent them before Jewish and Roman courts, and even into prison for this reason. The task of evangelism is the challenge of being a witnesses in the unbeliever's place of holding court. As we see in Acts, this can be a place of education or doing business, as well as an official court for passing judgment (Acts 19 and 16). The idea is that *God sends His witnessess before man's seats of judgment to proclaim God's judgment*, particularly through Jesus Christ.

Much has been said and written about evangelism, so I will not

---

1. See Appendix 7.

spend any more time on this phase of little-by-little covenant expansion. Besides, I have already spent some time developing this point in the fifth point of covenantalism (Chapter Five). The sword cannot hold the inheritance for the future; only education, missions, and evangelism can. Also, I pointed out in the Great Commission mandate that the Gospel was to be spread *household by household*, a very *bottom-up* approach to witnessing.

Covenant Lawsuit

It is the other bottom-up aspect of being a witness that I need to address, a negative side that is virtually unknown, or neglected. Bringing *testimony* can also become a *covenant lawsuit*. Taking dominion in a pagan society is frustrating at times — these days, most of the time! One of the greatest concerns is the "wicked people" — abortionists, pornographers, statist politicians, etc. — who stand in the way of the visible reign of Christ (Heb. 2:8ff.). How should they be dealt with? Because the Biblical covenant commands Christians to be lawful, they are not allowed to use violence, except in the event of self-defense and a legally declared war by proper civil magistrates. Are they, therefore, left only with what some Christian activists call "a smile and a 'God loves you'"?

No. The Bible specifies a special kind of *lawsuit* that can be filed with God against the wicked called a *covenantal lawsuit*. This Biblical concept is consistently used by the prophets, many of their books being structured according to the Deuteronomic covenant.[2] With a covenantal lawsuit, however, the five points of covenantalism are all turned toward accusations against lawless covenant-breakers and enemies of the Church, calling down God's sanctions on them. Yes, a covenant lawsuit asks God to *kill* the wicked. God destroys the wicked one of two ways: by conversion or destruction. So, a covenantal lawsuit is not "unloving." But it is the *Biblical method for taking dominion when opposition is met*! I began the "Dominion" section with the *covenantal mandates*. I close with what is perhaps the Christian's greatest weapon in the face of opposition: not a "carnal" weapon but a "spiritual" one (II Cor. 10:4), the covenant itself turned into a

---

2. Walter Brueggemann, *Hosea: Tradition for Crisis* (Atlanta: John Knox Press, 1968), pp. 55-105. In these pages, Brueggemann categorically proves that the prophets were using the Deuteronomic covenant as a model for their dealings with apostasy among the people of God. See also, James A. Sanders, *Torah and Canon* (Philadelphia: Fortress, 1972), pp. 54-90.

lawsuit before God. I use the Book of Hosea as a model. Before considering it, let us learn something about the prophets and Hosea in general.

Hosea: Prophet of the Covenant

When Solomon apostatized, the number 666 was used for the first time as the number of apostasy (I Kgs. 10:14). He became the "classic" example of Adam, who was created on the *sixth* day, and who departed covenantally from the Lord. Solomon's apostasy was nothing new, however, because Solomon was like the old Adam, who was the first man who gave up everything at the enticement of a fallen woman. In Solomon's case it was fallen *women*. God's judgment was to divide the nation, the same thing that was done at the Tower of Babel. Division is an effective way to restrain the power of sin. God used it time and again in the Old Covenant until Christ could come in history to reverse the powerful effects of sin.

The nation of Israel was divided into two separate countries: Israel to the north with ten tribes, and Judah to the south with two tribes. Although Israel to the north had more tribes on its side, it fell the fastest. There was not always safety in numbers. But Judah was not far behind. Neither was there safety in "small" numbers. When in sin, it really does not make any difference whether a group is large or small. During this period, God sent prophets to bring lawsuits against His divided nation. Some were sent to the north, and some to the south.

Hosea was a prophet sent to Israel, the ten tribes of the north, in the eighth century before the birth of Christ. He was sent at a time which should be considered the last "saving effort" toward Israel. Jeroboam II was on the throne. Although this king was evil, God made one last attempt to turn the nation from its sin (II Kgs. 14:25-27). Hosea was part of that "last call."

Years prior to this, God had promised Jehu that his sons would sit on the throne until the fourth generation (II Kgs. 10:30). Jeroboam II was the last king to be succeeded by his son. All six of the following kings were either succeeded by means of assassination or themselves succeeded an assassinated king. God gave Jehu four generations. Hosea's message was the final invitation in the fourth generation. This was the amount of time allotted for cursing (Ex. 20:5). At the end of these four generations, Israel was cut off and dispersed around the world, never again to be assembled as one unit.

Israel did not hear the message of Hosea, so God turned blessing into cursing.

The Prophet

Before developing the themes of the Book of Hosea, I need to explain the role of the prophet. He did basically two things. First, he was a *counselor* to God and man. The first time the word prophet is used in the Bible comes in Genesis 20:7. Abraham had gone back down to Egypt. God told Abimelech not to harm Sarah because Abraham was a "Prophet, and he will pray for you, and you will live." The role of prophet was to *intercede* for man. *He could go into the presence of God's high council-court and receive special entrance.* He would then be sent back to man to offer counsel.

Second, he delivered covenant lawsuit from God against man. He was a special messenger bringing God's "prophecy." Prophecy is a *covenantal action.* It delivers blessings and cursings. A better description is that prophecy is *promissory* in character, being in part conditional and in part unconditional. The promises are *conditional* in that they depend on covenant-keeping or covenant-breaking. Sometimes, for this reason, what God says will come to pass *does not happen.* When God said to Jonah that Nineveh would be destroyed in three days, it did not take place. Why? Nineveh repented during the forty days given them (Jon. 3:10). Did God lie? Did He just not know what was going to happen? No, on both counts. God cannot lie (Nu. 23:19). God knows what will happen ahead of time because He plans everything that does happen (Eph. 1:11). But, God is a covenant-keeping God. His prophecies, given through His messengers, are in terms of the covenant — *always.* He is hurling a lawsuit in the face of covenant-breakers.

Also, the promissory character of prophecy is *unconditional* whenever *messianic* in direction. For example, one of the marks of a prophet is that *his word always comes true* (Deut. 18:14-22). Whenever the prophet makes a specific prophecy about the coming of the Messiah, or anything to do with Him, it has to come to pass. If not, he is not a true "Messianic" prophet.

Hosea was an instrument in God's hand; he delivered the lawsuit to Israel. The form of this lawsuit is classic, being in the structure of the covenant. Not all the prophets follow the complete pattern, but they all began with this basic format. For example, they might start with the stipulations or ethical section. Maybe they start with what is called an ordeal of jealousy (Nahum). But the fact that the prophets veered from the structure in such set forms indicates that the covenant formed the background to their lawsuits.

Also, each prophet seems to speak to a particular commandment that is being broken. It is not as though other commandments are not being violated. Rather, all the given sins of the nation are viewed in terms of one key commandment. Hosea is an example of this. The primary commandment being broken is the seventh: "Thou shall not commit adultery." Through the book we will see that other commandments are being abused, but they are all arranged in terms of the seventh. Even so, however, Hosea follows the covenant to build his case — God's case — against the spiritual and ethical adultery of Israel.

The covenant lawsuit should be viewed as both a *prayer* to God and a *declaration* to the corrupt society. So the outline of Hosea, as a model lawsuit, should be understood as a guide for the Christian who wants to know what needs to be declared publicly.

The Covenantal Structure of Hosea

1. True Transcendence: 1:1-11
2. Hierarchy: 2:1-3:5
3. Ethics: 4:1-7:16
4. Sanctions: 8:1-9:17
5. Continuity (Inheritance): 10:1-14:9

1. True Transcendence (Hos. 1:1-11)

The first point that needs to be made in a covenant lawsuit is that God's offenders have failed to acknowledge God as the *transcendent Lord* of the world. The prophet Hosea begins this way.

Three of the transcendent/immanent themes come through in the first chapter. First, the name of the book is "Hosea," a variant of "Joshua," meaning *Yahweh is salvation*. This is the idea of redemption. God sends a prophet to redeem Israel whose very name is *redemption*. He is the "incarnation" of the Word of God to them. In his person he portrays a God who is distinct and present.

Second, the very first sentence of the book is, "The word of the Lord which came" (Ho. 1:1). Does this sound familiar to "In the beginning God created" (Gen. 1:1)? It should, because the same idea is intended. "Out of nothing" He created them, and "out of nothing" He redeemed them from Egypt. The "word," or *revelation*, came from

God, *distinct* from man, to perform both functions.

Here we see a very important prophetic principle. *Interpretation precedes fact.* God's Word is *before* history chronologically. His interpretation of history is *before* time, space, and everything (Eph. 1:4). All of life moves according to God's interpretation. Rejection of God's interpretation leads to cursing and acceptance to blessing. Either way, God's interpretation is first. Man is *presuppositional.* His presupposition *is* that the God of the Bible is true (Rom. 1:18ff.). He may be in rebellion to this interpretation, but he still knows it is true in his heart of hearts.

Third, the first chapter presents God as the One who *names.* God instructs Hosea to marry a prostitute. Why? Hosea is a covenantal head. Because he is not like the individual, we should not try to build a case from Hosea for marrying prostitutes, just as Ezekiel's running "naked" is not a model for *individual* behavior. What happens to Hosea is a symbolic message for Israel. This "incarnation" is in the negative. Out of his marriage to the harlot comes children. Specific names are given to them. In a play on words after Gomer has given birth to a son, God tells Hosea, "Name him, 'Lo-ammi.'" "Lo-ammi" means *not my people.* The point is that God's prophet who names gave his son a name implying *loss of identity.* He has the power to name and the power to *take away a name.* If Israel hears the message, the covenant will be re-created. If not, it will be destroyed. Only the God of the Bible could perform such transcendent/immanent actions.

2. Hierarchy (Hos. 2:1-3:5)

The second part of the covenant lawsuit should make clear that God's hierarchy has been violated. The real issue is a mediated system of judgment. God stands behind His authority; He stands behind it in history. Since hierachy involves history, specific historical events of God's faithfulness should be cited, as well as a record of disobedience on the part of the individual or group of individuals being filed against.

Hosea's lawsuit indicates the relationship between judgment and history by emphasizing the relationship between covenant faithfulness and peace with all the enemies around Israel.

Therefore, behold, I will allure her, bring her into the wilderness, and speak kindly to her. Then I will give her vineyards from there, and the valley of Achor as a door of hope. And she will sing there as in the days of her youth, as in the day when she came up from the land of Egypt. "And it will come about in that day," declares the Lord, "That you will call Me Ishi [My husband] and will no longer call Me Baali [My master]. For I will remove the names of the Baals from her mouth, so that they will be mentioned by their names no more. In that day I will also make a covenant for them with the beasts of the field, the birds of the sky, and the creeping things of the ground. And I will abolish the bow, the sword, and war from the land, and will make them lie down in safety. And I will betroth you to Me forever; Yes, I will betroth you to Me in righteousness and in justice, in lovingkindness and in compassion, and I will betroth you to Me in faithfulness. Then you will know the Lord" (Ho. 2:14-20).

Notice the "I will"/fulfillment pattern, and how God refers to *re-creation*, making a *new covenant* with the animals of the earth. In the Adamic covenant, this is the hierarchy section (Gen. 2). Here, God speaks of making a new creation out of Israel. He even compares it to redemption from Egypt.

The end of this passage highlights the major sins of Israel: idolatry and adultery. Notice that these two sins go together in Hosea's mind, just as they did at the end of the hierarchy section of Deuteronomy (Deut. 4:15-24). Remember also that the second and seventh commandments fall into the *hierarchical* category. To worship another God is to pursue another "groom." Hosea's bride symbolized the very kind of adultery God's "wife" (Israel) was committing.

3. Ethics (Hos. 4:1-7:16)

God likes to be reminded of His laws, and He desires that these laws be held up in front of the guilty. When John the Baptist, the last Old Covenant prophet, saw Herod in sin, he went before him in public and confronted him (Matt. 14:1ff.). So this part of the lawsuit should include a specific list of the infractions against God's Law.

Chapter four of Hosea mentions for the first time actual *commandments* that have been broken.

For the Lord has a case [lawsuit] against the inhabitants of the land, because there is no faithfulness or kindness or knowledge of God in the land. There is *swearing, deception, murder, stealing,* and *adultery* (Hos. 4:1-2).

Hosea also begins to do something else in this section that falls in the ethical category. In the very last verse of the third chapter, Hosea referred to David and the "sons" of Israel. This forms a transition into the first verse of chapter four that starts off with an address to the *"sons* of Israel." Both references turn our focus to the theme of "sonship," or *image-bearing*. "Sonship" is defined in terms of bearing God's image. The two main ways of bearing God's image are through the offices of priest and king.

The ethical section concludes with chapter seven, but eight forms a transition: "They have transgressed My *covenant* and rebelled against My *law*" (8:1).

4. Sanctions (Hos. 8:1-9:17)

The fourth part of the lawsuit asks God to pour out His sanctions on the wicked. Deuteronomy tells how God "blesses" and "curses." Both should be asked for, but in the case of the lawsuit, the specific curses should be requested and mentioned. Also, it should be kept in mind that Revelation speaks of "plagues" that are not referred to in Deuteronomy. These would also be appropriate sanctions to ask for.

The first verse of chapter eight opens, "Put the *trumpet* to your lips! Like an *eagle* the enemy comes against the house of the Lord" (8:1). This is how the sanctions section of Revelation began (Rev. 8:1-2). It starts with a series of angels blowing *trumpets*. This instrument announces, as in the case of Jericho, the coming *judgment* of God. In the case of Hosea, the judgment is coming against the once-faithful covenant nation, Israel.

The last verse of chapter eight continues the theme of judgment when Hosea says of Israel and Judah, "I will send fire on its cities that it may consume its palatial dwellings" (8:14). Although the whole book refers, off and on, to the judgment that will come to God's people, chapter 9 seems to be devoted *entirely* to the subject. It starts off, "Do not rejoice, O Israel, with exultation like the nations! For you have played the harlot" (9:1). Hosea goes on for the first time to mention the actual words "punishment and *retribution*" (9:7). Hosea's thrust is *sanction*.

Because Israel has "played the harlot," she will be *disinherited*. The last verse of chapter 9 says, "My God will cast them away because they have not listened to Him; and they will be wanderers among the nations" (9:17). The judgment has been passed and this means disinheritance. This sounds like the end of the judicial section in Genesis where Adam and Eve were cursed and sent out of the Garden. But, they were taken into a new inheritance because God had re-clothed them. Hosea's emphasis carries us smoothly into the next section.

5. *Continuity (Hos. 10:1-14:9)*

Finally, the lawsuit requests of God that He re-establish His covenantal continuity with the proper people and land. Furthermore, in the course of this prayer and announcement, God is asked to disinherit the wicked and drive them away through conversion or destruction.

The opening verse of chapter ten starts on the theme of *inheritance*. He says, "Israel is a luxuriant vine; he produces fruit for himself. The more his fruit, the more altars he made; the richer his land, the better he made the sacred pillars" (10:1). Israel appears to be rich in inheritance, but Hosea is mocking them. The richer Israel became, the more it used its inheritance to build liberal and pagan religion. The chapter follows with several declarations of *disinheritance*.

The great disinheritance God will bring will be *judgment on Israel's children*. He says, "Therefore, a tumult will arise among your people, and all your fortresses will be destroyed, as Shalman destroyed Beth-arbel on the day of battle, when mothers were dashed in pieces with their *children*" (10:14). This sounds cruel. But we must remember that God judges *covenantally*. As families are brought into the covenant as *family units*, so they will be judged together. This happened throughout the history of God's covenantal people. Korah, Dathan, and Abiram were judged together with their families (Nu. 16). Achan's family was burned with him (Josh. 7), and Ananias and Sapphira were judged as a covenantal unit in the *New Covenant* (Acts 5:1ff.). But, in each case, God gives the family opportunity to take a stand *against* the sinful covenant head. The covenant is made with individuals as well as groups.

As we have seen in each covenant, however, God makes for a way of escape. He offers a *new* inheritance. The last chapter of Hosea is one of the most beautiful expressions of God's promise of new salvation. But, *it is conditional* (14:1-3). Israel must return to the Lord to have all the blessings. Hosea closes with the following:

I will heal their apostasy, I will love them freely, for My anger has turned away from them. I will be like the dew to Israel; He will blossom like the lily, and he will take root like the cedars of Lebanon. His shoots will sprout, and his beauty will be like the olive tree, and his fragrance like the cedars of Lebanon. Those who live in his shadow will again raise grain, and they will blossom like the vine. His renown will be like the wine of Lebanon.

O Ephraim [symbol for firstborn son], what more have I to do with idols? It is I who answer and look after you. I am like a luxuriant cypress; From Me comes your fruit.

Whoever is wise, let him understand these things; Whoever is discerning, let him know them. For the ways of the Lord are right, and the righteous will walk in them, but transgressors will stumble in them (14:4-9).

Here the book ends with two classifications of people: covenant-keepers and covenant-breakers. These are the only two, each having opposite inheritances. The covenant-breakers may appear to be blessed on the "front end" of life. But in the end, they will lose everything forever. The covenant-keepers, on the other hand, may appear to have nothing on the "front-end" of life. But in the end, and even in this life, they have everything. Covenant-keepers get to be like Job: greatly tested but richly blessed in this life and the one to come.

Who Files the Lawsuit Today?

We should not leave our discussion of Hosea without bringing it into the New Covenant. The question is, "Who files the lawsuit today?" Can any individual curse someone he doesn't happen to like? Does the State file the lawsuit? Does the Church?

Jesus sheds some helpful light on these questions when He says, "Where two or three have gathered in My name, there I am in their midst" (Matt. 18:20). Two things stand out. First, the reference to "two or three" is a formula used for *legal* testimony in the Old Testament: "On the evidence of *two or three witnesses*, he who is to die shall be put to death; he shall not be put to death on the evidence [literally "mouth"] of one witness" (Deut. 17:6). Second, Jesus applies this formula at the end of the section on *Church discipline*.

Thus, we should conclude that a covenant lawsuit can only be brought in the context of a *Church court*, or worship service (also a Church court before God's throne), since the imprecatory (judgment) psalms (Ps. 83, 94) were intended to be used in worship. Individuals need witnesses in order to file a valid lawsuit with God, and certainly the State has no function in filing a covenant lawsuit before God. If someone wants to file an imprecatory lawsuit, he should appeal to the officers of the local church. If that church will not listen, one that will should be sought out. The imprecatory psalms are not to be treated lightly, nor *autonomously*. They have a two-edged nature to them. If they are abused, they could kill the user!

Conclusion

Hosea comes to an end on the theme of *legitimacy*, concluding our study of the covenant as a *lawsuit*. Each step of the way, I have tried to show the pattern of the covenant. Is it wrong for Christians to use the covenant lawsuit? Are not Christians supposed to "love the sinner and hate the sin?"

No! God hates the sinner as well as his sin (Ps. 11:5). And since the Church is the New Israel, Paul commands it to pray and sing the psalms (Eph. 5:19)—all of them, especially the imprecatory psalms that call down God's destruction and conversion of the wicked (Ps. 83, 74, etc.).

I have chosen a prophet to confirm that as Israel was built by the covenant, it was torn down on the basis of the covenant. Man gains dominion by covenant, and he loses it by breaking the covenant. Once again, as I have attempted to explain both the covenant and its application for dominion, we are reminded with richer understanding of Moses' words, "So keep the words of this covenant to do them *that you may prosper* in all that you do" (Deut. 29:9)! Now we know the words of the covenant are kept and applied in society *little by little*.

Appendix 1

THE TEN COMMANDMENTS

The Ten Commandments are called a covenant (Deut. 4:13). Let us see if the structure is the same as Deuteronomy.

First Five Commandments

Then God spoke all these words saying,

(1) I am the Lord your God, Who brought you out of the land of Egypt, out of the house of slavery. You shall have no other gods before Me.

(2) You shall not make for yourself an idol, or any likeness of what is in heaven above or on the earth beneath or in the water under the earth. You shall not worship them or serve them; for I, the Lord your God, am a jealous God, visiting the iniquity of the fathers on the children, on the third and the fourth generation of those who hate Me, but showing lovingkindness to thousands, to those who love Me and Keep My commandments.

(3) You shall not take the name of the Lord your God in vain, for the Lord will not leave him unpunished who takes His name in vain.

(4) Remember the Sabbath Day to keep it holy. Six days you shall labor and do all your work, but the seventh day is a sabbath of the Lord your God; in it you shall not do any work, you nor your son or your daughter, your male or your female servant or your cattle or your sojourner who stays with you. For in six days the Lord made the heavens and the earth, the sea and all that is in them, and rested on the seventh day; therefore the Lord blessed the sabbath day and made it holy.

(5) Honor your father and your mother, that your days may be prolonged in the land which the Lord your God gives you.

Second Five Commandments

(6) You shall not murder.

(7) You shall not commit adultery.

(8) You shall not steal.

(9) You shall not bear false witness against your neighbor.

(10) You shall not covet your neighbor's house; you shall not covet your neighbor's wife or his male servant or his female servant or his ox or his donkey or anything that belongs to your neighbor (Ex. 20:1-17).

214

Structure

How to structure the Ten Commandments has always been a problem.[1] Luther's Catechism, following Augustine, breaks some of the commandments up and re-groups them. The *Shorter Catechism* of the *Westminster Confession of Faith* (Presbyterian) splits the commandments between the fourth and fifth. This structuring has the most appeal because the first four pertain to God, and the last six refer to man in a general sort of way. But the first four commandments apply to man as well as to God. To keep the Sabbath Day is a "manward" activity. Christ said, "the Sabbath was made for *man*, and not man for the Sabbath" (Mark 2:27).

How about the next six commandments?[2] Even though they seem to be oriented to man, they are still primary obligations to God. The prophets refer to adultery as a "spiritual" problem. Israel's adultery with other gods resulted in "domestic" unfaithfulness (Mal. 2). The 4:6 structure does not hold up well either.

Besides, the fifth commandment has always been the real problem. All the others are expressed in the negative, "Thou shall *not*." The fifth is stated in the positive "Honor your father and your mother." The question is: "Why?" It could be because it heads up the beginning of the "manward" commandments. The commandment heading up the "Godward" commandments is in the negative. Problem: the "manward" commandments also begin with a negative.

Why try to break the decalogue into two groups at all? God communicates with a *double witness*. It takes two witnesses to convict someone (Nu. 35:30; Deut. 17:6). This "two-fold witness" concept is everywhere. For example, there are two copies of the Ten Commandments placed in the ark (Deut. 10:5), two cities (city of God and city of man). Even the language of the Bible is written in *parallelism* (i.e. The Psalms and Proverbs). This is so much a part of God's manner of communication that the interpreter should instinctively look for it.

---

1. Notice that I have not referred to the divisions as "tables" of the law. Kline has conclusively demonstrated that the "tables" were actually two copies of the *same* law. See *Structure of Biblical Authority*, pp. 117-120.

2. U. Cassuto, *A Commentary On The Book Of Exodus* (Jerusalem: The Magnes Press, 1951), p. 249. Cassuto basically goes with a God/man division of the commandments. He notes that the first and the tenth commandments have to do with loving "God" and loving "man" (your neighbor) respectively.

In and of itself, however, the fact that the commandments can be divided into two even groups of five is not enough to persuade us. It would not be absolutely necessary to have two groups with the "same" number. Here is the value of knowing the covenant structure, for the commandments follow the pattern twice.

First Five Commandments

1. First Commandment: True Transcendence

One of the three ways God makes His transcendence known is by redemption. The other two are by creation and revelation. Here, the first commandment has to do with *redemption*. God delivered Israel from Egypt. Israel always looked back on this incident as their definitive salvation. How did God save them? He defeated the false gods of Egypt. The conflict was one of true transcendence, which means that it involved immanence.

Israel had had an important relationship to Egypt. Joseph was the son of *revelation* (Gen. 39:1ff.). He received dreams, and lived by God's Word. Israel's other sons resented this. They sold Joseph into slavery, and he ended up trapped in a pit. Symbolically, he died. But God resurrected him in Egypt. Through God's *revelation*, Joseph rose to the second in command of the greatest nation in the world.

The Egyptians soon turned against God and His people. Israel found itself in slavery. All of this came to a "showdown" between God and the gods of Egypt. The transcendent/immanent themes emerge. God met Moses on Sinai in the burning bush. He was present with Moses. Through this presence, He triumphed over the false gods of Egypt, and demonstrated His transcendence. The God of the Israelites was unlike any of the Egyptian gods. He was truly God, distinct in His Being.

But the basic transcendence theme attached to the redemption concept is *resurrection*. Israel was raised up, after being dead in Egypt. Israel was raised up before the other nations. Being brought out of Egypt was a form of "new life," another resurrection idea. In all of this, we discover God's transcendent character manifested through the great Old Covenant work of redempion. We will see this again in the great New Covenant work of redemption, Christ's salvation of the world through His own Death and Resurrection.

2. Second Commandment: Hierarchy

The second commandment moves to the next principle of the covenant, a hierarchy of obedience ("worship and serve"). In the Deuteronomic covenant, the hierarchical section closes by associating rebellion to the sin of idolatry. Moses says, "So watch yourselves carefully, since you did not see any form on the day the Lord spoke to you at Horeb from the midst of the fire, lest you act corruptly and make a graven image" (Deut. 4:15-16). Thus, the second commandment follows the same pattern, connecting worship and submission, "service" (Exod. 20:5).

The history of Israel's redemption is also the backdrop. God forbids worship of any sort of idol. The specific outline is "from heaven above to the earth, to anything under the sea or earth." It is possible that the commandment is written this way to counter a "hierarchy" among the Egyptian false gods. They worshipped life above, below, and especially the Nile itself. Birds and animals of the Nile were worshipped because it was believed that the "Great River" was a serpent providing life to the world above, below, and all around. Clearly this refers to the imagery of the serpent in the garden, a pagan hierarchy. Even the way God condemns idolatry develops a certain "false" hierarchy.

God's hierarchy places all authority in Him. Anyone else only has delegated responsibility. Transcendence is not shifted from God to man, or to creation for that matter. Egyptian religion had a hierarchy of authority that placed the Pharaoh in the center of the world. He was half god and half man, a perfect "false" incarnation. He mediated life to the world. The animals were simply "emanations" from him, possessing a little "less" deity.

This created a pyramidal hierarchy with man at the top of the pyramid. The pyramid structure is not itself inherently bad, since it is the "mountain model" found throughout the Bible.[3] The pyramid was simply a cheap (or shall I say, rather expensive) copy of God's mountain dwelling. But God's mountain-pyramid always has God on top of the mountain. His hierarchy begins with God, not man. To worship a "created" thing is to place creation at the top of the mountain. The result: tyranny like that of Egypt.[4]

---

3. Richard J. Clifford, *The Cosmic Mountain In Canaan and The Old Testament* (Cambridge, Massachussetts: Harvard University Press, 1972), pp. 25-28.

4. R. J. Rushdoony, *The One and the Many*, pp. 36-37.

3. Third Commandment: Ethics

The third section of the Deuteronomic covenant stipulates what is involved in obeying God. The pagan system, growing out of a "chain of being" approach, is inherently manipulative. This commandment has to do with not manipulating the "name of God." When would the name of God be taken in vain? In false oath-taking. To "swear" in the Bible is to take an oath. Jesus criticized the Pharisees for swearing by all sorts of things and taking so many false oaths (Matt. 5:33-37). They tried to manipulate God's name.

What is a name? A name in the Bible represents the person. The *power to name* is the *power to control*. God named Adam. Adam named the animals and Eve. This made man God's vice-regent in dominion. But the *power to name* is the *power to have authority over the thing that is named*. Therefore, any time the name of God was tampered with, it indicated an attempt to manipulate Him. Actually, to worship a false god re-names and re-constitutes the true God. God does not want to be re-named, and He certainly cannot be manipulated.

The Pharaoh renamed Joseph (Gen. 41:45). Nebuchadnezzar's official over the eunuchs renamed Daniel and the three Hebrew youths (Dan. 1:7). When a man came under a pagan king's authority in the Old Testament, at least to serve in a position of leadership under him, he was renamed by that king. God renamed Abram to Abraham and Jacob to Israel, a sign of His authority over them.

The commandment here forbids a manipulative approach to God. It does not forbid oath-taking per se (i.e. in the courtroom). It condemns swearing to "emptiness" or "vanity." When someone makes a false oath, he is attempting to manipulate God's name for his own end. Even though man tries, he cannot control God. It is the other way around. Nevertheless, false oath-taking is ultimately a reflection on Him, making Him seem to be empty. How? When someone who is actually lying says, "May God strike me dead, if I am telling a lie," and, if he does not fall down dead, but is later found out to be a liar, God does not "seem" to have stood behind His name. If man obeys God's stipulations, however, he will not need to try to manipulate God's name. Blessing and whatever man needs will come through a proper ethical relationship to Him.

4. Fourth Commandment: Sanctions

The fourth commandment regulates the Sabbath. What was the Sabbath? Originally, it was the day when God "blessed" the world in a special way (Gen. 2:1ff.). The word "blessing" ties the day to one of the two judicial *sanctions* of the covenant (Deuteronomy 28). This makes the original Sabbath a day when man was to receive God's benediction. Instead, man disobeyed and the Sabbath Day became a day of judgment. The curses of Genesis three were issued. So, throughout history, the Lord's Day (Sabbath Day) is a time of judgment. It is like that final day, "the Day of the Lord."

This commandment has to do with honoring a time of special judgment. One day in seven should be devoted to it. Double sacrifices were offered because Israel made special reflection on her sins (Num. 28:1-8). The comments about working on the other days orient even man's work toward a time of judgment. Indeed, this is the direction of history.

5. Fifth Commandment: Continuity

As already noted, the fifth commandment is positive. The emphasis is on tangible continuity, *inheritance*, since to "live long on the earth" was the legacy given to Israel. Why longevity? The curse of death broke down generational continuity, requiring that covenantal faithfulness be sustained over many generations.

Historical extension of the faith was broken down. Think how easy it would be to sustain a system of belief if the founders lived for 500 years. This would be like still having Martin Luther alive. All those years that liberal German, Lutheran theologians were corrupting orthodoxy, Luther could and would have confronted them and probably turned them over his knee. (They would have needed a lot more than that.) But the point is that longevity was critical to sustaining the family inheritance. Because death entered the world, a system was needed to *transfer* the inheritance. It is in the *transferral* that the many problems of inheritance can be seen.

Although, it seems that death is also *pro-covenantal*. After the Flood, lifespans shortened. The common grace to pagans lasts three to four generations, then they fall or revolt. The blessings to the faithful go on for a thousand generations. Thus, covenant-keeping compounds far longer than covenant-breaking. If the evil ones lived five hundred years per generation, their hand would be strengthened: two thousand years of compounding. So this commandment has to do with inheritance, an issue of *legitimacy*. Obedient sons and daughters receive the inheritance, the blessing of the previous commandment.

The first series of commandments follows the structure of the covenant. Without having to force the commandments, I believe the reader can easily see how God ordered them around the five parts of the covenant. The second half of the commandments does the same.

The Second Five Commandments

6. The Sixth Commandment: True Transcendence

God returns to the transcendence theme. How? Unlawful killing of another human being was expressly forbidden because "Whoever sheds man's blood, by man his blood shall be shed, For in the *image* of God He made man" (Gen. 9:6). In fact, the "ethical" section of the Noahic covenant is summarized under this one commandment, summing up all of God's demands.

The key is in the word *image*. Man is the image of God. Unique to God's creation and unlike any other aspect of His handiwork, man is a picture of God. Man shows God's transcendence and immanence. To kill man is analogous to killing God. All rebellion is an attempt to kill God. Satan tempted man to become like "God." Between the lines of Satan's offer was the idea that the true God would be *displaced* (Gen. 3:1ff.). So the second set of commandments begins with a commandment against eradicating God's transcendent/immanent representation in man.

7. Seventh Commandment: Hierarchy

The Deuteronomic covenant made a specific connection between idolatry and adultery. The end of the second section calls attention to the second commandment, reminding Israel of the prohibition against "idolatry" (Deut. 4:15-19). Moses gives as a reason, "For the Lord your God is a consuming fire, a *jealous* God" (Deut. 4:24). "Jealousy" is a response to any kind of marital unfaithfulness. Indeed, there was a special "ordeal of jealousy" (Nu. 5). Since the people of God are His "bride," worshipping other gods would be analogous to sexual unfaithfulness in marriage. God's proper response would be "jealousy."

The ideas of worship and marriage are expressed in the old

Anglican form of the marriage ceremony where the bride pledges, "I worship thee with my body."[5] Sexual faithfulness is a form of service, like the faithfulness of service in worship.[6]

Adultery is a violation of God's hierarchy. Marital faithfulness is a mutual *submission* (familial hierarchy) to one another. Paul says,

> But because of *immoralities* [adultery], let each man have his own wife, and let each woman have her own husband. Let the husband fulfill his duty to his wife, and likewise also the wife to her husband. The wife does not have *authority* over her own body, but the husband does; and likewise also the husband does not have *authority* over his own body, but the wife does (I Cor. 7:2-4).

Adultery is due to rebellion against the authoritative *hierarchy* within marriage. A man and woman are to submit their bodies to one another, the best defense against adultery and "immoralities." To "cut off" one's spouse is nothing more than an attempt to be *autonomous*.

8. Eighth Commandment: Ethics

The third section of the Deuteronomic covenant "stipulated" how to be consecrated through "ethics." In other words, God's *boundaries* are ethical, separating the clean from the unclean. As long as God's people lived by these ethical boundary lines, they would be victorious.

Ethics is contrary to a "manipulative" world-and-life view. In the third commandment we saw that man is forbibben to "manipulate" the Name of God.[7] The eighth commandment, which parallels both the third section of the covenant and the third commandment, speaks to another form of "boundary violation." Stealing is manipulative. Taking something that is not yours is a failure to relate to people on *ethical* terms, and a failure to honor property of others.[8]

Paul says, "Let him who steals steal no longer; but rather let him labor, performing with his own hands what is good, in order that he may have something to share with him who has need" (Eph. 5:28). There are two problems with a thief. He will not *work* and will not *give*. Both require *ethical* dealings with people. *To work* means one submits himself to the laws of work: perseverance, showing up on

---

5. *The Book of Common Prayer.*

6. James Jordan, *Law of the Covenant* (Tyler, Texas: Institute for Christian Economics, 1984), pp. 18-19.

7. *Ibid.*, pp. 132-33.

8. *Ibid.*, pp. 204-5.

time, willingness to learn, diligence, etc. *To give* means taking what has been earned and helping someone in need.

A thief, on the other hand, takes a manipulative approach. Instead of working, he seeks to manipulate through conning, deception, and various other forms of theft. He certainly doesn't give to others, and if he happens to, he does so to further *his* need, not the other person's. Ultimately, a thief believes money is magical: not the means to an end, but the end in itself. This is why all tyrannies are based on theft. The "Robin Hood" approach is a form of manipulating what belongs to one group to re-distribute it to another.

9. Ninth Commandment: Sanctions

The Deuteronomic covenant is ratified by sanctions in the fourth section, to be received in an "official" context, probably a "courtroom." Furthermore, this judgment was received at a Sabbath time, Pentecost.[9] Thus, in this commandment, "bearing false witness" also conjures up the picture of a courtroom scene. Where would one be likely to bear false witness? It would probably be brought in the same legal environment of passing judgment, a formal trial or hearing. This could also be done informally, telling lies about someone in the congregation or who lives down the street.[10] But even this setting is judicial because a judgment is passed. "Bearing false witness" interferes with and perverts judgment. How? False witness causes blessings to fall on those who deserve a curse, and vice versa.

10. Tenth Commandment: Continuity

Notice all the items that are forbidden to covet. They all have to do with a man's inheritance. In Old Testament times, the wife was made an heir of the covenant through an adoption procedure. She actually became the "sister" of her husband. Abraham was not lying to Pharaoh after all (Gen. 20:2) when he called Sarah his "sister." This practice was done to assure the woman's receiving part of the inheritance, contrary to the pagan practices of considering a woman's value as being less than a man's. So, when an Old Testa-

---

9. *Ibid.*, p. 58. Also, See Jordan's, *Sabbath Breaking and the Death Penalty* (Tyler: Geneva Ministries, 1986). He connects the fourth and ninth commandments in terms of the "sanctions" idea.

10. R. J. Rushdoony, *Institutes of Biblical Law*, pp. 598-600. Rushdoony has an interesting section on the relation between "slander" and the 9th commandment.

ment man coveted the wife of another, he was cutting into his neighbor's inheritance. In Israel, this disrupted everything because each family received a particular piece of land and inheritance when Canaan was conquered under Joshua. To covet one's covenant brother's family and possessions was to rob the inheritance granted by the covenant itself. Here the last commandment ends on a note of finality.

The second five commandments follow, without much explanation, the basic pattern of the covenant, completing a perfect double witness.

Priest/King Distinction

One final observation about the commandments should be made. The fundamental difference between the two halves is that the first has a priestly emphasis, while the second is kingly. A priest was fundamentally a *guardian* of the presence of the Lord. Adam was told to "till and *guard*" the garden (Gen. 2:15). We know that "guarding" is a priestly function because the same Hebrew word refers to the Levite's responsibility (Lev. 5).

The first five commandments have to do with things which priests were specifically to guard: the Lord's transcendent/immanent character, the worship of God, God's name, the Sabbath, and family inheritance. What does the last point have to do with guarding? The priesthood was the guardian of the family. Inheritance left without an heir went to the Levites. In the New Covenant, the care of widows and orphans belonged to the Church, not the State. Both Israel and the Church are called priesthoods (Ex. 19:6; I Pet. 2:5). Protecting the family inheritance is a priestly function. This is why Jesus so severely chastised the Pharisees for allowing the abuse of parents' inheritance (Mark 7:1ff.).

The second five commandments have to do with the oversight of the king. He was the one, for example, to implement the discipline for breaking these commandments. He would have also been involved with "first table" offenses, but they would have come through the priesthood, the special guardian of God's House.

This structure, priest to king, is the way man dominates. As a general principle, he must be a servant to be a leader. One should not think of this process as anything other than the way of the covenant. Man covenants his way to dominion. When man keeps God's commandments, he is living by the covenant. When he lives by the covenant, he has dominion.

Conclusion

The Ten Commandments express God's law in a covenantal way. There are five parts to the covenant, and so God's ten laws follow the covenant twice, each re-enforcing the other.

Can we find this five-fold pattern anywhere else? The next appendix jumps to the Psalms. It, too, has a Deuteronomic structure as we shall see.

Appendix 2

PSALMS

From Adam forward, each leader of Israel becomes a "new" Adam — Noah, Abraham, and Moses being examples. They even introduce their time period to a "new" covenantal regime. But all of these Old Covenant men cannot deliver the world from sin because they are prior to Christ, the last "New Adam." So, the flow of the Old Testament is that each "new" Adam turns out to be like the first, undergoing some type of major fall into sin.

The pre-eminent Old Testament new Adam and type of Jesus Christ, however, is *David*, the second king of Israel. More is written about and by him than any other person in Scripture. The bulk of Israel's history is concentrated on his activities. The fifty-five chapters of I & II Samuel, 29 chapters of I Chronicles, and a few other chapters in I Kings and II Chronicles are almost devoted entirely to him. And, where he is not explicitly referred to, the context is either building to or away from something happening in his life.

Then there are the Psalms, the longest book in the Bible, with 150 chapters designed to be sung in worship. Messianic in orientation, *warsongs of the Prince of peace*,[1] the majority of them were written by David himself. Its text is divided into *five* smaller books, a division virtually undisputed, dating back before the time of Christ.[2] There is

---

1. This expression is actually the title of one of the best commentaries on the Psalms: R. M. Benson, *Warsongs of the Prince of Peace* (New York: E. P. Dutton & Co., 1901).
2. William G. Braude, *The Midrash on the Psalms* (New Haven: Yale University Press, 1959), I, p. 5. Braude comments on a Midrash from the Talmudic period on Psalm 1, "As Moses gave five books of laws to Israel, so David gave five Books of Psalms to Israel: the Book of Psalms entitled *Blessed is the man* (Ps. 1:1), the Book entitled *For the leader: Maschil* (Ps. 42:1), the Book, *A Psalm of Asaph* (Ps. 73:1), the Book, *A prayer of Moses* (Ps. 90:1), and the Book, *Let the redeemed say* (Ps. 107:2)." Also, Michael Dahood, *Psalms I*, Vol. I (Garden City, New York: Doubleday, 1965), pp. XXX-XXXI, "Perhaps the oldest explicit testimony to the fivefold partition of the Psalter occurs in a poorly preserved liturgical fragment 1 Qumran 30 dating to the turn of the Christian era." D. Barthelemy and J. T. Milik, *Qumran Cave I, Discoveries in the Judean Desert*, I (Oxford, 1955), p. 133.

225

a good possiblity that Ezra was the one who organized the Psalms according to this arrangement.[3]

Most modern translations now include this division. Why five? I believe this great collection of psalms *follows the covenantal pattern* of Deuteronomy. Let us now consider the structure of the Psalms according to the following outline.

The Covenantal Structure of the Psalms

Book I (1-41): True Transcendence.
Book II (42-72): Hierarchy.
Book III (73-89): Ethics.
Book IV (90-106): Sanctions.
Book V (107-150): Continuity.

1. True Transcendence (Ps. 1-41)

The Psalms begin with a "sanction" word, "blessed," placing the entire book in the context of covenant renewal on the Sabbath Day of worship. Remember, the fourth commandment pertains to the Sabbath and corresponds to the "sanctions" section of the covenant.

Be this as it may, the Psalms open on one of the three transcendent themes: *creation*. The setting of Psalm 1 is a "garden" and "trees planted by water" (1:3). Sound familiar? The Psalmist speaks of a new *genesis*, or beginning, "how to become a new creation in God's new garden." We are called back to the garden where there was the first tree of life. The psalm wants us to see David's beginning as being that of a new Adam. All those who receive (meditate on) the Law of God become "miniature" new Adams. Ultimately (eschatologically) this psalm is about Christ, who was the "Tree of Life," and one who "did not sit in the seat of scoffers."

Another pronounced "transcendent theme" stands out. The first psalm contrasts those who meditate on God's truly transcendent Word, and those who "sit in the counsel" of man's *revelation*. The Deuteronomic covenant began with the same contrast. God's Word was distinguished from Moses' words. In this regard, Psalm 1 is virtually identical to Deuteronomy 1:1-4.

3. R. K. Harrison, *Introduction to the Old Testament* (Grand Rapids: Eerdmans, 1969), pp. 986-87. Harrison notes that although the actual length of the Psalms has been debated, the book division was probably made by Ezra and could be considered part of the text.

Psalm 2 turns to another transcendent issue. God "sits in the heavens and laughs" at the nations (Ps. 2:4). It concludes with, "Worship the Lord with reverence, and rejoice with trembling. Do homage to the Son, lest He become angry, and you perish in the way" (Ps. 2:11-12). These lines speak of a God who sits above the heavens and offers His Son, through the Incarnation, the redemption of the world. Here is the third transcendence idea: *redemption*. The whole first book carries this theme through and closes on a psalm that talks about God's ability to lift out of *sin, sickness, and trouble* (Ps. 41). Great outworkings of God's redemptive power: this is a demonstration of His transcendence and immanence.

Psalms 3 and 4 continue the redemptive emphasis. Psalm 3 is a morning prayer, and Psalm 4 is the evening prayer. Prayer is a means in accomplishing God's redemptive purposes, illustrated by Christ's prayer in the Upper Room and the Garden of Gethsemane (John 17-18). But why do the Psalms have listed "morning and evening" prayers at this juncture? The tone draws us back to the first days of creation. The first creation is ordered from "evening to morning" (Gen. 1:5). Could it be that the new prayer vigil expressed in Psalms 3 and 4 reflects a new structure of the creation day from morning to evening, paralleling the "sunrise" of the Son of God, a morning to evening progression? I think this is very likely.

Moving on in the first book, Psalm 8 continues the "true transcendence" emphases, speaking of the wonderful creation of man, and a better creation of the "new" man, Christ. Transcendence even opens and closes the psalm: "O Lord, our Lord, How majestic is Thy name in all the earth" (1:1,9).

From this point on in Book I, the Psalms turn the reader's attention to the theme of "deliverance," a theme which comes to maturity in the next book.

2. *Hierarchy (Ps. 42-72)*

The first psalm of the section introduces the same topics in line with the hierarchical principle of the Deuteronomic covenant. Psalm 42 opens Book II: "As the deer pants for the water brooks, so my soul pants for Thee, O God. My soul thirsts for God, for the living God; When shall I come and appear before God? My tears have been my food day and night, while they say to me all day long, 'Where is your God?'" (Ps. 42:1-3).

The second part of Deuteronomy summarizes a "wilderness ex-

perience" in the life of Israel, when God taught them about His faithfulness by delivering them from all kinds of enemies. Psalm 42 reflects a similar time of great testing in the Psalmist's life, when Saul
was chasing him in hot pursuit. Saul was God's representative, and
he was in conflict with another representative. David was the new
heir. People around him were saying, "If you're such a hero, why
doesn't your God get you out of this?" But David knew that if God
could help him kill a giant like Goliath, He could certainly remove
Saul from his path. David was caught in the wilderness experience of
conflict between two representatives, one in the process of apostasy
and the other in the process of victory. Yet, God was taking him
through a time which would prove *His faithfulness*. It was also a time
for David to be responsively faithful.

For his faithfulness, God gave him the opportunity to build His
house. Book II of the Psalms continues the basic theme of "trusting
in a time when deliverance is needed." Psalm 71, the second to the
last of this section, concludes on the note, "In thee have I taken
refuge; Let me never be ashamed" (Ps. 71:1). God heard this request.
When David failed him at the end and was not allowed to go ahead
with the building of the Temple, God was faithful to his *son*, Solomon. The very last psalm of this section is by and about Solomon
(Ps. 72). David had been true to God's hierarchy. God made David's
name live on as part of His hierarchy through Solomon.

Book II concentrates almost exclusively on the concept of "deliverance of the Lord's representative." Certainly, this idea appears in
Book I and some of the other books. But, roughly eighty percent of
the psalms of this section develop the theme of deliverance. Each
time, the Psalmist comes to the conclusion that "God will deliver His
anointed." In the Deuteronomic covenant, Moses called Israel's attention to the same principle. For example, Moses said, "But the
Lord said to me, 'Do not fear him [Bashan], for I have *delivered* him
and all his people and his lands into your hand' " (Deut. 3:2). Moses
was God's hierarchical representative, and he asked for the same
thing as David (Deut. 2:31; 3:3).

So, the Deuteronomic structure of Psalms continues to hold true.

3. Ethics (Ps. 73-89)

The third section of the Psalms unmistakably follows the covenantal pattern of Deuteronomy. The entire section starts with a
psalm on the *ethical cause/effect* theme (Ps. 73). The end, or effect, of

the wicked is contrasted with that of the righteous. In Deuteronomy, we saw the same. The third section of the covenant recapitulated the stipulations of the covenant, the Ten Commandments. Covenant-keepers received life. Covenant-breakers end in death. The Psalmist concludes the first psalm of the third book, "For, behold, those who are far from Thee will perish; Thou hast destroyed all those who are unfaithful" (Ps. 73:27).

We also saw in Deuteronomy that one of the ethical cause/effect emphases was that only the *son* can fulfill God's commandments (p. 61). Only the true son, or image-bearer, can implement the law and conquer. In the third section of Deuteronomy, all three images of sonship—prophet, priest, and king—are discussed. The third book of the Psalms speaks of a true image-bearer to come. We find the great sonship chapter, Psalm 80. Written by Asaph, Levite (the first-born son of Israel [Ex. 32]), the psalm speaks of Israel as God's true son. Asaph writes, "O God of hosts, turn again now, we beseech Thee; Look down from heaven and see, and take care of this vine [Israel], even the shoot which Thy right hand has planted, and on the *son* whom Thou hast strengthened for Thyself" (Ps. 80:14-15).

It could be argued that there are other psalms on "sonship" in other sections of the Psalms. But Book III seems to bring out the theme more clearly because it closes with probably the most power-ful expression of the Davidic covenant as a covenant of "sonship." It is the only place in Scripture that specifically refers to David's rela-tionship to God as being a "covenant." The psalm says,

He [David] will cry to Me, Thou art my Father, My God, and the rock of my salvation. I also shall make him My *first-born*, the highest of the kings of the earth. My lovingkindness I will keep for him forever, and My *covenant* shall be confirmed to him. So I will establish his descendants forever, and his throne as the days of heaven. If his sons forsake My law, and do not walk in My judgments, If they violate My statutes, and do not keep My commandments, then I will visit their transgressions with the rod, and their iniquity with stripes (Ps. 89:26-32).

This statement pulls the ethical emphasis together. David was God's son. His sons were expected to obey God's stipulations, the Ten Commandments. If they didn't, there would be discipline. So, the final Psalm of Book III closes on this note. It follows the basic pattern that leads to the next principle of the Biblical covenant. Psalm 89 is about the cutting of the covenant. The covenant-cutting theme sets the tone for the *judicial* aspect of the covenant. Psalm 89 is the perfect transition.

4. Sanctions (Ps. 90-106)

Book IV of Psalms highlights the *judicial* theme. More than in any other section of the Psalms, the sanctions are mentioned. Both Psalms 103 and 104 begin, "Bless the Lord oh my soul." Man blesses God because God first blessed him. The remainder of those psalms speak of God's rich benediction on man.

Most of the other psalms of this section are imprecatory. An imprecatory psalm invokes God's curse on His enemies. Reasons are given and then a request is made to vindicate and carry out immediate vengeance on those who are attacking God's people. Psalm 94 begins,

O Lord, God of vengeance; God of vengeance, shine forth! Rise up, O Judge of the earth; Render recompense to the proud. How long shall the wicked, O Lord, How long shall the wicked exult? They pour forth words, they speak arrogantly; All who do wickedness vaunt themselves. They crush Thy people, O Lord, and afflict Thy heritage. They slay the widow and the stranger, and murder the orphans. And they have said, "The Lord does not see, nor does the God of Jacob pay heed" (Ps. 94:1-7).

Book IV ends with Psalm 106. It is somewhat of a complete history of Israel. In a way, all of the covenantal themes come together, but the psalm ends on the note of Israel's being disinherited from the land. Another receives the final blessing of the Lord (Ps. 106:40-48). This carries out the judicial sanctions and pushes into the final part of the covenant.

5. Continuity (Ps. 107-150)

The final book of the Psalms ends on the inheritance theme. In this section, we find the most quoted psalm in the New Testament, "The LORD said to my Lord, 'Sit at My right hand until Thy enemies are made a footstool under Thy feet'" (Ps. 110:1). What does this have to do with inheritance? The "LORD" is God the Father, and "my Lord" is Jesus Christ, God the Son. Jesus Christ goes to the right hand of God the Father at the Ascension (Acts 1:6-11). He is not to come back "until" all the enemies of God are defeated. His estate passes into the trusteeship of the saints. This matches what we have previously observed. At the end of all the other covenants, they speak of a new inheritance being given. As Adam was cast out of one realm and into another, so Christians are taken into the new inheritance which Christ systematically gives them, the earth (Matt. 5:5).

The principle of continuity is underscored by the "Psalms of Ascent" in this section (Ps. 120-134). These are psalms meant to be sung on the way to Passover in Jerusalem. They are called Psalms of Ascent because Jerusalem was on a mountain. One had to climb God's mountain while he made his way to the Passover. This was the Feast of the great meal with God. It commemorated the disinheritance of the Egyptian's inheritance, the loss of their firstborn, and the new inheritance of Israel, the Promised Land. The Passover meal was the primary symbol of continuity and discontinuity.

So, these are psalms to be sung on the way to one's true inheritance. They taught many principles of walking with God. Every year was begun with Passover, and every year marched forward to another festival time when the mountain would be climbed again. History was always moving upward, toward God. This was the Israelites' true hope.

The Psalms close with a final call to worship, but the next to the last psalm is a powerful statement of the final *disinheritance* of the apostate, and the reward of the *new inheritance* to the righteous.

Let the godly ones exult in glory; Let them sing for joy on their beds. Let the high praises of God be in their mouth, and a two-edged sword in their hand, to execute vengeance on the nations, and punishment on the peoples; To bind their kings with chains, and their nobles with fetters of iron; to execute on them the judgment written; This is an honor for all His godly ones. Praise the Lord! (Ps. 149:5-9).

Remember how the Psalms began in the garden, and then Psalm 2 started off, "Why are the nations in an uproar?" Answer: they are trying to war with the God of heaven and earth, but they are fighting a losing proposition. Psalm 149 says what will happen. The kings of the earth will be brought down by God's righteousness. How specifically? The civil magistrate bears the "two-edged" sword (Rom. 13:1ff.), and the priesthood (Church) takes the Gospel. One is the ministry of blessing, the other of cursing. Both are needed to bring the world to the Davidic King who is ultimately Christ.

Again we see the value of covenantal theology. Without understanding the principle of "image-bearing *representatives*," the reader could abuse this psalm. But God does not give every responsibility to every individual. Biblical society operates by representation, avoiding tyranny on the one hand, and anarchy on the other. So Psalm 2 raises the question, and Psalm 149 gives the ultimate answer. The illegitimate will be driven off the earth, and the true legitimate heirs will take possession of what rightfully belongs to them, final continuity and discontinuity being set up.

Conclusion

Psalms has a Deuteronomic structure. We are safe in concluding that the Old Testament continues to follow the covenantal pattern.

But does it continue into the New Testament? Someone might be saying at this point, "I agree that Deuteronomy is the structure of the covenant in the Old Testament, but things change in the times of Jesus, don't they?" Do they? Let us now consider in the next three appendixes the structure of one of the Gospels, an epistle, and the Book of Revelation. Then we will be able to see if this covenantal pattern extends into the age where the "New Covenant" Christian lives!

Appendix 3

MATTHEW

Every "Adam" up to the time of Christ had failed to redeem man. The first Adam's sin led to death, and his death spread to the whole world (Rom. 5:12). He *legally* represented the rest of humanity. Before each person was even born, he was guilty of the "original sin" of Adam. Like the old Puritan primer says, "In Adam's fall we sinned all." Adam's own family bore the consequences, as brother killed brother.

But God had promised a "Seed" (Gen. 3:15). Not many "seeds," but one Seed who would come to redeem the world (Gal. 3:16). Every mother waited to see if her son would be the savior. What were they really waiting for? A *New Adam*. Not only would this New Adam save the world, but he would raise up faithful sons to dominate the earth.

Was it Seth, Adam's replacement son for Abel? No, Seth failed to be the new Adam and provide true sons. Within a few generations, his sons were marrying covenant-breakers. Their offspring were so vicious and corrupt that God was willing to destroy His entire creation (Gen. 6:1ff.). God found one righteous man left, Noah.

Was it Noah? No, but in a way he was. The world was delivered by his ark. He started to re-build the world in God's image. Before long, however, one of his sons apostatized, bolted from the faith, and started another line of covenant-breakers. The power of sin was greater than grace. The Tower of Babel episode plunged the world into another horrible fall. Noah's life came to a sad end. He proved to be like the "old" Adam. There was still no New Adam.

How about Abraham? No. Yet, Abraham seemed to begin the world all over again after the Tower of Babel had thrown everything into "confusion." The Tower of Babel created the need for a new priesthood. God chose the Hebrews. Abraham was circumcised and given a "seed," Isaac. The Messianic line was narrowed. But the fact that Isaac came meant Abraham was not the New Adam. He died like the rest. Also, the line of the Patriarchs, Abraham's successors (Isaac, Jacob, etc.), wound up in serious trouble. Jacob's sons turned on the one faithful son, Joseph, sold him into slavery, and a famine (death) came to the land. Joseph ended up in Egypt. Eventually, he rescued the Patriarchs and his whole race, when God's revelation to him resulted in his being second in command to Pharaoh. Before long, however, Joseph had died, his sons had failed, and Israel was in bondage in a foreign land.

Who would save them? Moses? No. He certainly was the next deliverer, but in the end he also died. He successfully led Israel out of bondage, across the Red Sea, and on their way to the Promised Land. But Moses was like the old Adam. His impatience and anger caused him to fall. He died outside the Land of Promise. A new savior was needed. Who would he be? Joshua? Samson? Gideon? These were all likely candidates, but each could not save Israel or the world from its sin. What was the answer? Israel asked for a *king*. The first one was Saul whose life ended in apostasy. The second became the most powerful king in the history of Israel.

Was the new Adam David? No. Prohibited by God from building His house, he died. But his beginning was glorious. He was the "man after God's own heart." His remarkable career indicated that he was going to deliver Israel and set up the kingdom of God. When he was crowned the "son of God" (II Sam. 7), the "Davidic Millennium" began, a time roughly 1,000 years before the birth of Christ (Matt. 1:1ff.). His millenium began a time of unprecedented peace, but it was short-lived. He too fell, and all his sons apostatized. Only Solomon came back to the faith. Even so, by the middle of this millennium, in the sixth century before Christ, Israel was in captivity. David had not succeeded any better than the very first Adam. God brought His covenant lawsuit against the nation time and again through His prophets. Israel would not repent, so He judged them with captivity and slavery to foreign powers (Deut. 28:60-68).

During captivity in Babylon, half way through David's millennium, God revealed to Daniel that a Messiah would come in another 500 years or so. He would make a new *covenant*.

Seventy weeks [literally "sevens" = approximately 490 years] have been decreed for your people to build your holy city (Jerusalem), to finish the transgression, to make an end of sin, to make atonement for iniquity, to bring in everlasting righteousness, to seal up vision and prophecy, and to anoint the most holy place.

So you are to know and discern that from the issuing of a decree to restore and rebuild Jerusalem until Messiah the Prince there will be seven weeks and sixty-two weeks; It will be built again, with plaza and moat, even in times of distress.

Then after the sixty-two weeks [the sixty-ninth week] the Messiah will be cut off and have nothing, and the people of the prince who is to come will destroy the city and sanctuary. And its end will come with a flood; even to the end there will be war; desolations are determined.

And He will make firm a *covenant* with the many for one week, but in the middle of the week He (Christ) will put a stop to sacrifice and grain offering (by His death); and on the wing of abominations will come one who makes desolate, even until a complete destruction, one that is decreed, is poured out on the one who makes desolate (A.D. 70 [Dan. 9:24-27]).

Daniel had prayed that God would be faithful to His *covenant* (Dan. 9:4). He wanted his people to be sent back to Jerusalem, but he also wanted to know exactly how long they had to turn away from their sins. Answer: they had until forty years after the death of the Messiah which would be approximately 490 years from the "decree" referred to, the prophecy God was revealing to Daniel.[1] So, God told him that there would be the coming of the Messiah, and that His true atonement would stop the sacrificial system of the Temple. This also meant the end of Israel's religion, the end of the holy city Jerusalem and the Temple, the place of sacrifice.

The prophecy of Daniel sums up the complete failure of Israel to be the New Adam. In fact, it brings to an end all of the "Adams" of history who had proven not to be the true sons of God, and draws Biblical history to the time of Christ. When Christ came, apostasy had again filled the land. Israel was run by demon-possessed apostates (John 8:44). Yet, in spite of the previous Adams' lack of success, the coming of the true New Adam had been progressively revealed, each new fall being followed by more redemptive light.[2]

---

1. Meredith Kline, "The Covenant of the Seventieth Week," *The Law and the Prophets*, ed. John H. Skilton (Philadelphia: Presbyterian and Reformed, 1974), pp. 452-69. Kline argues that the 490 years of Daniel ought to be viewed in a more symbolic sense, although not entirely to the exclusion of a more literal reference. His point is that 490 should be understood in a covenantal context. To the Hebrew, 490 is ten Jubilee cycles indicating a fulness. That is why I use the word "approximately."
2. Geerhardus Vos, *Biblical Theology* (Edinburgh: Banner of Truth Trust, [1948] 1975). Vos's thesis is that Revelation is *progressive*, gradually unfolding more of the New Covenant until Christ comes in history. Actually, I believe that the Old Testament is the constant re-publishing of the first covenant with Adam, necessitating a New Covenant. As each re-publication of the Old Covenant fails, therefore, the New Covenant draws closer and becomes progressively clearer.

Finally, Christ did come, and the covenant to which Daniel referred, a New *Covenant*, was sealed.

Jesus and the Deuteronomic Covenant

Daniel confirms that Jesus was coming to establish a covenant. From Jesus' own lips, it was called a "new" covenant. At the Last Supper, taking the cup He said, "This cup which is poured out for you is the *new covenant* in My blood" (Luke 22:20). What was this "covenant" to which Christ referred? Matthew gives an indication by the fact that he structured his account of the Gospel according to the Deuteronomic covenant.

Matthew arranges his book in *five sections* around Jesus' five discourses or sermons (Matt. 5-7; 10:1-42; 13:1-52; 18:1-35; 23-25). He repeats a key phrase at the close of each "book" and/or sermon to mark the end: "It came to pass when Jesus had finished these sayings" (7:28; 11:1; 13:53; 19:1; 26:1). R. V. G. Tasker, in his excellent commentary on Matthew says, "This is in effect another way of saying, 'Here endeth the first (or second, etc.) book of the oracles of Jesus the Messiah.'"[3] Matthew clearly follows some kind of five-fold structuring.

Why five? I believe Matthew develops a *covenantal framework* of the life of Christ. The book organizes around the five points of covenantalism. Thus, Matthew's Gospel simultaneously arranges according to Deuteronomy and the Pentateuch. Some work has been done comparing Matthew to the Pentateuch,[4] but none (to my knowledge) develops the book according to Deuteronomy. For the remainder of the chapter, let us compare the Deuteronomic model to Matthew.

---

3. R. V. G. Tasker, *The Gospel According to St. Matthew* (Grand Rapids: Eerdmans, 1978), p. 19.

4. B. W. Bacon, *Studies in Matthew* (London, 1931), pp. 80ff. and *passim*. Bacon was one of the first to make the observation that there were five parts. He even went further and said that the five sections of Matthew parallel the five books of the Pentateuch. Austin Farrer makes a similar observation with the exception that he proposed six sections, "On Dispensing with Q," in *Studies in the Gospels*, ed. D. E. Nineham (Oxford, 1954). Louis Bouyer, *The Spirituality of the New Testament and the Fathers* (New York: Seabury, 1982), Vol. I, pp. 92-93, also refers to the work of Farrer and agrees that Matthew has a Pentateuchal structure. For an additional comparison of Bacon and Farrer, see M. D. Goulder, *Midrash and Lection in Matthew* (London: SPCK, 1974), pp. 171ff.

The Covenantal Structure of Matthew

True Transcendence: Matthew 1:1-7:28
Hierarchy: Matthew 7:29-11:1
Ethics: Matthew 11:2-13:53
Sanctions: Matthew 13:54-19:2
Continuity: Part I—Matthew 19:3-26:1
     Part II—Matthew 26:2-28:20

1. *True Transcendence (Matt. 1:1-7:28)*

Matthew begins his Gospel by emphasizing transcendence. Remember that there are three common ways by which God distinguishes Himself and establishes His Lordship: creation, redemption, and revelation. Matthew opens his Gospel by the first two but definitely focuses on the revelation theme, just as we saw in the Deuteronomic covenant.

First, the Genesis *creation* appears in the introductory statement, "The book of the *genealogy* of Jesus Christ" (Matt. 1:1). The word "genealogy" is from the Greek word "genesis," meaning origin or lineage. It is the same word after which the first book of the Bible is named. Genesis is divided into ten sections that end, "these are the *generations* of" (Gen. 5:1; 6:9; 10:1; 11:10; 11:27; 25:12; 25:19; 36:1; 36:9; 37:2).

Second, the *redemption* theme appears in the announcement of the coming of Jesus Christ to Mary. Matthew emphasizes Joseph, a man who is caught in a moral dilemma but is delivered by God's revelation. Twice this happens. He decides to divorce Mary because she is pregnant (Matt. 1:19-25), and he has to flee to Egypt to escape the wrath of Herod, a descendant of Esau: the firstborn of Isaac (Matt. 2:1-15). Apparently, Matthew intends the reader to make the connection back to the first Joseph (Jacob's son) who experienced similar moral dilemmas, and was delivered by special revelation (Gen. 38-50). He too was taken to Egypt to escape the wrath of his elder brothers (the firstborn). Yet, Israel was sent to Egypt to escape judgment during the famine. Later, they came up out of Egypt at the Exodus for redemption.

Third, Matthew emphasizes the *revelation* theme of transcendence more than the others by means of Jesus' sermon that closes this section: the Sermon on the Mount. As Deuteronomy opened by pointing out that the words of the Deuteronomic covenant were transcendent (Deut. 1:3), from God not man, so the thrust of the first sermon contrasts Jesus' interpretation of the Law with the words of men, the "interpretations" of the Pharisees. Some have mistakenly thought that He was comparing His words to the teachings of Moses. This is not true. To pit Christ against Moses results in pitting Scripture against Scripture. As Daniel Fuller has observed, "It makes one section of Scripture anathematize another portion."[5] Moreover, Christ says, "Do not think I came to abolish the Law or the Prophets" (Matt. 5:17). Careful reading of the "you have heard it said . . ." statement, shows that Moses did not teach these ideas. Rather, they were distorted interpretations of him.

The conflict had become one of God's Word against the words of man. The Pharisees had elevated their own interpretations and writings above Scripture. Christ spoke as Divine interpreter showing that the Pharisees were wrong. This proved that God's Word and His Son are truly transcendent and immanent. Man's words are neither. By so doing, Jesus re-established the Deuteronomic covenant and placed Himself at the Head as the new Moses. At the end of the book, like Moses, He died before entering the new Canaan (the whole world), but unlike Moses He did not remain dead. He rose to become the true Joshua. From the beginning of Matthew's Gospel, therefore, we see how the author self-consciously structured according to the Deuteronomic pattern.

At the end of the sermon, we read, "The result was that when Jesus had finished these words, the multitudes were amazed at His teaching: for He was teaching them as one having *authority*" (Matt. 7:28-29). This hinge draws to a conclusion the true transcendence segment and takes us to the next subject: *hierarchy*.

2. Hierarchy (Matt. 7:29-11:1)

Matthew follows Book I with the theme of *hierarchy*. Matthew 8 takes us right to the idea of authority. Beginning with the account of the Leper, we read of an encounter which is the classic passage on "authority," the story of the Centurion. A Centurion came to Christ because his servant was lying at home, paralyzed and suffering much pain (Matt. 8:6). Christ said He would be willing to come, but the Centurion told Jesus that he was not worthy to have Him under his roof. Then the Centurion made a remarkable comment. He

---

5. Daniel P. Fuller, *Gospel and Law* (Grand Rapids: Eerdmans, 1980), p. 69.

said, "Just say the word and my servant will be healed. For I, too, am a man under *authority*, with soldiers under me; and I say to this one, 'Go!' and he goes, and to another, 'Come!' and he comes, and to my slave, 'Do this!' and he does it" (Matt. 8:8-9). Jesus was taken by his comment and said He had not seen "faith" like this in all of Israel.

The Centurion understood authority in terms of the power of *mediation*. He gave an order, and the servant, or the one to whom the command was given, carried out what was commanded. The Centurion could therefore extend his authority over great distances. He saw that Christ had a similar but even greater authority. Jesus was able to bring things to pass with His Word. Through the "Word," life (or death) could be mediated to someone. The Centurion says, "Just say the *word*." The Roman officer believed in a mediated system of government. The following passages contain a series of healings where Christ mediates judgment unto life and death. For example, not only does Christ heal the Centurion's servant, but He heals Peter's mother-in-law (Matt. 8:14-17). He also judges unto death when He casts out and effectively destroys the demons of the Gadarene demoniac (Matt. 8:28-34).

The concept of a mediated system of authority comes to full force during Jesus' second sermon. He names and then commissions His disciples to exercise His authority on the earth (Matt. 10:1-15). They have the power to bless and curse. Any city that does not receive them will be judged worse than Sodom and Gomorrah (Matt. 10:15). By placing a harsher judgment on the cities that refuse Christ's ordained mediators of authority, the sermon parallels the second section of Deuteronomy, with one exception. In Deuteronomy, Moses was head of the covenant. In Matthew, Christ is the Head. His authority is being applied to the earth. This explains why judgment intensifies in the New Covenant.

Matthew concludes Book II with a reference to the role of the *prophet*. The disciples are compared to the prophets. Christ promises that anyone who receives His servants receives His authority and the reward will be great (Matt. 10:40-42). This points us toward the ethical section.

3. Ethics (Matt. 11:2-13:53)

The ethics segment of Deuteronomy concentrated on the *fulfillment of righteousness*. Three subordinate ideas formed around this concept: conquest, consecration, and image-bearing. Matthew makes all of the same emphases by starting Book III with the account of John the Baptist, the prophet (Matt. 11:2-19). Why the prophet and what does this have to do with the ethical theme? The prophet was the *embodiment of the Word of God*. Literally, he was a miniature incarnation of the *fulfillment of righteousness*. He reminded the people of the basic *ethical cause/effect relationship*. He did so by means of a covenant lawsuit.

Additionally, the prophet was a special image-bearer. Remember, the image-bearer was tied to sonshsip in the third section of Deuteronomy (p. 61). Only a son could properly image the Father. Sonship was purely in terms of ethics and not any physical or methaphysical reflection. The one who obeyed was the true image-bearer and son of God. When all of God's sons turned away, the prophet was always there to recall to the minds of God's people that they needed to live like "sons." Since he was the incarnation of the Word of God, he represented living sonship to them.

Matthew also develops the fulfillment of righteousness theme in the third section around the difficult ethical question of the Sabbath (Matt. 12:1-14). By placing this sequence here, Matthew focuses our attention on the heart of the covenant, law. The Pharisees accused Jesus of changing the law of the covenant (Matt. 12:2). But He turned their arguments against them and said, "Have you not read in the Law, that on the Sabbath the priests in the temple break the Sabbath, and are innocent? But I say to you that something greater than the temple is here" (Matt. 12:5-6). So the ethics of the Old Covenant had not changed, only its application. Jesus was the new temple and that meant that the Sabbath could be broken in His presence. Since He is the true Rest of God, however, the Sabbath continues forever in Him. Christ had become the Law of God. Ironically, when Christ was present, the Sabbath was broken and kept simultaneously. How could this be? He declared Himself the "Lord of the Sabbath" (Matt. 12:8).

Finally, Matthew concludes the ethics section with Jesus' third sermon. He uses the medium of parables to present the fulfillment of righteousness in the coming of the kingdom. Remember that Moses taught that conquest came as a result of faithfulness to the righteousness of the covenant in Deuteronomy. In the same manner, strong ethical as well as dominical concerns surface in Jesus' words. He begins with the famous "parable of the soils" (Matt. 13:1-23). The message is simple. The Word of God is the seed that falls in different types of soils. Only the soil that perseveres in obedience becomes fertile ground for the birth of the kingdom. Jesus perfectly fulfills this parable in the narrowest sense in that He completely fulfilled the righteousness of the Father and gave birth to the kingdom of God. In its broadest application, however, the followers of Christ would be the new soil in which the kingdom would be born.

Jesus continues to use parables to weave ethical faithfulness together with the coming of the kingdom. He finishes on the parable of the dragnet (Matt. 13:47-50). At the "end of the age" the kingdom of God will be fully established when the wicked are separated from the faithful on the basis of fulfilled righteousness (Matt. 13:49). The parallel with Deuteronomy continues in full force.

4. Sanctions (Matt. 13:54-19:1)

Matthew's fourth section of his book attests to the *sanctions* theme. Immediately we see sanction and counter-sanction at the end of the 13th and 14th chapters. The evangelist returns to the "prophetic" theme with a discussion about how a "prophet is not welcome in his own home town" (Matt. 13:48-54), provoking the question "Why?" The prophet is not welcome because he brings sanctions by means of covenant lawsuit. Not a very popular role. As a matter of fact, Jesus' own friends and family sanctioned Him by disregarding His teaching and miracles. With this introduction, Matthew prepares us for the sanction emphasis.

In the very next chapter, the first full chapter of this segment, he tells us about the beheading of John the Baptist. John is the prophet who has brought covenant lawsuit against King Herod. In the sanctions section of Deuteronomy, I said that this function was to be performed by the "witness" of the covenant. As a "witness," John publically prosecuted the king (Matt. 14:4). The king had John put in prison, and Herodias had him put to death. John had sanctioned and the king had counter-sanctioned. When Christ learned of the prophet's death, He withdrew. But instead of letting the people starve by the loss of His presence, He gave them blessing sanction in the feeding of the five thousand (Matt. 14:13-21). Christ countered the sanction of Herod, which took away the Word, by providing a better sanction in the sacrament of communion.

The same pattern of sanction and counter-sanction repeats itself through the remainder of the section. For example, in chapter 15, the Pharisees initiate covenant lawsuit against Jesus, charging Him with breaking the tradition of the elders (Matt. 15:2). Christ counters with a sanction of cursing, calling them "hypocrites" (Matt. 15:7). In effect, He was issuing His own *covenant lawsuit*, thus picking up where John the Baptist had left off. In the following section, again Jesus withdraws and feeds the blessing sanction of communion to the 4,000. Chapter 15 parallels the sanction/counter-sanction pattern of chapter 14.

Finally, Jesus concludes the sanction section with His fourth sermon (Matt. 18). The topic is *church discipline*, most certainly a sanction theme. He leads into the discussion by talking about the need to excise that member that causes the rest of the body to stumble (Matt. 18:6-14). He even starts with a sanction word, "woe," meaning "curse" (Matt. 18:7). Then He presents the actual process of discipline (Matt. 18:15-20), concluding on how the unrepentant should be excommunicated. But Jesus closes His sermon on the very practical note of forgiveness (Matt. 18:21-35). Why? *Forgiveness* is the sanction of *blessing*, the appropriate response to the one who has responded properly to the sanction of cursing. The sermon ends with the familiar refrain added by Matthew, "And it came about that when Jesus had finished these words" (Matt. 19:1).

5. *Continuity (Matt. 19:2-28:20)*

The final section breaks into two halves: covenantal discontinuity (Matt. 19:2-26:1) and covenantal continuity (Matt. 26:2-28:20). Because the book climaxes in the greatest continuity and discontinuity of history, this is the largest section. Matthew begins first with the complete disinheritance of Israel through repeated emphasis on judgment. Then, he concludes the book with the Death and Resurrection of Christ, the establishment of new heirs, and new inheritance.

A. *Discontinuity*

The opening passage of this section sounds a clear note of covenantal discontinuity. Matthew 19 starts with the great divorce question. Divorce is the covenantal process of creating discontinuity. Specifically, divorce cuts off inheritance. While the Pharisees are asking questions about divorce between man and woman, Jesus answers in such a way as to turn the matter to the issue of inheritance. He argues that true inheritance can only be found in the kingdom of God (Matt. 19:12).

In the same context, we find the rich young ruler coming to Christ to find out how to "obtain eternal life" (Matt. 19:16). The word "obtain" means "inherit" because in the Lukan account it says, "What must I do to *inherit* eternal life" (Luke 18:18). Jesus tells him that he must give up his inheritance (everything that he has) to have eternal life. In other words, he loses his inheritance to gain God's. Of course the new inheritance includes the old plus an expansion. Jesus says as much when He tells His disciples in the same context, "And everyone who has left houses or brothers or sisters or father or mother or children or farms for My name's sake, shall receive many times as much, and shall *inherit* eternal life" (Matt. 19:29).

The key to this encounter is that *the rich young ruler represents Israel*. Israel's inheritance via the Old Covenant had become its god. It worshipped the land, namely its own inheritance, committing the ancient sin of Baalism. Jesus called them to repentance, therefore, by forfeiting what they had come to worship. As a result, His inheritance would be their previous land plus the whole world. One would think that such an offer would not be refused. Israel did refuse and was disinherited. More to the point, Israel refused because they were envious of the fact that God was willing to include the gentiles into His inheritance. In the parable of the vineyard, those who grumble because they receive the same amount as the man who comes late in the day are fired (Matt. 20:14). They are Israel, receiving covenantal discontinuity.

For the next several chapters, one section after another pronounces judgment and total discontinuity between God and Israel. First, Jesus enters Jerusalem, cleanses the temple, and curses the fig tree, a symbol of Israel (Matt. 21:1-22). Second, He tells the parable of the landowner where the wicked tenants who kill the prophets and and the owner's son are brought to a wretched end, and the owner rents out the vineyard to other vinegrowers and pays the proceeds (inheritance) at seasons (Matt. 21:41). Third, Jesus tells another parable about a man who shows up at the king's wedding feast without wedding clothing on. He is thrown out of the "kingdom" (Matt. 22:1-14). The man represents Israel being cut off from its inheritance. Fourth, Jesus pronounces eight "woes" (curses) over Jerusalem (Matt. 23:1-39). Fifth, Jesus gives his last sermon of the book and describes the actual destruction of Jerusalem. Its total devastation implies the complete discontinuity we have been examining. Then finally, Christ applies the destruction of Jerusalem to the final judgment of the world where the wicked receive their just rewards: total disinheritance (Matt. 25:31-46).

B. Continuity

Unique to the fifth section of Matthew, Matthew attaches his usual formula to the end of Jesus' sermon (Matt. 26:1). But it is not the end of the book or section. He has discussed total discontinuity, but now he directs his attention to covenantal continuity. It begins with the institution of the Lord's Supper at the time of *Passover*. Remember, this meal originally disinherited the Egyptians, and transferred the wealth of the wicked into the hands of the Israelites. Jesus' meal and death is the Passover in reverse. This time, the Jews are disinherited, and the Gentiles receive the wealth of the Jews. We can say that through Jesus' taking of man's discontinuity — loss of inheritance due to the Fall — the world receives continuity.

Jesus, of course, is the "lamb" without blemish. After the meal, He is led to be slaughtered. The First-born Son dies — not the first-born of the Egyptians, but the First-born of God. But this First-born does not stay in the grave. The first-born of the Egyptians had all died (Ex. 12:30). They were helpless. God's First-born rises again at dawn, the time the original Passover march was to have begun. On this Resurrection Day, however, Christ begins a triumphal march into Jerusalem. He gathers His people and holds another meal. This time the inheritance is regained. Continuity is created with the covenant-keepers.

Matthew concludes his book with the Great Commission, drawing both the section of the covenant and our study of Jesus' covenant to a close. The best statement of the Great Commission is found at the end of Matthew. This is the new dominion charter attached to the end of the covenant: a statement of the Church's new inheritance. We saw the same thing at the end of Deuteronomy. Jesus appears as the new Joshua commanding His army to take the land that belongs to them. A significant shift has taken place, one from the Land of Palestine to the *world*. Since this Commission is structured according to the covenant, I will develop it later. Nevertheless, Matthew verifies that the Gospel ends in dominion in the form of another mini-covenant, proving *dominion by covenant*.

Conclusion

Matthew follows Deuteronomy's covenant structure. Without a doubt, the structure of the two books is parallel. But the theological ramifications are important. It means the New Covenant is not completely new in structure and content. It builds on the Old Covenant, making the New simply a refurbishing of the Old.

But someone might say, "The Gospels, for the most part, are still in the Old Covenant economy, coming just before the death of Christ where the transition from Old to New took place. Does the Deuteronomic covenantal pattern still continue to influence the rest of the New Testament? How about the epistles? They don't have this structure do they?" Yes they do, and with a simple over-view of the book of Romans, I believe we will see the pattern again.

Appendix 4

ROMANS

Paul's letter to the Church at Rome is probably the most important of all the New Testament epistles. Why? Because Paul systematically presents *the doctrines of the Christian faith*. Nowhere else in the Bible do we find such an ordered treatment. For the new convert, Romans plants his feet solidly in the most important doctrines of the faith. For the older Christian, the book is a constant reminder of the basics that have to be returned to over and over again.

For our purposes, Romans is laid out in the form of the *covenant*. The structure of the epistles is similar to what we saw in the prophets. They all vary somewhat, but it is apparent that the five points of covenantalism are the basic organizing structure. In Romans, Paul follows the covenant in detail.

The Covenantal Structure of Romans

True Transcendence: Romans 1:1-17
Hierarchy: Romans 1:18-11:36
Ethics: Romans 12:1-15:33
Sanctions: Romans 16:1-2
Continuity: Romans 16:3-27

1. True Transcendence (Rom. 1:1-17)

Paul introduces himself as a "Bond-servant of Christ Jesus, called as an Apostle, set apart for the gospel of God" (Rom. 1:1). Without any delay, Paul makes certain that he communicates to the Romans the *transcendent* character of his ministry and message. Neither came from himself or man, but from God, from *without*. On the other hand, his ministry and message have the presence of God. In the past, we have seen covenants open on a *redemptive* note. Paul has been "hand-picked" by God to be an Apostle, involving the tran-

246

scendent creator of the universe in the life of His messenger. So, his communication to them is distinct (transcendent) and bears the evidence of the presence (immanence) of God.

One other interesting factor about the opening section of Romans is that although it emphasizes the first part of the covenant, it also has the over-all pattern of the covenant. Note that Paul's introductory thoughts follow these themes.

True Transcendence: (v. 1)
"Bond-service," "calling," and being "set apart."

Hierarchy: (vv. 2-4)
Historical development of "promise" through the Incarnation.

Ethics: (v. 5)
Paul's ministry to produce "obedience."

Sanctions: (vv. 6-15)
Sanction of "grace to you" (v. 6). Special prayer of blessing also emphasizing sanction.

Continuity: (vv. 16-17)
"To the Jew first" and then the "Gentile" refers to the continuity and discontinuity of the coming of the Gospel. The true child of faith comes by *faith* (v. 17).

Many times the Bible includes the covenant structure on a miniature scale within one of the sub-points. Paul begins his letter this way. Romans starts where the other covenants have — with Paul's own calling, the Incarnation, and prayer emphasizing transcendence and immanence — but the section progresses along the five points of covenantalism. At the conclusion of Paul's prayer, an "amen" is implied, although not expressly stated so as not to break the continuity. Paul actually inserts an "amen" at 1:25, but it seems to be in relation to "blessing God," and not in connection to his prayer mentioned in 1:10ff. At the next two transition points, however, Paul will use the word "amen" (Rom. 11:36; 15:33).

The transition out of the transcendence section and into the hierarchy is, "For I am not ashamed of the Gospel, for it is the power of God for salvation to everyone who believes, to the Jew first and also the Greek. For in it the righteousness of God is revealed from faith to faith; as it is written, 'But the righteous man shall live by faith'" (Rom. 1:16-17). Paul addresses three issues, one summing up his introduction, and the others pointing forward to the largest section of the book.

First, Paul summarizes transcendence when he says "Righteousness is *revealed* from faith to faith." The theme of revelation is one of the three ways God manifests His transcendence and immanence. What is revealed? The "righteousness of God," which is none other than Jesus Christ. In a way, this statement is the theme of the book.

Second, this draws us to the *historical* part of Paul's comment: "Revealed from *faith to faith*." He even adds, "The Jew first and also the Greek." This historic progression of Jew to Gentile is the development of Old to New Testament. This opens the way for the second section of the book.

Third, Paul refers to *justification by faith*. This is an issue of authority, a hierarchical idea that is unfolded for the next several chapters. The full verse of Habakkuk from which Paul quotes reads, "Behold, as for the *proud* one, his soul is not right within him; But the righteous shall live by faith" (Hab. 2:4). The context in Habakkuk is *pride*. A proud man is one in rebellion to God's authority. In contrast to him, a righteous man lives by faith, meaning he *submits* to the Lord. Paul's quotation of Habakkuk leads us into the next section.

2. Hierarchy (Rom. 1:18-11:36)

The hierarchical part of the covenant addresses God's authority and history's confirmation of this hierarchy. The following section, which runs from 1:18 to 11:36, is a development of these Deuteronomic ideas. Paul begins,

For the wrath of God is revealed from heaven against all ungodliness and unrighteousness of men, who *suppress the truth* in unrighteousness, because that which is *known about God* is evident within them; for God made it evident to them. For since the creation of the world His invisible attributes, His eternal power and divine nature, have been clearly seen, being understood through what has been made, so that they are without excuse. For even though they *knew* God, they did not honor Him as God, or give thanks; but they became futile in their speculations, and their foolish heart was darkened. Professing to be wise, they became fools, and exchanged the glory of the incorruptible God for an *image* in the form of corruptible man and of birds and four-footed animals and crawling creatures.

Therefore God gave them over in the *lusts* of their hearts to impurity, that their bodies might be dishonored among them. For they exchanged the truth of God for a lie, and worshipped and served the creature rather than the Creator, who is blessed forever. Amen (Rom. 1:18-23).

Man's problem of rebellion to God's authority is analyzed as manifesting itself in two ways: *idolatry* and *adultery*. Paul's comments in the first chapter address both ideas. Turning from the Gentiles, Paul speaks in regard to the Jews, and adds in the next chapter, "You who say that one should not commit *adultery*, do you commit *adultery*? You who abhor *idols*, do you rob temples?" (Rom. 2:22). These are precisely the same concepts taught by the second and seventh commandments. It was pointed out in our study of the Ten Commandments that each commandment dealt with one of the points of covenantalism, the five points being covered twice. The two commandments that fall in the *hierarchy* category are prohibitions against idolatry and adultery. Paul casts man's sin in terms of these commandments.

This also means that salvation is considered in this light, specifically *justification* (Rom. 3-5). In these chapters of Romans, Paul quotes Genesis: "Faith was reckoned to Abraham as righteousness" (Gen. 15:6). The context of Genesis follows the theme of submission. Genesis 14 concludes with Abraham's bowing his knee to Melchizedek, a type of Jesus Christ. Abraham's faith was pictured as the supreme act of submission to God. Indeed, later when Abraham is asked to offer his own son, we see again the close relationship between faith and submission. To believe God is to submit to His hierarchy.

When Paul comes to Romans 6, the influence of the second section of Deuteronomy continues. He uses the analogy of *slavery*. One never leaves a state of slavery or submission to authority (Rom. 6:15ff.), being either a slave to sin or righteousness. Then, Paul opens the next chapter with an analogy about marriage. The marriage analogy is an extension of the laws connected to the seventh commandment and defines the limits of *submission* to the authority of the Law. Finally, Paul ends the justification discussion with the next chapter (Rom. 8), developing how one is *empowered to submit to God* through the Holy Spirit.

Paul finishes the hierarchical section by a lengthy discussion of "ethnic" Israel's apostasy (Rom. 9-11). He starts by pointing out that the covenant was originally made with them and belongs to them (9:4). But they fell away because they "did not pursue it by *faith*" (9:32). This is another way of saying they did not submit to God's authority. They are so rebellious that they will not return to faith and submission until the Gentiles have been converted (Rom. 11:25ff.).

This section, considered as a whole, is actually a history of salvation: first the Gentiles and then the Jews. This historic tone is consistent with the hierarchical category of the covenant. Paul proves that history confirms God's hierarchy of salvation through faith in Christ.

Paul ends the hierarchical section with *Amen*. This time the "amen" is not implied, but stated (11:36). We should be careful not to put too much emphasis on Paul's use of "amen," because he expresses it at other points when a shift in subject matter is not implied. Not only does the structural marker indicate the section is finished, but Paul now moves from the hierarchical/authority theme to a different emphasis, indicated by his "hortatory" style. The literary shift is the primary reason for seeing the break in Paul's thought at this point.

3. Ethics (Rom. 12:1-15:33)

Consistent with the other ethical sections of the covenant, Paul lays out the program for conquest by setting forth stipulations, by correcting aspects of the image-bearing offices of king and priest, and finally by specifying his personal plan of conquest.

Paul starts with such stipulations as, "Present your bodies as a living sacrifice . . . Do not be conformed to the world . . . Let love be without hypocrisy . . . Be devoted to one another . . . Rejoice with those who rejoice . . . Do not take revenge . . ." (12:1-21). The following chapter even restates many of the Ten Commandments (13:9). Clearly, the *ethical* tone of Paul's letter is felt.

But Paul also addresses the two Adamic offices of the cultural mandate. First, he addresses kings. He talks of the proper obedience to kings or "magistrates" and their corresponding responsibility (Rom. 13:1ff.).

Second, he addresses priests. He discusses problems in the Church at Rome which were due to some who still wanted to apply some of the Old Covenant's clean/unclean boundaries. Paul's argument is: because the curse has been lifted through Christ's death, all food is open to man (Acts 10). The wall between Jew and Gentile is broken (Eph. 2:11ff.). The Gentile's food can be eaten because *he is eaten by the Gospel* (see reference to "mouth" in Rev. 3:16). To continue to maintain the dietary laws as a point of *law* is a fundamental denial of Christ's Resurrection. If a person maintains them as a point of *conviction*, he should be given deference and treated as a "weaker brother" (Rom. 14:1-23).

Paul concludes this section by returning to some general stipulations. Then he speaks of his personal program for conquest in the spread of the Gospel by outlining his plans to go to Spain, Jerusalem, and finally to Rome (15:22-29). He closes with another "amen" (15:33).

4. Sanctions (Rom. 16:1-2)

The judicial section is short and expressed in the form of a *commendation*, or special "blessing" (16:1-2). Paul "commends" Phoebe, a diaconess, who is entrusted with the responsibility of bringing the Word to them, Paul's letter to the Romans. She does not hold the *office* of deacon: rather, she holds a special *appointment*. This was one of the unique functions a woman could have in the early church. Paul's comments fall in the "sanction" category because Phoebe was sent with special blessing to bring the special blessing, the Epistle to the Romans.

5. Continuity (Rom. 16:3-27)

True to the form of so many of the epistles, Paul concludes his letter with a long list of names. Why? Continuity is maintained. Remember that the *continuity* section establishes the true heirs. In this case, Paul "greets" several people. He expresses his *approval*: "Greet Prisca and Aquila, my fellow workers in Christ Jesus, who for my life risked their necks, to whom not only do I give thanks, but also the churches of the Gentiles" (16:3); "Greet Epaenetus, my beloved, who is the first convert to Christ from Asia" (v. 5); "Greet Mary, who has worked hard for you" (v. 6); "Greet Andronicus and Junius, my kinsmen, and my fellow prisoners, who are outstanding among the apostles, who also were in Christ before me" (v. 7); "Greet Apelles, the approved in Christ" (v. 10); "Greet Rufus, a choice man in the Lord" (v. 13).

There are many more listed here, but these are special greetings' citations. These are the people in the local church at Rome who would most definitely carry it forward. But Paul mentions some who are not so noteworthy. He says, "Now I urge you, brethren, keep your eye on those who cause dissensions and hindrances contrary to the teaching which you learned. . . . And the God of peace will soon crush Satan under your feet" (16:17-20). Why doesn't Paul list their names? He does not want to give them permanent place among the honor roll listed above. He is singling them out, however, to point out the "bastards" of the community who not only break down *contin-*

uity but will lose it themselves if they don't change.

Paul also makes a comment that goes all the way back to Genesis three, "The God of peace will soon crush Satan under your feet" (16:20). God had told Eve that her "seed" would crush the head of the serpent (Gen. 3:15). This curse was part of the judicial sanction and the promise of continuity in the legitimacy section. Here Paul does the same. While cursing the "trouble-makers," he makes a *promise of continuity* that Satan will be destroyed.

One final comment. This list establishes the principle of Church rolls and records. The Bible is full of *rolls of membership*. The Book of Numbers begins and ends with one, and any time the nation is re-constituted, lists start to appear. Why? There can be no discipline, meaning excommunication, if there is nothing to be disciplined from. How can someone be cast out if he is not a member? He can't. Today when the *absence* of church rolls is in vogue, the conclusion is that there really cannot be effective discipline. Sure, discipline can be abused, but the abuse does not nullify its use. Also, records keep track of any judicial proceedings for future generations. The Roman Catholic Church has a long record of all its court cases. Unfortunately, Protestantism doesn't! Since Biblical law is applied through a "precedent" system, these records are invaluable. They help future generations to determine how to make decisions. They help to maintain the proper continuity.

Conclusion

Paul follows the pattern of the covenant in his letter to the Romans. His thought is so ordered by it that he even develops his sub-points in this fashion. Most students of the Bible will notice that most of the epistles, especially the Pauline ones, follow the Deuteronomic structure. But one last portion of the Bible remains to be considered, perhaps the most controversial of the Bible, Revelation. Is the last book ordered according to the covenant? It would seem that if my thesis is right, that the five points of covenantalism are indeed the structure of the covenant and of the Bible itself, then the final book of Scripture should have this pattern somewhere. Not only does the Book of Revelation have the pattern, the whole book follows the Deuteronomic pattern. And it is one of the most obvious examples in the New Testament, indeed in the entire Bible.

Appendix 5

REVELATION

The Deuteronomic model of the covenant is carried into the New Testament. Two prime examples are Matthew and Romans. Now, last but not least is perhaps the clearest presentation of the covenant in the New Testament. The Book of Revelation conveniently falls into five sections.

The Covenantal Structure of Revelation

True Transcendence (Preamble): 1:1-20
Hierarchy (Historical Prologue): 2:1-22 (7 churches)
Ethics (Stipulations): 4:1-7:17 (7 seals)
Sanctions (Ratification): 8:1-14:20 (7 trumpets)
Continuity (Succession Arrangements): 15:1-22:21 (7 bowls)

Understanding Revelation as a covenant is the single most helpful insight about its structure. How so? The Book of Revelation is about an awful judgment on the earth. Fire and brimestone fall; a great battle called Armageddon is fought; even the dragon, Satan, is finally cast into the pit. If any book is about judgment, Revelation is.

The covenant model, however, connects this judgment with the *covenantal lawsuit* concept.[1] A covenant lawsuit was brought against someone who had made covenant with God, broken it, and been unwilling to make amends. When this happened, God sent messengers to file the suit—normally three, since two or three witnesses were needed to obtain a conviction (Deut. 17:16). But in this case of God's lawsuit against someone, the witnesses announced a *verdict already reached* in the Lord's High Court of heaven. Revelation opens in this context, using the covenant structure to present the terms of judgment.

---

1. In Chapter 14, I discussed at length the concept of "covenantal lawsuit."

Who is the judgment against? First, the student of Revelation should realize that the language of the book itself restricts the prophecies, almost exclusively, to the *first century*. Revelation begins, "The Revelation of Jesus Christ, which God gave Him to show to His bond-servants, *the things which shortly must take place*" (Rev. 1:1). Then, at the end of the book, the nearness of all the prophecies of Revelation is again underscored when John says, "The Lord, the God of the spirits of the prophets, sent His angel to show to His bond-servants *the things which shortly must take place*" (Rev. 22:6). Anyone, therefore, who takes the Bible seriously, should recognize that the prophecies of Revelation concerned the *immediate future*.

Second, having established the time brackets, we see that the specific judgments of Revelation are against the *Old Covenant people, the animal sacrifice system, and its center, the Temple in Jerusalem*. Everything in the book focuses on the destruction of the Old Covenant, particularly Jerusalem, the heart of the Old Covenant religion. Then, after an elaborate discussion of the annihilation of the old "holy people," the book concludes on a description of the "new" Temple, and Holy City (Rev. 21-22).

Most modern students of Revelation generally have a "futurist" perspective of Revelation, so this interpretation might seem novel, but the view I have proposed for Revelation, called a "preterist" interpretation, is not new. Commentaries are being published now which indicate that this was one of the standard views of the church through the ages.[2] I will leave the details of this thesis, however, to David Chilton, a theologically orthodox thinker who has just completed a commentary on Revelation, *The Days of Vengeance*.[3]

Nevertheless, having explained "who is being judged" in Revelation, my concern is to show that the book follows the Deuteronomic pattern. Of course, this would support a "preterist" interpretation. If Revelation is a covenant lawsuit against God's Old Covenant people, we would expect the Apocalypse to take this form.

---

2. Eugenio Corsini, *The Apocalypse* (Wilmington, Delaware: Michael Glazier Inc., 1983). Corsini, a Roman Catholic scholar, presents a brief summary of the early Fathers and then proceeds to develop Revelation in terms of a "preterist" model. Also, see J. Massyngberde Ford, *The Anchor Bible: Revelation* (Garden City, New York: Doubleday, 1975), and Jay Adams, *The Time is at Hand* (Phillipsburg, New Jersey: Presbyterian and Reformed, 1966).

3. David Chilton, *The Days of Vengeance* (Ft. Worth, Texas: Dominion Press, 1987).

1. *True Transcendence (Rev. 1:1-20)*

Indeed, Revelation begins like the Deuteronomic covenant. John opens, "The *Revelation* of Jesus Christ" (Rev. 1:1); Deuteronomy starts with, "Moses spoke . . . all that the Lord *commanded* [revealed]" (Deut. 1:3). One does not have to strain to detect the parallel between the Sinai "revelation" and the Apocalypse.[4] Moses had just come from the presence of God where he had received the written Word of God a second time. John is lifted up before the transcendent Christ—in a graphic glorious description (Rev. 1:14-17)—to receive the second "revelation" about the destruction of Jerusalem, the first having been given at another mountain in the Olivet Discourse (Matt. 24:1-51).[5] The preamble of both books, therefore, opens with statements indicating that the "words" are distinct, one of the three ways the covenant presents the principle of *transcendence*.

There are also some other important parallels about the historic situation of Deuteronomy and Revelation. Revelation is addressed to the New Covenant people—"to the seven Churches" (Rev. 1:4)— to tell them once again of destruction coming on the "ancient religion." The destruction came in A.D. 70, so the contents of Revelation had to have been written before the collapse of Jerusalem. This means there were approximately forty years between the death of Christ and the destruction of the Old Covenant capital, from the definitive redemption to the actual clearing away of the old religion.

This was precisely the situation with Israel, as the nation sat on the borders of Canaan, when Moses gave them the "second revelation." There had been forty years between their definitive redemption from Egypt and the new entrance into Canaan. But the land of Palestine represented the old ancient religions and their perversions of the original covenant. Israel was entering with a "new" covenant,

---

4. Kline, *Structure of Biblical Authority*, pp. 73-74. Kline says, "The Book of Revelation is replete with treaty analogues from its opening preamble-like identification of the awesome Lord Christ; through the letters to the churches, administering Christ's covenantal lordship after the manner of the ancient lawsuit; on through the elaborately expounded prophetic sanctions which constitute the major part of the book; and down to the closing documentary clause and canonical curse."

5. The key to this chapter is the near demonstrative pronoun, "this generation" (Matt. 24:34). Also very important is the fact that the Markan account of the Olivet Discourse clearly describes the same events in terms of the destruction of Jerusalem, A.D. 70. See Chilton for a further description. Also, J. Stuart Russell, *Parousia* (Grand Rapids: Baker, 1983), pp. 66-114.

one that had just been renewed and signified by the very name of Deuteronomy, "second" law.

Many other parallels could be drawn, but Revelation definitely begins according to the structure and influence of Deuteronomy. Moses is God's "servant" delivering the transcendent words of the covenant, and John is the new messenger in the transcendent presence of the Lord, revealing a new, better, "renewed" message about the end of the ancient religion.

2. Hierarchy (Rev. 2:1-22)

The second section of the Deuteronomic covenant develops the hierarchy of lordship which is confirmed in history. Revelation contains all these elements in its second section, the seven letters to the churches.

First, they have to do with a hierarchy. The letters are addressed to an "angel," properly translated "messenger" (*angelos*), and symbolically portrayed as a "star" (Rev. 1:20; 2:2). Who are these "stars," or "messengers" of the churches? The fact that they "receive" the letters indicates that they are "elders," not angels. William Hendriksen says,

> The "angels" cannot indicate the messengers of the churches sent to visit John, as the Scofield Bible holds. Then the expression: "To the angel of the church at . . . write" (Rev. 2:1 for example) would have no meaning. Again, real angels, heavenly beings, cannot be meant. It would have been rather difficult to deliver the book or its epistles to them! . . . For an excellent defense of the view that these angels refer to the bishops or pastors or ministers of the churches, see R. C. Trench, *Commentary on the Epistle to the Seven Churches in Asia*, pp. 53-58.[6]

Since the recipients were "elders," a hierarchy is implied. The "elders" were to convey the message to their churches and implement discipline. Furthermore, the "messengers" (elders) of this section in Revelation are the same "messengers" of Revelation 8-11 who pour out judgment on the earth. In other words, the representatives in God's hierarchy become a means to issue some kind of imprecation against the enemies of the New Covenant people. Perhaps Im-

---

6. William Hendriksen, *More Than Conquerors* (Grand Rapids: Baker, [1939] 1977), p. 73, note 16. See also, Moses Stuart, *Commentary on the Apocalypse* (Andover: Allen, Morrill, Wardwell, 1845), Vol. II, pp. 55-56.

precatory Psalms were used—Psalms laid out in the covenant law-suit structure designed to bring judgment on God's enemies (Ps. 83) —or some other "maledictory oath." Whatever they did, we are introduced to a hierarchy in Revelation 2-3.

Second, these letters to the churches also have a *historical* flair to them, each church having Old Testament allusions that seem to follow the history of the Old Covenant. Corsini says,

It has been sometimes noticed that there is a sort of *historical progression* in the Biblical allusions, a history of salvation beginning with Adam and finishing with Christ. Each episode refers to some progressing moment in the history of salvation . . . fitting John's continual and central concern to show that the coming of Christ is the perfection and replacement of the Old Testament economy.[7]

The following is a brief overview of the history indicated.

1. Ephesus. Reference is made to the *Fall, garden,* and *curse* (Gen. 2:17-3:19) in the phrases, "Remember then from what you have fallen" (2:5), "I will grant to eat of the tree of life which is in the paradise of God" (2:7), and "Your works, your toil and your patient endurance" (2:2).

2. Smyrna. The historical period seems to be the *captivity in Egypt.* The "ten days of testing" (2:10) refers to the 10 plagues of Egypt (Exod. 7:14ff.). Also, Christ speaks of Himself as "dead and has come to life," an allusion to the Exodus where Israel was dead and then resurrected.

3. Pergamum. The next period is the time of the *wilderness wanderings* with reference to the "manna" (2:17; cf. Exod. 16:32ff.). Also, during this period, there was the Balaam and Balak episode (2:14; cf. Num. 25:1-2).

4. Thyatira. A time of prosperity and apostasy approximates this epoch of history during the *reign of the kings.* The mention of "Jezebel" indicates the era when Israel "tolerated apostasy" (2:20; I Kgs. 16:31ff.).

5. Sardis. The time is the latter *prophetic* period, judging by the comments hinting at a small group of people, a "remnant" (3:4; Isa. 1:9, 6:13; 65:8ff.).

6. Philadelphia. The history probably refers to the return of the Jews *after exile.* The "key of David" indicates that people are coming

7. *The Apocalypse,* pp. 104-105. Emphasis mine.

back to a city to open its doors (Rev. 3:7). Yet, when they return, they encounter false Jews, "a synagogue of Satan" (3:9; Ezra. 4; Neh. 4, 6, 13).

7. Laodicea. These are the times from A.D. 30 to A.D. 70, a period of great apostasy and "lukewarmness" (3:16).[8] The language of Revelation 3 parallels the Mosaic description of Israel's being "spewed" out of the land (cf. Rev. 3:16 with Lev. 18:24-28; and Luke 21:24). God told Israel that he would "spit" them out of the land the day they apostatized. In A.D. 70, God kept His promise.

Why does God record all of this history in terms of the seven churches? Again, we must remember the parallel between *Israel's preparation to enter the land*, Deuteronomy, and the *Church's position before* A.D. 70. The Church was being prepared for new territory, just as the Israelites had been before they entered the Promised Land. They did not listen, and a new people of God were raised up. God wanted His New Covenant people to remember the history of His hierarchy. As He had disciplined His children under the Old Covenant, so He would chastise them in the new age (Heb. 3:7-13).

Finally, regarding this hierarchical section of Revelation, each letter is laid out like a miniature covenant, following the five-fold structure. Take the first letter as an example, the Church at Ephesus (2:1-7).

1. *Preamble*: "The One Who holds the seven stars in His right hand (True Transcendence), the One Who walks among the seven golden lampstands" (2:1).

2. *Historical Prologue*: "I know your deeds" (history of compliance with the hierarchy; 2:2-4)

3. *Stipulations*: "Remember therefore from where you have fallen, and repent [consecration], and do the deeds (ethics) you did at the first" (2:5a).

4. *Sanctions*: "Or else I am coming to you, and will remove your lampstand out of its place [application of sanctions in covenant lawsuit] — unless you repent" (2:5b).

5. *Succession Arrangements*: ". . . To him who overcomes [perseveres in continuity with covenant], I will grant to eat of the Tree of Life [sacramental continuity], which is in the Paradise of God" (2:6-7).[9]

---

8. Chilton, *Days of Vengeance*, pp. 134ff.
9. *Ibid.*, pp. 98-99.

3. *Ethics (Rev. 4:1-7:17)*

The third covenantal principle is *consecration through obedience to the Law*, the stipulations of the Deuteronomic covenant. Revelation 4-7 follows these emphases, beginning with a scene around the throne of God where the "Holy, holy, holy" response stresses consecration (Rev. 4). The next chapter specifically mentions the Ten Commandments, a "book" written on both sides (Rev. 5:1). So the "ethical" concentration is obvious. Again, however, this section provides a "covenant within a covenant," the entire segment following the five points of covenantalism.

A. *True Transcendence (Rev. 4)*

Revelation 4 begins the ethical section with the first point of covenantalism. John was commanded to "Come up here" (4:1). Worship starts with the *votum*, "the call." Everyone is called to come into God's presence and offer true worship. Once John reaches heaven, he encounters the transcendent/immanent Lord. God is sitting on His "throne," transcendent (4:2). His *presence* (immanence) is also manifested by His "holiness." Everyone is singing, "Holy, Holy, Holy, is the Lord God, the Almighty, Who was and Who is and Who is to come" (4:8).

In the other covenants we have found that three events are used at the beginning of the covenant to convey God's transcendence and immanence: creation, redemption, and revelation. John witnesses God as the mighty creator. The last verse of the chapter closes, "Worthy art Thou, our Lord and our God, to receive glory and honor and power; for Thou didst *create* all things, and because of Thy will they existed, and were *created*" (4:11).

The Adamic covenant had begun the Bible with creation, and now the last book of the Bible emphasizes this theme. Why? God is getting ready to destroy the world through the judgments to come in the next few chapters. He is not going to destroy the creation, but instead He will judge it unto new life. The world will be re-made by the application of the covenant.

B. *Hierarchy (Rev. 5:1-5)*

The hierarchical sections of the covenant emphasize God's authority and the "I-thou" relationship between God and His people. God's hierarchy requires *submission*. Often a "command/fulfillment" pattern is used to show God's authority to speak something into existence, the building of His creation house (Gen. 1:3ff.), or the destruction of the world (Gen. 6:11ff.). Revelation 5:1 opens with an "unfulfilled challenge." This chapter shifts from heavenly adoration to a challenge by a "strong angel" for anyone to "open a book" that has been sent to the throne (5:1ff.). No one is strong enough to open it, and this is the point. There is only One who comes and has the *authority*, Jesus Christ (Rev. 5:5).

C. Ethics (Rev. 5:6-14)

The third section of the covenant usually contains stipulations that *consecrate* and become the *program for dominion*. Through these laws, *ethical boundaries* are established that separate the clean from the unclean.

John turns his attention to the "book." The document is not just any book; it is the *Ten Commandments*. John explains that this scroll is written on the *front and back* (5:1). The only other "book" with writing on the front and back is the Ten Commandments. Moses writes, "Then Moses went down from the mountain with the two tablets of the testimony in his hand, tablets which were written on *both sides*; they were written on one side and the other" (Ex. 32:15). Now we can see why Jesus was the only One who could break the seals. The "new song" that everyone sings says "He is the lamb that was slain" (5:9). He was the only One "worthy" to open the book because He was the Redeemer, the One who satisfied all the just demands of the Law.

After it has been determined that Jesus is the only One strong enough and "pure" enough to break the seals, He comes and "takes the book" from God the Father (5:7), *applying it toward the conquest of the enemies*.

D. Sanctions (Rev. 6)

This part of the covenant has to do with *judgment* by means of the sanctions, the breaking of the seals. After being broken, they cause six awful judgments to begin to fall on the earth, the sixth coming when martyrs at the throne of God say, "How long, O, Lord, holy and true, wilt Thou refrain from judging and avenging the blood on those who dwell on the earth" (6:10). Their call to be "avenged" brings the sixth judgment, the "great day of wrath" (6:17).

The saints play an important role, therefore, in having the seals broken. Their request for God's *vengeance* brings direct judgment to the wicked. Normally, since God's people receive the sanctions, the wicked are also simultaneously cursed, or "sealed."

Probably, God's people break the seals on the wicked by praying, singing, and speaking the *imprecatory psalms* at this time of the service. The *imprecatory psalms* are Scriptures devoted entirely to calling down God's vengeance and judgment on the wicked. Psalm 94 opens with the following.

O Lord, God of *vengeance*; God of *vengeance*, shine forth! Rise up, O Judge of the earth; Render *recompense* to the proud. How long shall the wicked, O Lord, how long shall the wicked exult? They pour forth words, they speak arrogantly; all who do wickedness vaunt themselves. They crush Thy people, O Lord, and afflict Thy heritage. They slay the widow and the stranger, and murder the orphans. And they have said, "The Lord does not see, nor does the God of Jacob pay heed" (Ps. 94:1-7).

God is the blood avenger of His people. In the Old Testament, when a relative was murdered, the next of kin was asked to be a "blood avenger" (Nu. 35:12; Deut. 19:6-12). God's justice was "recompensed" when the nearest of kin killed the murderer. The Psalmist speaks of God as having this role for the saints. Did this change in the New Covenant? No, the New Covenant saints cry out for God to be their "avenger" (Rev. 6:10). Also, Paul commanded the Ephesians to greet one another with psalms (Eph. 5:19), so they, even the imprecatory ones, are still applicable in the New Covenant.

This is the way to dominion. By praying the imprecatory psalms in the sealing part of worship, the seals are broken on the wicked. How powerful is worship and the prayers of the saints? So powerful that God judges the world on this basis. This is a theology of love, even though it may not seem like it. God says He "hates" the wicked (Ps. 11:5). If a person believes the Word of God, then he should realize that God does not love everyone. He only loves His people. God shows His love for the righteous by *avenging them*. He kills the wicked through *conversion or death*. When the wicked are cleared off the earth, the righteous receive their inheritance (Matt. 5:5). This prepares us for the last section.

E. Continuity (Rev. 7)

The last section of the covenant establishes continuity and discontinuity. Consistently, this has been done through the sacred meal. After the house is built and the boundaries are set up to divide between clean and unclean, the Lord comes to His house and applies the sanctions of blessing and cursing. Then He sits down with His people, eats a meal, and distributes the inheritance to the faithful sons.

Revelation 7 is the legitimacy section of this worship scene. It starts by listing the 144,000 of the remnant *tribe by tribe*. This census is the numbering method used at the *end of the Book of Numbers*, a book beginning with the census, forming a transition from Leviticus and into the fifth book of the Bible, and ending with a numbering of the nation because the door to the fold has closed, and it is *time for war*.

The meal, however, is the heart of the continuity section. Is a meal involved? Yes, the "remnant" is gathered around the throne and one of the elders says the remnant will never "hunger" again. Why? They are eating a meal with God forever. He says to John,

These who are clothed in the white robes, who are they and from where have they come? And I said to him, "My Lord, you know." And he said to me, "These are the ones who come out of the great tribulation, and they have washed their robes and made them white in the blood of the Lamb. For this reason, they are before the throne of God; and they serve Him day and night in His temple; and He Who sits on the throne shall spread His tabernacle over them. They shall *hunger* no more, neither *thirst* anymore; neither shall sun beat down on them, nor any heat; for the Lamb in the center of the throne shall be their shepherd, and shall guide them to springs of the water of life; and God shall wipe away every tear from their eyes" (Rev. 7:13-17).

The "remnant" runs the kingdom. At Revelation 7, they are small in number. Some of their number have even been martyred for the faith. Martyrdom is an attempt on the part of the bastard sons to disinherit the true sons. The ones persecuting the saints are mainly the Jews in coalition with the Roman Empire. Both groups are "bastards." They have been disinherited by God and can only come back to the "fold" by faith. Instead, they try to disinherit God's people by premature death.

Remember, continuity and discontinuity are established at the meal. Either the blood of Christ is eaten symbolically or another "blood" becomes the communion meal. The bastard sons try to establish continuity through the shedding of the blood of the saints. Biblical continuity comes through Christ's blood, however, and the bastards' attempts are unsuccessful. The martyrs still end up at the meal of God in heaven; they still receive the inheritance. In fact, they receive it *sooner.*

All five parts of the covenant have been recapitulated. Finally, I should note that the stipulations section of Deuteronomy requires attendance at the annual sacred feasts: Passover (Deut. 16:1-8), Pentecost (Deut. 16:9-12), and Tabernacles (Deut. 16:13-15). The stipulations section of Revelation follows the same pattern. Chapter five centers around the "Lamb that was slain," Passover. Chapter 6 is the breaking of God's law on the earth, paralleling the Pentecost Feast that commemorated the *giving of the Ten Commandments.* Significantly, the synagogue reading for Pentecost was Habakkuk 3, the unleashing of a series of judgments on the earth.[10] Revelation 7 culminates the festival year with imagery referring to the Festival of Booths (Tabernacles) and multitudes before the throne of God with "palm branches" in hand (Rev. 7:9).

The "ethics" section comes to a close and leads into the fourth part of the covenant.

4. Sanctions (Rev. 8:1-14:20)

The next literary break in the structure of Revelation falls at the beginning of the "trumpet" section (Rev. 8:1), flowing out of the seventh seal. In Deuteronomy, the fourth part of the covenant explained the ratification process. Kline calls attention to the fact that the sanctions of the suzerain treaties are called "woes and weals."[11] Revelation 8-14 contains three "woes" (11:14).

Israel ratified the covenant through a self-maledictory oath of covenant curses (12) called the dodecalogue (Deut. 27:15-26). Revelation matches the dodecalogue with twelve angels who bring judgment. The trumpets section opens with an angel, breaking the seal that leads to seven other angels blowing trumpets (8:7, 8, 10, 12, 9:1, 13, 11:15). The sanctions conclude with five angels of doom (14:6, 8, 9, 15, 17), and then return to the original angel of "fire" that began these calamaties (14:18).

The section begins with trumpets because these were used to announce the coming of God's judgment. The Greek word is the same used in the Septuagint for the "ram's horn" of the Old Testament (Josh. 6:5; Exod. 19:13; Lev. 25). The ram's horn came from one of

---

10. M. D. Goulder, *The Evangelists' Calendar: A Lectionary Explanation for the Development of Scripture* (London: SPCK, 1978), p. 177.

11. *Structure of Biblical Authority,* p. 140.

the primary animals of sacrifice. After the animal atoned for the people of God, its horn was blown to signal judgment to those who were not covered by sacrificial blood. When the people of God failed to sacrifice, they were drawn near to the Lord for judgment, for example, at Mt. Sinai (Ex. 19:13). But, mostly the horn signaled judgment to the nations, symbolized at the Feast of Trumpets, which preceded the last festival of the year (Booths), and marked the Judgment Day of History.

The judgmental character of the horn also explains why it was the instrument used to defeat Jericho (Josh. 6:4). The blowing of the horn brought the judgment of God. And so, in Revelation, the angels blow trumpets that bring awful judgment on the earth. Notice the parallel between the curses of Deuteronomy 28 and Revelation 8-14. Deuteronomy says,

> If you are not careful to observe all the words of this law which are written in this book, to fear this honored and awesome Name, The Lord your God, then the Lord will bring extraordinary *plagues* on you and your descendants, even severe and lasting plagues, and miserable and chronic sickness. And He will bring back on you all the diseases of Egypt of which you were afraid, and they shall cling to you. Also every sickness and every plague which, *not written in the book of this law*, the Lord will bring on you (Deut. 28:58-61).

The Deuteronomy sanctions, therefore, provide a background for the sanctions in Revelation. Some of the "plagues" are just as the ones that fell on Egypt, but there are "others" that are not previously described. Revelation 8-14 details a few "plagues" very similar to the ones that affected Egypt: hail and fire falling on the earth (Rev. 8:7), and water turning to blood (8:8). But most of the "plagues" are quite different from the Egyptian ones, just as Moses had promised.

Finally, the sanctions section of Revelation refers to "marks" of ratification. Several references speak of a "mark" of the beast, placed on the head or the hand of those who follow him (13:17; 14:9). This "mark" was used to form a false covenant, resulting in the application of the sanctions in a covenant lawsuit (Rev. 14:10ff.). In fact, the judgments only fell on those who did not have a "seal of God on their foreheads." This language takes us back to Genesis, where the curse sanction is applied to the "head" of the serpent (Gen. 3:15).

Thus, the sanctions section of Revelation continues to follow the pattern of Deuteronomy. When, however, we arrive at the fifth section, the Deuteronomic influence is extremely obvious.

5. *Continuity (Rev. 15:1-15:21)*

The continuity section of Deuteronomy arranged succession from one generation of leaders to another. Continuity was established between Moses and Joshua. Moses went before the Lord in the form of a "Song of Witnesses," also called the "Song of Moses" (Deut. 32), testifying of the succession that was being made.

John notes a shift to the fifth and final section of Revelation by a movement from the seven trumpets of plagues to the *seven bowls* (Rev. 15:1-16:1). As usual, one series of seven opens into the next on the last of the series. At this point, the company around the throne of God begins to sing the *Song of Moses* (Rev. 15:3), matching the structure of Deuteronomy perfectly. But the transition is from Israel to the Church, so the heavenly congregation also sings, the "Song of the Lamb," the new captain of the host, which reads,

Great and marvelous are Thy works, O Lord God, the Almighty; Righteous and true are Thy ways, Thou King of the nations. Who will not fear, O Lord, and glorify Thy name? For Thou alone art holy; For all the nations will come and worship before Thee, For Thy righteous acts have been revealed (Rev. 15:3-4).

A transition prepares to take place. The last section of Revelation speaks of the final destruction of the Old Covenant and the "nations" that are ready to come to the Lord once Israel is dealt with. This shift occurs by means of the sacred "bowls," or "chalices." We saw in the Matthean covenant that the final section made the successional arrangements at the Lord's Table, where the "chalice" was served. Indeed, the "chalice" was the means of continuity and discontinuity. How?

Jesus gave His disciples the "cup of blessing" which was the inauguration of the New Covenant (Lk. 22:20; I Cor. 10:16). The application of the blessing sanction transferred inheritance because the "cup" often represented *inheritance*. The Psalmist says, "The Lord is the portion of my inheritance and my *cup*" (Ps. 16:5). The Biblical "cupbearer" was therefore not just a wine sipper, testing the cup for poison, but a guardian of the king's estate.

Famous Old Testament figures held this position—Joseph, Daniel, Nehemiah—and were "trustees" of the king's estate. Nehemiah was unhappy. The king wanted to know why. Nehemiah told him that Jerusalem had been torn down, and so he was given a *covenant grant* (Neh. 2), the *Holy City of Israel.* Why would the king do such a thing? Nehemiah had been his "cupbearer," and had held all of the king's properties in trust. Nehemiah was *given his land* because he had been *faithful to the king.* This is precisely what happens with the disciples. They become guardians of the cup, the Lord's estate. For their faithfulness, they receive their own property and land. The "cup of blessing" symbolized the entire estate of the King of kings.

Jesus is quickly betrayed after the "cup of blessing" is given. The "cup" actually turns into an *ordeal of jealousy.* Jesus notes a betrayer, or "bastard," in their midst. Judas is identified in terms of the cup when Christ says, "But behold, the hand of the one betraying Me is with Me on the table" (Luke 22:21), "that is the one for whom I shall dip the morsel and give it to him" (John 13:26). Christ served this first communion by dipping the bread in the "cup of blessing," signifying the transferral of inheritance from one person to the next. Judas quickly betrayed the Lord, "Satan having entered into him" immediately after he ate (John 13:27).

In the last section of Revelation, the "bowls" are poured out on the Old Covenant city and people. Even Satan meets the judgment of these bowls (Rev. 20). As Jesus used the "chalice" to create continuity with the faithful, and reveal discontinuity with the "bastards" of the covenant, the continuity section of Revelation does the same.

The "chalices" create continuity between God and His people by the destruction of the Old Covenant worshippers, the Great Whore and the Beast. At the end of the continuity section, the new Temple, City, and home of God's elect appears, a city which invites those who want to live there to come in (Rev. 22:17). No longer is the covenant exclusively Jewish. The "nations" (Gentiles) are ready to come in, sit down, worship, and eat at the new "Tree of life" (Rev. 15:4).

Conclusion

This completes our study of the patterns of the Deuteronomic covenant. How appropriate that we end on the Book of Revelation. John's message was forged on the anvil of the Mosaic pattern, the five parts of the Apocalypse perfectly matching the five sections of Deuteronomy.

One matter remains to be considered in the *covenant* half of this book. I have demonstrated that the Deuteronomic covenant continues into the New Testament and have noted the parallels. But, does this mean there are no changes in the New Covenant? Are we still supposed to sacrifice animals? Should we go to church on Saturday instead of Sunday?

In the next appendix, we will examine these questions and many more, seeking to understand the relationship between Old and New Covenants.

Appendix 6

OLD COVENANT/
NEW COVENANT COMPARISON

We have overviewed the covenant. The whole Bible contains its structure and content. The fact that the New Covenant is called a "covenant" indicates continuity. But, does this mean there are no differences between the Old and New? No. Hebrews 8 is a chapter that helps us to summarize the similarities and dissimilarities. But before we engage in this comparison, I should explain the designation: Old and New Covenants.

The Two Covenants

There are two and only two covenants in the Bible, and they are called Old and New. Immediately, two issues are raised. How do we determine the number of covenants? And, what distinguishes these covenants from each other?

First, as to the number of covenants, the Bible only speaks of two. Some students of the covenant have tried to specify more because covenants are made with specific individuals such as Noah, Abraham, and David. But these are merely the *re-establishment* of the first covenant made with Adam, the Old Covenant. For example, God says to Noah according to the New American Standard Version, "I will *establish* My covenant with you" (Gen. 6:18). But the Hebrew ("heqim" not "karath") should be properly translated, *confirm*.[1] So God "confirmed" an already existing covenant. This means that covenants exist in the Bible where the literal word "covenant" is not used.

More importantly, the original covenant made with Adam is re-

---

1. Warren Gage, *The Gospel of Genesis* (Winona Lake, Indiana: Carpenter Books, 1984), p. 30.

268

peatedly "confirmed" with replacement "Adams" (Noah, Abraham, etc.) so that there is essentially one covenant (the Old Covenant) until a true different and New Adam (Jesus) arrives. Some of the confusion results from the fact that each of these newly confirmed covenants anticipates with greater clarity the New Covenant. They are progressive in nature. Although the covenantal head (i.e. David etc.) has a fall and dies like Adam, each one progressively reveals more about the Christ to come. So, David was still part of the Old Covenant because he fell and died, but he was also the culmination of the greatest type of Christ. Every time God confirms the first covenant with a new individual, He adds more revelation until the final Revelation comes and transforms the Old Covenant into the New.

Second, as to the distinguishing features of the covenants, many explanations have been attempted by theologians. Perhaps the most common is "covenant of works and covenant of grace," found in the *Westminster Confession of Faith* (VII.2), the standard confession of the historic Presbyterian Church. "Covenant of works" refers to the period before the Fall of Adam. Supposedly, he related to God according to works. After the Fall, however, God implemented the "covenant of grace." This distinction is extremely misleading. "Covenant of works" is simply not adequate to describe Adam's relationship to God. Meritorious salvation before the Fall is not in question because Adam was already saved. So then it becomes "works" in the sense of obedience. Adam was supposed to obey to receive the blessing of God, but so is the post-Fall man. God always deals with man on the basis of grace, and grace always involves faithfulness.

It is much better to stick with Biblical distinctions. Scripture explains the differences between the covenants around the two heads or Adams: Adam and Christ. The Old Covenant was made with *Adam*, and the New Covenant was made with *Christ*. To be more specific, we can apply the five-fold covenantal model. Since Hebrews 8 uses the designations "first" or "former" (by implication "old") and "new," it is a logical place to examine the differences. The shortness of the chapter makes it easy to write it in full below. I have placed the basic outline in the text. Notice how the word "for" forms a grammatical boundary for many of the segments, helping us to see that even the comparison between two covenants in this chapter has the covenantal structure.

The Covenantal Structure of Hebrews 8

True Transcendence

Now the main point in what has been said is this: we have such a high priest, who has taken His seat at the right hand of the throne of the Majesty *in the heavens*, a minister in the sanctuary, and in the true tabernacle, which the Lord pitched, not man. For every high priest is appointed to offer both gifts and sacrifices; hence it is necessary that this high priest also have something to offer. Now if He were on earth, He would not be a priest at all, since there are those who offer the gifts according to the Law; who serve as a copy and shadow of the heavenly things, just as Moses was warned by God, "See," He says, "that you make all things according to the pattern which was shown you on the mountain."

Hierarchy

But now He has obtained a more excellent ministry, by as much as He is also the *mediator* of a better covenant, which has been enacted on better promises. For if that first covenant had been faultless, there would have been no occasion sought for a second. For finding fault with them, He says, "Behold, days are coming, says the Lord, When I will effect a New Covenant with the House of Israel and with the House of Judah; Not like the covenant which I made with their fathers on the day when I took them by the hand to lead them out of the land of Egypt; For they did not continue in My covenant, and I did not care for them, says the Lord."

Ethics

"For this is the covenant that I will make with the House of Israel after those days, says the Lord: I will put My *laws* into their minds. And I will write them on their hearts. And I will be their God, and they shall be My people."

Sanctions

"And they shall not teach everyone his fellow citizen, and everyone his brother, saying, 'Know the Lord.' For all shall know Me, from the least to the greatest of them."

Continuity

"For I will be merciful to their iniquities, and I will remember their sins no more." When He said, "A new covenant," He has made the first obsolete. But whatever is becoming obsolete and growing old is ready to disappear.

1. *True Transcendence (1-5)*

Hebrews 8 begins with the transcendence theme. The High Priest of the New Covenant sits in the *heavens* in a *heavenly* temple "which the Lord pitched, not man" (Heb. 8:1). The contrast between the Old and New Covenant is the contrast between an earthly temple, priesthood, and sacrifice, and a *heavenly* temple, priesthood, and sacrifice. The first is a copy, and the second is the original (Heb. 8:5). Heaven and earth are distinguished from one another, just as we have seen that God and the creation were distinguished in the Deuteromic covenant. The "heavenly" character of the original gives it transcendence.

In the first covenant, the garden was a copy of the heaven around the throne of God, called a "glory cloud" (Ezek. 1:4-28). Earth was a copy of heaven. How do we know? The tabernacle and temple were simultaneously pictures of earth and heaven (Exod. 25-27).[2] Inside the tabernacle, a blue ceiling represented the blue sky. Trees that symbolized people lined the walls (Ps. 1:3). In the center of the Holy of Holies stood the ark, the throne of God. So the tabernacle was a picture of what the world was supposed to be, *ordered space around the throne of God*. The garden was supposed to have been the same. Originally, it was. Everything was arranged around the Tree of Life, God's throne.

But even though the garden was the throne of God, it was still only a *copy*. Its transcendence was reflective, not original. The garden was heavenly, not heaven. The difference is quite significant. Heaven*ly* means influenced and characterized by heaven. Heaven is the source. The serpent tempted Adam and Eve with original transcendence, deification (Gen. 3:5). He wanted to make earth into heaven, a utopia. Adam and Eve bought his proposition with all that God had given them. They set out to make earth into heaven instead of carrying out the cultural mandate, which would have made earth like heaven, a reflection, not the original. They wanted earth to be the original. Consequently, they fell into sin and death and with their every effort marred what imaged God. The heavenly garden became *earthly*.

God restored them and provided models of a heaven*ly* world. As I have already pointed out, the tabernacle and the temple were

---

2. Meredith Kline, *Images of the Spirit* (Grand Rapids: Baker, 1980), pp. 13-26.

microcosms of a world controlled by heaven. But they were never able to restore creation. The Old Testament told the story of man's Fall over and over again. Even when Christ came, He found a land that was anything but space controlled by heaven. Israel was demon-possessed and controlled from below! The chosen people had become earthly.

Hebrews 8 says that God provided a better covenant because this covenant is "heavenly," meaning truly transcendent. Christ is the New Covenant: the temple, sacrifice, and High Priest. He restores heavenly rule to the earth again. Since the temple is in heaven, all men have access; there are no zones of holiness kept from the common member. The throne of God is open and available. Thus, man can go straight to the origin of transcendence. Moreover, he can act as a true image (copy) of original transcendence. The "heavenlyness" of the New Covenant draws out the first contrast between the Old and New Covenants.

2. Hierarchy (6-9)

The hierarchical section of Hebrews 8 begins, "He [Christ] is a mediator of a better covenant" (Heb. 8:6). We have seen that hierarchy has to do with the *mediation of judgment to history* through *representatives*. In the Old Covenant, Moses and sacrifices mediated life and death. In the end, they all mediated death because the Old Covenant ends in the death of Christ. But Christ is the new mediator. Through His priesthood the Church, He mediates life to the world through the Word and sacrament. His mediation is far superior to the old mediators. All men have direct access to Him, and His sacrifice is permanent and complete.

The second section of Hebrews 8 also weaves the issue of *authority* into it. As we have already seen time and again: history and authority have a dynamic relationship to one another. Just like the second point of the covenant in Deuteronomy, the writer speaks to Israel's rejection of God's authority and their subsequent excommunication (I Cor. 10:8). He refers to the days of the Exodus when Israel apostatized and was cast out, whereas the New Covenant is different. What is the difference? This will not happen to the New Covenant Bride and people.

The first covenant had a "fault." Notice that the flaw is not in the covenant itself, but in the *people*. The text says, "Finding fault with *them*" (v. 8), meaning the "new" Adams of the Exodus who turned out to be just like the "old" Adam, they were no longer "cared" for (v. 9). The New Covenant, however, is more *permanent*. The implication is that God would never throw off the true New Adam, Jesus Christ, and His Bride, the Church. The contrast in historical situation is really between an *age dominated by Adam*, and an *age dominated by Christ*.

The historical comparision by age is critical to understanding how the New Testament often speaks of the Old Covenant. Serious theological errrors can be made if this is not understood. For example, how often have modern Christians heard that the Old Testament man as an "individual" was not filled with the Spirit? This section of Hebrews 8, however, demonstrates that Old and New Covenant comparisons do not focus primarily on *individuals*. There were individuals who did not fall away in the wilderness and were saved by faith, like Joshua and Caleb. And, there are individuals who get excommunicated in the New Covenant, like the incestuous man in I Corinthians 5. Often when the Old Covenant and New Covenant are compared, it is not in the sense of the *individual* per se. The entire *age* is being contrasted to another *age*.[3] Given this rationale, Pauline language takes on fresh meaning. Paul talks about the age of the "letter" which is "fleshly" and kills, in contrast to the age of the Spirit which creates life (II Cor. 3:1ff.). Does he mean the Old Testament Divine *Law* is sinful and wicked because it "kills"? No. He is merely describing the Old Covenant period as a whole, which rejected the Spirit of God and died out. On the level of individuals, there were "Spirit-filled people" who were saved in the Old Testament (Ps. 51:11). Yet, the historic situation was different, because prior to Christ, the Spirit had not been released in a new sense. As an age, the New Covenant period depicted the Spirit as being poured out on the whole table of nations (Acts 2:9-11).

So, the historical difference is that God's first bride was Israel of the Old Covenant. As a *people*, she was divorced and excommunicated. Since God could never do this to His own Son on a permanent basis — even when Christ died and was cut off, God raised Him from the dead — the New Covenant Bride will never be cast aside. Individ-

---

3. Richard B. Gaffin, *Centrality of the Resurrection* (Grand Rapids: Baker, 1978), pp. 107ff. Gaffin, building on G. Vos, "The Eschatological Aspect of the Pauline Conception of the Spirit," *Biblical and Theological Studies* by the Members of the Faculty of Princeton Theological Seminary (New York: Scribner's Sons, 1912), pp. 209-255, refers to Paul's use of "flesh" (*sarx*) in the sense of an "age," making it equivalent in many references to the "old age," Old Covenant. Vos says, "It (*sarx*) is an organism, an order of things beyond the individual man, even beyond human nature" (p. 255).

uals may fall away, but the Church became God's final bride. The Church as the Church will never apostatize!

From the historic point of view there are two Israels, yet one true Israel. How so? The writer says God will make a "new" covenant with *Israel and Judah* (v. 8). In one sense this "newer" covenant was made with Israel when they returned from captivity in Babylon (Jer. 31:32). Remember, the writer to the Hebrews is quoting Jeremiah who prophesied before and during the captivity. But in a strict sense, the New Covenant was made with the Church. When Jesus inaugurated the Lord's Supper He said, "This cup which is poured out for you is the *new covenant* in My blood" (Lk. 22:20). This means the "Israel and Judah" of the New Covenant is the *Church*. The Church is the true son of Abraham and the new "Israel of God." Paul says, "If you belong to Christ, then you are Abraham's offspring, heirs according to the promise. . . . Neither is circumcision anything, nor uncircumcision, but a new creation. And those who walk by this rule, peace and mercy be upon them, and upon the Israel of God" (Gal. 3:29; 6:16). Paul's comments lead us to believe that there is only one *true Israel* through history, the "faithful!" There are two historic Israels, but one true covenantal Israel.

This brief section in Hebrews has helped us to see a very important *historic difference* between the covenants. One was made with Adam and was temporary. The second was made with Christ and became permanent. The latter mediates a better judgment in history.

3. Ethics (10)

The principle of comparing Old Covenant *age* to the New Covenant *age* carries into the ethical. Remember, the ethics section of Deuteronomy speaks of the heart of the covenant as being the *fulfillment of righteousness*. This concept is pulled into the New Covenant. Jeremiah says the Law of God will be written on the "heart" of the New Covenant man (Jer. 31:33). Does this mean the law is not on the heart of those in the Old Covenant? No. David says, "I delight to do Thy will, O My God; Thy *Law* is within my heart" (Ps. 40:8). What is so unique about the New Covenant?

The law was not "incarnated" in Adam. Christ became the *embodiment* of the Law of God: the Word made "flesh" (Jn. 1:1, 14). He carried the Law in His person, unlike Adam, and became the incarnated Law! Again it should be stressed that there were *individuals* who had the law written on their heart in the Old Testament

(Ps. 40:8). But as an *age*, the law was far from them because it was the age of the first Adam. Before the historic outpouring of the Spirit, there was no power to implement the law in its fulness. The New Adam, Jesus Christ, brought a change. Since *He* incarnated the Law, His followers were much more "law oriented," God's standard being more deeply imprinted on them *in Christ*.

Christ is therefore the key to understanding the similarities and differences between the ethics of the Old and New Testaments. The *similarities* are in Christ. A question, however, is provoked by Pauline literature. Paul says that the Law is nailed to the cross (Col. 2:14). Does this mean the Old Testament Law is no longer binding on a New Testament Christian? No. There was no piece of paper on the cross with the Ten Commandments written on it. Where were they written? They had to be in the Person of Christ. So, when He died they died with Him. But when He was raised, *they were raised with Him*. Only, the Law of God was raised in greater glory and power. Now when someone breaks a commandment, he is violating Christ, not just a tablet of stone!

All of the law dies with Christ and all of it is raised with Him. So, how do we account for *differences*, like clean/unclean boundaries, food laws, and sabbath days? Christ is raised with a "transfigured" body. Thus, the incarnated law is also transfigured, or changed. How do we keep straight what is altered?

One, the *heremeneutical principle*. Old Testament law carried through, unless the New Testament made a change. For example, Old Testament food laws were changed. All of these pointed to the death of Christ and created boundaries that were altered because of His death. The Jew/Gentile boundary had to be maintained to protect the priesthood (the Jews) from being corrupted. But after Christ came in history, and the power of the Spirit was poured out in greater measure because of His Resurrection, the boundary was broken down. It was no longer needed (Eph. 2:11ff.). Peter was shown a giant tablecloth with all kinds of Gentile animals on it and told to eat. Then he helped Cornelius, a Gentile (Acts 10:1ff.). The food laws changed, but there was still a food law in the New Covenant. It became the Lord's Supper. The Church was commanded to eat this food and not to participate in any other pagan "communion meal" (I Cor. 10:19-20). Furthermore, it was told that "all" things had become clean. God told the Church to eat *everything* just as the Gospel would consume all things!

Two, the *historical principle*. The historical situation changed.[4] Christ redeemed the whole world. The Promised Land was no longer "holy" ground exclusively. Thus, laws endemic to a Hebrew republic were no longer necessary, while laws conducive to a Christian republic carried over; the redemption of Christ facilitated the spread of the kingdom into the nations. Actually, laws tied to the Hebrew *family* dropped off, whereas laws with a *multi-national* character extended forward. How so? The Old Covenant was styled around the *family-unit*. The Hebrew people were actually one large extended family: hence, laws like the law of the "kinsman redeemer" and nearest of kin "avenger of death" were important. Cast as such, both were closely connected with the preservation of the Hebrew seed-line through which the Messiah came. Essentially, they ended with Him.

But the avenger of death concept demonstrates the shift from family to *multi-national* organization in the New Covenant. The New Testament drops the *family* avenger of death concept. In its *general equity* (general *equivalent*), however, it pulls through. Paul argues in Romans that the "avenger" is the State. Notice the slide from family to nation. The historic situation of the New Covenant changes. The family of God expands from a nuclear unit to the people of God, multi-national in scope. The Church replaces the role of the original Adamic family by "making disciples of the *nations*" (Matt. 28:19-20). Thus, the historic change of situation pulls over the *general equity* of Old Testament law.

Three, the *personal principle*. Personal commitment to the law of God deepens in the New Covenant. Quoting Jeremiah, Paul says, "I will write them [Old Testament laws] on their *hearts*" (Heb. 8:10). Transfigured Torah is etched on the heart of every New Covenant believer (Jer. 31:33). Since David is an example of an Old Testament man who internally possesses the law, the New Covenant intensifies the internalization of the law of God through the dramatic work of the Spirit of God. It comes in greater fulness in the New Covenant.

Keeping in mind the relationship between Old and New Covenant, *fulfillment of righteousness* is clarified. It is in and through Christ. Yet, the covenant is still ethical at its center. Man comes to God through Christ's fulfillment of righteousness, and then having done so, is expected to "keep His commandments" (I John 2:3-4).

---

4. *Law of the Covenant*, pp. 11ff.

4. Sanctions (11)

In Deuteronomy, the sanctions are focused through a self-maledictory oath taken by the Lord of the covenant and consigned to the vassal. At this point, our attention is not drawn toward the contrast between circumcision and passover in the Old Covenant and baptism and communion in the New Covenant. I devote appendixes 8 & 9 to this subject. But Hebrews 8 has a broader contrast of the sanctions. What does the conversion of the nations (8:11) and the death of Christ have to do with sanctions (Heb. 8:12)? Let us begin with Hebrews 8:11.

Conversion of the nations. The promise of world-wide dominion of the Gospel is itself a sanction. The writer's comments about the far-reaching effect of the New Covenant—that so much success would result that there would be no need to ask people if they are Christians—is the unfulfilled Old Covenant *blessing* of dominion over the nations of the world. At one of those key transferral-of-blessing points, Jacob *blessed* his sons (Gen. 48:1-49:33). Remember, the blessing was *seed and environment*: the latter necessitating some kind of international influence of the covenant. He said to Judah, the ancestor of Jesus, "The Scepter shall not depart from Judah, nor the ruler's staff from between his feet, until Shiloh [Jesus] comes, and to *Him* shall be the *obedience of the peoples*" (Gen. 49:10).

It is the same blessing given in Deuteronomy, "The Lord will open for you His good storehouse, the heavens, to give rain to your land in its season and to bless all the work of your hand; and you shall lend to many nations. . . . And the Lord shall make you the head and not the tail" (Deut. 28:12). The blessing is that through the application of the covenant, other nations of the world would have to come to Israel. This was fulfilled in the days of Solomon when nations came for counsel and wisdom (I Kgs. 10:1). But Solomon apostatized, and even though he returned, Israel of old never again returned to this glory.

Multi-national success was promised to another. Isaiah was told, "Now it will come about that in the last days, the mountain of the house of the Lord will be established as the chief of the mountains, and will be raised above the hills; and *all the nations will stream to it*" (Isa. 2:2). When were those "last days"? Hebrews says, "In these *last days* [He] has spoken to us in His Son" (Heb. 1:2). Who is the moun-

THAT YOU MAY PROSPER

tain of Isaiah's prophecy? The writer to the Hebrews says it is Mount
Zion—that is, *Jesus Christ* (Heb. 12:22-29).

Thus, there is no doubt that what was promised to the Old Covenant by way of sanction was fulfilled in Jesus Christ. Israel failed to
dominate the peoples of the world, only experiencing brief success.
But the sanction of the New Covenant promises blessing that accom-
plishes the dominion which Isaiah referred to. Beginning with the
dominion success of Christ on the cross, the Gospel conquers the
nations of the world. Whereas the Old Covenant had dominion
through the application of the Law, the New Covenant has dominion
by appplying the Law *through Christ*. The Church takes Christ to the
nations, and thereby brings them to faith, "baptizing and teaching
them" the "commandments" (Matt. 28:19-20). The blessing sanction
of world-wide conversion has to occur before Christ can come back.
The Psalmist says, "The LORD says to My Lord, 'Sit Thou at My
right hand *until I make Thine enemies a footstool under Thy feet*'" (Ps.
110:1).

Even though the word "blessing" is not used, it is clear that
Hebrews 8:11 is an application of the fourth sanctions point of covenantalism. The next verse is more obvious.

Blessing of forgiveness. Hebrews 8:12 also fails to use the specific
word "blessing." But it clearly talks about *forgiveness*, "I will remember their sins no more." What does this have to do with the sanction
of blessing? For one, David expressly calls forgiveness a blessing,
"How *blessed* is he whose sins are forgiven, whose sin is covered
[same as "not remembered"]! How *blessed* is the man to whom the
LORD does not impute iniquity" (Ps. 32:1-2). For another, God's self-
maledictory oath called down the sanction of cursing on Himself.
God did not actually break the covenant, but He deliberately took
the curse sanction Himself to atone for His people's sin. Thus, the
comments of Hebrews 8:12 categorically refer to the sanctions section of Deuteronomy.

The great difference between the Old and New Covenant sanctions is the unlimited complete success of blessing. The senses of
Hebrews 8:11-12 could not take place in the Old Covenant, even
though they were anticipated. Here is another expression of the similarity and dissimilarity of the covenants. The sanctions of the Old
Covenant are fulfilled in the New: continuing forward (similiarity),
yet differing in that they come to their fullest expression through
Christ (dissimilarity).

Appendix 7

MEREDITH G. KLINE: YES AND NO

> In New Testament times there is no longer a simple coalescence of
> the authority structure of the covenant with that of any cultural unit.
>
> Meredith G. Kline[1]

In my development of the structure of the Biblical covenant, I
have particularly relied on Meredith G. Kline. Anyone who has
read his essays on the covenant structure will notice immediately
that I have adopted his outline of Deuteronomy. Clearly, my book is
not a commentary on Deuteronomy. It is unlike his work in the
Wycliffe Bible Commentary, an insightful study well worth meditating
on.[2] Rather, I attempt to isolate the various covenantal "principles."

Kline and I disagree about the applications and implications of
each of the five points of the covenant. We disagree to such an extent
that my book can legitimately be regarded as a rejection of Kline in
the light of Kline. Kline rejects the continuing New Testament authority of the covenant structure that he discovered in the writings of
Baltzer and Mendenhall. I, on the other hand, accept it.

The enigma in Kline appears most strikingly in *The Structure of
Biblical Authority.* On the one hand, he argues that the theme of the
covenant model of the suzerain treaties appears all through the
Bible; hence, it is the *structure* of Biblical authority. On the other
hand, he believes that Deuteronomy, as part of the Mosaic economy,
is an "intrusion" into history.[3] It is therefore temporary. It *cannot* by
his definition be extended into the New Testament, that is, unless his

---

1. Kline, *By Oath Consigned: A Reinterpretation of the Covenant Signs of Circumcision and
Baptism* (Grand Rapids, Michigan: Eerdmans, 1968), p. 100.
2. Rev. James B. Jordan informed me about Kline's chapter back in the early
1980s.
3. Meredith G. Kline, "The Intrusion and the Decalogue," *The Structure of Biblical
Authority* (Grand Rapids, Michigan: Eerdmans, [1972] 1978), pp. 154-71.

whole intrusionary premise evaporates. So, according to him, there are only bits and pieces of the structure in other places of the Bible, even the New Testament.

As a matter of fact, his references to other segments of the Scripture triggered me to look for the Deuteronomic structure in the New Testament. But he fails to see that the five-fold arrangement of Deuteronomy is a covenant model in *all* of its parts in *all* of the Bible. Thus, he is not able to come up with a precise covenant model for *all* of the Scripture. Is it a five-point model? Or is it a six-point model, with "depository arrangements" added?[4] He is not sure. I am not sure either; but I can be a lot more confident than he is. I find no six-point structure anywhere in the Bible; I see a five-point structure repeatedly.

Nevertheless, I am greatly indebted to him, as I am sure he is to Baltzer and Mendenhall, upon whom he largely depended for his insights. If he can make good use of the discoveries of a pair of theological liberals, I suppose I can make good use of the work of an amillennialist who rejects (or does nothing with) all five points of the covenant. Let me make myself clear by comparing his use of each of the five points with my use of them.

Transcendence

One major difference is my treatment of the first part of the covenant, as indicated by the word "transcendence." This difference is easy to pinpoint. Kline does not discuss the topic; I make it the covenant's fundamental point: the Creator-creature distinction. He does not develop the theme that the distinction between what God said and what Moses said points to the doctrine of transcendence. He says only this: "Ancient suzerainty treaties began with a preamble in which the speaker, the one who was declaring his lordship and demanding the vassal's allegiance, identified himself. The Deuteronomic preamble identifies the speaker as Moses (v. 1a), but Moses as the earthly, mediatorial representative of Yahweh (v. 3b), the heavenly suzerain and ultimate Lord of this covenant."[5] That is all he says — no development, nothing. This is a good insight, as I have

---

4. *Ibid.*, pp. 49-51.

5. Meredith G. Kline, *Treaty of the Great King: The Covenant Structure of Deuteronomy* (Grand Rapids, Michigan: Eerdmans, 1963), p. 50.

tried to show in my book, but in Kline's book of 149 pages, there ought to have been more, if the author intended to *do* anything with the insight.

Hierarchy

He does not relate the hierarchical structure of the Mosaic court system to the rebellion of Israel. Consequently, he misses the frame of reference for this second point. He does not call it hierarchy. He includes it as part of the historical prologue. He does not see why God begins the whole section with the hierarchical passage (Deut. 1:12-18). What is crucial is the court system of Israel. He does not ask or answer the question that I regard as crucial: *Why does this historical prologue begin with a presentation of Israel's court system?*

Again, my criticism is that he only briefly mentions part two of the covenant structure, and then he does nothing with it. He does not ask the obvious question concerning the law courts. Thus, his book makes no application of his insight. All he says is, "This reason for righteous administration of justice is at the same time a reminder of the theocratic nature of the Israelite kingdom, a reminder that God was the lord who was making covenant anew with them this day."[6]

Why does he fail to develop this theme? One obvious reason is that he believes that this Israelite theocratic kingdom and its laws represented an intrusion into the plan of God for the ages — something not carried over into the New Testament. He does not want New Testament judicial reminders "that God is the lord who is making covenant anew with *us* this day." I do want such reminders.

Ethics

Kline does not discuss the whole principle involved in Biblical ethics, namely, that *there is an ethical cause-effect relationship.* Kline does not believe that such a relationship is visible in history. Whatever cause-and-effect relationship there is, is known only to God. To mankind, such relationships supposedly are inscrutable. I think it is appropriate here to cite Gary North's observations concerning Kline's view of ethical cause and effect:

If you preach that biblical law produces "positive feedback," both personally and culturally — that God rewards covenant-keepers and punishes

---

6. *Ibid.*, p. 53.

covenant-breakers in history — then you are preaching a system of positive growth. You are preaching the progressive fulfillment dominion covenant. Only if you deny that there is any long-term sustainable relationship between external covenant-keeping and external success in life — a denial made explicit by Meredith G. Kline — can you escape from the postmillennial implications of biblical law.

North then observes in a footnote that

Kline says that any connection between blessings and covenant-keeping is, humanly speaking, random. "And meanwhile it [the common grace order] must run its course within the uncertainties of the mutually conditioning principles of common grace and common curse, prosperity and adversity being experienced in a manner largely unpredictable because of the inscrutable sovereignty of the divine will that dispenses them in mysterious ways."[7] Dr. Kline has obviously never considered just why it is that life insurance premiums and health insurance premiums are cheaper in Christian-influenced societies than in pagan societies. Apparently, the blessings of long life that are promised in the Bible are sufficiently non-random and "scrutable" that statisticians who advise insurance companies can detect statistically relevant differences between societies.[8]

It is precisely the cause-and-effect relationship between external covenant-keeping and external success, and external covenant-breaking and external judgment, that the Book of Deuteronomy's ethics section is all about (Deut. 8). It is also what God's judgments in history are all about (Deut. 28:1-14): sanctions.

Sanctions

Let Kline speak for himself (though he is not very clear at this point):

The kingdom of Israel was, of course, not another Caesar-kingdom but, uniquely, the kingdom of God institutionally present among the nations. Its earthly and cultural form was symbolic of the ultimate integration of culture and cult in the world of the consummation. The judicial infliction of cultural sanctions by its officers typified the final messianic judgment of men in the totality of their being as cultural creatures. This institutional symbolization of the final judgment and eternal kingdom disappeared from the earthly scene when the Old Covenant gave way to the New. In this age

---

7. Kline, "Comments on the Old-New Error," *Westminster Theological Journal*, XLI (Fall 1978), p. 184.

8. Gary North, *Dominion and Common Grace* (Tyler, Texas: Institute for Christian Economics, 1987), p. 138.

of the church, royal theocratic authority with its prerogative of imposing physical-cultural sanctions resides solely in Christ, the heavenly King. The judicial authority of the permanent special officers whom Christ has appointed to serve his church on earth is purely spiritual-cultic.[9]

Here is where Kline's implicit antinomianism becomes explicit. What about Romans 13? What about the ministers of justice appointed by Christ to protect His Church, as well as to protect all men in their "non-cultic" activities? Paul writes of God's appointed authorities, which includes (though is not limited to) civil magistrates:

Let every person be in subjection to the governing authorities. For there is no authority except from God, and those which exist are established by God. Therefore he who resists authority has opposed the ordinance of God; and they who have opposed will receive condemnation unto themselves (Rom. 13:1-2).

When Paul reminds us that rebels will receive condemnation, he is reminding us, using Kline's words, that the kingdom's "earthly and cultural form was symbolic of the ultimate consummation. The judicial infliction of cultural sanctions by its officers typified the final messianic judgment of men in the totality of their being as cultural creatures." *The State legitimately inflicts sanctions, acting as God's appointed agent.* These sanctions point directly to God as the final Judge. This did not end with the Old Testament. This is why Paul calls the civil authority a *minister of God.* "For he [the authority] is a minister of God to you for good. But if you do what is evil, be afraid; for he does not bear the sword for nothing; for he is a minister of God, an avenger who brings wrath upon the one who practices evil" (Rom. 13:4).

The problem is this: What is the nature of the sanctions in the New Testament age? Kline cannot show why or how something in the New Testament restricts to the Mosaic economy the dual sanctions of Deuteronomy 27-28. My question is simple: What principles govern God's historical judgments in this New Testament era? Silence in this case is not golden. Kline does not see any New Testament civil applications. Specifically, he does not see the civil sanctions as being tied to a system of covenantal adoption. (He does make one important covenantal application of his insights regarding the dual sanctions of the covenant: the covenantal basis of New Tes-

9. *By Oath Consigned*, pp. 100-1.

tament infant baptism.)[10] It is his intrusionist thesis again — an out-working of his self-conscious rejection of Biblical law in the New Testament.

Continuity

Continuity means continuity *over time*. But he has already said that there is no cause-and-effect relationship between the covenant and *historical* sanctions in New Testament times, which he defines strictly as an era of "common grace." So, if there are no personal cause-and-effect relationships, then there certainly are no "cultic" cultural relationships.

This means that there can be no earthly progress over time. One generation does not bequeath God-sanctioned blessings in a system of positive, long-term growth and development. There is no "positive feedback" economically, politically, or culturally. Remember his position: "And meanwhile it [the common grace order] must run its course within the uncertainties of the mutually conditioning principles of common grace and common curse, prosperity and adversity being experienced in a manner largely unpredictable because of the inscrutable sovereignty of the divine will that dispenses them in mysterious ways."[11]

Inscrutable sovereignty in this case means "no growth, no judgments, and no predictability" in the historical working out of the kingdom of God. In short, *no postmillennial hope*. He is adamant about this, as he insisted in his ill-fated attempt to cross intellectual swords with Greg Bahnsen.[12]

---

10. Kline, *By Oath Consigned*, ch. 5.

11. Kline, "Comments on the Old-New Error," *Westminster Theological Journal*, XLI (Fall 1978), p. 184.

12. "Along with the hermeneutical deficiencies of Chalcedon's millennialism there is a fundamental theological problem that besets it. And here we come around again to Chalcedon's confounding the biblical concepts of the holy and the common. As we have seen, Chalcedon's brand of postmillennialism envisages as the climax of the millennium something more than a high degree of success in the church's evangelistic mission to the world. An additional millennial prospect (one which they particularly relish) is that of a material prosperity and a world-wide eminence and dominance of Christ's established kingdom on earth, with a divinely enforced submission of the nations to the world government of the Christocracy. . . . The insuperable theological objection to any and every such chiliastic construction is that it entails the assumption of a premature eclipse of the order of common grace. . . . In thus postulating the termination of the common grace order before the consummation, Chalcedon's postmillennialism in effect attributes unfaithfulness to God, for God

I have already indicated that the Book of Revelation is divided into the five-point covenant model. It is highly significant for the proper use of Kline's insights that David Chilton asked me in the fall of 1985, "Do you think that the Book of Revelation is divided into this five-point structure?" I thought that it was, and the two of us worked through the Revelation together. I highly recommend the reader to Chilton's monumental book, *The Days of Vengeance*, in which he states the postmillennial position as eloquently as anyone ever has.

Conclusion

Kline wants to ignore the effects of the Gospel over time. He especially wants to destroy cause and effect in God's judgments in history. His rejection of the New Testament validity of points two through five of the covenant is grounded in his hostility to Biblical law (#3), law courts governed by Biblical law (#2), the judgments of God in history based on Biblical law (#4), and the success of covenant-keeping societies over generations (#5).

For these reasons, I take issue with Kline's work on the covenant. He vaguely — and I stress *vaguely* — refers to the five points of the covenant, but he refuses to draw any implications. Why? *Because the only believable implications point directly to the theological system developed by his theological rivals, the "theonomic postmillennialists," or Christian Reconstructionists.* This is why I depend on Kline in order to reject Kline's conclusions — or lack thereof.

Hence, "Meredith Kline: Yes and No." Mostly "no." In terms of New Testament Biblical social theory in general, completely "no."

---

committed himself in his ancient covenant to maintain that order for as long as the earth endures." Meredith G. Kline, "Comments on an Old-New Error," pp. 183, 184. Cited by North, *Dominion and Common Grace*, p. 90.

Appendix 8

COVENANT IN THE FLESH
(Old Covenant Sacraments)

The main Old Covenant sacraments are *circumcision and passover*, called sacraments because they signify and seal the covenant. Other "symbols" in the Old Testament signify, but these sacraments have a special "sealing" function. How do we know they are more than symbols?

Circumcision carries a *sanction*, a real judgment, with it. A *self-maledictory* curse was applied to the one who either was not circumcised, and should be, or the one who broke the covenant of circumcision. In either case, the person would be "cut off" (Gen. 17:11). Remember, *the "self-maledictory" oath is a pledge of faithfulness*, the punishment being the curse of the covenant. It is called *self*-maledictory because the individual takes the curse (malediction) on himself. Circumcision is the *judicial* phase of the covenant, as we saw in the Abrahamic Covenant, ratifying the covenant by the direct application of the sanctions.

Passover is also more than a symbol. A real transfer of *inheritance* takes place through this meal. Passover, including all other "food" sacraments (manna, sacrifices, etc.), is the *legitimacy* section, establishing continuity and discontinuity between the true and false heirs. Like circumcision, Passover "cut off" the false heirs (Gen. 17:14). No "leaven" could be eaten at this meal. The Israelites were to "cut it off" (Ex. 12:8). So these "rites" are more than mere ritual. They are covenantal exercises that affect the destiny of each family and individual involved.

My purpose for studying the sacraments at this point is simple. The sacraments can be analyzed separately, since they are the *visible* manifestation of the five points of covenantalism. My purpose, however, is to take each sacrament as it fits into the overall covenantal structure. Circumcision demonstrates the judicial phase, and Passover the legitimacy aspect of the covenant. I intend to show that these sacraments form a transition into the New Covenant. Each has its fulfillment in Christ. Furthermore, since Passover in particular closes on the disinheritance of the "bastards" of the covenant, we will be set up for the ministry of Christ. John the Baptist, Christ, and His disciples encountered "sons" of the covenant who were being disinherited and new "sons" who were being included. As we shall see, Jesus re-created the world through the five points of covenantalism. We begin with circumcision.

Circumcision (Boundary Sacrament)

Circumcision is the primary symbol of boundary, representing a "line" that is crossed to get into the covenant. Where do we see the idea of boundary? First, the Flood was a form of circumcision, being called the "cutting" off of the world (Gen. 9:11; 17:14). It is further significant that God gave a "rainbow" as a symbol that He would never do this again. The "rainbow" formed a circle of water around the earth, much like circumcision cuts a line around the organ of procreation.

Second, when Israel marched into the Promised Land, the parting of the Jordan river, a boundary, is called a "cutting" (Josh. 3:13). Again, the same Hebrew word is used to describe the "cutting" of circumcision. Then, after Israel had entered the land, God commanded the people to circumcise themselves (Josh. 5:2-9). This circumcision is followed by the "circling" of Jericho. There seems to be a theological connection. The boundary performed on the land at the Jordan river and the people at Gilgal ("wheel") is finally placed around the unbeliever. So circumcision was a boundary applied to the "flesh."

The "Flesh"

Circumcision was applied to the *"flesh* of the foreskin" (Gen. 17:11). Encircling the "flesh" with a bloody cut symbolized a new boundary, the boundary of the covenant. Why the emphasis on "flesh"? The Old Covenant was made with the "flesh." Adam, who was created flesh—actually from the "dust" of the ground (Gen. 2:7) —was the covenantal representative. When Adam fell, the "flesh" became a term of derision, meaning *the Old Covenant itself had fallen into disrepute.* Shortly after the Fall, man was referred to as "flesh" in a negative sense. God describes the pre-Noahic situation: "My Spirit shall not strive with man forever, because he also is *flesh*" (Gen. 6:3).

The war between "Spirit" and "flesh" had begun. The battle would not be definitively won until the Spirit was poured out in all His fullness in the New Covenant. Even then, however, the conflict would still be between them progressively (Gal. 5:16ff.).

During the Old Covenant, God continued to provide new "Adams" and bring man back into the covenant, each time attempting to overcome the "flesh" because the covenant had been originally made with the "flesh." *Circumcision was a means of doing this by actually placing the covenant in the flesh.*

The purpose was to "kill" the flesh so that it might be "resurrected." But, we should remember that there are *dual* sanctions: cursing and blessing. Circumcision brought automatic results but not automatic salvation. The ritual demanded faithfulness, and by itself it could not save. If the recipient did not persevere, he was cut off. His circumcision became a sign of *judgment unto death.* But, if he continued in faith, circumcision became a *judgment unto life.* The "cut" brought the sanction of "blessing" (Gen. 17:16). Through this judgment ordeal would come life or death, depending on the faithfulness, or lack thereof, in the person being circumcised. Three legal realities, however, were accomplished.

(1)

Circumcision brought about a judicial form of new life, *adoption.* The skin removed was called the "flesh." We have already seen the theological importance of this term. It represented man's sinful "dead" condition. By "killing" the "flesh," new life could begin.

Abraham's case is a clear example. Sarah's womb was dead. He was unable to *procreate.* Also, all men, even babies, are born *dead in sin.* David said he was "conceived in sin in his mother's womb" (Ps. 51:5). The reality of man's sin was that babies were born *sinful,* further meaning that there was no way that a child could become the "child of the covenant" through any *natural process.* Remember, mere *birth* in the home did not make the child a member of the covenant. He was born covenantally dead. How did he become a member of God's family? A legal process of *adoption* had to occur. Since circumcision performed the function of bringing someone into the covenant who was not "naturally" related to God, it amounted to *legal adoption.*

No child "naturally" belongs to God, not if we take seriously the statements about being born in sin. There is no such thing as an "age of accountability." The Bible nowhere teaches such a make-believe doctrine. Paul says specifically that Esau was hated by God in his mother's womb, before he had done good or evil (Rom. 9:11,13). Age had nothing to do with Esau's judicial accountability before God. He was a son of Adam; Adam had already been judged guilty. What is astounding is not that Esau was judged guilty, but that Jacob was judged not guilty in the womb. That is God's grace in action.

Further, notice that *dedication* of the child was not enough. Dedication would have been just the dedication of a "dead" baby. Remember, God looks at life *covenantally*. That baby may have been the healthiest child on earth, but until covenantally claimed by God, it remained forever *separated from Him*. This cleavage was *covenantal death*, not cessation of existence. So if a child was to be part of the covenant, he had to come through *adoption*, or legal life.

What about daughters? Obviously they could not be circumcised. Daughters came into the covenant by way of representation. The male covenantally represented the whole family. Remember, the woman symbolized the bride. The bride could not save herself. She needed a "groom," symbolizing Christ, to come and save her. Through the death of His flesh, the Bride is therefore adopted. But circumcision could only kill the "flesh." After Christ's circumcision death, not just the "fleshly foreskin" is removed: the whole body, the Church, dies with Him (Rom. 6:1ff.). His circumcision went beyond Old Covenant circumcision, becoming a baptism that applied to male and *female*. Both received the sign and were adopted into the new house.

Even though circumcision was applied to children in the Old Covenant, however, the child was required to continue in the faith. There was the possibility that he could fall away, like the ones in the wilderness (I Cor. 10:5ff.). Circumcision brought a dual sanction, not automatic salvation. The child was legally adopted, but could still be *disowned*, precisely what God did to Israel when He adopted the gentiles.

(2)

Second, circumcision symbolized the *whole sacrificial system*, or salvation. How? It removed *shame*, performing a function that the "bloody sacrifice" accomplished. After Joshua had the Israelites circumcised at Gilgal, before they entered the Promised Land, the Lord said, "Today I have *rolled back the reproach* of Egypt from you"

(Josh. 5:9). This "reproach" is literally *shame*, like Adam's and Eve's shame, experienced when the forbidden fruit was eaten. How was this shame covered? Through a bloody sacrifice. Circumcision, therefore, stripped away the old fleshly clothing through a bloody ordeal, providing new clothing. What became of the "clothing"? I think we have to see this ultimately as Christ Himself. His death was simultaneously the circumcision and baptism of the world (Col. 2:11-13). To be baptized in Christ is to put on His clothing (Gal. 3:27). So until Christ came, Israel was still in a state of nakedness, being circumcised, but in need of clothing to cover what was removed.

(3)

Three, circumcision judgment represented a *final judgment*. God told Abraham that an uncircumcised person would be "cut off" (Gen. 17:14). The idea is that God would cut off the organ of reproduction, symbolically killing, if the foreskin was not removed. Immediately after God promised destruction to Egypt's firstborn, we read:

Now it came about at the lodging place on the way that the Lord met him [Moses] and sought to put him to death. Then Zipporah took a flint and cut off her son's foreskin and threw it at Moses' feet, and she said, "You are indeed a bridegroom of blood to me." So He [Angel of Death] let him alone. At that time she said, "You are a bridegroom of blood" — because of the circumcision (Ex. 4:24-26).

God was willing to *kill* Moses, even after He had called him out to lead His people out of Egypt. Why? Remember, *dominion is by covenant*. Just as we saw the need for Israel to be circumcised before the Promised Land could be conquered, so Moses' son had to be circumcised before he could conquer the Egyptians. God wants His people to live in covenant faithfulness, and He promises that He will go before them and destroy any and every enemy.

God's people must meet judgment *up front*. Circumcision represented a real judgment. But it provided a covenantal umbrella that avoided the great final judgment of sin. It was simple: a man received the symbolic judgment of final death, and as long as the recipient persevered in faithfulness to God, eternal death would not come. The promise to Israel was that as long as they were faithful to their circumcision, they would not be "cut off." In the end, they fell away, and God did cut them off. But they didn't have to perish.

Jesus' death was the *substitutionary* circumcision of the world. Paul says,

> And in Him you were also circumcised with a circumcision made without hands, in the removal of the body of the flesh by the circumcision of Christ; having been buried with Him in baptism, in which you were also raised up with Him through faith in the working of God, who raised Him from the dead. And when you were dead in your transgressions and the uncircumcision of your flesh, He made you alive together with Him, having forgiven us all our transgressions (Col. 2:11-13).

When Christ was born, the Jews had almost been cut off. The Jews were given opportunity after opportunity to trust in Christ's circumcision. They didn't. But when the New Testament begins, *Israel* is living in an *uncircumcised condition*. Judgment is all around. The land has turned to a "desert"—Mark's description of Israel (Mark 1:1ff.). Mark goes on to structure his book according to thirteen individual healings (1:21; 1:29; 1:40; 2:1; 3:1; 5:1; 5:21; 5:25; 7:24; 7:31; 8:22; 9:14; 12:46). Only one has to do with a Gentile, symbolizing that the Gentiles would be raised up after the Jews. The rest are Jews who have physical conditions like blindness, lameness, and dumbness, that represent the curses of the covenant (Isa. 35). Israel had apostatized and faced the judicial judgment that circumcision represented.

The Old Covenant closes on the note of being "cut off." The world needed to be truly *circumcised*. The sanction was working into disinheritance. This brings us to the second sacrament and the *legitimacy* section of the covenant, the segment in which the *meal of inheritance* normally fell.

Passover (Food Sacrament)

Passover was actually another form of circumcision. The continuity between them is expressed in the following passage.

> Now it came about when they had finished circumcising all the nation, that they remained in their places in the camp until they were healed [revived]. Then the Lord said to Joshua, "Today I have *rolled away the reproach of Egypt* from you." So the name of that place is called Gilgal ["wheel"] to this day. While the sons of Israel camped at Gilgal, they observed the Passover on the evening of the fourteenth day of the month on the desert plains of Jericho. And on *the day after the Passover*, on that very day, they ate some of the produce of the land, unleavened cakes and parched

grain. And the manna ceased on the day after they had eaten some of the produce of the land, so that the sons of Israel no longer had manna, but they ate some of the yield of the land of Canaan during that year (Josh. 5:8-12).

The relationship between the two Old Testament sacraments is twofold. First, the continuity between the two sacraments can be seen in the phrase, "rolled away the reproach of Egypt" (v. 9). Passover and circumcision were *bloody* rites. As already mentioned, "removal of shame" took place in the Garden of Eden by means of a sacrifice. At the first Passover, the blood of the sacrificial lamb was placed on the door that the Angel of Death would *pass over*. Then the sacrificial lamb was eaten. This sacrifice averted death the same way the first animal sacrifice pushed away the death of Adam and Eve. So both passover sacrifice and circumcision removed "shame."

Second, the Joshua passage shows that circumcision led to Passover. Circumcision had to come first. One could not eat of the Passover unless he was circumcised. The "stranger in the land," for example, could live in the midst of God's people if he kept the civil law. But until circumcision, he could not eat the Passover meal.

So, there is a relationship between the two sacraments. Both were part of a covenant in the flesh, or a "rolling away of shame." The two are similar yet have their own distinct emphasis. Circumcision established covenantal union, while Passover and the other sacramental meals preserved this union through communion. At this point, we turn to Passover as another place where the covenant is legitimated.

Continuity

Legitimate heirs received inheritance and continuity in terms of obedience to God's Passover requirement. The illegitimate heirs, the bastards, were disinherited through the Passover and all other sacramental meals. The original Passover account reads,

It is the Lord's Passover. For I will go through the land of Egypt on that night, and will strike down all the first-born in the land of Egypt, both man and beast; and against all the gods of Egypt I will execute judgments—I am the Lord. And blood shall be a sign for you on the houses where you live; and when I see the blood I will pass over you, and no plague will befall you to destroy you when I strike the land of Egypt. Now this day will be a memorial to you, and you shall celebrate it as a feast to the Lord; throughout your generations you are to celebrate it as a permanent ordinance. . . .

Sanctify to Me every first-born, the first offspring of every womb among the sons of Israel, both of man and beast; it belongs to Me. . . . Remember this day . . . and nothing unleavened shall be eaten. . . . Now it shall come about when the Lord brings you to the land of the Canaanite, as He swore to you and to your fathers, and gives it to you, that you shall devote to the Lord the first offspring of every womb . . . And Moses took the bones of Joseph with him, for he had made the sons of Israel solemnly swear, saying, "God shall surely take care of you; and you shall carry my bones from here with you" (Ex. 12:11-14; 13:1-19).

All of the issues of continuity and discontinuity are found in this passage.

(1)

Passover created continuity and discontinuity between the first-born of God and the first-born of the Egyptians. The first-born sons of Egypt could keep inheritance only on the basis of obedience to God. When they refused to obey, their inheritance was lost because of death. Also, the Israelites' journey was financed with the first-born inheritance of Egypt. The people left and were able to take all the gold of Egypt they could carry.

The Israelites were never to forget that *their inheritance came by covenant*, not by natural succession. First-born status was based on *obedience to the Lord*. The text above says that the reason for unleavened bread was a "firstfruits" commitment that Israel would dedicate everything to the Lord when the land was reached. This bread symbolized that Israel was in compliance with the Passover and the commandments of God. Once the land was reached, this symbol of ethical separation was the primary requirement for remaining in the land and keeping the inheritance.

(2)

The Passover meal established continuity and discontinuity within Israel. While Moses was on the mountain receiving the commandments, the Israelites ate an idolatrous *communion* meal, which in effect became a false passover. They committed idolatry and adultery at the same time. Remember, these two commandments parallel each other in the Ten Commandments Covenant, the second and seventh falling in the hierarchical category. We can see how the Passover meal that had been eaten became an *ordeal of jealousy* type of meal. What happened?

The Israelites became impatient. They took their new inheritance from Egypt and made an idol, fashioned after a sacrificial animal, the ox. They offered false sacrifices and worshipped it. As Paul says, "The people sat down to eat and drink [false passover], and stood up to play" (I Cor. 10:7). This idolatry made God jealous. To the second commandment on idolatry is attached the statement, "I, the Lord thy God am a jealous God" (Ex. 20:5). God sent Moses down the mountain. When he arrived, he "threw the tablets from his hands and shattered them at the foot of the mountain. And he took the calf which they had made and burned it with fire, and ground it to powder, and scattered it over the surface of the water, and *made the sons of Israel drink it*" (Ex. 32:19-20).

This procedure is the ordeal of jealousy described in Numbers 5 regarding a woman suspected of adultery. This is a process of disinheritance. All of the meals in the wilderness became part of a "spiritual food and drink" category (I Cor. 10:3-4). In an extension of the true Passover, the Israelites drank a mixture of their sin, plus its judgment (the commandments), and its purification (the water). It seems from what follows that this was to reveal those who were unrepentant. After drinking the solution, Moses used the Levites to execute judgment. Going among the Israelites, approximately 3,000 were put to death. How did the Levites know whom to kill? They probably had a "swollen stomach" like the guilty woman in the ordeal of jealousy (Nu. 5:27). As a result of this judgment, the true heirs were established through *continuity*.

(3)

Passover created continuity with the future. Exodus 12 says, "This day [Passover day] will be a memorial to you, and you shall celebrate it as a *permanent ordinance*" (Ex. 12:14). Passover restored the family. As the children participated in the Passover, they were told the meaning of the meal. The father said in effect, "You get to eat because of what the Lord did for me" (Ex. 13:8). To cut off the children would not make sense because this would be a complete denial of what the Passover was all about: a future inheritance for the covenant people. The future was in the covenant child. *No children meant no future: no land or anything else.* If the children were not pulled up into the covenant, or if they turned away from the Lord, they would die and the land would be taken away. The Passover meal extended covenantal continuity.

The false passover meal at the foot of Mt. Sinai during Moses' absence had destroyed the families of the participants. As the death penalty was about to be carried out on the apostates, Moses said, "Dedicate yourselves today to the Lord — for every *man has been against his son and against his brother* — in order that He may bestow a *blessing* upon you today" (Ex. 32:29). The "blessing" was the transfer of inheritance. So, as Israel had lost its family continuity through an idolatrous meal, it would receive it back through faithful communion.

The covenant was legitimated in terms of a meal. As we have seen in previous covenants, at the end of the covenant, the *death of the covenantal head seals the disinheritance of the old heirs and the inheritance of the new heirs.* When Israel left Egypt, the "bones of Joseph" were taken. Remember, Israel had lived in the Promised Land once before. When Joseph died outside of the land, he needed to be returned to establish continuity. Joseph, in other words, had to be connected with Joshua. The same thing happened in the New Testament. John the Baptist died, representing the Old Covenant. Jesus Christ created continuity with the final Old Covenant Head. He died and was buried outside of Jerusalem, outside the land. After the Resurrection, He returned to the land, just as Joseph returned with Joshua. He established continuity with His new *army*.

When Christ was born, Israel was eating meals with the "golden calf" again. Israel had become like *a "new" Egypt.* Everywhere Jesus went, He encountered people cursed with plagues like sickness, demon-possession, and lameness. Jesus said their father was the devil (John 8:44). When they ate the Passover, or any sacramental meal, they were eating and drinking judgment to themselves. They would die just as their forefathers had. Christ told them who He was time and again. Like Moses, He went through the camp offering a time of repentance. They refused, and by His own birth, death, and resurrection, He removed the "flesh" (Col. 2:11-13). For those on the Lord's side, the ones who turned and trusted in Christ, His death and resurrection definitively accomplished salvation. Seventy A.D. was the progressive outworking of the destruction of the Old Covenant, which had become flesh, on those who wanted to remain in the wilderness of rebellion. But Christ did all of this not by the sword, but by His own covenantal death. Dominion over the apostates was through the application of the covenant.

Conclusion

Here is the end of the Old Covenant. We have called this chapter the "Covenant in the Flesh." Circumcision and Passover were designed to restore Israel, but they could not. They went the way of all the Old Covenant, the way of the flesh. Christ's appearance in history encounters a nation and world that had been consumed by the flesh. His circumcision/death was the only thing that truly changed the world.

Appendix 9

COVENANT BY THE SPIRIT
(New Covenant Sacraments)

The sacraments of the New Covenant are especially tied to the Holy Spirit. The Old Covenant sacraments were in the "flesh" (i.e. "foreskin") and ended in death. But when Christ died and rose again, the Holy Spirit was poured out on the earth as He never had been before. Does this mean individuals, prior to Pentecost, did not have the Holy Spirit? No, the Holy Spirit was "hovering" over the original creation (Gen. 1:2), leading Israel out of bondage from Egypt (Deut. 32:10ff.) and guiding the individual leaders of God's people. Jesus told Nicodemus that he needed to be "born of the Spirit" (John 3:1-5). When Nicodemus did not understand, Jesus rebuked him saying, "Are you a teacher of Israel, and do not understand these things?" (John 3:10). Being born again of the Spirit was nothing *new*. Nicodemus should have understood.

The difference between the Spirit's work in the Old and New Covenants is that the Spirit was given to the whole earth, to Jew and *Gentile* in the New Covenant. This was something *new*. Again it should be understood that it was not as though the Spirit had never gone to an "individual" Gentile, or individual Gentile nations (i.e. Assyria). There are plenty of examples in the Old Testament where a Gentile became a believer (Ruth 1; II Kgs. 5:1ff.). But never before, at least since the Tower of Babel, had Gentiles been made a part of God's *priesthood*. Because the Spirit went to the Gentiles, special signs, like speaking in tongues, accompanied it. Addressing the Church at Corinth, Paul says, "In the Law it is written, 'By men of strange tongues and by the lips of strangers I will speak to this people, and even so they will not listen to Me,' says the Lord. So then tongues are for a *sign*, not to those who believe, but to unbelievers" (I Cor. 14:21-22). Who were these unbelievers? Gentiles! Why was a sign needed? Because the Spirit of God was coming to them as well.

299

The Spirit had come in special measure, "given life" (II Cor. 3:6), and had life-giving *signs*. Ultimately, this is the great difference between Old and New. Baptism and communion are signs of Life through the Holy Spirit. The great transition point was the *resurrection of Christ*. After He was raised from the dead, He began to fill His disciples with the Holy Spirit (John 20:22). After He ascended to the right hand of God, the Holy Spirit was given to a broader circle at Pentecost. Jesus had said the Spirit would be left with man to be Christ's Presence on earth. The Spirit would overcome the "flesh." Certainly "individual" men still lived by the "flesh" and "died," but the contrasts of the New Testament between Old Covenant and New Covenant lay in the fact that the Spirit had been poured out on all of humanity. The Spirit would put down all *rule by the flesh*.

The *signs* of the New Covenant are symbols of the *Spirit*, not of the "flesh." There are two: baptism and communion. Why only two? Aren't there other symbols in the New Covenant? Yes, marriage is a *sign* of the covenant. Why isn't it a sacrament? Marriage is a symbol but it does not in any way *seal* into the covenant. Paul argues that one is free to marry or not to marry. Neither situation makes one more or less in covenant with Christ (I Cor. 7:8-24). Some churches include marriage as a sacrament, but only because they have a much *broader* definition of sacraments. This word should be reserved, however, for those covenantal acts which *seal* a person to Christ. These are *baptism and communion*.

Baptism (Boundary Sacrament)

We have already seen in the Great Commission Covenant that baptism is the new *sanction*. It represents the work of the Holy Spirit. Jesus says, "John *baptized* with water but you shall be *baptized* with the Spirit" (Acts 1:5). Paul says, "He saves us, not on the basis of deeds which we have done in righteousness, but according to His mercy, by the *washing* of regeneration and renewing by the *Holy Spirit*" (Titus 3:5). We should keep in mind the principle of the Trinity as we read such a passage. The "water" itself does not regenerate, but signifies *the incorporation of the believer under terms of the covenant*. It seals the believer covenantally to the Holy Spirit. Baptism warns the baptized: break the terms of the covenant by renouncing Christ, and you will perish by the terms of the covenant. Because baptism is a sanction, there are *dual* sanctions: blessing *and* cursing. Baptism seals to Christ, and is in this sense automatic, but it does not automatically create *salvation*.

How can this be? Remember the Trinitarian principle of *not separation but distinction* (p. 88). Salvation is not to be separated from the sacraments, but should be kept *distinct*, meaning God requires a life of faithfulness to accompany baptism. In this case, the believer receives the sanction of *blessing*. But if there is unfaithfulness as a result of the person's abandoning reliance on Christ, the *now-visibly revealed* unbeliever receives the sanction of *cursing*. In this regard, we see the similarity to and the difference from circumcision.

Cursing

Like circumcision, baptism is a "killing" ritual. Both symbolize the essence of the curse on man, *death* (Gen. 2:17). Paul makes the connection when he says,

In Him you were also circumcised with a circumcision made without hands, in the removal of the body of the flesh by the circumcision of Christ; having been *buried with Him in baptism*, in which you were also raised with Him through faith in the working of God, who raised Him from the dead. And when you were dead in your transgressions and the uncircumcision of your flesh, He made you alive together with Him, having forgiven us all our transgressions (Col. 2:11-13).

Circumcision killed the "flesh." At least, that was its intention. Only through the circumcision of Christ could its original purpose be accomplished. Yet, baptism replaces circumcision, also being a process of killing the "flesh." Paul says that we are "buried with Him in baptism."

Throughout the Old Testament, circumcision had anticipated baptism. Water was a *circular*, circumcision-forming boundary around the original creation/land. The Flood was referred to as a "cutting off" of the world. After the Great Deluge, God said, "All flesh shall never again be *cut off* by water of the flood" (Gen. 9:11). The Hebrew word "cut off" is the same one used to refer to the curse that falls on the one who is not circumcised (Gen. 17:14). So circumcision and water were *killing boundaries* in the Old Covenant.

Water was a constant source of *killing*. It killed the sons of Cain in the Flood; it killed the Egyptians at the crossing of the Red Sea. Jesus referred to His own *death* as a baptism. He said to His disciples, "Are you able to drink the cup that I drink, or to be baptized with the baptism with which I am baptized" (Mark 10:38). Christ's death was simultaneously a *circumcision and baptismal* curse.

Although circumcision symbolized death, baptism symbolized a greater death because it represented the death of Christ in a way that circumcision could not. How? It was *death unto life*. Paul says, "Do you not know that all of us who have been baptized into Christ Jesus have been baptized into His death? Therefore we have been buried with Him through baptism into death in order that as Christ was raised from the dead through the glory of the Father, so we too might walk in newness of life" (Rom. 6:3-4). Circumcision was death unto death. Baptism was *death unto life*.

So, baptism has greater *killing* power. It represents the Holy Spirit, whose Life is so powerful that instant death can come to the one who betrays his baptism. Of the early church we read:

> But a certain man named Ananias, with his wife Sapphira, sold a piece of property, and kept back some of the price for himself, with his wife's full knowledge, and bringing a portion of it, he laid it at the apostles' feet. But Peter said, "Ananias, why has Satan filled your heart to lie to the Holy Spirit, and to keep back some of the price of the land? While it remained unsold, did it not remain your own? And after it was sold, was it not under your control? Why is it that you have conceived this deed in your heart? You have not lied to men, but God." And as he heard these words, Ananias fell down and breathed his last; and great fear came upon all who heard of it. . . . And his wife came in, not knowing what had happened. And Peter responded to her, "Tell me whether you sold the land for such and such a price?" And she said, "Yes, that was the price." Then Peter said to her, "Why is it that you have agreed together to put the *Spirit of the Lord* to the test? Behold, the feet of those who have buried your husband are at the door, and they shall carry you out as well." And she fell immediately at his feet, and breathed her last (Acts 5:1-11).

How could Satan fill a baptized person's heart? Because baptism does not save anyone. Baptism represents the two-fold sanction of the Holy Spirit. To be united to Christ means great life or horrendous death, depending on the faithfulness of the one baptized. There was a similar incident with Achan in the Old Testament (Josh. 7). But even in that case, the *people* carried out the death penalty (Josh. 7:25). In the New Covenant, the Holy Spirit is more directly involved in the death of those who break covenant.

Baptism is a sanction of death. Like circumcision, it killed the "flesh," but unlike the Old Covenant sacrament, it killed *by the Spirit*.

Blessing

Water, however, is more than something which symbolically and covenantally kills. Water symbolically and covenantally *resurrects*. Water symbolizes the greatest *blessing* that could ever come to mankind: *life — victory over sin and death*. Paul says, "For if we have become united with Him in the likeness of His death, certainly we shall be also in the likeness of His resurrection" (Rom. 6:5).

Circumcision killed the flesh and adopted the recipient into the household. In this sense, it resurrected. But circumcision, as we saw at the end of the Old Covenant, failed to resurrect Israel. Christ's death went beyond circumcision, in that it actually resurrected the New Israel covenantally (representationally). This is implied in the symbolism of water in the Old Testament. When someone touched a dead animal, the law said,

The one who touches the corpse of any person shall be unclean for seven days. That one shall purify himself from uncleanness with the water on the *third day* and on the seventh day, and then he shall be clean; but if he does not purify himself on the third day and on the seventh day, he shall not be clean. Anyone who touches a corpse, the body of a man who has died, and does not purify himself, defiles the tabernacle of the Lord; and that person shall be cut off from Israel. Because the *water* for impurity was not *sprinkled* on him, he shall be unclean; his uncleanness is still on him (Nu. 19:11-13).

Such a ritual anticipated New Covenant baptism in several ways. First, this Old Testament *baptism* is called a *baptism* (Heb. 9:10). In the great chapter on the Resurrection, Paul says, "What will those do who are baptized for the dead? If the dead are not raised at all, why then are they baptized for them?" (I Cor. 15:29). The "baptism for the dead" was none other than the Old Covenant baptism in Numbers 19. When someone touched anyone who had died, he had to be symbolically *resurrected*, because death spread to death in the Old Testament.

Second, notice that this baptism was applied on the *third* day. Jesus was *raised* on the third day. He was the complete fulfillment of what Old Testament baptism typified, the resurrection.

Third, this baptism symbolically came from *above*, which is implied in the *sprinkling*. Resurrection is symbolized by the sprinkling or pouring mode. Notice that all throughout the Bible, only the pagans are drowned, or *immersed*. How were the sons of Cain killed in the Flood? By immersion. How were the Egyptians killed at the crossing of the Red Sea? By immersion.

God's people are always "sprinkled." At the Flood, the Ark was "rained on," or sprinkled. At the crossing of the Red Sea, the Psalmist says, "The clouds poured out water" on the Israelites (Ps. 77:17). Jesus was poured upon in the Jordan River because His baptism did not symbolize *conversion*. How could it? His was a baptism into the priesthood (Nu. 4:3). Priests were consecrated into the priesthood through special baptisms (Heb. 6:1; 9:10; Lev. 11:25). The method was by *sprinkling*. Moses says, "This is what you shall do to them to consecrate them to minister as priests to Me. . . . You shall bring Aaron and his sons to the doorway of the tent of meeting, and *wash them with water*" (Ex. 29:4). Because there was nothing big enough at the "door" to immerse the priests, the method was by *pouring*. This is why those Reformation churches that have emphasized *the priesthood of all believers* have traditionally poured or sprinkled people, rather than immersing them.[1]

Christ had said, "John baptized with water, but you shall be baptized by the Spirit" (Acts 1:5). When the Holy Spirit came, Peter quoted the prophet Joel, describing this event: " 'And it shall be in the last days,' God says, 'that I will *pour out* My Spirit upon all *flesh*' " (Joel 2:28-32 quoted in Acts 2:17ff.). Holy Spirit baptism is *pouring* or *sprinkling* because this symbolizes the *blessing of the Spirit*.

Circumcision blessed, but it did not have the power to bless the "flesh"; it only had the power to kill it. But Joel says that the Spirit would be poured out on all "flesh" (Joel 2:28-32). Baptism is a sign and seal of not only death, but the resurrection of flesh to become *true humanity*. When man is converted, he starts to act more like a human, and less like the "flesh," which has the characteristics of the "beast" (Dan. 7:1-8). Baptism is a symbol of the life-giving power of the Spirit. This blessing leads into the next sacrament.

Communion (Food Sacrament)

Communion is a *ritual meal* that portrays the power of Christ over death. Like the other covenants, the meal is the place for trans-

---

1. Those who baptize by immersion have argued that the Reformation churches (Lutherans, Presbyterian, and Anglican) were still unwilling to break ritually with Rome, which also sprinkled, have not understood the theological reason for retaining the early Church's mode of baptism. It was the Roman Church which was inconsistent with its own sacerdotal theology by retaining the mode of baptism used by the early Church.

ferring and memorializing inheritance. Communion is a memorial of Christ's Death and Resurrection. "Memorial" means *covenantal renewal*. The ancient suzerain treaties carved the covenant on a stone, leaving it in the land of the vassal. It served as a memorial that continuity had been established with the suzerain. The New Covenant makes communion the memorial. Paul says,

> The Lord Jesus in the night in which He was betrayed took bread; and when He had given thanks, He broke it, and said, "This is My body, which is given for you; do this in *remembrance* of Me." In the same way He took the cup also, after supper, saying, "This cup is the new covenant in My blood; do this, as often as you drink it, in *remembrance* of Me" (I Cor. 11:23-25).

"Remembrance" does not mean "memory." Rather, "remembrance" is a "memorializing" that renews the covenant. Biblical memorializing involves taking the Supper in a "worthy" manner. How is the Lord's Supper taken "worthily"? When is it *legitimate*?

Legitimate Communion

By this question I don't intend to imply that *communion* itself is not legitimate when taken "unworthily." Paul's language indicates that the *recipient* of communion may not be legitimate. In the case of the Corinthians, some were "sick and dying" because they were *not communing*. Paul explains three violations that rendered a communicant an illegitimate, or bastard of the faith. Keep in mind the following points are expressed in the negative because this is the way Paul states them.

First is the *failure to commune*. What were the Corinthians doing? Paul says, "When you meet together, it is not to eat the Lord's Supper, for in your eating each one takes his own supper first" (I Cor. 11:20-21). Very seldom is this context recognized. So often this passage is read just before the Lord's Supper, when it actually applies primarily to those who are *not* taking communion. The Corinthians were treating communion as a regular meal of their homes. The Church is *not the family*. To reduce the Church to the family is to "bastardize" everyone who takes the meal. What does this say about churches that profess to be churches but never take communion? The members are ritually proclaiming themselves to be bastards of the faith, or illegitimate sons. The Lord's Supper is not an option. It is to be eaten by Christians because it is the place of life (John 6:52-59), life brought about by the Spirit of God (John 6:53, 63). It is to be eaten often, preferably once a week (Acts 20:7-12).

Second is the *demonstration of unfaithfulness*. Paul says, "Let a man examine himself" (I Cor. 11:28). The command means *demonstration of faithfulness*. The word "examine" should be translated *demonstrate*. In other passages Paul uses the same Greek word where it is translated "prove." He says, "But let every man *prove* his own work, and then shall he have rejoicing in himself alone, and not in another" (Gal. 6:4). This is a fundamental aspect of *Christian self-government*. Self-government is basic because to make a covenant with God always involves taking a *self-maledictory oath*, which is what baptism is.

This presents quite a contrast to the modern idea of the Lord's Supper as a form of *contemplation* — with lights turned down low and quivering organ music in the background. Communion is not contemplation; it is *covenant renewal*. It is therefore a manifestation of the communicant's ritual reaffirmation of his self-maledictory oath. Yet many people take communion who have never heard of a self-maledictory oath. In most churches, anyone can walk in off the street and have communion. He may be a professing Christian who believes and practices abortion. But as long as he is "fully clothed and in his right mind," he can receive communion. Paul's statement, however, indicates that one becomes an illegitimate communicant if he does not demonstrate his faith. Where does this begin? At baptism, because it is the definitive covenant-cutting ceremony. How is it continued? Through obedience. It is the Church officers' job to find out if the people communing have demonstrated their covenant to Christ.

Third is *no accountability to the government of the Church*. Paul says, "For he who eats and drinks, eats and drinks judgment to himself, if he does not *judge* the body rightly" (I Cor. 11:29). The word "judge" means *discern* (I Cor. 4:7; 6:5). The New American Standard Version simply says "discern the *body*" because some manuscripts understood this to be the "body of the Church." But whether it means discern the mystical or political body of Christ, Paul clarifies what he means when he says, "If we judge ourselves rightly we should not be judged" (I Cor. 11:31). How does the Church "judge itself"? Through the disciplining process of Matthew 18. Jesus says,

> If your brother sins, go and reprove him in private; if he listens to you, you have won your brother. But if he does not listen to you, take one or two more with you, so that by the mouth of two or three witnesses every fact may be confirmed. And if he refuses to listen to them, tell it to the church;

and if he refuses to listen even to the church, let him be to you as a Gentile and a tax-gatherer (Matt. 18:15-17).

When Church discipline is going on, the body is being "discerned," members are "judging one another." Where this is not happening, the members are being illegitimized. This makes local church discipline a very serious matter. The Church at Corinth was full of disciplinary problems. Paul had had to tell them to discipline one man who committed incest (I Cor. 5:1ff.).

These three principles of legitimacy were important to the life of the Corinthian Church. Why? As we have seen throughout the covenants of the Bible, continuity and discontinuity are created at the covenantal meal. The New Covenant is no different. Offense at the meal means loss of inheritance.

Continuity/Discontinuity

First, continuity/discontinuity is established with the *First-born*. Who is the First-born? Jesus. Paul says Christ is the "first-born among many brethren" (Rom. 8:29). Remember, the true first-born forms continuity. Throughout the Old Covenant it was always the second "Adam": Isaac not Ishmael, Jacob not Esau, etc. In effect, they became the first-born. But Christ was both the Second Adam and the First-born. The writer to the Hebrews says, "And when He again brings the *first-born* into the world, He says, 'And let all the angels of God worship Him'" (Heb. 1:6). Communion sets up continuity between Christ and the Church which is also called the "first-born" (Heb. 12:23). This continuity makes the Church the heir of everything that belongs to Christ, the whole *world*. There is a song, "We Are the World," which implies that everyone on earth is the world. Actually, the Church is definitively the world! Progressively, the Church is becoming the world by filling it and subduing it. In the end, anyone who is not a member of the Church will be removed from the earth.

Second, communion establishes continuity/discontinuity between the Church and world. The Passover Meal was a feast which *disinherited the Egyptians*. In the same way, communion is the new Passover meal which disinherits the world. How? While the Israelites were eating the lamb of the Passover, the Angel of Death visited the Egyptians. In a miraculous way, the Egyptians were defeated. When the Church communes with Christ, keeping in mind the principles of legitimacy mentioned earlier, the wicked are judged. The best illustration is toward the last part of the Book of Revelation. The last series of judgments are the "seven chalices" (Rev. 16:1ff.). These are clearly references to the "chalice" of communion.

The implication is that as the Church exercises discipline through its own communion, God begins to clear away the "clutter" on the earth. God pours out His vengeance on all those who oppose the Church. In a way, this is now happening in the Western world. For the first time in centuries, the Church is beginning to commune in disciplined fashion. It is not surprising to see God curse the world with a disease like AIDS. The same thing happened in the 14th century with the Plague. It happened again in 1493, when Columbus' crew brought Syphilis to Europe, and it spread across the continent within a decade. (In 1517, the Reformation began.) Judgment begins at the House of God. God weeded out Gideon's army before He allowed him to fight the Midianites. Discontinuity with the world, through communion, had to occur before any kind of continuity with the new world could be allowed. In other words, faithful communion with Christ clears away the "fleshly" world so that Christians can live in it.

Third, communion establishes continuity and discontinuity within the family. God claims whole families. We saw this earlier when I talked about "household baptisms." But baptism only applies the *sanctions*. Every member of the family is entitled to Christ's inheritance if he (or she) has been baptized. Paul says of the Red Sea baptism and communion, "*All* were baptized into Moses in the cloud and in the sea; And *all* ate the same spiritual food; and *all* drank that same spiritual drink, for they were drinking from a spiritual rock which followed them; and the rock was *Christ*" (I Cor. 10:2-4). The "all" means that each individual was baptized and ate the spiritual communion of Christ. Significantly, this context applies these principles to communion.

The Lord's Supper is for the whole family, providing they have already received the sanctions in baptism. To take communion before the sanctions is the same as attempting to have life apart from the sanction of death. This is a denial of the fundamental principle of *life through death*. For those who have been baptized, however, communion is part of the *inheritance*. Full family communion establishes continuity among family members. If the children are not allowed to commune, then they have no continuity with the rest of the family.

God's "Great Commission" to disciple the world, family by family, is cut short. How can the Church conquer the world when it unlawfully excommunicates the children of its own families? It can't. How can the Church inherit the earth (Matt. 5:5) if it disinherits the children of its own families? It can't. This is why family continuity is so important to the dominion of the world.

This concludes our study of communion. I have not attempted to define the sense in which Christ is present in the Lord's Supper. I can say that Christ is not physically present in the meal because the night He established the Supper and said, "This is My body," He was not speaking in a "physical" sense. Yet Scripture says that when the Supper is taken in faith, Christ has been eaten. This is a great mystery which neither rationalism nor irrationalism can comprehend. Even so, this meal is the covenantal process of legitimating the true and false heirs. Through the real presence of the Spirit at communion, it becomes a *covenant by the Spirit*.

Realism vs. Nominalism: Christ's Kingdom

I have argued that Christ's presence in the Lord's Supper is *representative* or covenantal. This breaks with the Roman Catholic view, the Lutheran view, and the modern "memorial only"[2] view.

The Roman Catholic and Lutheran views, despite their verbal differences, are essentially the same. They are heavily influenced by the medieval debate over realism and nominalism. Both the Roman Catholics and the Lutherans maintain that Christ must be humanly present in the bread and wine if the sacrament is true.[3] His presence must be *real*.

On the other hand, those who hold a nominalist view of the sacraments argue that the sacraments are only symbolic, strictly a present memorial to a past historic event. They argue that there is no "real presence" *representatively* (covenantally) of Christ in the sacra-

---

2. If those who defend the "memorial only" sacraments understood that the Biblical memorial is always *covenant-establishing* (baptism) or *covenant renewal* (communion), both of which involve the *self-maledictory oath*, they might be moved to find some other terminology besides "memorial."

3. According to one Lutheran scholar, "To say that the nature of Christ is personally present without his humanity is to deny that his humanity is part of his personality and the doctrine of the incarnation falls to the dust." Charles Philip Krauth, *The Conservative Reformation and Its Theology*, p. 350; cited by Cornelius Van Til, *A Survey of Christian Epistemology*, Vol. II of *In Defense of the Faith* (den Dulk Christian Foundation, 1969), p. 69.

ment of communion. Christ is present *nominally*, meaning symbolically and subjectively only. He is present in the sacrament only in
the sense that Christians ritually *remember* Christ's sharing a meal
with His disciples. The sacraments have no *power* apart from their
influence subjectively and psychologically over the people who par-
take in them. Christ is not *really* present in the sacraments.

This debate over the realism vs. the nominalism of the Lord's
Supper is analogous to the debate over the nature of Christ's earthly
kingdom. First, let us consider the "realist" view of Christ's millennial reign. Premillennialists say that Christ's presence in His kingdom must be a *real* presence: He must be humanly, physically present in order for His reign on earth to be manifested in history. In
other words, He cannot be said to be present in His earthly kingdom
representatively (covenantally) through His Church and the historical
manifestations of His Word, the Bible.

Second, let us consider the "nominalist" view of Christ's millennial reign. The nominalist view of the sacraments is exclusively subjective and psychological: the sacraments have no independent
power apart from the psychological commitment of those who par-
take in them. Similarly, amillennialists implicitly argue that Christ's
presence in His historic kingdom is only a *nominal* presence. It is
comprehended only by His Christian followers, who in fact experience increasing visible defeats historically. Cornelius Van Til's amillennial vision is representative: as time goes forward, the Church is
increasingly persecuted. "But when all the reprobate are epistemo-
logically self-conscious, the crack of doom has come. The fully self-
conscious reprobate will do all he can in every dimension to destroy
the people of God. So while we seek with all our power to hasten the
process of differentiation in every dimension we are yet thankful, on
the other hand, for 'the day of grace,' the day of undeveloped differentiation. Such tolerance as we receive on the part of the world is
due to this fact that we live in the earlier, rather than the later, stage
of history."[4] Or hear the words of the most prominent Dutch-Ameri-
can amillennial Bible commentator, W. Hendrikson, on chapter 20
of the Book of Revelation, the binding of Satan:

Now, please do not misunderstand our interpretation. We are not
stating that the world is becoming better and better and that by and by
nearly every one will join the ranks of Christ's army. Many will *hear* the

---

4. *Common Grace*, in *Common Grace and the Gospel* (Nutley, New Jersey:
Presbyterian & Reformed, 1972), p. 85.

Gospel, but will not *heed* it. Moreover, God's trumpets of judgment will not convert a world which is hardening itself in unbelief. The majority will ever be on the side of the evil one. We most emphatically reject the dream of a man-made era of peace, prosperity, and universal righteousness on earth preceding the second coming of Christ. Just as definitely do we repudiate the related idea according to which the almighty "law of evolution" will bring about an ever-upward trend in the course of civilization. . . . We repeat: the devil is not bound in *every sense*. His influence is not wholly or completely destroyed. On the contrary, within the sphere in which satan is permitted to exert his influence for evil he rages most furiously.[5]

When Hendrikson writes that "We most emphatically reject the dream of a man-made era of peace, prosperity, and universal right-eousness on earth preceding the second coming of Christ," he is ar-guing that there can be no covenantal, representative, *victorious king-dom* role of the Church in history. He dismisses "man-made" peace and prosperity, just as premillennialists do, with respect to the per-iod before Christ's second coming. He then dismisses an idea which he says is "related": evolutionary humanism. This is deliberately misleading. It is a disguised variant of that old lie that postmillen-nialism is liberalism. Furthermore, Hendrikson's pessimistic escha-tology is implicitly anti-covenantal. Here is my reasoning.

Covenant theology divides men into saved and lost, a division which is reflected in the sacraments. Covenant-breakers experience long-term defeat in history, and covenant-keepers experience long-term victory. We read in Proverbs:

> The righteousness of the blameless will smooth his way, but the wicked will fall by his own wickedness. The righteousness of the upright will deliver them, but the treacherous will be caught in their own greed. When a wicked man dies, his expectation will perish, and the hope of strong men perishes. The righteous is delivered from trouble, but the wicked takes his place (Prov. 11:5-8).

What are we to say as Christians, that the success of the right-eous in these verses is somehow man-made? This would be utter nonsense. Yet just such a nonsensical argument is used by Hen-drikson in his not-too-subtle rejection of postmillennial optimism. The historic victory of the righteous is not man-made; on the con-

---

5. W. Hendrikson, *More Than Conquerors: An Interpretation of the Book of Revelation* (Grand Rapids: Eerdmans, 1940), p. 228.

trary, it is *God-made*. It was established definitively at the cross (in history), affirmed visibly at the resurrection (in history), and manifested supernaturally at the coming of the Holy Spirit at Pentecost (in history). After all, Christ had told His disciples to remain in Jerusalem until the Spirit came, "for John baptized with water, but you shall be baptized with the Holy Spirit not many days from now. . . . [Y]ou shall receive power when the Holy Spirit has come upon you . . ." (Acts 1:5,8a). You would think from Hendrikson's comments that Christ had promised, "You shall receive impotence." Hendrikson's exposition, called *More Than Conquerors*, is in fact a defense of the idea of Church members as *less* than conquerors in history.

He is inescapably defending the idea that Christ's victorious kingdom is not *really* manifested in history; it is only *symbolically* victorious. It is only *nominally* victorious. The amillennialist asserts that Christ's authority over history is manifested only at the end of time, after a long progression of decline for the Church, at the very moment that the satanic forces have surrounded her (Rev. 20:8-9).[6] Only at the close of history is Christ's absolute authority manifested in history. Thus, amillennialism's so-called "realized eschatology" is historically an *unrealized* eschatology: Christ's Church is *defeated* historically.[7]

To avoid the inescapable implication of covenant theology that such a defeat of Christ's Church is therefore also *representatively* (covenantally) a defeat of Christ in history, amillennialists must implicitly deny the representative character of the Church and its members' (supposedly increasingly ineffective) cultural activities in history. Amillennialists may verbally affirm the covenantal nature of the sacraments, but by denying the covenantal nature of the sacraments' *culture-transforming effects* in history through the Church's visible victory, they thereby implicitly *deny* the covenantal nature of the sacraments, for the sacraments testify to Christ's victory in history.

The traditional Reformed or Calvinistic view of the sacraments, I contend, is the Biblical view. Like the Biblical view of Christ's historic kingdom authority, it is covenantal. It is therefore a *representative* view. In the sacraments, Christ is spiritually present, not humanly

---

6. R. B. Kuiper, *The Glorious Body of Christ* (Grand Rapids, Michigan: Eerdmans, 1958), p. 277.

7. For a critique of this amillennial view, see Gary North, *Dominion and Common Grace* (Tyler, Texas: Institute for Christian Economics, 1987), ch. 5.

or bodily present, and something really happens in history. The covenant has meaning and influence in history. Its sacraments change history because they are effectual. They are not mere symbols. Christ attains special presence through the representative meal of His people. The Biblical view therefore abandons both realism and nominalism. It is instead a covenantal view.

The Covenantal View of Christ's Kingdom

The Biblical view of the kingdom is equally covenantal. It is also a *representative* view. It is therefore also *hierarchical*. In His kingdom, Christ is spiritually present, and manifestations of this victorious kingdom appear in history. The covenant has meaning and influence in history, sacramentally and eschatologically. The kingdom of Christ on earth is more than a symbol, yet He is not physically present. He attains visible sovereignty through the historic victory of His representatives, His people. He does not attain visible, historic *defeat* through His representatives. The Biblical view therefore abandons both realism and nominalism. It is instead a covenantal view.

Fundamentally, both premillennialism and amillennialism deny the representative character of God's people as Christ's kingdom representatives. Every Christian must affirm that all true authority is in Christ. But if the Church's visible authority is forever limited in history (pre-second coming), then the amount of submission required of Christ's hierarchy is also limited. We know the general principle that *with greater authority comes greater responsibility*, yet modern pessimillennialism denies the increasing responsibility of the Church over the affairs of history. Covenant-breakers grow more powerful as time goes by; hence, the Church has progressively less responsibility before God to exercise responsible authority. As the disciples began the Great Commission Covenant with their own submission at the feet of Christ, so must the present-day Church. To the degree that this Church believes in the full authority of Christ in heaven and on *earth*, it will worship and submit to Him on *earth*!

As a curiosity, let me note a few oddities. First, those who hold the doctrine of the real presence of Christ in the Lord's Supper historically have been amillennialists (nominalists) eschatologically. They have explicitly denied the increasing visible manifestation of Christ's institutional rulership in history. Second, in this century, those fundamentalists who have held to a "memorial only" view of Christ's sacraments (nominalism) have generally been realists with respect to Christ's earthly kingdom: He must rule in person, bodily, for the promised millennial blessings to take place.

A third oddity has been the amillennial Calvinists: Europeans and especially the Dutch. They have officially held to the traditional Reformed view of the sacraments: covenantal representation — neither real presence nor memorial only. They have rejected both nominalism and realism *sacramentally*. But with respect to Christ's kingdom on earth, they have become nominalists. (They were originally postmillennial.)

Perhaps the greatest oddity of all has been the Dutch-influenced amillennial Reformed Presbyterians who still hold officially to the Westminster Confession of Faith. Their creedal position, unlike the Continental European Dutch creeds of the sixteenth century, was written by the Puritans in England, and is therefore comprehensively covenantal. The Puritans were overwhelmingly postmillennialists, and therefore they believed in a covenantal kingdom on earth: the authority given to Christ by God the Father will be progressively manifested in history *representatively* by Christ's Church. The Westminster standards (1640s) are postmillennial, which is why Carl McIntyre and the newly formed Bible Presbyterian Church in 1937 rewrote the eschatological section of the Westminster Confession to conform it to traditional premillennialism. The Larger Catechism of the Westminster Confession calls on *all* Christians, as representative priests, to pray for the coming of a postmillennial kingdom:

> In the second petition, (which is, *Thy Kingdom Come*,) acknowledging ourselves and all mankind to be by nature under the dominion of sin and Satan, we pray, that the kingdom of Satan may be destroyed, the gospel propagated throughout the world, the Jews called, the fulness of the Gentiles brought in . . . (Answer 191).

Are we to say that such prayers, prayed in history by saints on earth, cannot and will not be answered in history? The expositions of Romans 11 by postmillennial covenant theologians Charles Hodge, Robert Haldane, and John Murray teach that these prayers *will* be answered in history. The Church will manifest *progressively* in history the victory which was given to Christ *definitively* at His resurrection. What we see represented in the sacraments — the victory of Christ over sin and death (baptism), and the participation of the Church in a victory celebration (the Lord's Supper) — we will also see in every area of life as God's kingdom principles are adopted by His Church. Jesus does not need to be bodily present on earth for His rule to become a historical reality.

Conclusion

This chapter is named "Covenant by the Spirit." Both sacraments demonstrate the Spirit's work. Baptism is the picture of the regenerating power of the Spirit of God, forming a *boundary between life and death*. Everything that the Spirit does is represented in baptism.

Communion is the food of life. Jesus says in the same context He refers to Himself being the "Bread of life" that the "Spirit gives life" (John 6:53, 63). When communion is taken in faith, "life" results: it becomes the "food of life." Christ nourishes His Church through the life-giving power of the Holy Spirit.

Both sacraments of the New Covenant result in the life of the world. Circumcision and Passover could only end in death, the destruction of Christ, who is the true first-born son. First-born sons must die. But Jesus did not stay in the grave. His baptismal death was unto life. His baptism not only kills, it resurrects. Communion extends the Resurrected Christ in the life of the believer and then out into the world so that the sacraments of the New Covenant make the whole world alive again. The great promise of Christ is that He will not come back until the world is dominated by the Church (Ps. 110:1; I Cor. 15:20-28).

What this really means is that the sacraments of the New Covenant *do what they symbolize*. Baptism applies sanctions to the Church which ultimately affect the world. Communion feeds life to the Church which kills and transforms the sinful world into the new garden. If God is Sovereign, then the power of the Holy Spirit is invincible. Nothing can overcome the Spirit. As the song goes, "Grace is greater than all my sin." It should also say that "grace is greater than all the *world's* sin." This is the great accomplishment of the *Covenant by the Spirit*!

Appendix 10

THE COVENANT STRUCTURE OF
THE THIRTY-NINE ARTICLES

The *Thirty-Nine Articles* are the official doctrinal statement of the Anglican Church. Written by Thomas Cranmer, they were adopted in final form in 1571. They have not significantly been changed since then, although the prayer book has undergone some minor revisions. They have survived the "isms" of Twentieth Century better than any other doctrinal statement coming out of the Reformation.

The *Thirty-Nine Articles* are consciously or unconsciously marked by the theology of the Reformation, what Perry Miller calls "Federal theology." How do I know? The articles logically break down according to the five-fold model of the covenant. Rev. John Howe, rector of Truro Episcopal Church in Fairfax, Virginia, in *Our Anglican Heritage*, says they may be grouped in *five* sections:

> 1-5 (The Trinity)
> 5-8 (Authority)
> 9-18 (Judicial Theology)
> 19-36 (The Sacraments)
> 37-39 (Property)[1]

The words in parenthesis are Howe's; they are part of fuller explanations in his section on the *Thirty-Nine Articles*. *His* words use some of the same terminology that I have utilized to explain the covenant, certainly without any prompting from me. His book has been out for nearly ten years.

As far as I know, Howe's division of the *Thirty-Nine Articles* would be generally accepted. The structure is quite obvious because the subject matter shifts at logical points. But let us consider the em-

---

1. John W. Howe, *Our Anglican Heritage* (Elgin, Illinois: David C. Cook Publishing Co., [1977] 1983), pp. 45-47.

phasis of each section in light of the covenant structure. I think we will see fairly easily without forcing them that the sections of the *Thirty-Nine Articles* parallel the covenant model, making them a *covenant document*.

The Covenant Structure of the Thirty-Nine Articles

1-5 (Transcendence): Section one begins, "There is but one living and true God." The articles open with a discussion of the Trinity and the Incarnation. Could there be any clearer reference to the first point of covenantalism: transcendence? These articles describe God and who He is. They note His transcendence as well as His immanence.

5-8 (Hierarchy): The next section focuses on Holy Scripture and the creeds. These are the *authorities* of the Church. It should be mentioned that article seven briefly describes the relationship between Old and New Testament and in this context talks about the law. But the emphasis is not so much on law as it is on the *authority* of the Old Testament over New Testament Christians. This article is a direct attack on those deny any abiding validity (authority) of the Old Testament for New Testament believers.

9-18 (Ethics): The third part of the *Thirty-Nine Articles* addresses *judicial theology*. Section nine starts by presenting our *legal* identification with Adam. Then it talks about justification. And finally, it spends a considerable amount of time on "good works." Article fourteen says, "Voluntary works besides, over and above, God's Commandments, which they call Works of Supererogation,[2] cannot be taught without arrogancy and impiety."

19-35 (Sanctions): The fourth group of articles concentrates on the Church and particularly the *sacraments*. These are the sanctions of the covenant. I must break slightly with Howe's division at the thirty-sixth article. I think the section probably ends on the thirty-fifth because article thirty-six has to do with *succession*, the consecration of priests and bishops. This is a change of subject matter. And, as we have seen, the final section of the covenant is continuity, the *confirmation* of a successor.

---

2. Works added. The Catholic Church believes there can be works *beyond* the commandments themselves, a kind of "super" righteousness. But Reformation theology argues that the commandments are a reflection of the very character of God. There cannot be supererogation because it is impossible to be *holier than God*.

36-39 (Continuity): The final section of the articles has to do with aspects of continuity. They begin with the consecration of bishops and ministers (Article 36). Next, the role of the magistrate and the status of one's personal possessions (inheritance) are developed. Finally, article thirty-nine concludes on the *oath*. This may seem like a departure from the covenant structure, seeing the oath was discussed under the sanctions point of covenantalism. But we should keep in mind that instructions about the oath were also included in the fifth point, concerning allegiance to the covenant head and the reading of Scripture. Probably, the oath-article comes at the end because the *Articles* deal with the errors of Anabaptism at this point. And, closing on the oath emphasizes the need to subscribe to the *Articles*.

Whether the designers of the *Thirty-Nine Articles* were aware of this obvious covenantal influence or not, I don't know. I rather doubt it. Nevertheless, the document easily follows the pattern. The real value in understanding this covenant structure is theological. It means that the theological system of the Anglican Church is definitely Augustinian and Reformed. It is covenantal!

So what? Covenant theology keeps one from falling into Anabaptism at one end of the spectrum and Sacerdotalism[3] at the other end. In Anglicanism's case, it guards against the recurring Anglo-Catholic trends. For example, the liturgy of the Anglican Church is powerful. But unless it is understood as *covenant renewal*, it tends to become a *re-enactment* (not of covenant cutting) of the death of Christ. It becomes a magical ceremony where Christ is re-crucified. When this happens, the true strength of the liturgy is lost. This was the concern of the Reformers. This must be the concern of anyone who truly believes in covenant theology. And, I hope this will always be the concern of the Anglican Church. An understanding of the covenantal influence and structure of its most central doctrinal standard is the key to feeding and continuing this concern.

---

3. Roman Catholicism with its particular doctrine of transubstantiation.

SCRIPTURE INDEX

OLD TESTAMENT

NEW TESTAMENT

Mark			*Acts*	
10:39	133		10:15	90
12:46	293		15	161
			15:6-10	161
Luke			16	134
18:15-17	90		16:11-15	150
18:18	243		16:19	203
18:29-30	68		19:8-20	73
21:24	258		20:7-12	136, 306
22:20	236, 265, 274		22:16	89, 133
22:21	266			
22:49-36	77		*Romans*	
24:41-51	107		1:1	246, 247
			1:1-17	246
John			1:2-4	247
1:1, 14	274		1:5	247
1:12-13	94		1:6-15	247
3:10	299		1:10ff.	247
3:15	299		1:16-17	247
6:47	82		1:18	181, 248
6:52-59	305		1:18b	188
6:53	63, 305, 315		1:18ff.	188
6:63	305		1:18 - 11:36	246
8:36	177		1:18-23	248
8:44	235, 297		1:18-32	132
11:50	47		1:19-31	188
13:26, 27	266		1:24	183
13:34a	131		1:25	247
17-18	227		1:26-28	183
20:22	300		1:29	189
			1:29-32	13
Acts			1:30	189
1:5	300, 304		1:30-31	189
1:6	203		1:32	181
1:6-11	230		2:14-15	183
1:8	202		2:22	249
2:9-11	273		3-5	249
2:17ff.	304		3:24 - 4:5	29
2:36	168		5:8	46
5:1ff.	154, 211		5:12	233
5:1-7	57		5:15	46
5:1-11	302		6	249
5:17-42	57		6:1ff.	291
8:14-24	75		6:1-7	115
9:4	169		6:4	133
10	250		6:3-4	302
10:1ff.	275		6:5	303

INDEX

Legitimacy, 103-105
Lesser magistrates, 130
Levi, 101
Leviathan, 126
Levinson, Robert E., 9n.22
Lewis, C. S., 72, 73
Lex talionis, 115, a62
Levy, Leonard W., 187n.9
Liberals, 106
Liebnitz, 69
Liturgy
   Book of Common Prayer, 221n.5
   church's, 46
   Cultural mandate and, 125
   life and, 108
   sacrifices and, 85n.10
Locke, John, xvii
Lohfink, Norbert, 2n.1
London Baptist Confession, 5n.8
Lord's Supper, 89n.15
Lot, 116
Lovejoy, Arthur O., 35n.9
Lumpkin, W. C., 5n.3
Luther, xvii, xviii, 219
Lutheran, 304
Lydia, 90, 150

Magic, 73ff.
Magician, 74-75
Mammon, 110
Manasseh, 98-99, 101
Manipulation, 75
Marriage
   contract, 147-48
   imputation and, 31
Marshall, John, 200n.4
Martin, Walter, 152n.6
Martyr, Justin, 132
Marxism, 70, 132
Masons, 14
Massachusetts Bay Colony, 190
Materialism, 70
Mathematics, 69
Mather, Cotton, 162n.4
Maupertuis, 38
Marsden, George M., 4n.3
Mayflower Compact, 195-96

Maynard vs. Hill, 8
McCardle vs. Mississippi, 10-11
McComiskey, Thomas, 81n.5
McIntyre, Carl, 314
Mediation
   capital *M*, 47
   sin offering, 85
   lower case *M*, 47
Mediators
   church, 57
   general, 48
   Capital *M*, 57
   special, 43
Memorial view, 309
Mendenhall, George S., 15n.30, 281, 282
Metaphysical religion
   continuity of being, 37ff.
   evolution and, 38-39
   Greek religion and, 37
   irrationalism and, 37-38
   Mormonism and, 37
   rationalism and, 37
   totem pole and, 36
   Middle Ages, 3, 69
Milik, J. T., 225n.2
Military, 52
Millennium, 234
Miller, Perry, xv, 4n.3, 5, 5n.10, 6n.14, 6n.15, 7
Milton, John, xvii
Missions, 131
Moab, 109, 117
Monism, 35
Mordecai, 97
Morgan, Edmund S., 3n., 4n.5, 7, 124
Mormonism, 37, 152
Morris, Leon, 119n.1
Moses, 59, 71
Mountain symbol, 129
Multi-national, 276
Murray, Charles, 9n.23
Murray, John, 314

Name
   baptism and, 93
   Christian, 93

He Shall Have Dominion
A Postmillennialism Eschatology
by Rev. Kenneth L. Gentry

The vast majority of those who call themselves evangelical Christians believe that the Church of Jesus Christ has been predestinated by God to fail in history. "It cannot possibly succeed!" Millions of Christians believe that the Church will be "raptured" soon, removing Christians from the turmoils and responsibilities of this life.

Ken Gentry argues otherwise in *He Shall Have Dominion*. He shows that Christians have many great things to accomplish for Christ before He returns bodily to earth.

Two centuries ago, Protestant Christians believed that they would die before Jesus came back to earth. This affected the way they thought, prayed, worked and saved. They built for the future. They were future-oriented. They were upper class. Today, many Protestants believe that Jesus is coming back soon, so they will not have to die. This belief affects the way they think, pray, work, and save. They are present-oriented. They are lower-class. Ken Gentry refutes this outlook, verse by verse.

He Shall Have Dominion is a positive book: positive about the future of the Church. It teaches that Christians will exercise dominion in history. It therefore teaches responsibility. This is why its message is hated. Today's Christians have been taught that they must flee responsibility, for Jesus' sake. They would rather believe that God has predestined His Church to failure than believe that they are personally responsible for transforming society. This is why the Church is so weak in our day.

584 pp., indexed, bibliography, hardback, $19.95
Institute for Christian Economics, P.O. Box 8000, Tyler, TX 75711